Voicing the Cinema

Film Music and the Integrated Soundtrack

Edited by
James Buhler and Hannah Lewis

UNIVERSITY OF
ILLINOIS PRESS
Urbana, Chicago, and Springfield

1 2 3 4 5 C P 5 4 3 2 1
∞ This book is printed on acid-free paper.

Library of Congress Cataloging-in-Publication Data
Names: Buhler, James, 1964– editor. | Lewis, Hannah, 1985- editor.
Title: Voicing the cinema: film music and the integrated soundtrack / edited by James Buhler and Hannah Lewis.
Description: Urbana: University of Illinois Press, 2020. | Includes bibliographical references and index. |
Identifiers: LCCN 2019035094 (print) | LCCN 2019035095 (ebook) | ISBN 9780252043000 (cloth) | ISBN 9780252084867 (paperback) | ISBN 9780252051869 (ebook)
Subjects: LCSH: Motion picture music--History and criticism. | Film soundtracks. | Voice in motion pictures.
Classification: LCC ML2075 .V63 2020 (print) | LCC ML2075 (ebook) | DDC 777/.53—dc23
LC record available at https://lccn.loc.gov/2019035094
LC ebook record available at https://lccn.loc.gov/2019035095

Voicing the Cinema

Contents

Acknowledgments

This book had its origin in a conference, Voicing the Soundtrack, held in honor of David Neumeyer's retirement, in spring 2016 at the University of Texas at Austin. The collection underwent a number of revisions to enhance clarity and improve the thematic focus of the papers, and we added several new contributors. We are grateful to Douglas Dempster, Dean of the College of Fine Arts, and Mary Ellen Poole, Director of the Butler School of Music, for their support of the conference. We are also grateful to the Center for American Music for providing funds, both for the conference and for a subvention to facilitate the publication of a larger collection. We would like to thank several conference participants who did not contribute essays to this book for their thoughtful contributions to the broader scholarly conversation that led to this volume: Daniel Goldmark, Claudia Gorbman, Frank Lehman, Martin Marks, Scott Murphy, Michael Pisani, and Thomas Schatz.

Many thanks to Daniel Nasset, our editor at the University of Illinois Press, for his enthusiastic support of the project and his willingness to work with us as the volume continued to grow in size and scope, and to the anonymous readers of the manuscript, who provided valuable feedback that proved crucial to our framing in the volume's introduction. Nancy Albright, our copyeditor, ensured that the volume was polished and consistent across chapters, and Marika Christofides helped manage the various moving parts of putting the manuscript together. Thank you also to the happy hour crew, Charles Carson, Eric Drott, and Marianne Wheeldon, for their convivial company and general advice. Hannah would like to thank Ojas Vyas and Jim would like to thank Leslie Bush for their moral support, as always.

Voicing the Cinema

Introduction

Voices in, of, and on the Cinema

James Buhler and Hannah Lewis

The Voice and the Cinema

Over the past three decades, the study of the film soundtrack has developed into a rich scholarly discipline, characterized by diverse approaches and methodologies drawn from such fields as musicology, music theory, film and media studies, and sound studies. As an object of theoretical focus, the voice has helped correct the long-standing ocularcentrism of film theory discourse. Yet, the voice as a narrow concept is itself problematic in that it limits our understanding of how it functions among the various components of the soundtrack. Traditionally, the voice has been given great deference in production, even as dialogue has been denigrated in film theory. This has led to a curious conceptual framework for the soundtrack where the default state of synchronized dialogue in filmmaking is treated as a merely redundant figure or even as a profoundly ideological delusion in film theory. Understood as part of an integrated soundtrack—that is, a soundtrack where the various components have a sense of being planned or composed and where sound design and music are blended into a kind of conceptual unity—the voice (dialogue in particular) assumes a somewhat different role and allows for a more complex and interpretively richer conceptual framework. Many films—and increasingly in contemporary cinema of all sorts—downplay the centrality of dialogue even as the soundtrack as a whole assumes a crucial role in these films' spectacle. This volume aims to reconsider and broaden our notion of what the voice as a concept can do for studies of film music and sound.

The essays in this volume build on existing scholarship on music and film sound, with particular attention to the concepts of the voice in cinema and the integrated soundtrack. The word "voicing" in our title is multivalent. By voice we mean something broader than spoken dialogue, or even the singing voice. It describes the voice in the usual sense of the term, but we also include issues of critical interpretation: "giving voice to," allowing various practitioners to speak, to have a voice, and so forth. Voice is also a useful concept when considering a film's production, one that gets at the complicated nature of—the real polyphony underlying—film's corporate authorship; with respect to the soundtrack, we might identify and distinguish the voices of the sound designer, the sound mixer, the composer, the orchestrator, the music supervisor, or the director.

This conceptual broadening gives rise to a set of questions that guide this volume: How does the voice affect music in the cinema? What is the cinematic significance of the singing voice? How do music and dialogue interact in cinema? To what extent, if any, is silent film affected by the voice? To what extent can we think about music and sound as adding distinctive voices to filmmaking? Talking film, as the term implies, has long centered the dialogue, but recent commercial films show considerable movement away from this idea. Does the voice have the same status in contemporary postclassical film? Do the soundtrack and its various components shift over time? Or, put another way: In what ways can attention to dialogue, music, and sound help us understand the soundtrack as a site of constructing meaning in cinema? What effect does genre have on the soundtrack? How, if at all, is the voice set differently outside of Hollywood? To what extent can we say that a compilation score represents the personal voice of a director? How do competing creative voices—the director, composer, or orchestrator, for instance—play out in a film's final version, or its critical or scholarly reception? Finally, how do we as scholars give voice to the soundtrack? We believe that considering these various definitions of voice together allows for deeper insight into the work of the soundtrack.

The Routine of the (Speaking) Voice

The voice has long been an object of focus of many theoretical approaches to sound in cinema. Scholars such as Michel Chion, Mary Ann Doane, Kaja Silverman, Mladen Dolar, and Michal Grover-Friedlander have contributed to our understanding of how the voice structures a film's narrative and impacts the spectator's experience of a film. These scholars all approach the voice from a psychoanalytic perspective, in particular adopting significant elements of Jacques Lacan's theories, which have been tremendously influential in film theory's focus on the visual, to understand the soundtrack.[1] By turning their attention to theoretical concerns surrounding the voice in cinema, these figures worked to expand film theory's scope beyond the visual workings of cinema.

The concept of voice and the variety of kinds of voice in films have made for a rich subject of study, but the special qualities of film dialogue itself have received less attention, and film theory has generally been hostile to dialogue, or, if not hostile, then mostly uninterested in documenting its potential contributions. Dialogue connects closely to issues of narrative, and this is perhaps one reason for the relative lack of attention: the importance of dialogue to film narrative threatens film theory's investment in the image as the aspect of the film object that matters most. Dialogue, film theorists from Rudolf Arnheim and Béla Balázs to Siegfried Kracauer and Jean Mitry declare, belongs to the theater and is an uncinematic figure whenever it determines the constructive principles of film. At any rate, Sarah Kozloff, the foremost scholar of film dialogue, notes that many film scholars ritually chant the visual dominance of cinema "like a charm to ward off evil."[2]

Beyond the hostility to dialogue as an uncinematic figure, the fact that spoken dialogue is a mundane part of the soundtrack—that which because it seemingly speaks for itself can go without saying—also accounts for its relative neglect. (Dialogue has been much more neglected than music in scholarship on film.) Still, during the transition to sound, dialogue was one of the most interesting features of the talkies, a fact highlighted early by both theorists and filmmakers, whether it was celebrated or decried. Stephen Heath notes "the law of the speaking subject" that orients filmmaking—blocking, shot composition, editing, etc.—around the presentation of dialogue and the impression of embodiment that makes the voice appear a property of the image.[3] Dialogue also distinguishes the silent film from the sound film: in the former, words belonged to the character; in the latter, the soundtrack divided them between character and actor. This divide between character and actor forms the basis for what Mary Ann Doane calls the "fantasmatic body," the image of the unified body that the film promises and encourages audiences to identify with even as that body threatens to dissolve back into the heterogeneity of the constituent parts.[4] This divide was a particular challenge during the transition to sound, and the mechanical synchronization that welded voice to body was fraught, liable to dissolve character into the actor on the one hand but susceptible to counterfeit on the other. In 1929, Mark Larkin announced "the truth about voice doubling" (that it occurs) and unleashed a minor scandal when audiences learned the voices they heard in films did not necessarily correspond to the bodies they saw on screen,[5] and cultural anxiety over this truth was sufficiently high that it could form the premise of one of Hollywood's most remarkable films on itself, *Singin' in the Rain* (1952), whose story insists on an ethical practice that united actor with voice even as its actual production practice violated such ethics quite drastically.

Even within the category of spoken dialogue, the voice takes on a range of nuances and varied roles, extending its function beyond that of purely conveying narrative. Early in the sound era, Béla Balázs had noted the importance of dialogue delivery. If dialogue was "the least edifying element of the sound film,"[6] Balázs also thought that what counted was the performance, the manner of delivery: "In film, what attracts our interest is less what a person says than the sound of his voice. . . . [W]hat is decisive is not the content, but the acoustic, sensuous impression."[7] Then, too, Balázs recognized the importance of recording: "Sound film dialogues differ from other dramatic dialogues in that they are uttered only once, and once and for all. Every nuance of intonation is final and fixed for all time."[8] The recorded voice has significance as its own phenomenon; but recording and mixing practices have likewise evolved within mainstream narrative cinema to take the importance of voices into account and to make them into bearers of narrative significance.

Vococentrism and the Voice in the Cinema

In his recent book, *Meaning and Interpretation of Music in Cinema* (2015), David Neumeyer clarifies how the various elements of the soundtrack work themselves out on the structure of the soundtrack. Developing an insight from Michel Chion, Neumeyer claims that narrative sound film is "vococentric"—that the soundtrack is constructed in a hierarchical fashion to ensure clarity of narrative meaning, which is most often carried by the dialogue. Neumeyer moves beyond Chion's conception, however, when he argues that the soundtrack is also a fully constructed entity that has priority over any of its individual components; therefore, any interpretation and understanding of music in the cinema must take into account music's role within the integrated soundtrack.[9] In mainstream narrative cinema, film music and sound are regulated on the soundtrack by this vococentric principle. More specifically, audiovisual narrative media generally subjugate music and sound effects to the voice, since the latter is the principal source of narrative information on the soundtrack.

The principle of vococentrism does not mean that the voice will always be the most prominent sound in the mix. Often the status of the voice seems destabilized on the soundtrack, much like the face in the image, as it is in a constant process of being centered and decentered. But such destabilization can also serve to reinforce the principle at a higher level, since vococentrism insists only that the voice will form the ground of the interpretation—that its decentering will be understood as meaningful and as an expressive effect—not that it will always be centered.[10]

One such example is the synchronization of dialogue. Dialogue is most commonly synchronized because under the system of vococentrism, synchronization is typically a sign of pertinence. That is, synchronization has historically been an important device that establishes a hierarchy in both image and soundtrack: all things being equal, objects in the image that make sounds will attract visual attention, and sounds that have clear sources in the image will take precedence on the soundtrack. Even in a crowd, we recognize any figure that has synchronized speech as important and belonging to the foreground and other bodies in the crowd that do not emit synchronized sounds as belonging to the background. But the presumption of synchronization also means that nonsynchronized speech bears special import, often carrying affective as well as structural significance. In audiovisual analysis, for instance, we distinguish voice-off and voiceover especially as important modalities of the voice outside synchronized dialogue. The voiceover, as analyzed by Pascal Bonitzer, does not require the typical grounding of a voice in an onscreen body, thereby granting it a seeming omniscience or even omnipotence. Bonitzer expands this analysis to the voice-off, suggesting the latter retains attributes of this power so long as the voice-off is maintained.[11] Chion develops this idea into the figure of the *acousmêtre,* the acoustical being, which gains power by seeming to have access to special knowledge, namely, the placement of the camera, that is denied to other characters.[12] Also working from Bonitzer's conception, Mary Ann Doane notes the subversive potential of the voice-off, which calls into question the order of the image.[13] Ultimately, however, these nonsynchronized instances of dialogue only briefly and locally destabilize vococentrism, and at a larger level of analysis the local displacement reinforces the vococentric principle, namely the voice's dominant role in narrative interpretation.

The ubiquity of vococentrism in commercial filmmaking since the transition to sound does not mean that all cinema is vococentric. Indeed, the silent film and early sound film are not vococentric. The former is structured only by muteness, the absence of the voice and rudimentary dialogue displaced to text, and the latter is bound to the rule of mimetic synchronization that does not allow for meaningful displacement or decentering.[14] Thus, Julie Brown, in her essay for this volume, reveals the many manifestations of "voice" in the silent era, many of which required a broad kind of apprehension, rather than traditional listening or a hierarchical order of the sort vococentrism commands. Many early sound films experimented with pushing against the voice's inherent pull within the soundtrack, as Hannah Lewis suggests in her study of early French sound film in this volume. Experimental cinema has often challenged the principles of vococentrism or purposely offered alternative solutions for structuring the soundtrack. Some international filmmakers have resisted vococentrism and offered a critique of its inherent anthropocentrism and embodiment of certain western (capitalist) ideals. Thus, in her essay on *Dersu Uzala* (1975), Brooke McCorkle shows how Kurosawa Akira's attention to natural soundscapes decenters the human voice and so also unsettles the conventions of vococentrism.

Certain forms of popular contemporary cinema also seem to break with the principle of vococentrism in various ways. As James Buhler notes in his contribution, even as contemporary action film follows the facial centricity of "intensified continuity," the soundtrack typically centers explosions and other affect-laden sound effects or music, but the displacement of dialogue from its usual dominant position in cinema does not seem especially meaningful nor is it always deployed as an expressive effect. Certainly, the displacement often functions that way. In his essay, Eric Dienstfrey, for instance, suggests that in *The Martian* (2015) the dominance of dialogue by effects in the climactic rescue scene serves to "amplify the astronaut's life-threatening predicament." Yet not all or even most contemporary action films suppress dialogue for this kind of expressive effect. Often, the diminishment of dialogue in contemporary action film seems more allegorical—a recognition of speech's limitations and inadequacy compared to matter's explosive, kinetic potential—than expressive in character. Then, too, the body reacts to its verbal inarticulateness by becoming an affective surface. But if cinema has reached an end of vococentrism, as Buhler suggests in his essay, there are other ways that the voice continues to structure our thinking. Even in a postclassical cinema (if such a thing exists), sound and image come together into a sort of post-vococentrism, where the voice continues to exercise an influence, even as it is called into question.

The Spectacle of the (Singing) Voice

The nuances of dialogue delivery sometimes take on even greater importance, causing the voice to function as spectacle, its sound signifying something other than the meaning of its words. Screams are an obvious example, and Chion notes their structural importance to the sound film in his category of the "screaming point."[15] In her essay on Kurosawa's *Dersu Uzala*, Brooke McCorkle extends another of Chion's claims to point out that one of the effects of watching films in a language you don't understand is that it emphasizes the extra-semantic aspect of language, so that the signification divides into the delivery of tone and grain on the one hand and a visual subtitle of sense on the other.[16]

The singing voice accomplishes something similar, dissolving the boundary of dialogue and music. Writing from a Deleuzean perspective, Amy Herzog has detailed, in her 2009 book, how the hierarchy between narrative and spectacle can shift in what she calls the "musical moment" in film.[17] In theories of film narrative, spectacle is traditionally opposed to narrative: it is generally a figure of excess, a counter-narrative force that suspends or retards the unfolding of narrative in order to increase intensity and memorability of certain moments within narrative.[18] Spectacle is therefore frequently celebrated for its subversive potential even as it is also regulated so that it does not threaten the overarching narrative order.

The singing voice is often of this kind: characters sing when dialogue fails to say what the narrative requires, and the singing voice can also offer an erotic spectacle, which is why the femme fatale in film noir is frequently a singer. In this respect, vococentrism allows such figures because it assumes that the singing voice, but also the scream, taps a subversive power.

The singing voice also offers other sorts of appeal, for instance, as a way of representing interiority. In her essay, Robynn Stilwell argues that because films that center on female protagonists frequently have to trace an inward journey, the traditional mode of film narrative realized in externalized action does not work very well. The spectacle of the singing voice in a film such as *Frozen* (2013) allows the film to represent this inward journey. Cari McDonnell's essay argues for a similarly important function of lip-synced songs in 1980s teen films. Even in staged performances, the voice becomes a kind of spectacle, particularly the singing voice. The operatic singing voice has been the subject of substantial scholarly treatment—particularly because its presence as spectacle seems in many ways at odds with the otherwise naturalistic and narrative-bound role of the speaking voice in cinema.[19] In her essay for this volume, Marcia Citron deftly shows how director Ingmar Bergman's presentation of arias in *The Magic Flute* (1975) differs from dialogue in important symbolic ways. This kind of differentiation between song and dialogue occurs with the film musical as well.

Music and the Voice of the Cinema

Another important aspect of the voice in cinema is the way in which it is part of a singular technical apparatus: the soundtrack. This conception can lead to a traditionally integrated soundtrack, where sound effects and music are sublimated so that the voice, the conveyer of narrative information, is at the top of the hierarchy. It can also end up highlighting the fact that music is recorded and so part of the apparatus of the film.

One of the interesting things about the recorded musical score is its disembodied quality—that it seems to come "from nowhere"—and the bodily absence of musicians or an obvious emanating source for the music makes it distinct from other elements within the soundtrack. Even the voiceover, which shares a similar disembodied character, seems to connect more straightforwardly with the rest of the film because its commentary is articulated in words. Moreover, often the character delivering the voiceover belongs to the story, such as in *Rebecca* (1940), *The Uninvited* (1944), or *Laura* (1944). But even when this is not the case, as in the newsreel-like narration that opens *Casablanca* (1942), the voiceover casts the images we see into a series seemingly derived from the words. In *Casablanca*, the narration locates the place of Casablanca within the Second World War's circuit of intrigue, whereas the accompanying music suggests more of the suffering of those who had the misfortune of being forced to follow that circuit. But the connection of the music is far more attenuated and more difficult to dislocate in place and time than is the case with voiceover. The music often seems to represent something concrete in the image, such as the (diegetic) feeling of a character. Yet the sound source of the music also has no place in the image. Writing during the transition to sound, Rudolf Arnheim worried that "hear[ing] the voice of a young girl sitting alone in the forest accompanied by a large orchestra, [the audience] quite rightly wonders how such luxury comes to exist in the wilderness."[20] This was a common anxiety for filmmakers in the early years of synchronized sound, as exemplified in a well-known anecdote (hyperbolically) recounted by Max Steiner about the "wandering violinist" found in the back of a love scene.[21] As the practice codified, however, filmmakers found it less and less necessary to justify the presence of nondiegetic music, and it became part of the convention at least in part because on a monaural soundtrack music generally made a better background for dialogue than did either silence or realistic ambient sound and so it supplemented the principles of vococentrism.

Such disembodied accompanying music is often called "background music," and narratology terms it "nondiegetic" because the sound does not have its source in the diegesis. Though the very concept of music in film as "nondiegetic" has been contested, perhaps most notably by Ben Winters, Jeff Smith in his essay in this volume argues for its continued importance as a category and suggests that it is particularly vital to the construction of a vococentric soundtrack.

As noted, synchronization marks a figure in an image and sound on the soundtrack for attention. Vice versa, elements that are not synchronized tend to move into a background situation, and music in film follows this pattern. Thus, a diegetic performance is often foreground; accompanying music is usually background. But just as the voiceover has a special power that derives from being unbound by the image, so too the disembodied character of nondiegetic music can give it the potential for voice. Under classical film theory, this aspect of nondiegetic music was called its *commentative function*. Film music's commentative function is strong enough that it not only offers insight into a film's narrative, it also sets up spectators' expectations as to how an individual film will work based on music's role in articulating broader generic expectations. Janet Staiger suggests that music plays an important role in the ways spectators construct and understand a film's genre; in her essay, she offers a multidimensional approach to genre theory that argues for the importance of a film's musical style in its affect and inflection.

Production and the Voice on the Cinema

Because of the way it relates to meaning and hierarchy, "voice" is also a useful metaphorical conceit for thinking about relations within the soundtrack. Such voices are often spectral—when we attend to them we are "hearing voices"—and have to be drawn from the film either through listening for fissures in the soundtrack where different voices come into contact or by examining archival materials such as production documents to discover unexpected presences in the film and its production history. David Neumeyer's analysis of *The Uninvited* notes the ghostly doubling of the famous main theme in the film.

Voice can also serve as a clarifying metaphor in thinking about issues of authorship and production. Where dialogue divides the voice between character and actor, so too music divides between the commentary of the narration and the utterance of the composer, sound designer, mixer, and so forth. In mainstream narrative cinema, the "voice" of music is generally subdued and subordinated in narrative film, but like a secondary character it occasionally takes over. And like the actor, the "voice" of the composer—the musical particularities that distinguish a composer's style—is frequently distinctive enough that it is not wholly absorbed by the film even when properly subordinated to narrative. The voice of the composer—and sometimes, as Nathan Platte shows in his essay, the composer's collaborators—is a metaphorical extension of voice in part because the music does not have the same kind of bodily presence with respect to actors' voices. Though music in film may function closer to something like the voiceover, the idea of a composer bringing something to a film remains similar to the way an actor brings a voice as something special and distinctive. It is even possible to consider the voice of the audio mixers and sound technicians, whose contributions to a film's soundtracks are frequently overlooked. For instance, Katherine Quanz examines correspondence between recording engineers in Hollywood and London regarding the sound design of *Fiddler on the Roof* (1971), uncovering a seemingly obscure debate over mixing standards that had both important practical and aesthetic implications. Such voices barely register in the film itself, but they go to the heart of the filmmaking process, testify to the collaborative nature of the enterprise, and remind us that technical workers have interests to defend as well as expertise to share.

Voice is therefore a valuable concept for considering distinctive contributions by technical personnel and composers, and, by extension, auteur directors.

Auteurism has been a useful, albeit reductive, concept for considering the unifying presence of a singular director, who is usually not all that singular in reality. The typical concept for organizing discourse on auteurs is "vision," but we might also think about their contributions in terms of voice. For directors, "voice" is more metaphorical and is lodged less in the particularity of sound structures than in special emphases in the relations among the elements of the soundtrack. But if certain directors have developed an approach to the soundtrack that seems unique to them—a Hitchcock film sounds like a Hitchcock film no matter who composed the score, worked on the sound effects, or voiced the dialogue—this "voice" of the director is worthy of attention as well. We can also say that a director may "speak through" a larger corporate body of a film studio to create a more unified, singular conception that ensures the polyphony remains harmonious. Even if auteur theory is ultimately an invented concept, there does seem to be a "trademark" that distinguishes particular films that come under a director's name, which can often be heard in a film's soundtrack. Julie Hubbert, for instance, in her essay, argues for the distinctiveness of Michelangelo Antonioni's use of popular music in *Zabriskie Point* (1970), noting the lengths the director went to find the music to make his conception. Likewise, Erik Heine claims that director Peter Weir frequently makes distinctive and effective use of slow movements of piano concertos to present a voice of innocence that otherwise would be silenced by repressive social institutions.

This Volume

Considering these many different conceptions of "voice" can therefore provide new perspectives on how we consider the relationship between voice and cinema, broadly defined. Each contribution in this volume defines "voice" somewhat differently and so attends to different voices—the actor's voice; the singing voice; the voice of the mixer, composer, director; the voice of genre; the voice of the institution itself; and the soundtrack's vococentrism. When examined as a whole, they provide a flexibility and nuance to the concept that offers new understandings of the relationship between voice, music, sound effects, and the integrated soundtrack as a whole.

The four essays of Part One, "Historical Approaches to Technology and the Voice," address the ways in which the voice has been constructed historically in films both representationally and through its mediation by technology. During the silent period, the status of the voice was representationally uncertain and highly variable, which led to a great deal of experimentation with voice's role in narrative cinema. Julie Brown argues that it is more productive to consider the voice of the silent cinema in terms of apprehension than audibility since the voice was often represented even as its sound was absent. In the second essay, Hannah Lewis covers the contested nature of the voice in early French sound film and considers the ways in which the speaking voice and the score were at odds. She looks at how music could silence the voice in a way that resembled silent film practice but took on a different coloring in the context of sound film practice in films such as René Clair's *Sous les toits de Paris* (1930) and Jean Grémillon's *La Petite Lise* (1930). Julie Hubbert argues that the high-fidelity movement of the 1950s and '60s changed how filmmakers grounded the narrative work of the soundtrack. A new desire for sonic complexity in film sound design led to a collapse of distinctions between musical genres, and between the previously distinct elements of the soundtrack, and the commentative voice of the orchestral underscore was increasingly assigned to preexisting commercial recordings. Katherine Quanz examines the rerecording process for *Fiddler on the Roof*, focusing on the internal communications between two sound departments on different sides of the Atlantic and providing insight into the attitudes and aesthetics of the different departments during a time when Hollywood's role as the center for postproduction of commercial films was being contested. Her examination of correspondence between rerecording engineers helps us gain a deeper understanding of the role of the mixer in the sound of the film.

Part Two establishes how the singing voice has been distinguished as a special sound object in cinema. Three essays analyze a variety of uses of the singing voice and the variety of representational strategies that have been deployed to situate it aurally and visually. Marcia Citron focuses on sound design in Ingmar Bergman's *The Magic Flute,* one of the better-known opera films that originated as a television production and was released the following year for the big screen. She considers how the film uses sound (rather than just music) to construct meaning. In particular, she argues that the direct recording of the dialogue creates an interiorized quality found in other Bergman films, which contrasts with the prerecording of the musical numbers. The combination of these two techniques yields a range of aesthetic effects that Citron documents and analyzes. Cari McDonnell examines lip-sync performances in 1980s teen films. These sequences serve a similar function to performance numbers in the classic musical, but the use of existing recordings ties the performance more closely to the commercial basis of the music industry, resulting in a fusion of identity with commerce into a distinct affective configuration. Robynn Stilwell explores the treatment of the girl's voice in several contemporary animated films and shows how music intersects with voice in these coming-of-age stories.

The papers of Part Three interrogate what it means for a filmmaker to have a distinctive voice—the voice of an "auteur"—and how it manifests sonically and narratively in the soundtrack. Nathan Platte addresses this from the standpoint of composer Max Steiner and examines how collaboration with orchestrators and other composers served to create a more powerful and distinctive compositional "voice." At the same time, the division of labor created anxiety over the ownership of this voice since credits were less than straightforward and the myth of singular composition meant that divided authorship cast doubt on the quality of that compositional voice. David Neumeyer analyzes music's narrative functions in the well-known horror film *The Uninvited*, where themes become involved in the doublings common to the horror genre. He also explores the voice of composer Victor Young, through the film's musical theme, which later evolved into the jazz standard "Stella by Starlight." Whereas Platte and Neumeyer look at a specific composer, the other two essays in this section consider how directors create distinctive authorial voices through aural imagination. Brooke McCorkle shows how Kurosawa Akira deployed a series of sounds to represent specific environmental soundscapes, endowing nature with a voice. Erik Heine examines Peter Weir's use of preexisting classical music and looks at how slow movements of piano concerti come to represent innocence and an escape from repression in Weir's films. From three different national contexts, the essays in this section reveal different ways of considering authorial voice in studies of the soundtrack.

The papers in the final section consider the conceptual entwining of voice, spectacle, genre, and narrative. Janet Staiger looks at hybrid genres of horror to argue for a multidimensional approach to understanding narrative formulas and how music and voice articulate those formulas through the production of affect. Romantic horror is a particularly good genre for illustrating the instability of genre categories because of the way sound and music, particularly popular song, in these films work with the genre of horror but also with the genre of romantic comedy. Eric Dienstfrey introduces the concept of monocentrism to account for the stability of stereo and surround mixes along vococentric lines that privileges the intelligibility of dialogue. He discusses how *Forbidden Planet* (1956) challenged the developing monocentric norm in the 1950s and looks at the treatment of dialogue in the surround mix of *The Martian* in order to show how departures from vococentric principles serve expressive effects.

Jeff Smith focuses on music's narrative functions, returning to the classical division between diegetic and nondiegetic music considered in terms of the vococentric principle that underlies the conception of the integrated soundtrack. He evaluates Ben Winters's argument against the concept of nondiegetic music, taking issue with Winters's counterintuitive claim that music belongs in an essential respect to the diegesis and arguing instead that the concept of the nondiegetic is crucial for understanding a wide variety of sound treatments in the cinema. James Buhler considers the contemporary situation of vococentrism in the age of intensified continuity. Although the visual style of intensified continuity has been centripetal, reinforcing the central place of the face in the image, Buhler argues that the intensified style of the soundtrack by contrast is largely centrifugal, decentering the voice from its position in classical style. Addressing the long-standing historical significance of vococentrism that has been articulated in the other essays in this volume, Buhler identifies a number of traits of contemporary soundtracks and suggests that the end of vococentrism aligns with other significant themes of current filmmaking.

Notes

1. Michel Chion, *The Voice in Cinema*, trans. Claudia Gorbman (New York: Columbia University Press, 1999); Mary Ann Doane, "The Voice in the Cinema: The Articulation of Body and Space," *Yale French Studies* 60 (1980): 33–50; Doane, "Ideology and the Practice of Sound Editing and Mixing," in *The Cinematic Apparatus*, ed. Teresa de Lauretis and Stephen Heath (Milwaukee: MacMillan Press, 1980), 47–56; Mladen Dolar, *A Voice and Nothing More* (Cambridge: MIT Press, 2006); Kaja Silverman, *The Acoustic Mirror: The Female Voice in Psychoanalysis and Cinema* (Bloomington: Indiana University Press, 1983); Michal Grover-Friedlander, *Vocal Apparitions: The Attraction of Cinema to Opera* (Princeton, N.J.: Princeton University Press, 2005). See also James Buhler, *Theories of the Soundtrack* (New York: Oxford University Press, 2019), chapter 8, esp. 246–56.

2. Sarah Kozloff, *Overhearing Film Dialogue* (Berkeley: University of California Press, 2000), 9.

3. Stephen Heath, *Questions of Cinema* (Bloomington: Indiana University Press, 1981), 178, 201.

4. Doane, "The Voice in the Cinema," 34.

5. Mark Larkin, "The Truth about Voice Doubling" (1929), in *Celluloid Symphonies: Texts and Contexts in Film Music History*, ed. Julie Hubbert (Berkeley: University of California Press, 2011), 138–44.

6. Béla Balázs, *Early Film Theory: Visible Man and The Spirit of Film*, ed. Erica Carter and trans. Rodney Livingstone (Oxford: Berghahn Books, 2010), 208.

7. Ibid., 194.

8. Ibid., 207.

9. Chion, *The Voice in Cinema*; David Neumeyer, *Meaning and Interpretation of Music in Cinema* (Bloomington: Indiana University Press, 2015). On the integrated soundtrack, see also Liz Greene and Danijela Kulezic-Wilson, eds., *The Palgrave Handbook of Sound Design and Music in Screen Media: Integrated Soundtracks* (London: Palgrave Macmillan, 2016).

10. Neumeyer, *Meaning and Interpretation of Music in Cinema*, 101.

11. Pascal Bonitzer, "The Silences of the Voice (*A propos* of *Mai 68* by Gudie Lawaetz)," in *Narrative, Technology, Ideology*, ed. Philip Rosen (New York: Columbia University Press, 1986), 319–34.

12. Chion, *The Voice in Cinema*, 17–29.

13. Doane, "The Voice in the Cinema," 37–43.

14. James Buhler, *Theories of the Soundtrack*, 24.

15. Chion, *The Voice in Cinema*, 77–80.

16. On the singing voice, see Roland Barthes, "The Grain of the Voice," in *The Responsibility of Forms*, trans. Richard Howard (Berkeley: University of California Press, 1991), 267–77.

17. Amy Herzog, *Dreams of Difference, Songs of the Same: The Musical Moment in Film* (Minneapolis: University of Minnesota Press, 2010).

18. Neumeyer, *Meaning and Interpretation of Music in Cinema*, 30.

19. See, for instance, Marcia Citron, *Opera on Screen* (New Haven: Yale University Press, 2000); Citron, *When Opera Meets Film* (Cambridge: Cambridge University Press, 2010); Grover-Friedlander, *Vocal Apparitions*; Jeongwon Joe and Sander L. Gilman, eds., *Wagner and Cinema* (Bloomington: Indiana University Press, 2010); Jeongwon Joe and Rose Theresa, eds., *Between Opera and Cinema* (New York: Routledge, 2002); David Schroeder, *Cinema's Illusions, Opera's Allure: The Operatic Impulse in Film* (New York: Continuum, 2002); and Jeremy Tambling, *Opera, Ideology and Film* (New York: St. Martin's Press, 1987).

20. Rudolf Arnheim, *Film Essays and Criticism* (Madison: University of Wisconsin Press, 1997), 51.

21. Max Steiner, "Scoring the Film," in *We Make the Movies*, ed. Nancy Naumburg (New York: Norton, 1937), 219.

Part One

Historical Approaches to Technology and the Voice

Chapter 1

Apprehending Human Voice in the "Silent Cinema"

Julie Brown

In the silent cinema, moving pictures had no soundtracks, nor, when exhibited, were they subject to consistently applied sonic accompaniments; least of all did they have an established sound hierarchy in which voice occupied a particular place—central or otherwise. Many early moving pictures were conceived as "attractions" rather than principally as vehicles for narrative, while others—including "attractions"—involved the material visualization of sound; indeed, for Isabelle Raynauld, the latter is what permits us clearly to differentiate early from later cinema.[1] Yet sounding voices could also be added in the moment of exhibition, at the fairground or in the theater or cinema, and this could be done in a variety of different ways. During their first thirty years, the moving pictures therefore afforded the representation of voice and vocality by means of diverse cinematic and theatrical systems.

In this chapter, I outline the many manifestations of cinematic "voice" in the silent cinema. Among others, these include speaking within a "hearing" screen world to which the audience is nevertheless deaf; intertitles; bodily gesture; typed words on the screen; live voices in the theater variously describing the moving pictures, reading out title cards, or lip-syncing dialogue or song, and so forth. I draw on Brian Kane's reconceptualization of "voice" as *Phoné* to theorize voice in the silent cinema in a way that moves beyond notions of vocal silence and audience deafness.[2] For Kane, *Phoné* "is distinct from three other terms with which voice is often described": *echos*, *topos*, and *logos*—that is, roughly speaking, sound, site, and meaning. What Michel Chion describes as "elastic speech," but which we can expand to silent cinema "voice," might therefore be better conceptualized as a series of techniques necessitating a constant movement between different manifestations of *echos*, *topos*, and *logos*, created via various technologies or techniques (*technê*).[3] Because *echos* is sometimes entirely absent in the silent cinema, I also draw on Nicholas Cook's account of the inherently multimodal character of meaning apprehension, arguing that this fundamental aspect of human communication was exploited by the silent cinema such that "apprehension" is a more apt word than "listening" to describe how silent cinema's representational systems for voice become intelligible to the viewer.[4]

Voice in the Silent Cinema

As a first step toward theorizing early cinematic "voice," let us start with a few observations to clarify its nature. Silent cinematic voice is resolutely different from sound cinematic voice principally because the theatrical setup is different. Michel Chion argues that in sound cinema the suture effect leads to the image governing the triage of different types of sound, including voice.[5] We can all doubtless think of exceptions, but we would also probably recognize the typical scenario of synchronous sounds being "swallowed up" by the fiction, in the way Chion describes: you hear a sound and look for a potential screen source. In sound film, "it's as if the voice were wandering along the surface, *at once inside and outside*, seeking a place to settle," Chion suggests—"especially when a film hasn't yet shown what body this voice normally inhabits."[6] In this situation, sounds "from the proscenium" or "the pit" that are *not* visualized on-screen gain the spotlight because "they are perceived in their singularity and isolation."[7]

During the first thirty years of cinema, we can assume neither the same sight and sound relationship nor the same role of voice in cinematic entertainments. Film performance (as I prefer to describe silent film exhibition) did not have an invisible apparatus. The performers involved in film screenings were almost always visible, in one way or another, and so even attempts to render on-screen voices materially in the theatrical space created a kind of "off-screen" space by default; actual off-screen sound would likewise be located elsewhere in the theater. This is in contrast to the off-screen vocal sound of sound cinema, which in most cases comes from the same *actual* place as the other sounds—a central loudspeaker. Sonorous voice heard in the moment of "exhibition" or early performance only rarely coincides and "locks" with the image. Because of the many forms that voice took, the early film theater would not have been conducive to sutured listening, nor to comprehension of the screen as source of sound and voice triage.

Those many forms of voice included sonorous voices heard during the moment of exhibition, what Raynauld describes as "materially visualized" voice as part of onscreen scenarios, and a range of other techniques for representing word and speech, including and exceeding those described in Chion's account of "elastic speech."[8] It is useful to start with a short overview of the silent cinema's complex representational system for voice, approaching it along two axes: one that recognizes the defining feature of silent film exhibition, namely, that voices can be both heard and unheard; another that recognizes that voices can pertain directly to a moving picture entertainment, and/or be part of the wider mixed program. As Nicholas Hiley reminds us, over the first twenty-five years of projected moving pictures "the basic unit of exhibition was not the individual film but the programme."[9]

Of the unheard cinematic voices that relate directly to the moving pictures themselves, most fall into the category of on-screen visual effect and can pertain to fictional worlds and nonfictional worlds or can involve direct (performative) address. In fact, early screen scenarios often involved both fictional world and direct audience address, especially comedies and other entertainments transferred to screen from the popular entertainment stage.

Material Visualization of Voice

As Raynauld and others have revealed, the human voice, speech, and sound in general were constantly present in the scenarios of moving pictures during the first thirty years, and from the first decade of moving pictures, these scenarios "took place intradiegetically in a hearing world and not in a 'deaf world.'"[10] This "visualized sound cinema," as she calls it, showed or implied sound of a wide variety of sorts—from noises, to music, to voice. Films produced by Pathé 1907–1914, Georges Méliès (her particular focus), and others not only often implied sound that might go on in any "real world" situation but also included "sonorous events," that is, actions involving sound that carry narrative information and affect the course of the scenario. As she notes, film scenarios and films themselves did not wait for technological developments permitting perfect synchronization between image and sound in order to attempt to tell stories that were simultaneously visual and sonorous.

Mouthed Dialogue

The classic on-screen visual effect for voice is that of on-screen actors speaking or singing to each other in the hearing world that is the film set. Raynauld has debunked the myth that actors generally spoke randomly on set. Interested in what early actors of the silent screen were doing when they moved their lips, she performed a comprehensive study of screenplays and films written in France between 1895 and 1915, and found that more than half of the scripted titles and stories in the Pathé catalogue that were not actualities, sports, or travel films (1,925 out of 3,346) were what she felt able to term "early sound screenplays."[11] Of the screenplays she was able to pair with their corresponding films, it transpired that the dialogues were indeed those "intended to be performed by the actors." We also know that mouthed dialogue was often particular to the scene filmed because some early filmmakers wrote about asking actors to enunciate slowly and deliberately if they wished certain words to register.[12] Although it can be difficult for the audience to lip-read what the actors are saying, often and especially with films dating from after the late aughts, the meaning of the movement of their lips is more or less deducible—especially in the case of shouts, or simple phrases. A fragment may even be recognizable in a neighboring title.

But it was not simply a matter of voice being represented in a mute medium as an accidental byproduct of the photographic capturing of both fictional and nonfictional human happenings from the "hearing world." A remarkable facet of early films is how common scenarios in which voice and spoken word play a pivotal role were. According to the *American Film Institute Catalog of Motion Pictures Produced in the United States* (*Film Beginnings, 1893–1910*),[13] even before 1910 at least ten films with "voice" in the actual title were distributed in the United States; many more included music or singing in the title (six with the word "sing" or "singing"), and dozens with music or musicians, as follows:

1905 *His Master's Voice*
1906 *Voice of Conscience*
1907 *What His Girl's Voice Did*
1908 *His Daughter's Voice*
1908 *A Voice from the Dead*
1908 *The Voice of the Heart* [Italy: Aquila Films. *La voce del cuore*]
1909 *The Voice of the Violin*
1910 *A Powerful Voice* [Gaumont]
1910 *A Voice from the Fireplace*
1910 *The Voice of the Blood* [Itala Films]

And as Raynauld reports, many of the scenarios of early French films depended upon hearing particular words, such as Pathé's *Erreur de porte!!* (1904), which involves a character who hears or is told something that he would not have heard and who sees his life changed by that sound event.[14] In several films, Méliès comically thematizes the figure of the "talking head," which was a routine part of both spoken theater and moving pictures. The lips and head move; they are just severed from a body. In *L'Homme à la tête en caoutchouc* (The Man with the Rubber Head) the head speaks to Méliès (Figure 1.1a), in *L'Oeuf du sorcier* (The Sorceror's Egg)

Figure 1.1: (a) *L'Homme à la tête en caoutchouc* (The Man with the Rubber Head, 1901); (b) *L'Oeuf du sorcier* (The Sorceror's Egg, 1902).

and in *Le Chevalier mystère* (The Mysterious Knight), the head likewise doesn't stop moving, smiling, speaking to the magician (Figure 1.1b).[15]

The 1911 Italian comedy *Pik Nik ha il do di petto* (*Pik Nik as King of the High C*),[16] about a man with a stupendously loud voice, brings several of these traits together to comedic ends. Although we cannot hear Pik Nik's voice, his vocality is a "shown sound," to borrow Raynauld's terminology.[17] We see bodily gestures consistent with the production of an enormous sound: deep breath, wide opening of the mouth, and straining to produce a loud sound. To confirm our reading of that body language, other on-screen characters in the film's "hearing world"—our listening surrogates—react to his enormous vocal volume, and other things also happen as a result of it: characters fall over (Figure 1.2a), roofs cave in (Figure 1.2b), windows blow out, automobiles go into reverse, and so forth.

Figure 1.2: *Pik Nik ha il do di petto* (1911). (a) Characters fall to the strength of the voice; (b) the voice causes the roof to cave in. Courtesy of the Desmet Collection, EYE Filmmuseum, the Netherlands, with kind permission.

The Phonograph

Not only actors speaking to each other but sound technologies such as phonograph players or telephones could also indicate the intradiegetic presence of a voice. In *Il gramofono di Polidor* (Italy, 1912) a man pretends that he can sing beautifully by miming to a recording played on a gramophone unseen by other on-screen characters. In the final scene, Polidor uses foliage to hide the gramophone from his on-screen audience and mimes a concert, to which they react. Reflecting a thinking that is not only audiovisually apt for the film but recognizes the potential for trickery inherent in the technology, the gramophone crashes to the ground from its hiding spot, thereby revealing to the on-screen audience, *Wizard of Oz*–like, the technological ruse.

Speaking with the Body

Physical gesture can also assist in visualizing the presence and quality of a mute speaking or singing voice. In other words, voice might be rendered in an embodied form—as pantomime or melodramatic bodily gesture—as a replacement for the absent voice, instead of, or in addition to, speaking on the set. In 1907 George Méliès identified the importance of an actor's bodily gestures in conveying meaning when "the camera is the only viewer":

> There is no longer an audience for the actor to address, either verbally or with gestures. . . . Actors must realize that they have to make themselves understood to the deaf viewers watching them while remaining completely silent. Their performances must not be showy and yet be very expressive. Few gestures are used, but they must be very distinct and clear. They must create perfect physiognomies and strike just the right pose. I have seen many scenes performed by well-known actors who were not good because the principal element of their success, speech, is lacking in the kinematograph.[18]

Notwithstanding the uncomfortably ableist implications of Méliès's language choice, historians and theorists have increasingly taken his lead in thinking about these films in terms of their comprising a hearing world to which the audience is rendered deaf.[19] In English, we retrospectively describe the first thirty years of the moving pictures as "silent cinema," ignoring the many sounds created in the theatrical moment; in many other languages these moving pictures are characterized as "mute" (*cinéma muet, Stummfilm, němý film*), the ableist language to which Méliès's own term refers. None of these terms is ideal, as I will suggest later with reference to a more multidimensional mode of comprehension.

Text

Printed words on the screen could materialize voice in numerous ways. Until the conventions of title cards developed, this might be quite artisanal, as in Edwin

Porter's *College Chums* (1907), which uses printed words to convey speech content and suggest spatial location. A telephone conversation is rendered via two people located in the top left and right corners of the screen, with the words of their conversation floating through the space (Figure 1.3). As Bernard Perron notes, this is a version of the more common split-screen idea that aimed to represent on one screen connections between two diegetic spaces before the development of narrative editing (which linked spaces via cuts): divided sets or screens "directly juxtaposed scene and off-scene."[20]

Although used earlier by individual exhibitors and even distributed earlier by some manufacturers, intertitles came into general use from about 1910, and became the norm in the teens.[21] Either made by the exhibitor locally, or provided with films by the manufacturer, they enabled film to become independent of a lecturer (discussed later)—whether as an announcer between items on the program or as an explainer of scenario and later narrative content. In addition to providing film credits and serving to introduce characters and even whole scenes, title cards served to clarify the actual meaning of the voices otherwise embodied on-screen. Between 1910 and 1914 "dialogic intertitles" emerged, in lowercase and using quotation marks. They reported speech directly or indirectly and/or provided brief narrative commentary. They could also attempt to convey something of the sonic effect of speech—using size of the printed word to serve as a "code for the reading eye"—or "vocal cues" (to use Chion's term) dramatizing how a film audience might listen internally, whether to a text version of on-screen speech—such as Figures 1.4a and 1.4b from Murnau's *Sunrise* (1927), variously (a) hesitant and (b) insistent—or to an emphatic commentary—such as Figure 1.4c from Captain J. Noel's *The Epic of Everest* (1924).

Figure 1.3: *College Chums* (1907).

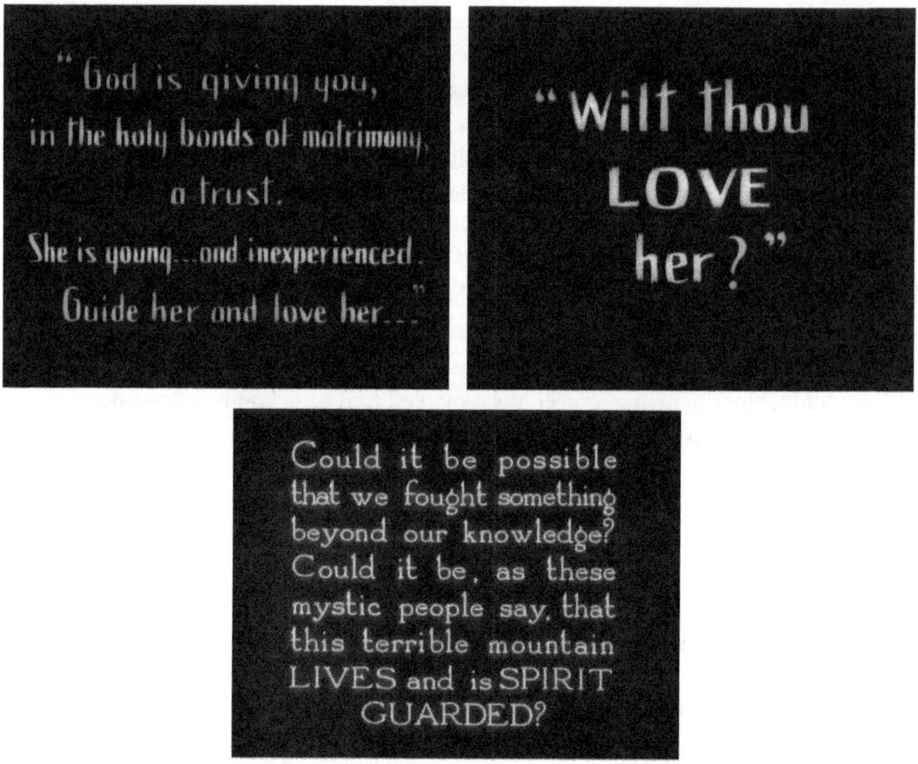

Figure 1.4: (a) *Sunrise* (1927): hesitant dialogue card; (b) *Sunrise*: insistent dialogue card; (c) *The Epic of Everest* (1924): emphatic commentary.

For Chion, however, such expressive title cards did not provide signals as to pronunciation; rather, they dramatized the impact the word(s) were supposed to have and therefore how we should understand them.[22] The "voices" translated into different types of title cards also commanded different levels of attention, according to Chion, and this is a level of narrative nuance that was lost with the onset of the sound film. They could give little snatches of information (e.g., "Afternoon") or conjure up a "narrator" who could be relatively detached—even ironic. Often, the "voice" expressed through the intertitle's commentary was "smarter than the characters."[23]

Sonorous Voice in the Theater

We need to move away from the screen itself, however, for there were many audible voices in the silent cinema, and they were as likely to relate to other entertainments on the mixed program as to the moving pictures themselves. Cinematic voices emanated from in front of, to the side of, or even behind the screen for a range of purposes including the performance of illustrated songs (a staple of the nickelodeon in the United States) and a range of other entertainments that varied according to year and type of venue but which included potentially singers, actors, and comedians; from the mid-teens a live prologue might also have included some sort of voice. And especially in the first fifteen to twenty years of the moving pictures, an overall showman might have held the show together—and possibly also lectured to individual films.

The Voice in the Theater

One of the most common of these voices was that of a live spoken commentator (that is, a film lecturer or describer), who might have provided a commentary to the physically moving lips or bodies on-screen, probably lecturing from in front of the screen and to the side. Such a lecturer might have described scenes, spoken concurrently with the film, or spoken between films. Even once title cards had developed, a lecturer might have read titles aloud or summarized them, as if "indirect speech" in a novel.[24]

In early cinema, voices extended to actors speaking and singing in hybrid moving picture–theatrical productions. Alfred De Manby's Kinemacolor film *Mephisto*, accompanied by "music selected entirely from Gounod's *Faust*," was shown at the Scala Theatre in London in August 1912 in just such a hybrid form. The full-page advertorial in *Kinematograph and Lantern Weekly* describes the character Mephisto being revealed when the curtain rises in a "beautifully staged scene," only to disappear from the stage and for Kinemacolor to present the first part of the story: "The disembodied presence of Mephisto appears on the screen."[25] Only when we return to the staged cavern does Mephisto reappear there, where he "calls forth the aid of Wine." The multimedia work ends with Mephisto in his cavern on stage singing, "Mankind is mine; the world is mine." This description suggests a live theatrical voice floating in location, from onstage source to perhaps hidden source occasionally "swallowed up" by the on-screen fiction, much as in the sound cinema described by Chion.

Around the same time, actors sometimes lip-synced dialogue live, usually from behind the screen, creating an effect of synchronized speech and approximations to realism that astonished many audiences. "The Humanovo" and "Ta-Mo-Pic" (Talking Moving Pictures) were two such troupes in the United States.[26] Live singing voices synchronized with moving pictures were also found. According to a report in *Kinematograph and Lantern Weekly*, as late as November 12, 1925, in the United Kingdom, Bristol exhibitors running larger houses added atmosphere to their films by making use of singing *to* the picture.[27] Feeling by that stage that people came to their cinemas to see the film, they seemed less keen than some on the reemergence elsewhere of interest in variety turns which, being an addition to their programs, also necessitated a special license.

Musical Mimicry

Musical mimicry of the human voice was also sometimes used. Cinema organists sometimes tried to mimic the human voice from the pit using the *vox humana* stop. This short-resonator reed stop has a long history on the pipe organ and is so named because of its supposed resemblance to the human voice; it was usually used in churches to evoke the impression of a singing choir or vocal soloist. For music columnist Arthur Roby in the British trade paper *The Cinema*, "There is no better imitation of the human voice to be found."[28] British cinema organist Reginald Foort recalls creating actual dialogue:

> One of the best effects I remember getting in a silent picture was in the sentimental situation at the end, when the repentant wife returned to the home and the husband quietly greeted her with: "Hello, Mary," and she replied: "Hello, Joe." I succeeded in reproducing these two phrases in their respective registers in such a way that the audience really got an impression of the characters speaking.[29]

Composers of original scores took this type of musical mimicry a step further and sometimes drew on classical techniques, such as creating an orchestral melody with rhythmic patterning to represent direct speech, thereby making the dialogue in title cards if not speak, then almost sing. Fiona Ford has written about Edmund Meisel's use in *Der heilige Berg* (1926) of "declamatory melodies with exact or near-exact rhythmic replication of the dialogue exchanges in the intertitles"—and his return to the technique in *The Crimson Circle*, which was rereleased in 1929 with dialogue, sound effects, and a postsynchronized score.[30] However, this technique was used at least a year earlier in London in an original score by Frederick Laurence to the Soviet fairy-tale film, *Morozko* (1924, shown in London in 1925 as *Morosko*). The key sequence is a simple exchange between Moroz (Father Frost) and Marfushka while she is abandoned by her stepmother in the forest in the depths of winter. Moroz tests her manners and patience by repeatedly asking, "Are you warm?" to which she politely and stoically replies, "I am warm." The exchange is repeated three times as a type of incantation, and for this Laurence creates a beautiful lyrical melody, the opening of which is exactly patterned for the key phrase (Figure 1.5). The film version adapted for screening in London does not survive, only a Russian-language print does. And although a separate list of the English translations of the title cards is likewise lost, for this moment the score includes a specific quotation ("Are you warm?"), so we know the phrase with which Laurence was working here. It is not possible to know exactly how the rest of the phrase was translated, but "dear Marfushka" or "my dear maiden" would all translate the Russian and fit with the melody as it continues.

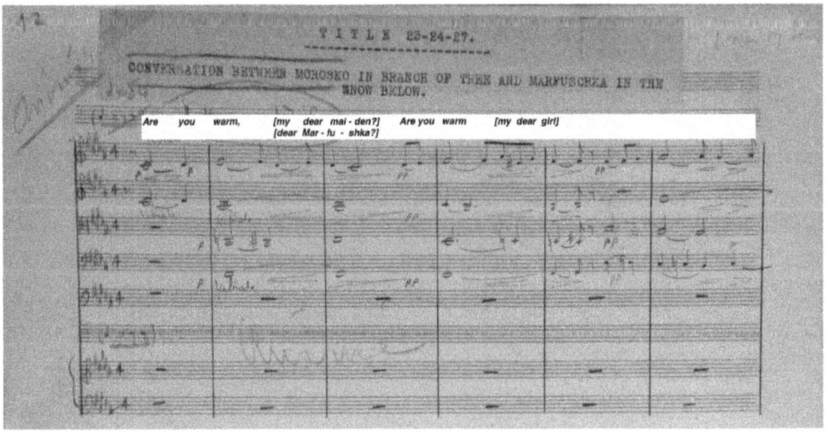

Figure 1.5: Frederick Laurence, original music for 1925 London screenings of *Morozko* (1924). Reproduced with kind permission of Anthony Laurence.

Silent Film and Techniques of the Voice

As this admittedly non-exhaustive outline suggests, there were many types of voice in the silent cinema and many placements for it. On-screen these were *translations* of embodied ways in which intelligible communication, including actual vocalization, takes place: linguistic communication is either substituted or amplified by gesture or written word. In the theatrical space, it could be re-created live by real people, summarized as part of a live third-person commentary, or mimicked by musical instruments. Other conventions were iterative. For instance, Chion argues that mimed gestures were often not so much a code that translated the content of what was being said, as a way of "show[ing] with the whole body that one was speaking" at all.[31] And in order to convey that a sound persists over a period of time while other events happen, repeated shots of the sound-making person or object were often shown, a formal byproduct of which was the creation of patterns of "refrain-shots." Raynauld wonders whether the almost over-loquacious talking heads in certain early films—notably Méliès's "talking head" trick films—sometimes talk more than they do in later "talkies" in order to mimic verbal exchange especially well, just as the bodily gestures of melodrama exaggerate real bodily expression.[32] And as she also notes, early films often afford the audience a virtual listening position via one of the on-screen characters. Although this device can be important in later sound films, too, in the silent cinema such a character could serve an especially crucial role as what she calls "the spectator's delegate in the story" precisely because the audience could not hear in the same way. Such on-screen listening surrogates might simply acknowledge the very presence of voice or might go further and register something of its spoken (or sung) content or quality—as in the *Pik Nik* example discussed earlier.

Voice typically commanded attention via two or more visual markers (such as moving lips and title cards, or moving lips and lecturer), and often in two or more physical spaces in the theater (screen and proscenium, or screen and pit). When materially present from the proscenium or pit, voices were not only physically and hence potentially conceptually isolated from the screen but often provided an alternative focus of visual attention. More rarely, but certainly sometimes, they were materially present behind the screen. Voices played important roles in rendering moving pictures comprehensible to audiences, and eventually in creating narrative, but they also featured in entertainments on the mixed program.

Because of the way in which voices were constantly emanating from different locations and serving different functions, Brian Kane's recent reconceptualization of "voice" as *phoné* is helpful in approaching the silent cinema—though with a modification. As I noted at the beginning of this essay, Kane distinguishes voice as *Phoné* from *echos, topos,* and *logos,* which constitute its sound, site, and meaning. *Phoné,* he argues, "is constituted by the spacing of *echos, topos* and *logos,* supplemented by *technê*"—this last encompassing both technologies and techniques used to produce voice; *phoné* itself "involves the movement, or displacement, between these terms."[33] The various methods for materializing voice that I have outlined might therefore be conceptualized as a series of techniques necessitating a constant movement between different manifestations of *echos, topos,* and *logos,* created via various technologies or techniques in order to render silent cinema "voice."

The crucial adaptation that one needs to make to this model stems from the fact that vocal sound itself, *echos,* is sometimes entirely absent at the silent cinema. From one perspective, we could consider its various methods for materializing voice as prostheses for the absence of realistic synchronized vocal presence. For Chion, this does not prove a conceptual problem: listening in the silent cinema was always translation—theatrical sound effects and musical performance were never realistic.[34] This was equally true of music materialized on-screen and only made audible by musicians in the pit. Thus for him, listening involved a process of retranslation or retransposition of what was seen by means of the resources available. But to think of the representations of the silent cinema as always channeled through listening, translated or otherwise, seems a slightly perverse way to approach a form for which sound was not coming from the screen; it also encourages us to characterize early cinema via the ableist language of "muteness" and "deafness." If we approach it from another perspective, we could consider these various systems for conveying meaning—*logos*—as part of a complex, newly emergent, multimodal system of communication that was the moving pictures. As Bernard Perron puts it, the so-called silent cinema "may not truly appeal to hearing, but it appeals nevertheless to understanding."[35]

The dimension of "intelligibility," or "understanding," of interest to Perron is the role that materialized sound plays in the construction of early screen narrative. Before the conventions of continuity editing established themselves, the articulation of transitions between different spatial and temporal domains was very difficult. Spectators could not yet be expected to understand. The connection of spaces via on-screen materialized sound was a little easier to conceive, and what Perron called "transi-sounds" helped to forge connections between spaces, initially the adjacent spaces that had often been shown simultaneously in the one frame using a split screen. For Raynauld, the key loss to understanding for early cinema audiences was the loss of word's phatic function. Word was not entirely absent or useless in a story's structure: materialized in various other ways, "Word as a mode of verbal expression . . . ha[d] not lost its principal function which is to 'say.'"[36] Yet, as we have seen, it was not only words, spoken or sung by characters on-screen, that were "saying." The many ways in which moving pictures sought to communicate meaning demanded what Nicholas Cook might call a multimodal environment of communication.[37] As part of a critique of the tendency in the age of technological reproduction to valorize listening modes that ignore the embodied nature of performances behind recordings, Cook points out that animals respond to a range of signs that might indicate danger—seeing, hearing, smelling, feeling—without making distinctions between one mode and another, and without relying on just one. If, as Raynauld notes, early cinema teaches us to look at sound, and above all to look at sound's impact on others, it goes well beyond that and encourages us to process materialized sound and sonorous information in the context of a richer multimodal approach to conveying and apprehending meaning. We are afforded a complex array of signs for creating the sense of sound; it is our job to read these together. The so-called "silent cinema" was arguably the cultural form *par excellence* to depend upon such a multimodal mode of communication. Thomas Elsaesser's observation about early film construction of actions in space and time equally apply to the sonic dimension of the entire first thirty years of film: namely, that in so-called silent film "[t]he impression of intelligibility . . . is not so much a question of how real that which is being filmed actually is (i.e., the documentary value of what is before the camera), but whether the system that governs its representation is intelligible to the viewer."[38] Film's efforts to render vocality intelligible included materialized voice, body language, live sonorous voice, written-down speaking and narrating voices, and both musically and sonically conventionalized vocal effects.

Funning and Knowingness

A 1918 manual, *How Motion Pictures Are Made*, stresses the engagement that so-called silent cinema required of its audiences: "With the words unspoken, the observer enters into the play and imagines himself a participator more than if some omniscient machine supplied them."[39] The type of multimodal narrative, or proto-narrative, engagement that I have touched on so far was only one aspect of that. Just as early moving pictures as a visual form need to be read alongside other earlier forms of visual culture, such as lantern slides, dioramas, and so forth, the same is true of early film sound cultures. So-called "film funners" in American nickelodeons depended upon audiences listening carefully to the pianist's accompaniment; in order to benefit fully from the entertainment provided, audiences needed to recognize the pianist's deliberate choice of popular songs whose lyrics bore a comic or ironic relation to what was on the screen. Individual scenes or entire films could be "funned" with musical puns that commented on the picture through the title, lyrics, or melody of the accompanying music—usually a popular song. Clarence E. Sinn reported in *Moving Picture World*, for example, that he'd watched a scene where the pharaoh's daughter discovers the baby Moses, at which point the pianist breaks out into the popular song "Oh You Kid."[40]

Cultural historian Peter Bailey has described the equivalent relationship between the performer and audience in British music halls as a culture of "knowingness." It involved a listening collusion between performer and audience, whereby the performer was playing to and listening for audience reaction and the audience was listening to the offering in a "knowing" way. A two-way communication created the performance. The performer used what was known and familiar, and the audience registered recognition through catcalls, shouts, or laughter which allowed for shortcuts and understatement to create pathos and humor.[41] Film funners likewise depended upon the audience's "knowingness" in order to listen to the popular song, recognize it, mentally interpolate the relevant lyric, and then enjoy the comic effect. In a Stanley Kubrick film, we would simply call this irony. However, his practice grows out of this type of collusive listening during live performances.

We might describe as "imaginary listening" our engagement with the various materialized voices that constitute "elastic speech." But as I have argued here, cinema voices go beyond modes of speech, and by adding the many live theatrical voices, also beyond the imaginary. We could try to salvage the *echos* of silent cinema's *phoné* by suggesting that on-screen visual effects of voices (moving lips, and graphically suggestive title cards) foster the creation of imagined voices, phantasmal voices, and phantasmal sound, a term Raynauld borrows from Oliver Sacks's account of the voices that deaf people who became deaf after a period of normal hearing are capable of hearing in their mind's ear.[42] It is a mental trace of a remembered sound world. However, the notion of phantasmal voice might then need to extend to the expressive type used in title cards, which can likewise create an implication of a sonic realm that is imagined internally by the audience member.

We don't need *echos* in our model of silent film voice. It is not that we don't listen in the silent cinema; we do, we listen a lot. And it is hard to disagree with Chion that silent cinema engendered a *discontinuity of listening*, where there were "often dramatic variations in attention and hearing, when a particular word or noise resonates differently from those that have come before."[43] Voice apprehension, which might or might not involve listening to the *echos* of Kane's *phoné*, seems a better concept for modeling audience attention to the highly stylized modes for conveying voice in the silent cinema. The systems for representing voice in silent cinema, and hence our route to apprehending it, may not always have entailed the sounds that we might think foundational to an intelligible concept of voice, yet such voices remain tantalizingly intelligible.

Notes

1. Isabelle Raynauld, "Présence, fonction et représentation du son dans les scénarios et les films de Georges Méliès (1896–1912). Mise en scène du son," in *Georges Méliès, l'illusionniste fin de siècle?* ed. Jacques Malthête and Michel Marie, Actes du colloque de Cerisy (Paris: Presses de la Sorbonne Nouvelle, 1997), 201–17 (205).

2. Brian Kane, "The Model Voice," in "Colloquy: Why Voice Now?" Martha Feldman, convener, *Journal of the American Musicological Society* 68, no. 3 (2015): 671–77. See also Kane, *Sound Unseen: Acousmatic Sound in Theory and Practice* (New York: Oxford University Press, 2014).

3. Michel Chion uses the term "elastic speech" in *Film: A Sound Art*, trans. Claudia Gorbman (New York: Columbia University Press, 2009), 11.

4. Nicholas Cook, "Seeing Sounds, Hearing Images: Listening Outside the Modernist Box," in *Musical Listening in the Age of Technological Reproduction*, ed. Gianmario Borio (Burlington: Ashgate, 2015), 185–202.

5. See, for instance, Chion, *The Voice in Cinema*, trans. Claudia Gorbman (New York: Columbia University Press, 1999), 3.

6. Ibid., 23 (emphasis in original).

7. Ibid., 4.

8. Chion, *Film: A Sound Art*, 11.

9. Nicholas Hiley, "'At the Picture Palace': The British Cinema Audience, 1895–1920," in *Celebrating 1895: The Centenary of Cinema*, ed. John Fullerton (London: John Libbey, 1998), 97.

10. Raynauld, "Dialogues in Early Silent Sound Screenplays: What Actors Really Said," in *The Sounds of Early Cinema*, ed. Richard Abel and Rick Altman (Bloomington: Indiana University Press, 2001), 69–78 (69).

11. Ibid., 70.

12. Ibid.

13. Patricia King Hanson, Kenneth White Munden, and Alan Gevinson, eds. *American Film Institute Catalog* (Los Angeles: University of California Press, 1993).

14. Raynauld, "Le 'sonore visible' dans les scénarios et dans les films Pathé dits 'muets,'" in *La firme Pathé Frères, 1896–1914*, ed. Michel Marie and Laurent Le Forestier, with Catherine Schapira (Paris: L'Association française de recherche sur l'histoire du cinéma, 2004), 213–18 (215).

15. Raynauld, "Présence, fonction et représentation," 208–9.

16. The print that survives in the Eye Filmmuseum, Amsterdam, is German: *Teddy Holzbock als Ritter vom Hoben C.*

17. Raynauld categorizes the intradiegetic materialized sound in these earliest films according to two key forms: "shown sound," where *the source* of the sound is *explicit*, and "heard/unheard sound," for which the sound source is implicit (invisible) and for which *reaction* to the sound might be filmed ("Le 'sonore visible,'" 216).

18. Georges Méliès, "Kinematographic Views" (1907), edited, with an introduction and annotations by Jacques Malthête, trans. Stuart Liebman and Timothy Barnard, in André Gaudreault, *Film and Attraction: From Kinematography to Cinema*, trans. Timothy Barnard (Urbana: University of Illinois Press, 2011), 133–52 (145).

19. Chion did this in 1982 in *La voix au cinéma* (Paris: Editions de l'Étoile, 1982), translated as *The Voice in Cinema*, 7–8. Isabelle Raynauld's subsequent work on deafness and the silent cinema informs his later foray on the topic in *Film: A Sound Art* (2009).

20. Bernard Perron, "The First *Transi-Sounds* of Parallel Editing," in *The Sounds of Early Cinema*, ed. Abel and Altman, 79–86 (84).

21. This short history of title cards is from Claire Dupré la Tour, "Intertitles and Titles," in *Encyclopedia of Early Cinema*, ed. Richard Abel (New York: Routledge, 2005), 326–31.

22. Chion, *Film: A Sound Art*, 12–13.

23. Ibid., 15.

24. For a comprehensive overview of film lecturing, see Joe Kember, "Professional Lecturing in Early British Film Shows," in *The Sounds of the Silents in Britain*, ed. Julie Brown and Annette Davison (New York: Oxford University Press, 2013), 17–37.

25. Kinemacolor Supplement to the *Kinematograph and Lantern Weekly*, August 29, 1912.

26. See Rick Altman, *Silent Film Sound* (New York: Columbia University Press, 2004), 169–70.

27. *Kinematograph Weekly*, Supplement, November 12, 1925, "The West Country," iv.

28. Arthur Roby, "It Pays to Play," *The Cinema* (July 8, 1920), 63.

29. Reginald Foort, *The Cinema Organ: A Description in Non-Technical Language of a Fascinating Instrument and How It Is Played*, 2nd edition (London: Pitman, 1932), 87–88.

30. Fiona Ford, "Edmund Meisel's 'Visual Sound' in *The Crimson Circle* (1929): The Case of the Vanishing Part-Talkie," in *The Sounds of the Silents in Britain*.

31. Chion, *Film: A Sound Art*, 4.

32. Raynauld, "Présence, fonction et représentation," 208.

33. Kane, "The Model Voice," 672.

34. As many have noted and Chion restresses, in *Film: A Sound Art*, 7.

35. Perron, "The First *Transi-Sounds* of Parallel Editing," 82.

36. Raynauld, "Présence, fonction et représentation," 210.

37. Nicholas Cook, "Seeing Sounds, Hearing Images," 185–202.

38. Thomas Elsaesser, "Early Film Form: Articulations of Space and Time—Introduction," in *Early Cinema: Space, Frame, Narrative*, ed. Thomas Elsaesser and Adam Barker (London: BFI Press, 1990), 11–30 (12).

39. Quoted in Raynauld, "Le 'sonore visible,'" 218.

40. Clarence E. Sinn, "Music for the Pictures," *Moving Picture World*, November 26, 1910, 12–27.

41. Peter Bailey, "Conspiracies of Meaning: Music-Hall and the Knowingness of Popular Culture," *Past and Present* (August 1994), 146. See also Peter Bailey, *Music Hall: The Business of Pleasure* (Milton Keynes: Open University Press, 1986); Anthony Bennett, "Music in The Halls," in *Music Hall: Performance and Style*, ed. Jacky Bratton (Milton Keynes: Open University Press, 1986), 1–22.

42. Raynauld, "Dialogues in Early Silent Sound Screenplays," 73.

43. Chion, *Film: A Sound Art*, 13.

Chapter 2

Silencing and Sounding the Voice in Transition-Era French Cinema

Hannah Lewis

"In actual movies," claims Michel Chion, "there are not *all the sounds including the human voice. There are voices, and then everything else.* In other words, in every audio mix, the presence of a human voice instantly sets up a hierarchy of perception . . . *the presence of a human voice structures the sonic space that contains it.*"[1] Just as human listening is by nature vococentric, so, too, is narrative cinema, and if a human voice is part of the sonic space of a film, "the ear is inevitably carried toward it, picking it out, and structuring the perception of the whole around it."[2] Building on Chion's claims of vococentric cinema, David Neumeyer more recently argued that vococentrism is a central tenet of an integrated soundtrack, which has direct bearing on the ways in which we understand music's role in film: "The sound track is constructed—the overriding priority in the classical system being narrative clarity, not acoustic fidelity—and it is hierarchical, with the voice (speech, dialogue) at the top, music and sound effects below."[3] Chion and Neumeyer mainly conceived of vococentrism in the context of classical Hollywood cinema, but the concept applies equally well to classical cinema in other national contexts. For the most part, in mainstream narrative cinema, the voice, the soundtrack's fundamental conveyer of narrative information, rests comfortably at the top of the hierarchy of sounds in cinema's integrated soundtrack.

In the late 1920s and early 1930s, however, during the first years of synchronized sound, this privileged role of the voice was far from a given. Although the voice was one of sound film's main attractions, it was not universally accepted as its most artistically interesting feature. Sound film became particularly contentious in France during this time, prompting widespread ontological debates about whether sound, particularly voices, would complete cinematic art or destroy it. Within this heated debate, two diverging aesthetics emerged in early French sound cinema: one that shared more affinities with silent film, and another that was proximate to live theater. Though neither approach was unique to France, French filmmakers were perhaps the boldest in experimenting with the extremes of each possibility. The treatment of the voice in each aesthetic, in turn, had a profound effect on the treatment of music within the soundtrack.

This essay examines these contrasting aesthetics of the voice in early 1930s French cinema, and the role that music played in each. Filmed theater, or *théâtre filmé*, emerged from the conception that sound cinema was primarily a recording medium and tended toward what James Buhler calls "mimetic synchronization," or "the demand that the source of the sound be accounted for in the image."[4] In French theatrical adaptations, the speaking voice dominated, taking precedence over all other elements of the soundtrack. This approach to the voice went beyond our traditional understanding of vococentrism: the predominance of voice in *théâtre filmé* left little space for music on the soundtrack, precluding the hierarchical structure of the integrated soundtrack upon which vococentrism is based. Film musicologists have paid scant attention to these films, since the predominance of the spoken word seems to leave little of musical interest. However, I argue that in *théâtre filmé*, speech, or *parole*, takes on almost musical qualities, folding music and sound effects into the voice itself. Theatrical cadence, in the context of the sound film, was transformed into something attractively modulated for the soundtrack. This kind of approach to the soundtrack was exemplified in adaptations like Jean Renoir's *On purge bébé* (1931).

On the other side of the debate were avant-garde filmmakers like René Clair and Jean Grémillon, who rejected the restriction of camera movement imposed by the model of mimetic synchronization and hoped to recapture some of the visual freedom characteristic of silent cinema. Clair and Grémillon, whose films *Sous les toits de Paris* (1930) and *La Petite Lise* (1930), respectively, told their stories with as little spoken dialogue as possible, incorporated music prominently into their soundtracks in order to *silence* the speaking voice. They frequently experimented with integrating different audiovisual modes that were usually kept distinct in early sound film—silence with musical accompaniment, talking, and singing—moving between them seamlessly within scenes. Though the intent may have been to strip the voice of its dominance within the soundtrack, these directors' strategic denial of the voice often granted it a much greater significance.

Neither of the diverging approaches found in early French sound cinema is characteristic of vococentrism as it came to be adopted as a principle in the classical style. Rather, by examining these early experiments with the voice on the soundtrack in the transition years, my analysis expands Chion and Neumeyer's concept of "vococentrism" to include different models of understanding the voice in cinema beyond those found in classical Hollywood and helps shed light on competing conceptions of the voice's role in cinema before practices became codified.

Ubiquitous Voice and Vocal Rhythm in *Théâtre Filmé*

In silent cinema, voice was most often suggested, represented indexically through the images of characters speaking, the text of intertitles, and the sounds of musical accompaniment.[5] Therefore, when sound film first appeared, talking—spoken dialogue that synchronized precisely with the moving lips of onscreen bodies—was one of its biggest novelties, precisely because it was something that silent cinema had been incapable of offering. As the very name "talkies" suggests, early sound films frequently highlighted and emphasized the synchronization of onscreen bodies and their perfectly matched voices.

This attention to the voice in cinema was not universally praised, to say the least. As I have argued elsewhere, the response to synchronized sound by French critics and filmmakers was particularly fraught, for reasons both economic and aesthetic.[6] Diverging discourses on sound film emerged in the late 1920s. Some spoke out as proponents of the new technology, seeing it as a broadening and perfecting of the limited art form of silent cinema. Perhaps the biggest proponent of *théâtre filmé* was Marcel Pagnol, a playwright whose highly successful stage play *Marius* was adapted for film in 1931. Pagnol wrote in 1930 that for theater practitioners, talkies would offer "a broadening of their art."[7]

Others lamented the havoc dialogue would wreak on the French film industry and, more generally, on film aesthetics: it threatened to destroy the very elements that seemed to define cinema, particularly the nuanced poetic quality of its form of visual expression. Filmmakers and critics wrote prolifically about the soundtrack, and theory and practice were intertwined, each influencing the other during this transitional period.

Theatrical adaptation was common internationally during the transition era, but it became particularly prevalent in France and continued well into the 1930s. Filmed theater emerged in part for expediency and in part because of the ways it showed off certain features of sound film. It was expedient because the theater provided endless source material that was easily adaptable for the screen. Additionally, in France, Paris was both the theatrical and cinematic center, which made it easy for actors to work on both stage and screen and, in some cases, to perform a role they had made famous on the stage for the film adaptation of the same story. Perhaps more importantly, filmed theater, particularly boulevard comedy, was a genre that heavily featured spoken dialogue, which best showed off the ability of the new technology to capture onscreen bodies and their synchronized voices.

Audiences loved these films: according to film historian Ginette Vincendeau, "the ability to hear [their] own language spoken . . . proved a source of unending pleasure for French audiences."[8] However, both at the time and especially in subsequent criticism and scholarship, the genre has been disparaged for its "uncinematic qualities": a focus on dialogue often came at the expense of camera movement, forcing static visuals that at the time seemed like an aesthetic step backward for the cinema, which had in the silent era developed a complex and multifaceted visual style. Critic François Mazeline wrote in 1928: "The Cinema is, by definition, a mute Art. It is a sort of ideographic writing; the opposite of the spoken word. To create a talking cinema is to create a bad rival to theater for poor neighborhoods."[9] A critic for *Ami du peuple* also saw theater and cinema as incompatible, writing that:

> Cinema is the art of movement.
>
> Theater is the art of the spoken word.
>
> Allow me to explain: in theater, only the spoken word is important. All the rest—mise-en-scène, the actor's performance, etc., only serve to showcase the spoken word.
>
> However, the spoken word is the enemy of movement.[10]

Scholars, too, have typically written off the *théâtre filmé* as crowd-pleasers with little cinematic value: Dudley Andrew writes that the theatrical model in French film was dominated by the star presence of the actors onscreen, "outweighing obligations to the film as a well-made object or work of art."[11]

The *théâtre filmé* model of sound film, that of mimetic synchronization, required that all sounds be sourced from within the image itself, that onscreen voices be paired with onscreen bodies. Because of its unwavering anchoring in the image, upon first listen, the soundtrack of the *théâtre filmé* seems of even less interest than the visuals. These films are verbocentric, to use Michel Chion's term, almost overflowing in their abundance of speech.[12] The voice monopolizes the soundtrack, leaving little room for a musical score or even sound effects. In doing so, however, the voice itself begins to take on musical qualities. *Théâtre filmé* soundtracks are rich with phrasing, variety of pitch and volume, contrasting timbre, cadences, and rhythmic variation.

Beyond the reaches of language and narrative, the grain of the voice—the materiality of the actors' vocal instruments—has its own affective impact.[13] This kind of musicalization of spoken dialogue was a feature of live theater before it was adapted for the cinema. Katherine Bergeron has pointed out the similarities between declamation and singing of French *mélodie* at the start of the twentieth century, suggesting that "we cannot really separate actors from singers in discussion of the French art of diction." In discussing stage actress Sarah Bernhardt's readings of poetry by Racine, for instance, Bergeron claims that a "strange kind of *mélodie* emerges from her tremulous cadences, with pitches and rhythms so true that they can easily be transcribed."[14] Audiences attended live theater in part because of the pleasure of hearing these musicalized voices.

The act of transposing theater to the cinema imported these musical qualities that were already present in live theater; but it also had a transformative effect that further enhanced the voice's musical qualities. Marcel Pagnol, who was one of the strongest proponents of filmed theater, acknowledged how actors' performances would take on different effects in the sound film, thanks to the microphone:

> Every spectator would hear the actor's words just as the little round box hears them when they are recorded; in a cinema hall there aren't a thousand spectators, there is only one.
>
> The consequences of this property are immense; for, from now on, we can achieve effects that have been unattainable onstage.
>
> First of all, we are no longer bound by the dimensions of the hall. . . . We can write a scene in whispers, and make it understandable to three thousand people, without changing the pitch and tone of the whispering. . . . Here's a new domain, . . . which can be conveyed without cries and large gestures, with a wonderful simplicity and a balance up to now unknown simply because it was impossible.[15]

By transposing a play to the cinema, actors could change their enunciation and delivery. They could modulate between softer, more intimate sounds to louder ones more quickly. Intimate dialogue was more effective on film than in a theater. Additionally, when plays were adapted for the screen, dialogue was frequently recast to include more dialogue exchanges between characters rather than lengthy monologues. Therefore, although dialogue in both live theater and cinema used musical principles in performing their voices, the recording apparatus—the act of recording captured by the microphone and played back via loudspeakers—enhanced the musical quality of voices onscreen.

In the sound film, therefore, the voice takes on additional function alongside that of being a conveyer of narrative information. It is an almost complete reversal of silent film, where music was tasked with doing the expressive work in the absence of voices; instead, in *théâtre filmé* the voice adds musical expressivity to the soundtrack. Rapid-fire dialogue especially accentuates the rhythmic, musical qualities of the spoken word.[16] Although the rule of mimetic synchronization often resulted in less frequent visual editing and a more static camera,[17] the quick exchange of dialogue between actors offered an aural equivalent to montage, anchoring the scene in sonic, instead of visual, contrast. Drawing on Barthes, Neumeyer and James Buhler argue that the grain can

> be deployed to create structural articulations as the characteristic sounds of individual voices interweave with one another as sound rather than meaning to become structurally significant on the aural plane of the sound track. In such cases, voices can recur like musical themes, and the changing mode of expression (anger, melancholy, gruffness, and so on) and form of address (public, private, formal, informal) resemble variants of musical themes and characteristic mood music.[18]

For Neumeyer and Buhler, the grain of the voice is "the opposing principle to vococentrism, the noisy oppositional ground vococentrism requires to establish the centrality of its order."[19] In the *théâtre filmé*, voices take on extra-verbal significance at the same time as they convey narrative information, playing on this tension, this noisy oppositional ground.

On purge bébé, Jean Renoir's first sound film from 1931, is a quintessential example. The film was an adaptation of a one-act play by Georges Feydeau, and starred well-known stage actors Marguerite Pierry, Jacques Louvigny, and Michel Simon. The film is a farce, focusing on the bourgeois Follavoine family. Mr. Follavoine is a porcelain salesman, who wishes to sell unbreakable chamber pots to the French army. He invites Mr. Chouilloux, an official with the army, to his house for lunch to close the deal. Unfortunately, Toto, Follavoine's son, happens to be constipated on that day, and despite Mrs. Follavoine's (Julie's) chiding, refuses to take his laxative. Feydeau's dialogue highlights the ridiculousness of the situation, commenting on the absurdity of bourgeois pretensions. The entirety of the film is set in the Follavoines' apartment and unfolds in real time.

Besides an infamous sound effect of a flushing toilet, there are very few sounds apart from spoken dialogue. Music appears only during the opening credits and at the very close of the film. A few diegetic sound effects occur—Follavoine throws a chamber pot down the hallway to demonstrate how unbreakable his porcelain is, only for the chamber pot to hit the ground and shatter with a huge crash—but when they do occur, they are startling because of their scarcity. Otherwise, dialogue dominates. Because of the limited physical action and dominance of spoken dialogue, the film relies heavily on theatrical aesthetics. (Renoir employed a range of camera angles, and the scene changes location from the office to Toto's bedroom to the living room; but Figure 2.1 shows how the camera often frames the actors in a presentational manner, as if they were on a proscenium stage.)

Yet in this film, the dialogue takes on additional secondary characteristics apart from narrative. The actors deliver their dialogue with a quick back-and-forth pace that is the source of much of the humor. There is a musicality to this upbeat,

Figure 2.1: Stage-bound visual aesthetics of *On purge bébé* (1931).

rhythmic pace of dialogue delivery. Additionally, the cadence of each actor's delivery creates a range of pitches, timbres, and phrases that function much like a musical score.

In fact, despite the absence of a musical score, we can analyze *On purge bébé*'s soundtrack *as if* it were music. This kind of musicality can be heard clearly toward the end of the film, when multiple characters speak in quick succession. Mr. Chouilloux tries to encourage Toto to take his laxative, and Toto tells him to shut up. Mr. Follavoine attempts to yell at his son, while his wife Julie yells at him for yelling. All four main characters speak during this brief moment (see Table 2.1).[20]

Much like the rest of the film, this moment is rife with speech but devoid of substance. They verbalize with little meaning behind their words. Instead, the voices' musical qualities take precedence. The conventionality and lack of substance to the speech allows the grain to come through with a certain prominence that reveals a different layer of vocal significance and signification. My loose transcription of the scene's dialogue, seen in Example 2.1, renders the musicality of the scene visually through musical notation. The characters' lines overlap in a rhythmic manner, the cadences of their voices rise and fall melodically, and the unique timbres of each voice contrasts each one with the others: Chouilloux's slightly gravelly sing-songy cadence (typical of Michel Simon), Toto's clear boy soprano, Follavoine's harsh admonishments, and Julie's melodic retort. This excerpt reveals how easy it is to pull out the nonverbal elements of speech present in the soundtrack.

Table 2.1. Dialogue and English Translation from *On purge bébé* (1931, dir. Renoir)

Chouilloux: Mon petit ami, quand j'avais votre âge . . . que j'étais un tout petit petit , quand mes parents me disaient de faire une chose, eh ! bien . . .	**Chouilloux:** Little man, when I was your age . . . just a little boy, when my parents told me to do something, well . . .
Toto: Ta gueule !	**Toto:** Shut up!
Chouilloux: Eh ?	**Chouilloux:** Eh?
Follavoine: Rien ! Rien ! Rien !	**Follavoine:** Nothing! Nothing! Nothing!
Chouilloux: Ah, pardon, pardon !	**Chouilloux:** Ah, sorry, sorry!
Follavoine: En voilà assez ! Tu vas me faire le plaisir d'obéir! Ce n'est pas un avorton de ton espèce . . .	**Follavoine:** That's enough. You will do as you are told, you little runt . . .
Julie: Ah, dit-on, dit-on, tu n'es pas fou, toi ?! Tu ne vas pas bousculer ce petit, maintenant ?	**Julie:** Ah, come on, are you mad?! You're not going to push around the boy now, are you?
Follavoine: Mais tu n'as pas entendu ? il a repondu 'Ta gueule !'	**Follavoine:** But didn't you hear? He told him to shut up!
Julie: Mais pas de croire il a repondu 'Ta guele ?' Quoi ? C'est français!	**Julie:** So, he said "shut up." So what? It's just French!
Follavoine: Oh !	**Follavoine:** Oh!
Julie: Oh ! Hm ! (to Toto) Mon pauvre chéri, va !	**Julie:** Oh ! Hm ! (to Toto) My poor dear!

Not all *théâtre filmé* completely lacked a musical soundtrack. But even in theatrical adaptations with more music than *On purge bébé*, dialogue-heavy moments functioned in much the same way, containing the same kind of musicality. The ubiquitous voice in French cinema slowly evolved by the late 1930s to a more integrated soundtrack, complete with musical underscoring and sound effects, even in films that were faithfully based on stage works. Although the ubiquitous voice became much less common after the transition era, similar approaches to the soundtrack have developed, in more limited contexts, since that time. For instance, the American screwball comedy of the 1930s, exemplified in films like *Bringing Up Baby* (1938) or *His Girl Friday* (1940), use speech in much the same manner.[21] To cite a more contemporary example, the famous dialogue exchanges of Aaron Sorkin's television and film scenes could be understood in this same manner. As intensely verbocentric films, we might consider them the most vococentric. However, when there is an overabundance of voice, other qualities beyond those that are purely semantic and narrative—such as those I highlighted in *On purge bébé*—become increasingly prominent. The pleasure of seeing and hearing these films is thanks in large part to the musical cadence of the spoken word.

Music as a Silencer of the Voice

To some filmmakers, sound film represented a major aesthetic step backward. The artistic developments of the 1920s had led to a blossoming of silent film as

Example 2.1: Musical transcription of dialogue in *On purge bébé* (1931).

a visual art form. From the representation of inner subjectivity found in French cinematic impressionism, to the visual abstraction advocated by proponents of *cinéma pur* ("pure cinema," an avant-garde movement that emphasized motion, shot composition, rhythm, and other visual elements over narrative), to the strange and dreamlike visual juxtapositions found in surrealist cinema, many filmmakers in France found cinema interesting precisely because of the *absence* of voice, or more precisely, because it did not rely on spoken or written language. Cinema, as a visual medium, could express in fascinating, beautiful ways, becoming its own language without relying on another, thereby creating its own form of abstract poetry.

For these filmmakers and critics, the dawn of the sound film—the introduction of the speaking voice to cinema—was possibly the medium's death knell. Voices

Example 2.1: (*continued*).

brought with them literalism, preventing the visual abstraction they believed necessary for cinematic poetry. Moreover, the audiovisual model of mimetic synchronization made sound and image redundant, presenting the same narrative information, which allowed neither sound nor image independent structural integrity. Lastly, the voice brought cinema more aesthetically proximate to live theater, which threatened to destroy its ontological specificity. These concerns were articulated quite vocally in the press, as I have detailed elsewhere.[22] But for all of these concerns, the same filmmakers anxious about sound film's future found its potential in its ability to re-create silent cinema's abstraction in both the sound and the image. Music was a strategic tool in achieving this goal: the musical score had the potential to disrupt, or even silence, the possibility of speech. Although this approach was less common than that of *théâtre filmé*, it represents an important and influential strain of theoretical discourse on the role of music and the voice during the early years of sound film.

René Clair was perhaps the most well-known proponent of this cinematic style. A silent filmmaker who championed film's abstract visual possibilities, Clair was initially resistant to the new technology, being adamantly opposed to bringing theater—particularly the spoken word—into the realm of film. But his very resistance prompted creative aesthetic responses to synchronized sound. Aiming to establish a fantastical screen poetry that maintained its cinematic abstraction and avoided an overemphasis on spoken language, he relied heavily on music, incorporating both instrumental and sung music into the story and the soundtrack in unusual, provocative ways, often to deny the speaking voice from gaining anything other than an incidental role.

This approach is evident in his first sound film, *Sous les toits de Paris* (1930). The film takes place in a working-class neighborhood in Paris, following Albert, a singer hawking music on the street corner, Pola, a Romanian woman he falls in love with, Albert's friend Louis, and a threatening gangster Fred. Released as "un film parlant et chantant, CENT pour CENT FRANÇAIS,"[23] the film is perhaps more accurately a part-talkie, since it contained many scenes without dialogue, consisting of pantomime with recorded musical accompaniment. In an article in late 1929, Clair articulated various techniques in the film that he self-consciously incorporated into his aesthetic, placing spoken dialogue last in the hierarchy: "I distinguish three kinds of scenes in my film: a purely visual scene in which sound plays the role of orchestral accompaniment; another in which the images are made comprehensible by means of [natural] sound; and a third in which speech is used either to produce a special effect or else to explain the action."[24]

Clair also frequently used music to cover up the possibility of speaking voices and other sounds on the soundtrack. This is apparent in the first scene, where the title song is first heard. "Sous les toits de Paris" establishes the film's setting and the motivations of the characters, but its presence also guarantees that the entire opening scene must unfold without dialogue. We first hear the song in the opening scene, quietly in the distance, beginning during the establishing shots of rooftops and the slow pan down to the crowd on the street corner. The voices are heard, but the lyrics are indecipherable. Instead, the neighborhood is introduced sonically through the accordion and the act of communal singing. The only lines of dialogue are Albert's, between performances of the song, to encourage the crowd of onlookers to sing along as he leads the crowd. While he sings, he subtly flirts with Pola, who has joined the group (Figure 2.2). As the song continues, we see Émile, a thief, picking an older woman's pocket, and then trying to pick Pola's pocket (Figure 2.3). Albert attempts to alert Pola by making gestures to her to close her purse, but she does not understand. Nevertheless, he never stops singing to speak to her, as if the song must continue at all costs.

Figure 2.2: Albert song-plugging on the street corner, *Sous les toits de Paris* (1930).

The song serves as a continuous backdrop for this unfolding drama, driving the scene and its primary conflict, while also acting as commentary on the events unfolding. Its incessant presence, no matter what happens visually, ramps up the tension. The song is repetitive—the verse and chorus have a similar melodic contour, beginning with a chromatic ascending gesture (Example 2.2)—and it is repeated ad nauseam, to almost humorous effect each time a new verse begins. In a later scene, the characters remark on the maddeningly repetitive tune, while humming the melody stuck in their heads. In its constant presence and repetition, Clair comments on the practice of song-plugging, or the insertion of a popular song into the soundtrack.[25] (Perhaps it is no coincidence that Émile is stealing money from people's purses while the characters sing.) The song takes over the

Figure 2.3: The pickpocket, *Sous les toits de Paris* (1930).

soundtrack, bleeding from scene to scene, and, even from apartment to apartment, as it seeps into each character's head, and, by extension, the audience's ears. Just as importantly, the song provides a narrative justification for the entire scene to unfold without the help of dialogue. Instead, Albert and Pola reveal their interest in each other through facial expressions and Albert his concern through hand gestures, much in the same manner as silent cinema. Therefore, Clair's use of a popular song both exploited the new capabilities of sound film while aiming to strip it of what he thought was its most facile features, using the singing voice to cover up the speaking voice.

In other scenes in the film, instrumental music overtakes the soundtrack. In many moments it serves as accompaniment to onscreen action, looking (and

Example 2.2: Verse and chorus, "Sous les toits de Paris," *Sous les toits de Paris* (1930).

sounding) much like a silent film, but within the context of a sound film it takes on a new power: it silences other sounds. In the first scene, for instance, after the song finishes, Albert goes to the pickpocket and speaks to him, asking for Pola's money back, and the pickpocket refuses. Then the musical accompaniment suddenly begins, as the two continue to argue and Pola realizes her money is missing, the music masking the more "realistic" soundscape that Clair had just established. In the opening scene, Clair presented a cinematic world where we can hear characters speak, and in this moment, he suddenly takes it away. It is not merely silent film background accompaniment, although it appears that way on the surface. Instead, Clair jumps right into these "silent" sections in the middle of scenes, using music to intervene into the mode of audiovisual narrative delivery. In these moments, instrumental music enacts a particular kind of silencing: a silencing of spoken word and of naturalistic sound effects in order to reassert the primacy of the image.

This kind of transition is different from Hollywood's "part-talkies" of the late 1920s. Transitional part-talkies, such as *Noah's Ark* (1928), one of Hollywood's first, would incorporate discrete scenes that featured synchronized dialogue or songs, and these scenes were often aesthetically unrelated to the rest of the film in both acting and cinematography styles, strictly segregating scenes into talking, singing, or silent sequences. Instead, in the opening of *Sous les toits de Paris*, Clair self-consciously switches from a "sound" to "silent" mode, right at the moment of Albert's confrontation with Émile. He mixes the modes within scenes rather than using scene transitions or moving into a song performance to demarcate the boundaries. The viewer might be prevented from hearing conversations, but the content of the conversations is not crucial for understanding what is going on during the scene. Part-talkies still frequently used intertitles in the silent sections of the films, but in *Sous les toits de Paris* there are no intertitles. Rather, the music's presence prompts a shift in attention and encourages different sensory priorities. It does so aggressively, making very clear to the spectator just what aspect of the soundtrack it is denying its spectators.

Jean Grémillon also aimed to downplay the voice and prioritize other sounds on the soundtrack. Although he was not as vocal about his resistance to dialogue as Clair, he believed the voice to be only one of a number of sonic tools in the director's toolbox. He wrote in 1931 that "The talking film and the sound film, in my mind, are the same thing, because a character who speaks doesn't interest me any more than a motor, a siren, etc. . . . The talking film newly poses the question of the construction of drama, of its means of expression, of its interpretation, and of montage."[26] Grémillon was a musician and composer by training, and he approached cinema from a composer's perspective: Colin Crisp claims that he understood films to be "potentially organized like symphonic movements in which, while not openly contrapuntal, the various sonorous elements interwove in the manner of musical lines of melody."[27]

In his 1930 film *La Petite Lise*, he used the voice sparingly, often denying the spectator vocal clarity and instead focusing on the mood and interiority of his characters. The film was disliked by its producer Bernard Natan, who gave it a limited release, and it received poor critical and audience reception and disappeared into obscurity; only recently has the film's reputation been recuperated and Grémillon praised for his poetic approach to mood and atmosphere and its daring use of sound. Dudley Andrew calls the film a "dark" and "prophetic" film, a "truly experimental piece of cinematic lyricism" that "orchestrates its melodrama like the libretto of an opera."[28]

The film is about Berthier, who is serving time for murder in a colonial prison in Cayenne. He eagerly anticipates reuniting with his daughter, Lise, upon his release. However, when he goes to live with her in Paris, he discovers that she has been making her living as a prostitute. She and her boyfriend André (a penniless musician) want to make a fresh start outside of Paris, but they need money to do so. They devise a plan to rob a pawnbroker, but their plan goes awry and Lise ends up killing the man. She tries to hide this fact from her father, but when Berthier discovers what has happened, his love for his daughter is so great that he decides to turn himself in for the crime and return to a life in prison to save her from the same fate.

Though dialogue is an important part of the soundtrack, Grémillon is not concerned with complete semantic clarity. The early prison scenes, for instance, feature overlapping dialogue—more realistic and atmospheric—when exact comprehension of dialogue is not necessary. Characters often speak their dialogue facing away from the camera, and at times, sound effects completely overpower the soundtrack, such as the frequent sounds of trains passing right outside Lise's small apartment, helping to contribute to the maddening sense of confinement of the characters' lives.

Grémillon also relies on the musical score to do much of the dramatic and emotional work. In several places in the film, music director Alexis Roland-Manuel uses different musical techniques to depict the strangeness and otherworldliness of the setting. The opening credits are accompanied by "exotic" sounding music: a solo female voice sings a melody in a minor mode, accompanied by drums and pitched percussion. The words are in French but are very difficult to understand, purposely obscured in the singer's diction. A male vocal ensemble enters, singing wordlessly. As the credits end a title card announces that we are in Cayenne, a French colony in South America, and we see an exterior shot of a colonial prison. The music continues as we see prisoners line up to reenter the prison building. The exoticist music brings the audience into the colonial setting of the first part of the film, but the lack of specificity of the musical style provides for them the emotional point of view of Berthier, who has lived for years in a foreign, unfamiliar place, helping the audience identify with his alienation. This is all accomplished without a single line of dialogue.

The opening scene's use of music to depict Berthier's alienation is paralleled in the final climactic scene, as Berthier struggles to decide what to do about his daughter's predicament. Grémillon uses diegetic music for dramatic ironic effect, to illustrate Berthier's inner emotional state.[29] Its presence also eliminates the possibility for extensive dialogue. In a nightclub, patrons dance to joyful, upbeat, Latin jazz music. Berthier enters and watches the dancing. Although he had planned to confront André, Lise begs him not to, and Berthier silently considers his next move. There is a brief flashback of Berthier's time in prison in Cayenne, all while the diegetic music continues to play in the background. The image cuts back to Berthier's anguished face, and as the music continues to play, we hear a voiceover of the prison warden's words from the beginning of the film—some of the only words in the scene—telling him that he is a free man. He joins the crowd, who are joyfully dancing, seemingly without a care in the world. The camera briefly cuts to Berthier's unhappy face, then back to the dancing crowd. The music continues as we see Berthier walk slowly into a police precinct and approach a police officer. We do not hear what he says, but based on his facial expression it is easy to deduce that he is entering the precinct to turn himself in for Lise's crime (Figure 2.4). The diegetic music in the club in this scene provides a point of contrast, as the happy upbeat music is anempathetic to Berthier's tragic dilemma. It also helps depict a scene where the primary conflict occurs internally. Rather than requiring dialogue, the diegetic music in this scene, paired with a visual depiction of Berthier's anguish, incisively portrays the tragedy of Berthier's situation as he makes his one last decision as a free man. It does so perhaps more realistically than dialogue, since Berthier's character would not be able to express this kind of emotional complexity in words.

Though Clair and Grémillon differed in approach, they both used music to deemphasize, sometimes even actively silence, the speaking voice. These filmmakers provided an alternative to *théâtre filmé*, by emphasizing the expressive power of the cinematic image. They worked to integrate the various modes of sound cinema—the "silent" scenes with a postsynchronized score, talking scenes, and singing—by breaking down the barriers that early sound film had erected to contain them and

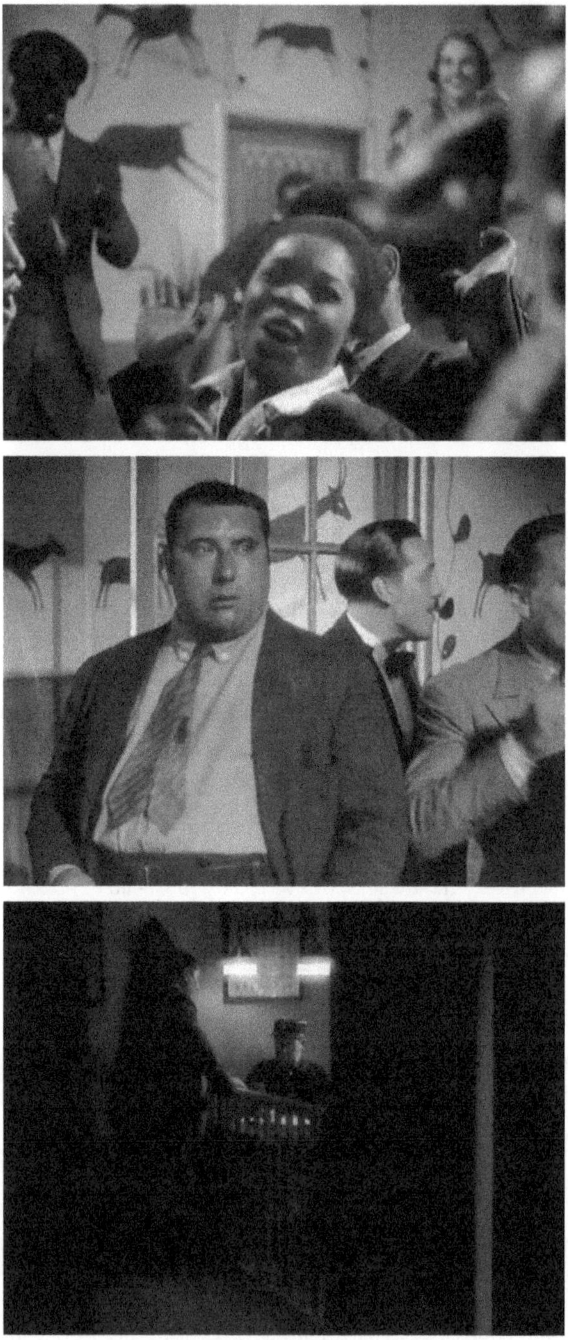

Figure 2.4: *La Petite Lise* (1930), final scene.

passing freely among them within individual scenes. Interestingly, this is what the modulated soundtrack (to borrow a term from Donald Crafton) of vococentrism would later do, although from a very different conception of the soundtrack.[30] In the scenes discussed above, music sometimes overpowered the speaking voice, becoming the dominant element of the soundtrack, but when the voice is silenced in this manner, it brings our attention and awareness to its lack even more fully. Ironically, in attempting to silence the voice, filmmakers like Clair and Grémillon heightened spectators' attention to it.

Conclusion

Although both theatrical adaptations and visually focused cinema where music dominated the soundtrack were not unique to French cinema, French filmmakers self-consciously experimented with the extremes that both options presented. For the proponents of filmed theater, the voice became the focus that structured everything around it: music, sound effects, and even image. Unlike classical cinema, however, this often resulted in a soundtrack that was not so much integrated into a vococentric hierarchy as it was a soundtrack singularly dominated by voices. In this case, the concept of the integrated soundtrack must be defined somewhat differently, since its integration is done across a single dimension. In this case, it is more productive to focus on the diverse sounds encompassed within the voice. On the other side of the spectrum, music became a tool for silencing the voice, covering up the possibilities for audiovisual realism and denying the soundtrack's role as a conveyer of semantic information. Yet, in silencing the voice, these directors created a noticeable absence that pushed the speaking voice further forward in the soundtrack's hierarchy.

To what extent, then, is vococentrism a helpful term for understanding the voice's role in the soundtrack in transition-era French film? Vococentrism as a principle for organizing the soundtrack did not fully take hold until the classical style was codified. As Buhler suggests in his article in this volume, vococentrism emerged as a principle that resolved certain difficulties with making films under the rule of mimetic synchronization.[31] Therefore, transition-era films cannot be considered traditionally vococentric. The diverging experiments in France emerged as early alternatives to the rule of mimetic synchronization that also suggest modes of organization that are not fully compatible with vococentrism. In other respects, we might consider the relevance of the term beyond the soundtrack itself. For one thing, the voice was an object of much debate in the press—anxiety, tension, fascination, fear, and celebration. One could say that, in its centrality as a topic of discussion (whether for or against its presence on the soundtrack), discourse on sound film in France (and in Hollywood, as well as elsewhere) was itself vococentric. Additionally, the experiments of the transition era can inform our ways of thinking about the voice's function in mainstream narrative cinema of the classical era, both expanding and clarifying how the voice structures the soundtrack and the image-track. They additionally point to alternatives to the vococentric model. These alternatives ultimately may not have won out in mainstream cinema, but during the experimental early years of synchronized sound film, they seemed manifestly possible as some of the infinite options for sound film's future.

Notes

1. Michel Chion, *The Voice in Cinema*, trans. Claudia Gorbman (New York: Columbia University Press, 1999 [1982]), 5 (emphasis in original).

2. Ibid.

3. David Neumeyer, *Meaning and Interpretation of Music in Cinema* (Bloomington: Indiana University Press, 2015), 3.

4. James Buhler, "The End(s) of Vococentrism," chapter 15 in this volume: 279.

5. Chion, *Film: A Sound Art*, trans. Claudia Gorbman (New York: Columbia University Press, 2009 [2003]), 4–5. See also Julie Brown, "Apprehending Human Voice in the 'Silent Cinema,'" chapter 1 in this volume.

6. Hannah Lewis, *French Musical Culture and the Coming of Sound Cinema* (New York: Oxford University Press, 2019).

7. Marcel Pagnol, "Les Ennemis du cinéma parlé," *Comœdia*, June 6, 1930, Bibliothèque Nationale de France, Arts du Spectacle (hereafter BNF-AS), Collection Rondel, 8-RK-671 (Le Cinéma sonore et parlant, 1er semestre 1930) (my translation). For more on Pagnol, see Lewis, *French Musical Culture*, 102–12.

8. Ginette Vincendeau, "The Art of Spectacle: The Aesthetics of Classical French Cinema," in *The French Cinema Book*, ed. Michael Temple and Michael Witt (London: BFI Publishing, 2004), 138.

9. François Mazeline, "Le cinéma parlant," *Rumeur*, April 30, 1928, BNF-AS, Collection Rondel, RK 656 (my translation).

10. L. P., *Ami du peuple*, August 24, 1928, BNF-AS, Collection Rondel, RK 656 (my translation). This idea, that theater is about words, and film about visual action, is a common thought expressed from the early debates of sound film through to the 1970s. It is unclear where this thought originated. It was implicit in silent film theory, but it may not have been made explicit before the sound film emerged as a commercial threat.

11. Dudley Andrew, *Mists of Regret: Culture and Sensibility in Classic French Film* (Princeton: Princeton University Press, 1995), 119.

12. Chion, *Film: A Sound Art*, 73. David Neumeyer argues that vococentrism includes both verbocentrism and other characteristics of the voice that are not related to language (*Meaning and Interpretation of Music in Cinema*, 12).

13. Roland Barthes, "The Grain of the Voice," in *The Responsibility of Forms*, trans. Richard Howard (Berkeley: University of California Press, 1991), 267–77.

14. Katherine Bergeron, *Voice Lessons: French Mélodie in the Belle Epoque* (New York: Oxford University Press, 2010), 187–88.

15. Marcel Pagnol, "The Talkie Offers the Writer New Resources," *Le Journal*, May 17, 1930, translated and reprinted in *French Film Theory and Criticism: A History/Anthology, 1907–1939, Volume II: 1929–1939*, ed. Richard Abel (Princeton: Princeton University Press, 1988), 56–57.

16. In this way, the soundtrack of *théâtre filmé* is not unlike spoken word poetry or rap in contemporary hip-hop.

17. The rule of mimetic synchronization was usually implemented with a choice of two visual editing styles: a long shot covering the scene, or cuts on dialogue lines from one character to another.

18. Neumeyer, *Meaning and Interpretation of Music in Cinema*, 102.

19. Ibid.

20. *On purge bébé*, bonus content on *La Chienne* DVD (New York: Criterion, 2016): 39:04–39:34.

21. Neumeyer writes of *His Girl Friday* that there is only music at the beginning and end of the film; but he, too, describes the dialogue musically, claiming that the "very active soundtrack is all talk, frequently at a frantic pace and often polyphonic (including several 'duets' and a virtuoso trio)." David Neumeyer, "Tonal Design and Narrative in Film Music: Bernard Herrmann's 'A Portrait of "Hitch"' and *The Trouble with Harry*," *Indiana Theory Review* 19 (1998): 102. On film dialogue in the screwball comedy, see also Sarah Kozloff, *Overhearing Film Dialogue* (Berkeley: University of California Press, 2000), 170–200.

22. Lewis, *French Musical Culture*.

23. Program, *Sous les toits de Paris*, Moulin-Rouge-Cinéma, Documents concernant le film "Sous les toits de Paris," BNF-AS, 8-RK-8809 (2). René Clair wrote the scenario and directed, and the "adaptation musicale" is credited to A. [Armand] Bernard (1893–1968), with "chansons nouvelles de R. Nazelles et de R. Moretti, éditées par Francis Salabert."

24. Clair, "Talkie versus Talkie," in Abel, ed., *French Film Theory and Criticism, II*: 40.

25. See Katherine Spring, *Saying It with Songs: Popular Music and the Coming of Sound to Hollywood Cinema* (New York: Oxford University Press, 2013). The song might have been incorporated for its Parisian popular style, suitable for the kind of setting Clair wished to evoke, but perhaps also because it epitomized the qualities that help popularize a song—catchiness, repetitiveness, and singability—to a point of excess.

26. Jean Grémillon, in *Ciné-Journal*, 1123, June 3, 1931, reprinted in Roger Icart, *La révolution du parlant, vue par la presse française* ([Perpignan]: Institut Jean Vigo, 1988), 159 (my translation).

27. Colin Crisp, *The Classic French Cinema, 1930–1960* (Bloomington: Indiana University Press, 1993), 113.

28. Andrew, *Mists of Regret*, 106–7.

29. Lewis, *French Musical Culture*, 138–41.

30. Crafton writes that the "new modulated sound track constructed a heterogeneous sensory environment, but one always dominated and unified by the voice." Donald Crafton, *The Talkies: American Cinema's Transition to Sound, 1926–1931* (Berkeley: University of California Press, 1997), 355.

31. Buhler, "The End(s) of Vococentrism."

Chapter 3

FM Radio and the New Hollywood Soundtrack

Julie Hubbert

Throughout the 1960s, as movie theater attendance and revenues continued to decline as they had since the war, film studio executives became increasingly interested in strategies that identified new markets and new sources of revenue. Of particular interest were population statistics and theater demographics that showed that 52 percent of the entire population of the United States was under the age of 30, but also that one of the groups with the strongest attendance records at the movies currently was the 18–24-year-olds.[1] Older adults had retreated to suburban America and to television, but younger viewers, teenagers rebelling against their parents' corporate appetites, were suddenly a reliable film audience.

In order to better monetize this increasingly profitable "youth" demographic, the studios began greenlighting films that they thought would specifically appeal to young audiences. Scripts that highlighted college life were still popular, but those that featured the growing counterculture, the "hippie" movement or campus protests, were given special attention. Executives even worried that the "campus revolution" phenomenon might subside before they could get the films finished.[2] As a result, Hollywood produced in quick succession a number of campus-centric youth pictures including *The Activist* (December 1969), *Zabriskie Point* (March 1970), *Getting Straight* (May 1970), *The Strawberry Statement* (June 1970), and *R.P.M.* (September 1970). As scholars of the period have noted, many of these films pursued unconventional visual techniques—shaky cinéma vérité-like camera work, fast swirling tracking shots, jump cuts, flash editing, nonlinear narrative structures—many borrowed from popular European filmmakers like Jean-Luc

Godard and François Truffaut.[3] What has received far less attention, however, is how unconventional the music was in many of these films. The use of rock music is often mentioned but little has been said about the eclectic range of musical styles and atypical music placements that also surface in them. MGM released two of these campus-centered "youth-cult" films in quick succession—*Zabriskie Point* and *The Strawberry Statement*. Although they were made by two vastly different directors with equally disparate budgets, the soundtracks for both films reveal how shifting music tastes and technologies were changing film music practices. In both films, the display of disparate musical styles and new listening practices was an essential part of marketing the revolution to youthful viewers. Both reflect the central influence of progressive rock, but their soundtracks are also distinctively shaped by one of the most galvanizing cultural forces in the late 1960s, the rise of FM radio, and in particular, the short-lived, revolutionary format called "free-form" radio.

FM Radio and the Counterculture

Although FM, the method of radio broadcasting sound that modulated the frequency of the waveform (hence the acronym FM) rather than the amplitude of the waveform (AM), had been available since the mid-1930s and offered superior quality sound and signal strength, it was largely ignored and underutilized until the mid-1960s.[4] Many radio station owners had FM licenses, but they used them to simulcast programming from AM stations, especially in rural parts of the country, or to broadcast educational or noncommercial material, religious or foreign language programs, or music that had small, specialized audiences, such as classical and jazz fans. For most radio station owners, FM had little or no commercial value, certainly nothing like the profits generated from AM radio.[5]

The fate of FM radio changed in 1964, however, when, as the AM spectrum began to be too crowded, the FCC issued a ruling that required station owners to end the practice of simulcasting. Suddenly stations owners were forced to generate new, original programming for their FM stations. Many owners objected to the costs of separate programming and resisted with legal delays, but when those were exhausted, the ruling finally went into full effect on January 1, 1967. With FM stations now forced to function independently from their AM counterparts, a wide variety of programming suddenly began to surface on FM radio. Some stations sought to mimic AM formatting and converted their classical stations and religious programs to more profitable popular music formats. Other station owners who were uncertain what kind of radio program could compete with AM used the opportunity to experiment with new content and formatting.[6] One of the most vocal and influential proponents of adventurous programming was a former AM radio disc jockey named Tom Donahue.

In the 1950s, Donahue had been a popular DJ on AM radio in the Washington D.C. and Philadelphia markets, but in the early 1960s he had been temporarily forced out of the industry when he became embroiled in a payola scandal. He reemerged a few years later in San Francisco as the voice of the popular AM radio station, KYA. When the FCC ruling went into effect in 1967, Donahue relocated to the sister FM station, KMPX, and began developing a new format, one that would correct the fundamental problems with AM radio.

Shortly after taking over KMPX, Donahue published a sweeping critique of AM radio, a manifesto that appeared in the second issue of *Rolling Stone Magazine* in November, 1967. Colorfully entitled "A Rotting Corpse Stinking Up the Airways . . ." Donahue's article identified two of the largest problems constraining contemporary radio programming:

> The bulk of popular music radio programming in this country today is devoted to absurd jingles that in their content are almost totally divorced from the kind of music the stations are playing, babbling hysterical disc jockeys who are trying to cram into a ten to fifteen second period the inane slogans that the program director has posted on the studio wall. The tempo is go! go! go!, the air is replete with such blather.[7]

Atop Donahue's laundry list of complaints was the observation that most of radio airtime was tightly controlled by corporate and business interests. Because radio stations generated most of their income by selling advertising space, listeners heard a preponderance of commercials. Stations themselves added to the frenzy by engaging in incessant self-promotion, shouting the station call sign in a distinctive way that would catch listeners' attention. By the mid-1960s, most AM radio programs were uniformly loud, noisy, full of commercials and DJ "chatter." A typical AM station, one study reported, "might in one hour play 22 commercials, 73 weather/time/contest announcements, repeat the stations call letters 58 times, [and] throw in a three-and-a-half-minute newscast."[8]

In AM formats, DJs also played music, up to a dozen songs per hour, but music was of secondary importance. Most playlists were determined by corporate market research and how well a song was selling or charting on *Billboard*'s or *Cash Box Magazine*'s Top 100 list. AM stations also typically played only hit "singles," short songs captured on 45 rpm records. Singles or 45s were preferred because their short two- to three-minute lengths and their predictable ABA structures facilitated frequent commercial breaks. As Donahue observed,

> The selection of music is almost invariably determined by what is happening in some other market. They will seldom take a chance on a new record, even when performed by a local group. Most stations today are playing from a list

> of approximately thirty records . . . few of them make any inquiry at all about LPs. If a record is selling that is more than seven inches in diameter, they don't care about it, don't want to hear, and most assuredly are not going to play it.[9]

Most stations played only a small rotation of popular hit songs. Songs that violated these criteria—in particular, songs that lasted longer than three minutes—were avoided because they constricted the number of commercials that could be aired. Songs by groups or singers not represented on the "charts" were deemed unmarketable and so were also rarely heard.

Donahue wanted to liberate radio formatting from commercial-based formulas by creating a new radio practice, a free-form format that would return FM to its early, noncommercial and educational roots. In this new format, DJs would be free to speak, and they would speak quietly instead of shouting. Commercials would be few and far between and primarily for local businesses, and DJs would determine their own playlists. At the heart of Donahue's manifesto was a mandate for creative programming that privileged music over advertising and marketing, a mandate he had already been putting into practice. In the past six months, he reveals:

> KMPX in San Francisco has been conducting a highly successful experiment in a new kind of contemporary music programming. It is a format that embraces the best of today's rock and roll, folk traditional and city blues, raga, electronic music, and some jazz and classical selections. I believe that music should not be treated as a group of objects to be sorted out like eggs with each category kept rigidly apart from the others, and it is exciting to discover that there is a large audience that shares that premise.[10]

Donahue's free-form format centered around two important changes. The first was a call to abandon the "singles only" formula in favor of playing "the best of today's rock and roll," which for Donahue meant albums, in particular, playing album "tracks" or "cuts." Many progressive rock groups in the mid-to-late 1960s were experimenting with song lengths and structures and with new ways of parsing up the roughly twenty to thirty minutes of recording time available on each side of an LP record.[11] Radio historians frequently cite examples of songs that defied AM radio play this way, including The Beatles' "A Day in the Life" (1967), which was well over five minutes long, or The Doors, seven-minute hit "Light My Fire" (1967), The Rolling Stones, eleven-minute song "Going Home" (1967), or Iron Butterfly's "Ina Gadda da Vida" (1968), which stretched the rock song to an incredible seventeen minutes. All of these songs were popular, but they were accessible only through album play. Record companies often made shorter versions of them for the radio, but because much of this music could not be edited—Jimi Hendrix's virtuosic solos; The Grateful Dead's long improvisations; Yes's 1973 double album *Tales from Topographical Oceans*, which had no tracks, just 4 LP sides—these long-playing "tracks" or "cuts" got little if any radio play.[12] As Dona-hue's wife Rachel remembers, playing long album cuts and whole sides was a defining aspect of the new free-form format. When Donahue took over programming at KMPX, he brought with him four cardboard boxes of albums because the station didn't own any LPs. It had only 45s.[13]

Stylistic eclecticism was another essential part of Donahue's free-form format. DJs should play a wide variety of musical genres including rock but also, as Donahue wrote in his manifesto, "folk, traditional and city blues, raga, electronic music, and some jazz and classical selections." Instead of repeating the same Top 40 songs, DJs were encouraged to choose selections from any style or genre of music and to organize them into programs however they wished. As radio scholar Jess Walker describes it, the free-form program typically offered a range of musical styles "that stretched from psychedelic to the baroque, in every sense of both words." A set could move from a "Buffalo Springfield song to a Mozart sonata . . . and mixed in and out with a Balinese gamelan piece . . . and then resolved with some blues from John Lee Hooker."[14] Sometimes the mandate for eclecticism was achieved between programs over the course of the day's programming. One DJ might play only progressive pop music, while others concentrated on jazz, classical music, novelty records, and country or folk selections.[15]

Radio historian Susan Douglas also points out that free-form FM radio flourished because it succeeded in transferring to broadcast radio listening practices that had previously been confined to classical music. Because FM was able to broadcast in stereo, and AM could not (and would not be able to until 1981), many popular music listeners, progressive rock fans in particular, began to adopt the same "attentive" listening practices their parents had adopted a decade earlier with introduction of high fidelity sound. The same desire for clarity, complexity, and perspective that stereo processes had introduced into the recording of classical music and jazz in the 1950s was now invigorating the reception of rock music with a few distinctive additions.[16] Free-form DJs encouraged listeners to turn up the volume of their radios, to immerse themselves in the music by playing it loudly. As one contemporary critic observed, "stereophonic FM, which surrounds the listener with sound, is purposely raised in volume by the young so that they can physically sense the vibrations of the audio waves."[17] As with album play on their home stereos, DJs encouraged listeners to play the radio "at the highest possible volume in order to fully appreciate the sound."[18] They were told to absorb the music by closing their eyes, and "lying on the floor between speakers" so that the "emotional and the cerebral could be . . . fused through the act of listening."[19] Free-form DJs also encouraged listeners to incorporate psychedelic drugs into the listening experience, marijuana in particular. "Getting stoned altered people's modes of emotional and cognitive processing," Douglas observes. "It allowed listeners to wipe the sensory slate clean . . . and focus more intensely on a single processing mode, the pure act of listening to music."[20]

Donahue's manifesto, with its clear antiestablishment and anticorporate undertones, also resonated with the egalitarian spirit of the counterculture movement. Young listeners also flocked to free-form FM because it offered an antidote to the contemptuous "commercialization that seemed to infuse and debase every aspect of American culture." They tuned in, Douglas points out, because they were "hostile to bourgeois values and the profit motives" of AM radio and television, and because music they heard on FM was pivotal "to their individual and generational identity, their sense of having a different, more enhanced consciousness about society, politics, and self-awareness."[21] Although this political ideology was at odds with the profit-seeking imperatives of station owners, because few owners thought at the outset that FM could be profitable, they largely tolerated experiments with free-form radio. As FM in general boomed, from an estimated 983 commercial FM stations in the country in 1962 to nearly 3,700 by 1976, and as revenues likewise increased from $19.7 million to over $543 million, free-form initially flourished.[22] From 1967 to 1969 nearly 300 free-form stations sprang up across the country. But by 1971, that number had plummeted dramatically to less than 25, and by 1973 free-form stations had all but disappeared.[23] One reason for its quick demise was that unlike other commercially oriented FM formats, free-form failed to generate revenues. The practice of playing more music and long album cuts with few if any commercials was simply not profitable. Without revenue from advertisers, lucrative corporation advertisements in particular, most free-form stations struggled to break even, even when many socially conscious DJs worked for free. By the mid-1970s, most station owners had forced their FM stations to adopt more corporate, advertising-based, AM-like formats that kept some elements of free-form: the occasional play of album cuts and a quiet, less aggressive DJ presence, while restoring frequent commercial breaks, the playing of hit singles, and even some automation.[24]

Free-form was also undone by censorship and the Nixon Administration's aggressive political attack on the counterculture movement. Beginning in the fall of 1970, Vice President Spiro Agnew made a series of public speeches blaming rock music and radio DJs for encouraging anti–Vietnam war demonstrations on college campuses, and for glamorizing obscene language, sexual promiscuity, and illegal drug use.[25] The Administration also pressured the FCC to exert greater control over radio programming, which they did by issuing a "public notice" threatening to revoke the broadcast licenses of stations that played what it labeled dangerous or decadent music. Donahue rebelled, staging an "all-drug" weekend at KSAN radio, ordering his DJs to play every drug-related song they could find and reading the Bill of Rights in between. Most station owners, however, not wanting to lose their increasingly profitable FM licenses, quietly asked station managers and DJs to comply and drew up "no-play" lists of music deemed too obscene or provocative to play.[26]

By 1973, free-form formats had also largely disappeared because their free speech policies were at odds with Nixonian politics. This short-lived experiment with free-form radio, with eclectic programming and progressive political thinking, however, had a profound effect on the musical tastes and listening practices of young Americans and altered the way youth audiences listened not just to music on the radio but music in other media too. Many film soundtracks from this same period reveal a similar experimentation with eclectic repertoire and immersive, stereo listening practices. Many film directors accessed the progressive sounds and practices of FM radio play in order to capture and sell the revolution to profitable youth audiences.

Free-Form Radio and the Film Soundtrack: *Zabriskie Point* (1970)

To some degree, the overlap between FM radio and the cinema in the late 1960s was influenced by the widely held perception that of all mass media, these two were the least corporate. A divide similar to the one that had sprung up between AM and FM radio, for instance, had also surfaced between television and film. Counterculture youth in particular were deeply suspicious of television and rejected it much along the same ideological lines as they spurned AM radio.[27] Its relentless commercial advertising made the articulation of a corporate agenda all too visible and manipulative. The perception of the cinema, however, was different. Youth audiences largely tolerated the cinema because its corporate manipulation was less visible and because the new and more liberal rating system the industry had just adopted in 1966 was allowing the film studios to distribute challenging, sensational, and unconventional films from Europe.[28]

Importing European directors, in fact, was another part of the studios' strategy to appeal to lucrative youth audiences. In 1968, United Artists had lured British director John Schlesinger to work in the United States; French director Jean-Luc Godard was also shooting parts of *1+1* (*Symphony with the Devil*) in the United States, an English-language film distributed by New Line Cinema.[29] When MGM reached out to Michelangelo Antonioni that same year, it was because he, too, was a director with an established appeal to youth audiences in America. His stark, high-modernist Italian films *L'avventura* (1960), *La Notte* (1961), *L'Eclipse* (1962), and *Il deserto rosso* (1964) were hits with art-cinema and youth audiences in the United States. Hoping to capitalize on this success, MGM studios entered into an agreement with Antonioni and producer Carlo Ponti to produce and distribute three English-language films. The first of these, *Blow-Up* (1967), shot in London with a British cast, was so racy it failed to get an MPPA rating. When MGM released the film anyway they were rewarded for their efforts when the film became a box-office hit.[30] As a result, with the second film, *Zabriskie Point*, the studios gave Antonioni even more room to experiment and an even bigger budget with which to do it.

When Antonioni began filming in September 1968, it was announced with great fanfare that the filmmaker would be turning his Marxist sensibilities on capitalistic America and examining the only worthwhile thing he found in contemporary American culture: the youth movement. *Zabriskie Point* was to be a film that was "indicative of a generation in semi-revolt; kids who have invented a free culture to grope with the madness of their elders." Antonioni was also anxious to experiment with American budgets and audience sizes. "I would really like to make a film for 12 million, maybe 20 million, why not? I need M.G.M.'s money, of course; in Italy, such things are impossible, even if there were anything interesting to film there."[31] Antonioni had no trouble using the capitalistic studio system to finance his anticapitalist critique, and the studios, likewise, had no difficulty tolerating his politics if they generated profits.

MGM gave Antonioni an impressive $7 million budget and nearly complete control of production, which stretched to nearly three years. A vague script, which finished with a critique of American overconsumption, the violent destruction of everything from luxury homes to common household items, underwent numerous rewrites, often to reflect political events that happened during the film's production—the protests at Columbia University in April 1968 and at the 1968 Democratic National Convention in August.[32] Production was slowed by problems with the mixed American and Italian production crews and by Antonioni's insistence on using real people instead of trained actors. Lead actors, Daria Halprin and Mark Frechette, had never acted before. Their "realness" was touted in the press, especially the story of how Frechette was spotted by a casting director while fighting at a bus stop in Boston.[33] Shooting was also interrupted when descriptions of Antonioni's quasi-orgiastic "love scene" in the Mojave Desert were reported in the press and the California State Police charged MGM with having violated the "Mann Act," which prohibits the transportation of minors over state lines for the purpose of filming "scenes of nudity or copulation."[34]

The production of *Zabriskie Point* was also shaped by the success of another youth picture that was released just as Antonioni finished primary filming in the summer of 1969. *Zabriskie Point* overtly alludes to *Easy Rider* in several ways, especially in the way that the film's countercultural protagonists find escape from corporate America in the empty, desert landscapes of California. MGM's marketing campaign clearly hoped the massive audiences that turned out for *Easy Rider* would come to *Zabriskie*. The publicity posters for *Zabriskie Point* had the same distinctive stars and stripes lettering and "Captain America" design featured on Peter Fonda's helmet and jacket.[35]

Many scholars have also noted how, like *Easy Rider*, *Zabriskie Point* also authenticates its examination of youth culture with a soundtrack full of rock music. On closer examination, however, while *Zabriskie*'s soundtrack does feature progressive rock, its differences from the *Easy Rider* soundtrack are numerous and noteworthy. Some of it echoes Antonioni's long-standing preference for musical sparseness, for silence instead of orchestral underscoring. As he told *Rolling Stone* magazine, "I don't like music that makes a commentary on the film. Of course, there will be rock music in the film as heard on the radio or record players. That's just natural. But I don't necessarily want a rock score. That would be too easy, too obvious."[36]

As he did with *Blow-Up*, Antonioni approached *Zabriskie* with a similar vérité-like intention of having music confined primarily to diegetic sources, car radios in particular. Unlike *Blow-Up*, however, he elicited the help of a "musical advisor," Don Hall, a popular disc jockey at an underground FM radio station in Pasadena, California. Hall worked at KPPC, Los Angeles' first free-form station, which had been launched in early 1968 in consultation with Tom Donahue. Since much of the film's action revolved around Daria's drive through the desert from Los Angeles to Phoenix, Antonioni asked Hall to construct an authentic program to play from her car radio. Although Daria's 1950s Buick would not have had an FM radio, Antonioni nonetheless wanted the repertoire and DJ chatter from the radio to realistically reflect the typical kind of underground radio programs that counterculture youth were listening to. He hired Hall specifically to re-create what rock historian David Fricke describes as "the catholic vitality of late '60s free-form radio" in the film's soundtrack.[37]

For Hall this meant first and foremost constructing an eclectic soundtrack, one that reflected the egalitarian ideals of early FM radio programming. Hall developed a playlist that clearly avoided "the stinking corpse of AM radio," and embraced Donahue's admonition to play an eclectic variety of musical styles. As Hall remembers it, "there was no idea, when we were doing the film, that a rock soundtrack meant everything had to be hard, intense, electric music. I was trying to do a soundtrack using the many different types of music that were being played on FM radio at the time."[38]

Hall's voice is literally heard in the film as the radio DJ that reports Mark's death, but his fingerprints are also on the repertoire choices that spill from Daria's car radio. His faux free-form program includes Roscoe Holcomb's hillbilly banjo-pickin' song, "I Wish I Was a Single Girl Again," taken from a 1968 Folkways recording called *Mountain Music of Kentucky*; the Youngbloods' "Sugar Babe" from their 1967 album *Earth Music*; John Fahey's "Dance of Death" from his 1964 album *The Dance of Death & Other Plantation Favorites*; The Rolling Stones' "You Got the Silver" from their 1969 album *Let It Bleed*; and a twangy, country-inspired 1968 instrumental "Mickey's Tune" from the little-known group Kaleidoscope, an underground favorite of Hall's. The 1950 recording of Patti Page singing the "Tennessee Waltz" was also Hall's choice, although he later regretted convincing Antonioni of the merits of Page's recording as it proved much more expensive to license than the Hank Williams version of the song MGM had in its catalogue.[39]

Reviewers in the countercultural press criticized Antonioni for an "aimless" and "poor use" of music, which they attributed primarily to the fact that most of the music is confined to jukeboxes and car radios.[40] Not all of Hall's authentic free-form playlist is so inaudible or diegetically limited, however. Several nondiegetic selections interrupt the film, bleeding in slowly to take over the soundtrack and often ending with shocking abruptness. The repertoire there, too, was suggested by Hall but placed by Antonioni during postproduction. The Grateful Dead were already an important concert band at the time, but their distinctive, long-playing improvisations had received virtually no airplay on the radio until they released their *Live/Dead* album in November 1969. Antonioni's decision to use an excerpt from the 23-minute track, "Dark Star," from the *Live/Dead* album, to play when Mark steals a plane and observes the urban chaos of Los Angeles freeways below, echoes the free-form preference for deep cuts and album play.[41]

The credit sequence and two long montages in the film were more problematic, however, and took Antonioni nearly six months to score. He wanted the sound of free-form radio here as well, but he also wanted music that could precisely match in length and mood the unconventionally long sequences. Although he said that he didn't want a rock score, he nonetheless "auditioned" groups from Hall's playlist to score the opening credits and the film's two long montages sequences. Hall suggested Procol Harum, but Antonioni chose Pink Floyd. He had met the group several years earlier in London while filming *Blow-Up* and had also been listening to the band's newly released LP *Ummagumma*.[42] When the group agreed to score the film, Antonioni flew them to Rome where, for the better part of the month of November, they recorded many takes for the three needed scenes. They recorded over an hour of instrumental music, most of it for the desert "love" scene and the final explosion montage. From these recording sessions, Antonioni used a cue entitled "Heart Beat, Pig Meat," and for the final explosion montage, he chose the group's reworking of an *Ummagumma* track called "Careful with That Ax Eugene," now even more cryptically titled "Come in Number 51, Your Time Is Up." A small bit of a third song, "Crumbling Land," was added to the car radio program. The rest of their work, however, almost an hour's worth, went unused.[43]

Antonioni rejected many takes Pink Floyd made for the film's long desert "love" scene, preferring instead to audition additional musicians. Most likely at Hall's suggestion, he flew guitarist Jeff Fahey to Rome, where the director showed Fahey only the film's "love" scene. Fahey did his best to score the scene, which Antonioni confusingly described as "young love, but in the desert where there's death" and Fahey described as "a really terrible and long skin flick." Antonioni rejected all of Fahey's work, however: six long tracks and forty-seven minutes worth of music.[44] In December 1969, with the film nearly two years overdue, Antonioni and Hall continued to audition groups to score the "love" scene, although now more conveniently in Los Angeles at MGM studios. It is not clear when Hall asked the group Kaleidoscope to record, but they were summoned, too. From the ten songs and nearly dozen takes they made for the scene, Antonioni took only one song, "Brother Mary," for the car radio and rejected the rest.[45] Antonioni also asked The Doors to write a new song just for the film, which they did and appropriately titled it "L'America," but he rejected this as well.[46] Hall made one final attempt and brought Grateful Dead guitarist Jerry Garcia into the MGM soundstage. Garcia, a film buff and fan of Antonioni's early Italian films, was eager to participate in the project. Although details about this session vary, Garcia improvised four takes for the "love" scene, two of which were immediately selected and fused together and placed in the film's soundtrack. Antonioni was instantly pleased with Garcia's improvisations. Garcia, however, was quite disappointed at how brief and uncollaborative the session was.[47]

The extraordinary attention Antonioni gave to selecting and placing the music in the montage sequences shows him interested in re-creating not just the intentionally eclectic repertoire of counterculture radio but also the new attentive, stereo listening practices that it was promoting. The montage sequences were difficult to complete because they were visually challenging, but also because they were sonically and musically unconventional. In the famed desert "love" scene, for instance, the camera pulls back to reveal a vast landscape teeming with additional lovemaking couples and groups. The surreality of the imagery is disruptive, but so is the length of the montage. Although montage sequences typically last one to three minutes, the desert "love" scene is an uncomfortable seven minutes long. Antonioni uses music conventionally to create continuity, but the improvisatory and unstructured quality of the music also allows it to function "sensorially." Antonioni uses Garcia's improvisatory guitar work, his wandering and unpredictable solo, to encourage a more attentive mode of listening, a heightened auditory experience. The montage is an unconventional audiovisual experience, one that prioritizes music and sound over narrative structure for an uncomfortably long time.

The film's final montage is equally "sensational." When Daria pauses from her car to imagine the destruction of her boss's luxurious desert retreat, the musical "score," which eventually suppresses all diegetic sound, is equally unconventional and arresting. The spontaneous and improvisatory nature of Pink Floyd's music, which becomes audible slowly and imperceptibly, forces the viewer into a different, more sensorial mode of listening. As the music slowly thickens in texture and crescendos, culminating in a loud, visceral and primal scream from lead singer Roger Waters, it takes on what film scholar David Fresko calls a kind of "radical spectatorial consciousness."[48] Like his European counterpart Godard, Fresko asserts, Antonioni also used the montage to question and challenge cinema's ideological and aesthetic foundations. What Fresko overlooks, however, is the degree to which Antonioni uses music to radically revise cinematic priorities. Antonioni lengthened the montage and foregrounded it with progressive rock music in order to prioritize sound, to give the film soundtrack the same kind of immersive feeling young listeners were experiencing with stereo albums and free-form programming on FM radio. He stretches the viewer's expectations by turning the montage into a long auditory spectacle. Pink Floyd and Jerry Garcia bring the "catholic vitality" of FM radio to the film soundtrack but they also import the long immersive listening practices being promoted by progressive rock music.

The new and overtly sensory nature of the music was not lost on MGM executives, who moved quickly to capitalize on it as a marketing strategy for the film's soundtrack LP. In the liner notes on the record jacket of the original LP release (MGM Records, SE 4668 ST), the president of MGM records, Mike Curb, claimed that "*Zabriskie Point* exists not as film but as an experience. . . . Antonioni draws his audience into his film, forcing his members to become involved participants rather than objective observers." The result, he concluded, is that "the film and the music are not really meant to be understood, but to be lived." One reviewer in the underground press went even further, lauding the soundtrack as a countercultural triumph over Western society's long history of privileging sight over other senses. The United States has become a capitalist nation of sightseers, but Antonioni's new film allows the viewers

> to feel their sense of Sight recede into a more harmonious balance with what they hear and read in the newspapers. Rock & Roll musicians turn their amps and instruments up to the danger level as they re-educate the young in the sense of Sound. Consciousness expanding chemicals allow young people to become aware of the infinite levels of Touch sleeping below the conscious surface.[49]

For counterculture youth, Antonioni's film represented a new cinematic experience, one that more closely resembled the heightened auditory experiences of progressive rock music.

Although MGM executives championed and even marketed the unusual, spectatorial shift the film's soundtrack helped to create, they were also clearly concerned it would affect their other corporate product—the commercial soundtrack album. Worried that the film had no "title song," and that its most marketable "singles" had been rendered inaudible in the film's car radio, studio executives had Top 40 and MGM artist Roy Orbison quietly write a conventional pop song for the film, a single entitled "So Young." Without either Antonioni's or Don Hall's knowledge, they inserted it at the last minute over the film's end credits.[50] They attempted to mitigate Antonioni's eclectic repertoire and long album cuts with at least one pop single conventionally placed for easy cross-promotion on AM radio. Although the Orbison song was not included on the official film soundtrack LP, the studio released it as a single with the supremely consumable subtitle "Love Theme from *Zabriskie Point.*" For all their efforts, however, just as the film failed spectacularly at the box office, both the LP and the Orbison single failed to make the charts.

. . . and *The Strawberry Statement* (1970)

Released just a few months after *Zabriskie Point*, and by MGM studios, *The Strawberry Statement* also centered on campus activism and sought to authentically capture the counterculture movement. Based on the best-selling memoir *The Strawberry Statement: Notes of a College Revolutionary* by James Simon Kunen, one of the student activists at Columbia University who occupied the president's office to protest the building of a university gym on a racially mixed neighborhood park, the film restages many of the book's events, including the central act of civil disobedience, which is brought to a violent conclusion when the police storm the building with tear gas and arrest more than 700 protesters.

Hoping perhaps to find a shorter and cheaper path to capitalizing on the youth movement than *Zabriskie*, MGM tapped two thirty-year-old newcomers to write and direct: Israel Horovitz, a young leftist playwright, and television director Stuart Hagmann. By the time the film was released, however, the ambition of reflecting and engaging youthful viewers had been dampened by several internal and external developments. Because Columbia University refused to give the studios permission to film on their campus, production took place instead on the UC Berkeley campus and in several neighborhoods in nearby San Francisco. The shooting was also marred by acts of "sabotage" when several rolls of film went missing from the labs while they were being processed.[51]

Real-life difficulties surrounding the production had an even graver impact, however. On March 6, 1970, a bomb exploded in a Greenwich Village townhouse in New York City, killing three members of the radical student group, The Weather Underground. At the end of April, President Nixon announced the invasion of Cambodia and an escalation of the war in Vietnam, a decision met with campus protests nationwide, which led on May 4th to the shooting deaths of four student protestors at Kent State University by members of the Ohio National Guard. As real student rebellion in the United States turned violent and deadly, MGM persevered with the release of the film, but they intentionally muted the theme of campus violence and protest, marketing the film instead as a contemporary love story set on a university campus.[52]

In *The Strawberry Statement*, director Stuart Hagmann, like Antonioni, employed visual strategies to signify the film's realist intentions. Although some of the camera work—fast zooms, swirling circular tracking shots—reflected Hagmann's television background, most of it had a cinéma vérité feel—shaky, handheld cameras, abrupt jump-cut editing, bad lighting, and poorly framed composition.[53] The film's soundtrack was also designed to have a youthful, vérité appeal. Although some scholars had described the soundtrack as "jumbled and incoherent," the mix of music styles and cinematic placements was intentionally designed to appeal to youth audiences.[54]

The film did not have a free-form DJ advising its soundtrack, but Kunen's book, as Hagmann pointed out, makes several references to free-form listening culture. On one occasion, Kunen notices, for instance, that The Animals' popular 1968 song, "Sky Pilot," was originally seven minutes long, but the concluding antiwar lyrics were cut from the three-minute single version of the song played on AM radio. He also criticizes AM radio for censoring songs and albums and for "anesthetizing" its listeners with inane chatter instead of informed political discussion about the war.[55] As Hagmann points out, "[Kunen's] book was very lucid. . . . It had all of this input from his surroundings. The pop songs he would hear on the radio!"[56]

Like free-form FM programming at the time, this film's soundtrack is similarly eclectic. Linda and Simon, the film's central protagonists, progressively listen to a variety of musical styles, from "Down by the River," a long cut from Crosby, Stills, Nash, and Young's recent, best-selling album *Déjà vu* (1970) to a concerto grosso in D minor from seventeenth-century composer Antonio Marcello. When Simon first enters his apartment, we see a hi-fi stereo and a record jacket, the commercial soundtrack for the film *2001: A Space Odyssey*, prominently displayed. Later, when Simon interrupts his roommate having sex with a young, liberated female activist, a cut from that album, Richard Strauss's 1896 orchestral tone poem *Also Sprach Zarathustra*, plays loudly, no doubt because Kubrick's film *2001: A Space Odyssey* had also become an important symbol of countercultural hipness. In *Rolling Stone Magazine* in the March and June 1970 issues, ads for the 1968 film with a new Leary-inspired tagline, "The Ultimate Trip," ran directly next to ads for *Zabriskie* and *The Strawberry Statement*. Free-form eclecticism is also on further display when Simon and Linda happen upon a spontaneous street performance, an amateur folk band comprised of several long-haired white hippies, the Red Mountain Jug Band, playing the classic blues tune "Gone Fishin'" on banjo, guitar, and an array of homemade instruments. As the camera observes an equally eclectic and intergeneration audience of young and old, working class and professionals, students and parents, all listening and dancing along, the music again serves to give the listeners in the film, and us, a communal and immersive experience of music.

Just as the music outlines free-form tastes, it also describes a range of listening practices. A few minutes after entering his apartment, Simon puts an album on the stereo, Neil Young's 1969 album *Crazy Horse*, and listens to a long nine-minute track, "Down by the River." He lies down on the couch and listens attentively, sometimes with a pillow over his head. Although we hear only two minutes of it, Simon's selection of this long improvisational album as well as his immersive listening practice of lying down, eyes closed, communicates his underground tastes and "hipness." The depth of Linda's countercultural commitment is also reflected in her listening habits, in a scene, for instance, where she playfully drags Simon into a record store to make him listen to some "far-out" music, the seventeenth-century composer Antonio Marcello. As the two squeeze into a listening booth, she puts headphones on both of them, and they both close their eyes to heighten the auditory experience. As we watch them listen, the sound of a Baroque guitar concerto suddenly expands to suppress all other sound on the soundtrack. Hagmann uses the depiction of immersive listening practices to disrupt the conventional hierarchy of the soundtrack, to privilege music over sound.

Unlike *Zabriskie*, however, this film also balances its experimental tastes with some conventional music practices. Although it begins, fashionably and vérité-like without a frame, plunging the viewer straight into a scene of college boys training and showering, when the opening credit sequence finally scrolls, it is accompanied by a "hit" pop song, Joni Mitchell's "The Circle Game," a two-and-a-half minute, ABA, pop single perfect for AM radio play, sung by Canadian folk singer Buffy St. Marie. Likewise, the film's three montage sequences are conventionally scored with hit pop singles—Crosby, Stills, Nash, and Young's "Our House," Neil Young's "The Loner," and "Something's in the Air" by Thunderclap and Newman. The film also uses several short episodes of underscoring to smooth over scene changes or to create tension. The fact that MGM attempted to package these bits of scoring, written by television composer Ian Freehairn-Smith, as freestanding songs on the soundtrack album is evidence of this film's shifting musical impulses. Unlike *Zabriskie Point*, it makes a significant attempt to retain aspects of the classical soundtracking, the strategy of using montage sequences to market music, "singles" especially. It positions music in ways that promote attentive listening but also in ways that encourage the purchase of songs and ancillary soundtrack profits. In terms of selling the sound of dissent, *The Strawberry Statement* charts a more successful middle ground than *Zabriskie Point* between counterculture and mainstream, rock and pop, protest and conformity, nonprofit and profit—a path that helped the film win the Jury Prize at the Cannes Film Festival in 1970 and its commercial soundtrack album achieve a respectable position on the Billboard charts.

This negotiation of integrating new countercultural listening with conventional soundtrack practices is also audible in the film's final scene. For nearly the entirety of the last twelve minutes of the film, we watch as the student protesters occupy the auditorium of the administration building. As they arrange themselves in rings of concentric circles, with Simon and Linda and other central figures in the middle, the police coalesce outside, getting ready to confront and arrest the protestors. At this point the students are united, not in protest, or even in listening, but in song. For nearly five minutes, as the police violently drag them one by one out of the building, the students sing loudly and repeatedly, one of the defining anthems of the counterculture movement, John Lennon's and Yoko Ono's new "Bed-In" protest song "Give Peace a Chance." Like *Zabriskie Point*, this film also ends with a radical sensorial experience, one that while undermediated, privileging singing over listening, live performance over hi-fidelity technology, is still strikingly long, free-form, and immersive.

Like *Zabriskie Point*, *The Strawberry Statement* also defines and authenticates its youthful protagonists through its soundtrack. In both films, the characters display distinctly countercultural listening practices. They consume an eclectic range of musical styles and forms, from classical orchestral music to contemporary folk and progressive rock music. Both soundtracks mirror the progressive programming of Donahue's free-form FM radio format. But they also articulate the unconventional listening practices that counterculture radio was encouraging. Just as each film's protagonists listen attentively to FM radios and hi-fi stereos, we, the film's viewers, are also asked to listen unconventionally, to privilege long, immersive, and interruptive montages and musical performances over conventional underscoring and framing. For these two films, but also for many other youth-oriented films from the late 1960s and early '70s, the "new" in the New Hollywood soundtrack wasn't just the inclusion of progressive rock music but a new approach to musically mediating the film experience. For many New Hollywood films, the soundtrack has been radically reshaped and grounded in both the stylistic eclecticism and the immersive listening practices of the counterculture movement.

Notes

1. David Cook, *Lost Illusions: American Cinema in the Shadow of Watergate and Vietnam* (Berkeley: University of California Press, 2002), 162–72. See also "Pix Must 'Broaden Market'; 18% of Public; 76% of Audience," *Variety*, March 20, 1968, 1; Abel Green, "B.O. Dictatorship by Youth: Kids as Talent and Consumers," *Variety*, January 7, 1979, 3, 36; and Stanley Penn, "Movie Makers See Box Office This Year in Low-Cost Timely Films Liked by Young," *Wall Street Journal*, March 27, 1970, 20.

2. See Rick Setlowe, "Campus 'Revolution' Themes Coming; First-to-Market Angle at Columbia," *Variety*, January 14, 1970, 6; Hank Werba, "Avemb Keys in Young Directors," *Variety*, October 8, 1969, 7; and Stuart Byron, "Polk ('Now' Generation) Begins; McLuhan

Quoter, Gal-Charmer; MGM's Gabby Annual Meet," *Variety* January 15, 1969, 3. Quoted in Aniko Bodroghkozy, "Reel Revolutionaries: An Examination of Hollywood's Cycle of 1960s Youth Rebellion Films," *Cinema Journal* 41, 3 (2002): 39–41.

3. Cook, *Lost Illusions*, 164–5; David Fresko, "Magical Mystery Tours: Godard and Antonioni in America," in *The Global Sixties in Sound and Vision: Media, Counterculture, Revolt*, ed. Timothy Scott Brown and Andrew Lison (New York: Palgrave Macmillan, 2014), 43–64; and Paul Monaco, *The Sixties: 1960–1969* (Berkeley: University of California Press, 2001), 74–75, 87–102.

4. Inventor Edwin Armstrong developed FM radio in the 1930s in partnership with RCA to fix many of the weaknesses of AM, especially its susceptibility to static and atmospheric and weather-related interference. See Jesse Walker, *Rebels of the Air: An Alternative History of Radio in America* (New York: New York University Press, 2001), 45–68; Peter Fornatale and Joshua E. Mills, *Radio in the Television Age* (Woodstock, N.Y.: Overlook Press, 1980), 119–21; and Susan Douglas, *Listening In: Radio and the American Imagination from Amos 'n' Andy and Edward R. Murrow to Wolfman Jack and Howard Stern* (New York: Random House, 1999), 259–67.

5. Douglas, *Listening In*, 262.

6. Before the FM boom in 1967, a handful of stations had developed alternative programming and formatting, like KPFA in Berkeley and KRAB in Seattle, both of which had been airing a mix of eclectic music and leftist political talk since the late 1940s. Mark Fisher, *Something in the Air: Radio, Rock and the Revolution That Shaped a Generation* (New York: Random House, 2007), 127–57, and also Walker, *Rebels of the Air*, 62–92. WBAI in New York City also had loose and colorful local programming, most of it coming from DJ Bob Fass, who had a weekly program called *Radio Unnamable* that featured an un-categorizable mix of talk, interviews, live performances, sound collages, political speeches, and music of all styles—classical, jazz, folk, country, ethnic, and popular.

7. Tom Donahue, "A Rotting Corpse Stinking Up the Airways . . .," *Rolling Stone Magazine*, 1, 2 (November, 1967): 14.

8. Fornatale and Mills, *Radio in the Television Age*, 127.

9. Donahue, "A Rotting Corpse," 14.

10. Ibid.; Douglas, *Listening In*, 268–74; and Walker, *Rebels of the Air*, 96–97.

11. Radio scholars often credit '60s folk singers with stretching song and recording lengths and cite Bob Dylan's 1965 recording of "Desolation Row," which was eleven minutes long, and Arlo Guthrie's 1966 ballad "Alice's Restaurant," which was 18 minutes, as early examples. See Fisher, *Something in the Air*, 160–1; and Fornatale and Mills, *Radio in the Television Age*, 127–28.

12. Long album "cuts" are frequently mentioned in contemporary articles on FM radio. See Caroline H. Meyer, "The New Respectability of Rock," *Broadcasting*, August 11, 1969, 46A-D; Jack Gould, "Around Country, FM Turns to Rock," *New York Times*, May 20, 1970, 33; and Larry Yurdin, "Waves upon the Ether," *Crawdaddy*, April 30, 1972, 30–35, and "Waves upon the Ether, Part II," *Crawdaddy*, May 14, 1972, 30–34. See also, Bill Martin, *Listening to the Future: The Time of Progressive Rock 1968–78* (Chicago: Open Court, 1998), 55–149.

13. Douglas, *Listening In*, 269; and Michael Keith, *Voices in the Purple Haze: Underground Radio and the Sixties* (Westport, Conn.: Praeger, 1997), 15–50.

14. Walker, *Rebels of the Air*, 93, 96.

15. Douglas, *Listening In*, 270–71.

16. Ibid., 263–67.

17. Listening at louder volumes was what separated young listeners from old, what created a "social schism between the generations." Gould, "Around Country, FM Turns to Rock," 33.

18. Fornatale and Mills, *Radio in the Television Age*, 130.

19. Douglas, *Listening In*, 274–75.

20. Ibid., 273; and Keith, *Voices in the Purple Haze*, 145–48.

21. Ibid., 268.

22. "The Rites of Passage Are All Over for FM Radio; It's Out on Its Own," *Broadcasting*, September 24, 1973, 31; and "The Upbeat Tempo of FM 1974," *Broadcasting*, October 7, 1974, 41–42. Quoted in Douglas, *Listening In*, 259 and 276.

23. Fornatale and Mills, *Radio in the Television Age*, 142.

24. "FM Rockers Are Taming Their Free Formats," *Broadcasting*, November 25, 1974; Steve Chapple and Joel Rogers, "The Rise and Fall of FM Rock," *Mother Jones*, May 1976, 55–61; and Ben-Fong Torres, "FM Underground Radio: Love for Sale," *Rolling Stone Magazine*, April 2, 1970. See also Walker, *Rebels on the Air*, 122–23; and Keith, *Voices in the Purple Haze*, 90–124.

25. Keith, *Voices in the Purple Haze*, 145–8. Douglas, *Listening In*, 281; and Fisher, *Something in the Air*, 166–72.

26. Douglas, *Listening In*, 278–79; Walker, *Rebels of the Air*, 122–30.

27. Fornatale and Mills, *Radio in the Television Age*, 129–30; Douglas, *Listening In*, 268; Gould, "Around Country, FM Turns to Rock," 33.

28. Monaco, *The Sixties*, 60–62.

29. Fresko, "Magical Mystery Tours," 43–44.

30. Peter Brunette, *The Films of Michelangelo Antonioni* (New York: Cambridge University Press, 2012), 23–24; and Seymour Chatman, *Antonioni, or, The Surface of the World* (Berkeley: University of California Press, 1985), 136–68.

31. Lawrence Bensky, "Antonioni Comes to the Point," *New York Times*, December, 15, 1968, D23. See also, Gene Youngblood, "Antonioni," *Rolling Stone Magazine*, March 1, 1969, 15–18.

32. "Zabriskie Point" Screenplays, April 1968 to February, 1970, Turner/MGM scripts, Z-1-Z-5; Margaret Herrick Library.

33. Murray Pommerance, *Michelangelo Blue, Antonioni Red: Eight Reflections on Cinema* (Berkeley: University of California Press, 2011), 172–78; and Ryan H. Walsh, *Astral Weeks: A Secret History of 1968* (New York: Penguin Press, 2018), 163–74.

34. Jon Lewis, *Hollywood v. Hard Core: How the Struggle over Censorship Saved the Modern Film Industry* (New York: New York University Press, 2000), 32.

35. Cook, *Lost Illusions*, 166–67.

36. Youngblood, "Antonioni," 16; Chatman, *Antonioni, or, The Surface of the World*, 3. In *Blow-Up*, the music is also spare and diegetically confined to club performances and hi-fi stereos.

37. David Fricke, "Liner Notes," *Zabriskie Point: Original Motion Picture Soundtrack* (Rhino Movie Music, R2 72462, 1997), 1–12. A full reprint is available at http://www.phinnweb.org/links/cinema/directors/antonioni/zabriskie/ (accessed March 22, 2018).

38. Ibid., 3–4.

39. Ibid., 10.

40. John Burke, "Fourteen Points to Zabriskie," *Rolling Stone Magazine*, March 7, 1970, 37. See also David Walley, "Cultural KaKa, Zabriskie Point and Other Non-Entities," *East Village Other*, February 25, 1970, 8.

41. Fricke, "Liner Notes," 3, 9–10. "Dark Star" was recognized and praised by countercultural reviewers. Burke, "Fourteen Points to Zabriskie," 37.

42. Pommerance, *Michelangelo Blue, Antonioni Red*, 188.

43. Fricke, "Liner Notes," 6–7; and Nicholas Schaffner, *Saucer Full of Secrets: The Pink Floyd Odyssey* (New York: Delta Books, 1991), 144.

44. Jeff Fahey, *How Bluegrass Music Destroyed My Life* (Chicago: Drag City Publishers, 2000), 160–85.

45. Fricke, "Liner Notes," 9.

46. Stephen Davis, *Jim Morrison: Life, Death, Legend* (New York: Gotham Books, 2005), 290.

47. Blair Jackson, *The Grateful Dead: The Music Never Stopped* (New York: Putnam Publishing Group, 1983), 167; Deborah Koons Garcia, "Liner Notes," *Zabriskie Point: Original Motion Picture Soundtrack* (Rhino Movie Music, R2 72462, 1997), 11–12; and Fricke, "Liner Notes," 8–9.

48. Fresko, "Magical Mystery Tour," 49–50.

49. Miller Francis Jr., "Zabriskie Point," *The Great Speckled Bird* 3, 14 (April 2, 1970), 6–7.

50. Fricke, "Liner Notes," 10.

51. Sam Blazer, "Amplifying the 'Strawberry Statement,'" *Los Angeles Free Press*, July 24, 1970, 33, 39.

52. Bodroghkozy, "Reel Revolutionaries," 41–42. The film premiered at Cannes just four days before Kent State, Hagmann notes, so they reedited the film, toning down some of its violence before the film opened in the United States in June. Justin Bozung, "Something in the Air, A Conversation with Stuart Hagmann about His 1970 Film *The Strawberry Statement*," TVStoreOnline Blog, March 27, 2015. http://blog.tvstoreonline.com/2015/03/something-in-air-conversation-with.html (accessed March 22, 2018).

53. Ibid. Although Hagmann claims much of the camera work was inspired by Truffaut, the film's final freeze frame being a good example, most contemporary critics of the film focused on its abrupt, fast-paced editing, which, with denigration, they tied to television commercial techniques. Judith Crist, "All That Glitters Is Not Nichols," *New York Magazine*, June 29, 1970, 54–55; and Dotson Radar, "A Razzberry for 'Strawberry'," *New York Times*, July 19, 1970, D9.

54. Bodroghkozy, "Reel Revolutionaries," 44. See also, Jesse Kornbluth, "Where Will 'Easy Rider' End Up," *New York Times*, October 25, 1970, D30.

55. James Simon Kunen, *The Strawberry Statement* (New York: Random House, 1968), 74, 89–102.

56. Bozung, "Something in the Air."

Chapter 4

Pinewood's *Fiddler* Fans Goldwyn's Folly

London's Battle for Postproduction Sound Business

Katherine Quanz

In 1972 Gordon McCallum from London's Pinewood Studios won the Academy Award for Best Sound for his work on the musical *Fiddler on the Roof* (1971). Following this win, *Variety* published a headline proclaiming "McCallum a Hero to U.K. Filmites." The article reports, "not only did the Pinewood studios dubbing mixer cop a sound award (shared with David Hildyard) for UA's 'Fiddler on the Roof,' but he had also been nominated for UA's 'Diamonds Are Forever.' He was a nominee last year, too, for 'Ryan's Daughter' (MGM)."[1] McCallum's status as an Oscar-winning film mixer demonstrated that British studios were capable of delivering Hollywood-style soundtracks.

Less than a year earlier, however, director Norman Jewison's decision to mix his musical in London was considered controversial in the industry. The British mix of *Fiddler* broke from Jewison's established relationship with the rerecording engineers at Hollywood's Goldwyn Studios. Moreover, his choice to rerecord the film in London was compounded by the decision to create a four-track stereo version for the musical. In order to convince producer Marvin Mirisch that the quality of the soundtrack would remain high, a sample reel from the film was sent from London to Goldwyn's technicians to review approximately two months before the final mix of the film—where all of the sound elements would be combined—was scheduled to commence. In effect, the review of the reel became Pinewood's audition to work in Hollywood, with their LA-based rival judging the results.

The soundtrack for *Fiddler* followed the typical division of labor for the creation of the soundtrack. First, the musical numbers were recorded at Anvil Studios in

London before the scenes were filmed; then these recordings were played back on the set as the actors performed each number. Next, location recorders captured the actors' nonmusical scenes on the set. After the filming was complete, the composer and arranger created and recorded the remainder of the music. While this was occurring, the dialogue editor began to clean the dialogue recordings and rerecorded some lines to boost intelligibility or to alter the performance. The sound editor added in sounds to enhance the visual image and to provide aural details for the onscreen actions and locations.

This essay focuses on the final stage, the rerecording, or dub, of the film. During this stage, the mixers, or rerecordists, combined all of the elements (dialogue, music, and sound effects) into a single cohesive soundtrack. Since the film was slated to be released in surround sound, the mixers also directed the sounds to the appropriate speakers. In sum, the rerecording mixers, McCallum and the uncredited John Hayward, were responsible for ensuring that the film's soundtrack matched the director's and producer's vision for the film, while maintaining maximum intelligibility of the dialogue. By focusing on the internal communications between two sound departments on different sides of the Atlantic, we gain a deeper understanding of the role of the mixer, in particular, the technical and diplomatic aspects of the job.

In this chapter, I examine the correspondence between the London and Los Angeles rerecording engineers regarding *Fiddler's* four-track sound design. This correspondence consists of two letters, one from the Los Angeles–based Goldwyn Studios and the other from London's Pinewood Studios, which are preserved in the Norman Jewison papers at the Wisconsin Center for Film and Theater Research. These two letters underline a simmering tension between two mixing facilities that were in direct competition with each other, while also pointing to issues of the gradual shift away from Hollywood as the center for production and postproduction of English-language commercial films. Consequently, the letters served to establish the status of each studio within the industry at a time of economic uncertainty.

The letters provide insight into the attitudes and views of the departments regarding the condition of the sample mix and their own aesthetic ideals. Unlike oral histories or interviews where practitioners recount their memories of events, often many years later, to promote their creative achievements and canonize their work, the letters document the exact exchange regarding the aesthetic traits of the soundtracks that occurred during a film's production. In these letters we hear the voices of the technicians as they work to persuade producers that their approach is the proper and professional one.

The first letter is signed by Donald C. Rogers, the assistant technical director at Goldwyn. Based on the contents of the letter, it appears to have been drafted in consultation with Gordon Sawyer, the director of sound at Goldwyn. This letter reveals a deep skepticism that their British counterparts were capable of producing a Hollywood-caliber soundtrack. The subtext of the letter suggests that Los Angeles sound technicians saw the British industry as a threat to their financial stability, as runaway productions were becoming the norm. Rogers's letter denigrates the quality of Pinewood's work in an apparent effort to prevent London from becoming an outpost for Hollywood sound. The sound department at Goldwyn was essentially defending its territory by attempting to forestall the era of runaway productions from becoming an era of runaway *post*productions.

The second letter is a response signed by Geoffrey F. Labram, the director of sound at Pinewood. This letter appears to have been written by a committee as Labram acknowledges the contributions of his team of engineers, including McCallum. Pinewood's response references industry standards for soundtrack creation and accuses Goldwyn of not adhering to the international soundtrack standards developed by Hollywood. Thus, Pinewood's sound team used the letter as a venue to argue that they understood the standards better than Goldwyn's mixers and that the quality of the soundtrack should be determined by the capability to understand and meet these standards rather than by the location of the mix facility.

The opposing ideals expressed in the letters signal the beginning of a reconceptualization of the identity of a Hollywood soundtrack. During the studio era, a Hollywood soundtrack was defined in a straightforward manner as a film that completed its sound editing and rerecording phases at a Hollywood sound studio. However, with the breakdown of the studio system, this definition became less clear, with studios outside of Hollywood creating soundtracks of similar quality for Hollywood. The letters suggest that the definition of Hollywood soundtracks was changing to include soundtracks that follow international standards set by the industry and that adhere to the general style of the industry, regardless of where it was mixed. Ultimately, this conflict positioned individual studio styles against international standards. The increase in competition for postproduction sound work led the sound teams at Goldwyn and Pinewood to each articulate their own definition of Hollywood-caliber cinema sound in their correspondence. The letters reveal how both Goldwyn and Pinewood asserted their value at a time when the definition of a Hollywood mix was in contention.

Postproduction Sound in the Post-Studio Era: Goldwyn's and Pinewood's Reputations

By 1971 Pinewood Studios had become an established facility for postproduction sound. The dubbing rooms were capable of producing both 4- and 6-channel soundtracks, in addition to monaural soundtracks. Pinewood, along with Elstree and Anvil Studios in London, was also outfitted with Dolby Noise Reduction technology,[2] a London-based innovation that the studio had previously used on

Ryan's Daughter (1970). And like the musical *Oliver!* (1968), *Fiddler* would take advantage of this British technology for the vocal recordings of the musical numbers, although the noise reduction would go unremarked by film critics reviewing both films.[3] Furthermore, Pinewood's mixers had been working on Hollywood productions for more than a decade. The studio's lead rerecording engineer, Gordon McCallum, was a seasoned mixer, having worked on the James Bond films, and six-track 70mm road shows such as Nicholas Ray's *55 Days at Peking* (1963) and Anthony Mann's *The Fall of the Roman Empire* (1964).

In contrast, during the 1960s and early 1970s, Los Angeles postproduction facilities were reestablishing business relationships following the dismantling of the studio system. Competition among LA-based facilities such as Goldwyn, Glen Glenn, and Todd-AO meant that sound engineers needed to develop and maintain their stable of clients. Complicating this situation was the decline in the number of studio-produced features each year and outside competition from postproduction houses in New York and London. This decline meant that maintaining existing relationships with producers was essential for the survival of studios, so it follows that Goldwyn would attempt to retain the Mirisch Company as a client.

Prior to *Fiddler*, Goldwyn was Mirisch's preferred rerecording studio. For instance, during the 1960s, Goldwyn's Clem Portman mixed *Kiss Me, Stupid* (1964), *The Hallelujah Trail* (1965), *Hawaii* (1966), *How to Succeed in Business Without Really Trying* (1967), and *The Party* (1968), among others, for Mirisch Productions. Likewise, although Marvin Mirisch provided Hal Ashby with final say over where the mix for his New York film *The Landlord* (1970) would be completed, he was encouraged to mix the film in Los Angeles at Goldwyn.[4] Consequently, Jewison's decision to mix *Fiddler* abroad would have signaled to Goldwyn that more Mirisch productions would be mixed elsewhere and that the studio would cease to be the preferred choice of the prolific production company. Goldwyn, therefore, had a huge incentive to try to derail Pinewood as a potential competitor.

Mixing in Britain

The postproduction files for *Fiddler on the Roof* offer a glimpse into how London was functioning as an outpost for Hollywood at the time. While it is not exactly clear why Jewison elected to mix *Fiddler* in London, there are several possible explanations. First, Clem Portman, the mixer with whom Jewison had previously worked at Goldwyn, suffered a mild stroke and his son, Richard, took over his role in 1970.[5] Before his stroke, Portman received an Oscar for Jewison's *In the Heat of the Night* (1967) and a nomination for his last collaboration with Jewison on *Gaily, Gaily* (1969). Portman was also Jewison's lead mixer for *The Thomas Crown Affair* (1968) and the mix came in about $2,425 under the $35,000 budget allocated for the sound dubbing and scoring.[6] Based on these numbers it appears that Goldwyn had established its reputation with Jewison in terms of both quality and efficiency. In his autobiography, Jewison praises the work done by Goldwyn on *In the Heat of the Night*, stating that the studio "was the best in the business in those years."[7] Jewison clearly respected Portman's work, but the mixer's stroke prompted the director to look for a new rerecording mixer, even if it meant leaving Goldwyn Studios.

Another, perhaps more important, reason for Jewison's move from Goldwyn to Pinewood was his own relocation to London. Jewison cites the political climate in the United States, especially the assassination of Bobby Kennedy, as his primary motivation for the move. It is not clear whether the transatlantic change of address influenced the selection of Pinewood—which he describes as "the center of filmmaking"—or if Jewison moved to London because he was filming there.[8] In either case, during the 1960s and 1970s, it was common for films to be shot on Pinewood's many sound stages and then mixed back in Los Angeles. *Cleopatra* (1963), *Doctor Zhivago* (1965), and *The Dirty Dozen* (1967) all made use of the sound stages in England, but were mixed in Hollywood, close to the producers' offices. However, as a Canadian citizen, Jewison may not have been able to work legally in the United States following his move to London, because, in a political statement to protest President Richard Nixon's and Governor Ronald Reagan's policies, Jewison returned all of his family's green cards to the State Department.[9]

Added to the convenience of Pinewood's London location was the benefit of lower costs in England. *Fiddler* was produced during an economic downturn, and as Amanda McQueen explains, many large-budget films were canceled or postponed due to financial issues. *Fiddler*'s production went ahead as scheduled, but the budget for the film was reduced by 20 percent.[10] McQueen notes that shooting the film on location in Yugoslavia and at Pinewood Studios in London was a cost-effective measure that had the added benefit of providing the realistic sets that Jewison desired. While the exact costs for mixing *Fiddler* at Pinewood are not available at this time, based on figures from 1988, London's sound studios were roughly two-thirds of the cost of their Los Angeles counterparts.[11] And this in turn would have recovered much of the 20 percent of the overall budget that had been slashed. Thus, it is likely that completing the postproduction sound at Pinewood aided in reducing the overall production costs.

The affordability and convenience of Pinewood made the studio an ideal location for the mix. However, the decision to have the LA-based rerecording mixers evaluate the work of their London competition was not a typical step, and the language in the correspondence suggests that this exchange was the first time the two studios had ever communicated. So, it is unclear why the sample soundtrack was evaluated by Goldwyn when Pinewood already had a relationship with United Artists and the Mirisch Company. McCallum had mixed the United Artists' Bond films, including the forthcoming *Diamonds are Forever*

(1971), for which he would receive his second Oscar nomination, and he had served as lead rerecordist on Billy Wilder's *The Private Life of Sherlock Holmes* (1970) the year before.

It is possible, however, that Wilder and McCallum did not have an amicable working relationship, as McCallum in his oral history alludes to one American director as problematic:

> One very famous Hollywood man, very famous and very talented, did something that I didn't approve of that, in my view, played a part in destroying the film. And he insisted on playing some music over, low—too low. I mean it's the only time it ever happened—so low as to be nothing more than an irritant on the track, for no other reason than he didn't like the score. . . . [I]t was most unsuccessful, so unsuccessful that it could have had a very bad effect upon me personally later on, because other people had picked that up and didn't know, of course, that it was not my fault.[12]

While it is unknown who the director was, if it was Wilder, that could explain why the producers of *Fiddler* wanted to see a sample reel from the film before the mix began. Moreover, McCallum's dissatisfaction with the mix of the unnamed film was not the only time that he disagreed with a director's choices. He opposed Anthony Mann's initial decision to remove the majority of Miklós Rózsa's score from *El Cid* (1961). In this case, however, McCallum was apparently able to convince Mann to restore much of the music to the film before its successful release.[13]

Mirisch may have requested the screening of the sample reel because *Fiddler* was slated for release in four-track stereo, and since the film was a musical, the soundtrack was of central importance. Moreover, *Fiddler* was the Mirisch brothers' largest production of the year and they had invested considerable resources into the film prior to the mix. It therefore stands to reason that the producers wanted the opportunity to evaluate the film's mix before its release, especially as the production was located on a different continent than the producers.

Finally, the screening of the reel took place in early April of 1971. Since McCallum was nominated for his work on *Ryan's Daughter*, he was likely in Los Angeles for the Oscars, which was held on April 15. The screening of the sample reel may have been intended to update the LA-based producers on the progress while the lead mixer was in town. Considering that editing and music recording were still underway at the time of the evaluation, and that there is nothing in the correspondence prior to the screening to suggest that the Mirisch brothers were concerned about the quality of the mix, it is possible that the screening was never intended to be an official evaluation of the soundtrack. While the current documents provide no indication as to the exact reason for the evaluation by Goldwyn or whether the screenings were even initially intended to be a venue to judge the quality of McCallum's work, the letters still provide a glimpse into the jurisdictional dispute between the two studios and allow us to hear the concerns and values of technical workers.

The Sound Departments Speak

Apart from oral histories, interviews, and technical articles, it is rare to locate documentation of the voices of the people who work in sound departments. While much can be gained by studying these documents, the correspondence between Goldwyn, Pinewood, and Mirisch provides a different perspective. On the surface these letters detail two different approaches to mixing the soundtrack, and in turn, each letter asserts a different definition of a Hollywood soundtrack: one based on location, and the other on industry standards. By positioning the letters within their industrial contexts and examining the voices of the writers, I reveal the tension surrounding these definitions.

In April 1971, the sample reel was screened in three different venues: Goldwyn Projection Room "A," Goldwyn Dubbing Theatre "C," and the Fox-Wilshire Theatre. Following these three screenings, Goldwyn's assistant technical director, Donald C. Rogers, sent a one-page letter directed to Mirisch and dated April 27, 1971. The letter opens with a note indicating that Mirisch requested the comments: "To reconfirm our conversation last Friday while viewing the temporary reel on 'FIDDLER ON THE ROOF', you asked me to make some comments with regard to the sound recording."[14] Through this opening, Rogers clarifies that the letter has been drafted only at the verbal request of Mirisch. There are no documents in the file to indicate why Mirisch would have requested this list, but three probable reasons stand out: (1) Mirisch was concerned about the soundtrack and wanted to ensure any issues were flagged and corrected early in the process; (2) Mirisch wanted to offer Pinewood the opportunity to respond to the criticisms raised by Rogers and Goldwyn's sound director, Gordon Sawyer, at the screenings; or (3) Mirisch was not concerned about the quality of the mix but wanted to ensure that the concerns of his longtime collaborators at Goldwyn were properly voiced. Regardless of why Mirisch requested the summary for Goldwyn, the letter provided the Los Angeles team with a venue for criticizing the British mix and created a record of Goldwyn's preferred mixing style.

In the letter, Rogers lists seven concerns with the screenings. The first three concerns outlined an issue with the balance of Pinewood's decibel and frequency levels: the overall recording level was 6 db higher than normal; there was a lack of low frequencies; and the high frequencies were too loud in the Goldwyn dubbing room. Fourth, Rogers suggests that the physical soundtrack material was of inferior quality and that different filmstock should be used.[15] Next, Rogers raised concern over the channel placement of the music: "The stereo music seemed to lack the separation to which we are normally accustomed," and "It was also noticed that the surround track was considerably low in level (approximately 6 to 8 db)."[16] Rogers's use of the phrase "we are normally accustomed" is usefully ambiguous, for while they are specifically talking about Goldwyn, the "we" implied that the views of Rogers and Sawyer reflected the opinions of the entire sound community in Hollywood. By stating that the soundtrack lacked stereo separation and was low in volume by 6 to 8 decibels, Rogers implied that Hollywood soundtracks tended to make fuller use of all available channels and that the rear channels provided sound at considerably high volumes.

Based on these points, it appears that for Rogers, Hollywood soundtracks should announce themselves to audiences by surrounding the filmgoers with sound. Such aural signals would justify to producers the money and time spent on the mix, while also serving to advertise the sound studio to filmmakers. Helen Hanson and Donald Crafton both note that during the classical era such stylistic choices were often part of each studio's individual house style and, in a period of increased competition, product differentiation helped to ensure the studio's survival.[17] Since Rogers's comments on the soundtrack for *Fiddler* center around informal measurements of decibels and frequencies (i.e., "approximately 4 db at 50 Hz" and "approximately 6 to 8 db"), he appears to have conflated his own preferences with Goldwyn's, and in turn, with Hollywood styles more broadly.

For his final point, Rogers clarified an issue that occurred at the Fox-Wilshire Theatre. The speakers were grouped together for a jazz concert, which changed how the mix sounded: "I examined the speaker system and found that the five speakers behind the screen had been pushed together because of a jazz festival which was being shown that night. The result was that we did not get a fair evaluation of the sound track in that theater."[18] This comment suggests that Rogers was trying to provide Mirisch with fair and balanced notes on the soundtrack by acknowledging the shortcomings of the final screening.

Despite acknowledging issues with the theater, in the final sentence of his letter Rogers counsels Mirisch to further review the quality of Pinewood's mix: "In closing, I would recommend that when you have completed a master for reel #1, or any other reel in the film, you have Pat Palmer send a copy to you so that it may be evaluated."[19] Interestingly, it is only at this point in the letter that Rogers notes that the temporary reel is not the actual mix. Rogers never acknowledges that the music recording and sound edit were still ongoing at the time he wrote the letter, nor that the official mix of the film was still more than two months away from commencing. Presumably, Mirisch understood that the temporary reel was incomplete, because there is no evidence in the files that Mirisch followed Rogers's advice to reevaluate Pinewood's work. Thus, although Rogers's letter insinuated that Pinewood's rerecording engineers were not capable of delivering a Hollywood-caliber multichannel mix, Mirisch did not seem overly concerned by the choice to mix the film in London. Perhaps this is because the Pinewood team felt compelled to respond to Rogers's letter a few weeks later.[20]

On May 19, 1971, Geoffrey F. Labram of Pinewood replied directly to Rogers and sent a literal carbon copy to Mirisch. By responding directly to Rogers, the Pinewood team was able to raise questions about inconsistencies in Goldwyn's practices under the guise of a desire to learn from their Hollywood counterparts. It is not clear why Labram wrote the letter instead of McCallum, but one reason may have been that as the head of the department Labram's role carried more weight and signaled that Pinewood would stand behind McCallum's creative decisions. Also, considering that Gordon Sawyer had Rogers, his assistant, sign the letter, the decision to have the head of Pinewood's sound department reply was presumably intended to communicate to Mirisch that the British team valued the project. McCallum was also not the most tactful person,[21] and it is possible that Labram was tasked to manage the response on behalf of the Pinewood team for this reason.

Labram addressed the letter to Rogers, as opposed to Mirisch. In so doing, Labram engages in a direct dialogue with Goldwyn: "I may say that the engineering staff here have read your remarks and received Gordon McCallum's report and observations with great interest."[22] From the beginning of the letter Labram announces that his entire team was involved in the response, as their investigations into Goldwyn's practices were central to Labram's rebuttal.

The letter continues by referencing sample reels of films mixed at Goldwyn and MGM Culver City that were given to McCallum for reference. The example films were ostensibly meant to help raise the bar of Pinewood's soundtracks. At this point, Labram asks for clarification on the standard to which the films were mixed: "we are interested to know what nominal frequency characteristic Goldwyn and MGM follow."[23] This question was asked, as Labram explains, because the Pinewood team found multiple inconsistencies in the way Goldwyn defined their typical mix. Compared to the industry standard test film, known as "RCFM,"[24] the Pinewood team found that Goldwyn's sample reels mixed their low frequencies several decibels below industry levels. However, according to a study conducted by another Hollywood sound studio, Glen Glenn, Goldwyn's lower frequencies were typically mixed at a much higher volume. And to better understand Sawyer's comments, the engineering staff at Pinewood measured the frequencies of the sample reels and compared the results with the industry standard test film:

> Comparing with the sample of your four-track, we find that you record 2dB lower at 50Hz and 7 or more dB lower at 10KHz than this standard, for equivalent levels at 1000Hz. In the recent Industry Frequency Standards Project, Glen Glenn found that your LF [low frequency] and HF [high frequency] recording characteristics were 6db and 2 ½ dB *higher* than RCFM, as we interpret the figures. These results are so conflicting that we wonder whether the

> sample Gordon brought back was typical, but in any event we should be most interested to learn if you depart from the standards defined by the RCFM film, and to what extent.[25]

In other words, when Pinewood analyzed the sample reels supplied by Goldwyn, they found that the studio was most likely using a variety of different pre-emphasis settings, rather than adhering to industry's standard setting. By pointing to these inconsistencies, Labram was insinuating that Rogers was hypocritical to criticize the volume of Pinewood's mix when, in fact, he and his colleagues at Goldwyn did not abide by consistent decibel levels.

Labram continues by clarifying that RCFM was the standard "in this country." The RCFM standard was created by Hollywood's Motion Picture Research Council during the 1950s and was subsequently endorsed by studios. Labram's use of "in this country" makes explicit that he knows the rules of creating a proper Hollywood soundtrack, while also questioning whether or not Goldwyn was following the standards of its own industry. Based on Labram's comments, it appears that mixers at Goldwyn employed a selection of curves much as they did in the studio era.[26] Thus, mixers could use different frequency settings based on the needs of the film. For instance, for a dialogue-driven drama, a specific curve might be employed due to the reliance on location recordings, while for a war film with multiple explosions, a different curve could be used to enhance the sound effects. It is probable that such practices were still in place during the early 1970s. By noting that Goldwyn typically deviated from the industry standard, Labram demonstrates that he was familiar with the propensity of Hollywood studios to use what film historian Eric Dienstfrey calls their own secret mixing recipes.[27] Moreover, Rogers was likely unaware that Goldwyn's films deviated so drastically from this standard.

Labram continues to defend the quality of Pinewood's sound work by mentioning McCallum's observations from the screenings and Pinewood's subsequent investigation:

> I understand that the Cinemascope print transferred at MGM sounded fine in their own dubbing theatre, but in your review room displayed similar hardness to the master. We find by measurement of the MGM test that it appears not to carry the LF pre-emphasis specified by the test film MF-1, the standard in this country (and possibly in your review theatre?). Can you throw any light on this?[28]

In this statement, Labram raises reservations about the quality of the transfer at MGM because it does not appear to adhere to the standards in the MF-1 test film (a companion standard to RCFM). In so doing, he questions the validity of the screenings, because if the transfer was not completed to the standard, then the Goldwyn team's comments were not an accurate reflection of the mix. The combination of referencing the Glen Glenn study and the standards, along with querying the validity of the screening, enabled Labram to effectively counter Rogers's charges that some frequencies were mixed too quietly.

Labram goes on to articulate the rationale behind the limited use of the rear speakers and the design of the music's mix. He states that it was Pinewood's practice to maintain as much of the integrity of the original recording as possible when creating the final sound design. He explains that because the location mixer and the sound editors provided lower levels for the surround channel, the rear speakers were quiet in comparison to the front speakers.

The lack of manipulation to the dialogue captured on set mirrors the recordings of Jewison's *In the Heat of the Night*. For instance, in the scene where Virgil Tibbs is chased by white supremacists into an empty warehouse, the sounds of the men's voices reverberate off the concrete walls and high ceilings. Jewison explains that this style was intentional: "I wanted sounds to match the movie's semi-journalistic approach. And that was what I got from the sound recordists and mixing back at Goldwyn Studios."[29] Arguably, this sonic style is reminiscent of the type of documentary sound captured by the National Film Board of Canada (NFB) and the Canadian Broadcasting Corporation (CBC), albeit a more polished version. Considering that Jewison began his career as a television director at the CBC in the late 1940s and early 1950s, this aesthetic inherited from the documentary may have been his preferred method for adding "realism" and "grit" to his feature films.

In *Fiddler* this approach to preserving the original on-set recordings is contrasted by the pristine studio recordings of the film's musical numbers. For instance, in "If I Were a Rich Man," Tevye dreams about what his life could be like as he belts out his imaginings to the accompaniment of a full orchestra score. The quality of the vocal recording positioned the voice in either a concert hall or a recording studio designed to sound like a lavish Broadway venue. For this song, the recording and mix of the music emphasize the fantasy of the lyrics. In contrast, the scene that follows relies on the location recordings to foreshadow the coming violence. Here, Tevye confronts news of antisemitism when he meets up with the other men in the village and one man discusses a news report of a pogrom in the Ukraine. For this scene, the voices of the men (apart from Perchik whose lines have been looped in postproduction for clarity) appear to have been captured on location in the village. They talk over each other and, due to the outdoor location, there is no reverberation to their voices. The gritty realism of the location recordings matches the theme of scene. The juxtaposition of these two sonic styles increases the likelihood that audiences will notice the narrative meaning of the scene. That said, while Jewison may have desired a sharp contrast between the fantasy of musical numbers like "If I Were a Rich Man" and the harsh reality of village life, the dichotomy of the studio and location recordings may have been a source of concern for both the Goldwyn team and Mirisch (and the contrast between these two styles may have been exaggerated in the test reel, especially as the looping had not yet been completed).[30] It is therefore possible that the comments from Rogers were meant as a means of solving this issue. However, as Labram explains, director Jewison ultimately had final say over the mix, and it is presumable that he preferred to use the soundtrack to accentuate such juxtapositions of fantasy and realism.

Similarly, the mix of the music reflects the manner in which the music recordists at London's Anvil Studio captured the performances. Labram explains that unless either the director or musical director requests an alternative approach, it was protocol at Pinewood for the mixer to follow the original design of the recording. Since the musical director, John Williams, would have been at all the recording sessions, he likely approved the recording setup and the initial recordings. Even though Williams was not yet a household name at the time he worked on *Fiddler*, he had already established himself in Hollywood as a musical renaissance man, working as a pianist (*Breakfast at Tiffany's* [1961], *To Kill a Mockingbird* [1962], and *The Pink Panther* [1963]), orchestrator (*The Apartment* [1960] and *The Guns of Navarone* [1961]), conductor (*Not with My Wife, You Don't* [1966], *Valley of the Dolls* [1967], and *Goodbye, Mr. Chips* [1969]), and composer (*The Killers* [1964], *How to Steal a Million* [1966], and *The Reivers* [1969]). Thus, as Walter Mirisch recounts, the *Fiddler* team was surprised and delighted that Williams desired to work on the project as the musical director: "So we were fortunate to get a brilliant musician to supervise the entire musical side of the picture."[31] Labram and the sound team at Goldwyn were likely aware of Williams's reputation as well, so by asserting that the placement of the music would be altered only if requested by Jewison or Williams, Labram maintained that the channel placement of the music had been approved by Hollywood experts.

Labram closes the letter by reiterating that, despite Goldwyn's insinuations, Pinewood adhered to the international standards that Hollywood had established, and that the British studio welcomed the opportunity to converse with Hollywood rerecording engineers regarding the best practices for soundtrack designs:

> In conclusion, I should like to express our pleasure in setting up this new transatlantic exchange of information, and to say that, whilst maintaining the closest agreement on standards amongst our own studios, we are anxious that the products of both countries should be compatible in every way.[32]

By accentuating the ideas of a "transatlantic exchange" and compatible international soundtracks, Labram reinforces the need for all mixers to adhere to the standards set by the industry. Pinewood's response communicated to Goldwyn and Mirisch that the British sound team was well versed in Hollywood standards and the industry's technical jargon. Labram left little doubt that they were fully qualified to work on Hollywood films. Because there is no further mention of the exchange in the archival records, and since the mix for the film at Pinewood commenced in June of 1971, it appears that Labram's response effectively argued that Pinewood's soundtrack would play well in theaters in the United States and abroad.

Moreover, there is no evidence that director Norman Jewison shared Goldwyn's concerns. Rather, he only raised *his* voice about the soundtrack following the first preview screening. Jewison notes, in a memo to the Dominion Theatre in London, that the mix produced lackluster results. However, Jewison goes on to report that his fears were quickly assuaged by a second screening in another London theater where the soundtrack was "brilliant."[33] This experience led Jewison to tackle the issue of ensuring the best possible reproduction of his soundtrack in movie theaters. To this end, he began a campaign to lobby Rank, Pinewood's parent company, to reconfigure their theaters, especially the Dominion Theatre in London where the first preview screening took place. Additionally, upon Mirisch's recommendation, Jewison had a memo prepared to provide directions for configuring the speaker system for the film.[34] The memo, which was sent to all theaters screening the film in four-track CinemaScope, highlights the importance of playing the mix in four-track sound and clarifies that the mono-track should be played only during emergency situations.

These acoustical details sent to theaters reveal the continued importance of the magnetic soundtracks almost twenty years after the arrival of CinemaScope. Rather than being a "frozen" technology from the 1950s,[35] the records of *Fiddler*'s exhibition demonstrate that the four-track version of the mix was exhibited in over 25 countries outside of the United States and in at least 33 première theaters within the United States and Canada in 1970.[36] This number is comparable to the 40 theaters that exhibited *Stars Wars* (1977) in Dolby Stereo during the blockbuster's first months of release.[37] *Fiddler*'s theatrical run therefore clarifies, in 1971, rather than being an obsolete technology, four-channel magnetic surround sound was a viable format for which audiences were willing to pay premium prices to enjoy. And around the world, so many eager audiences paid to hear McCallum's multichannel mix that the producers rereleased the film in 1979 with a remastered soundtrack to help promote the new Dolby Stereo format.[38]

Conclusions

This close examination of two letters by technicians demonstrates that it is possible to locate the voice of sound practitioners within an archive. While oral histories and trade papers can offer similar insight into the inner workings of postproduction studios, letters and memos record the actual words exchanged at the time a film was made. In order to fully understand the nuances in the communications, however, it is vital to position these documents within the industrial context in which they were exchanged. In this case, these documents showcase an important jurisdictional conflict between Los Angeles and London in the 1970s, one that has been overlooked in history. The terse letter drafted by the mixers at Goldwyn indicates that they felt their status in Hollywood was threatened by outsiders. The letters exchanged by the studios uncover just how contentious it was to mix a film outside of the United States in the early 1970s.

This jurisdictional conflict between London mixers and their stateside rivals continued well after the release of *Fiddler*. For example, in 1978 McCallum mixed *Superman* with two separate surround sound channels, often known as divided or "split-surrounds." But this achievement was overshadowed the following year by the release of *Apocalypse Now* (1979), as Walter Murch's use of split-surrounds for this film has received considerably more attention by American critics. In 1996, one of McCallum's former colleagues attempted to reassert Pinewood's rerecording mixers back into history of Dolby Stereo:

> Contrary to popular belief, it was Pinewood Studios that pioneered the next breakthrough in cinema stereo surround. We mixed with divided surround for an IMAX film [*Living Planet*, mixed in 1977 and released in 1979], (which also has the top centre speaker to allow vertical panning) and soon saw the potential for stereo surround. "Superman—The Movie" was the first feature film to be completed using Dolby 6 track 70mm with divided surround. . . . This system was subsequently employed on many prestigious films, most notably "Apocalypse Now."[39]

Despite these comments, McCallum's Oscar nomination for *Superman*, and Pinewood's history of working with Dolby, Murch and his team continue to take credit for the innovation. This example demonstrates that much like their colleagues at Goldwyn, Murch's San Francisco–based team was threatened by the work completed abroad. And like Goldwyn's letter, Murch's claims were presumably designed to deter producers from mixing their films in England.

Finally, this paper showcases the importance of *Fiddler*'s mix to the history of cinema. The film's Oscar win solidified both McCallum's and Pinewood's position within the international film industry. McCallum would go on to become a premiere mixer for Hollywood features, such as *Victor Victoria* (1982) and *Clash of the Titans* (1981), as would his colleagues at Elstree, Shepperton, and Twickenham, where films like *Alien* (1979), *The Shining* (1980), *Blade Runner* (1982), *The Fly* (1986), and *Batman* (1989) were mixed. Indeed, the Academy Award demonstrates that, despite attempts to undermine Pinewood by certain Hollywood engineers who felt threatened, Hollywood deemed the final soundtrack to be noteworthy, and in turn the London mixers were commended by their Hollywood counterparts. Thus, the definition of a Hollywood mix was changing from a soundtrack created solely in Hollywood to a Hollywood film with a standardized, high-quality mix, regardless of where the postproduction sound labor occurred.

Notes

I thank Jeff Smith for his comments on early drafts of this chapter.

1. "McCallum a Hero to U.K. Filmites," *Variety*, April 19, 1972, 33.

2. Ioan Allen, "The X-Curve: Its Origins and History: Electro-Acoustic Characteristics in the Cinema and the Mix-Room, the Large Room and the Small," *SMPTE Motion Imaging Journal* (July/August 2006): 267; Tim Blackham, "Film Sound Technique: Part Two Selecting Equipment," *Studio Sound* 13, 5 (1971): 239.

3. Blackham, "Film Sound Technique," 239.

4. Lee Katz to Hal Ashby, March 7, 1969, box 21, folder 5, Norman Jewison papers, Wisconsin Center for Film and Theater Research.

5. Richard Portman interview with Vincent LoBrutto, *Sound-on-Film: Interviews with Creators of Film Sound* (Westport, Conn.: Praeger, 1994), 43.

6. Cost and Budget, Thomas Crown and Company, July 6, 1968, box 16, folder 5, Norman Jewison papers, Wisconsin Center for Film and Theater Research.

7. Norman Jewison, *This Terrible Business Has Been Good to Me: An Autobiography* (New York: St. Martin's Press, 2004), 150.

8. Ibid., 175.

9. Ibid.

10. Amanda McQueen, "After 'the Golden Age': An Industrial History of the Hollywood Musical, 1955–1975" (PhD diss., University of Wisconsin–Madison, 2016), 80.

11. [Sound], *Dead Ringers*, 2000–001–05.0193, David Cronenberg Collection, TIFF Film Reference Library.

12. Gordon McCallum interview with Alan Lawson, *BECTU History Project*, October 11, 1988, 26–27.

13. Ibid.

14. Donald C. Rogers to Marvin Mirisch, April 27, 1971, box 31, folder 20, Norman Jewison papers, Wisconsin Center for Film and Theater Research.

15. Ibid.

16. Ibid.

17. Helen Hanson, *Hollywood Soundscapes: Film Sound Style, Craft & Production in the Classical Era* (London: British Film Institute, 2017), 78–110; Donald Crafton, *The Talkies: American Cinema's Transition to Sound, 1926–1931* (Berkeley: University of California Press, 1999), 360–73.

18. Donald C. Rogers to Marvin Mirisch.

19. Ibid.

20. A copy of the letter was forwarded to Jewison by Patrick Palmer, on behalf of Mirisch. Palmer wrote: "You might wish to discuss these comments with the people at Pinewood,

as well as with our Editorial Staff" (Patrick Palmer to Norman Jewison, May 3, 1971, box 31, folder 20, Norman Jewison papers, Wisconsin Center for Film and Theater Research).

21. G. Labram, "Obituary: Gordon K. McCallum Hon. Fellow BKSTS," *Image Technology* 71, 12 (1989): 549.

22. Geoffrey F. Labram to Donald C. Rogers, May 19, 1971, box 31, folder 20, Norman Jewison papers, Wisconsin Center for Film and Theater Research.

23. Ibid.

24. RCFM was a test film of the curve used to standardize magnetic film soundtracks to ensure uniform playback in theaters. The abbreviation *RCFM* is a code to indicate the test film is for research councils multifrequency magnetic film. For more, see Raymond Spottiswoode, *Focal Encyclopedia of Film and Television Techniques* (New York: Focal Press, 1969), 704.

25. Geoffrey F. Labram to Donald C. Rogers.

26. Eric Dienstfrey, "The Stereo Impulse: High-Fidelity Cinema and the Making of Modern Surround Sound Aesthetics" (PhD diss., University of Wisconsin–Madison, 2018), 111, 176.

27. Ibid.

28. Geoffrey F. Labram to Donald C. Rogers.

29. Jewison, *This Terrible Business Has Been Good to Me*, 150.

30. Patrick Palmer to Norman Jewison, Revised Post-Production Schedule Inter-Office Memo, June 12, 1971, box 31, folder 20, Norman Jewison papers, Wisconsin Center for Film and Theater Research.

31. Walter Mirisch, *I Thought We Were Making Movies, Not History* (Madison: University of Wisconsin Press, 2008), 307.

32. Geoffrey F. Labram to Donald C. Rogers.

33. Norman Jewison to Bryan Quilter, September 6, 1971, box 31, folder 20, Norman Jewison papers, Wisconsin Center for Film and Theater Research. Norman Jewison to Eric Pleskow, September 7, 1971, box 31, folder 20, Norman Jewison papers, Wisconsin Center for Film and Theater Research.

34. Projection, Sound and Curtain Cue Sheets, box 31, folder 20, Norman Jewison papers, Wisconsin Center for Film and Theater Research.

35. John Belton, "1950s Magnetic Sound: The Frozen Revolution," in *Sound Theory Sound Practice*, ed. Rick Altman (New York: Routledge, 1992), 154–67; Mark Kerins, *Beyond Dolby (Stereo): Cinema in the Digital Sound Age* (Bloomington: Indiana University Press, 2011), 24–28.

36. Premieres and Release Dates, February, 1970–March, 1973, undated, box 32, folder 15, Norman Jewison papers, Wisconsin Center for Film and Theater Research.

37. Jay Beck, *Designing Sound: Audiovisual Aesthetics in 1970s American Cinema* (New Brunswick: Rutgers University Press, 2016), 200.

38. Presumably the Dolby Stereo rerelease of the film was a conversion of the original four-track mix. Due to Pinewood's relationship with Dolby, this process was likely completed at Pinewood and reviewed by McCallum before release.

39. Graham V. Hartstone, "Experiences with Surround Sound," Paper presented at the *100th Convention of the Audio Engineering Society*, Copenhagen, May 11–14, 1996, 2.

Part Two

The Practice of the Singing Voice

Chapter 5

Vococentrism and Sound in Ingmar Bergman's *The Magic Flute*

Marcia J. Citron

Ingmar Bergman's film of Mozart's *The Magic Flute* was originally made for television to mark the fiftieth anniversary of Sveriges Radio. Swedish audiences watched it on New Year's Day 1975, and later that year a version was created for cinema. Distributed worldwide, the movie earned praise from many quarters—musicians, audiences, and critics—and would become a landmark of opera-film. In spite of its significance, however, it has received little serious critical attention, with two exceptions. Musicologist Jeongwon Joe explored the movie with an eye to postmodernism and presented extensive information on its genesis, aims, and features. Part of her dissertation, Joe's discussion remains the go-to source for a comprehensive introduction to the work.[1] The other important study is by Jeremy Tambling, a scholar of comparative literature, in his foundational monograph *Opera, Ideology and Film*.[2] As the title suggests, it focuses on politics and culture, and the Bergman portion emphasizes Brechtian qualities and the film's capitulation to bourgeois values in its commemorative function.

One of the striking elements of Bergman's *Magic Flute* is its use of sound, and this essay is devoted to the idea that sound is critical to Bergman's opera-film, connecting it to his cinema as a whole. The movie is not a lightweight aberration, as some would have it, but an important film that has been underestimated because of its happy ending. I argue that the sound design in *The Magic Flute*, including the passages of spoken dialogue, is crafted to express and even exaggerate the serious side of Mozart's opera. In its exploration of human psychology and despair, this *Magic Flute* is unquestionably Bergmanesque.[3]

Across the film, the *mise-en-bande* works closely with image, usually empathetically, in shaping Bergman's conception. Sound functions as much more than "added value," Michel Chion's concept of what sound contributes to image,[4] but as a key expressive element whose absence would have produced a very different film. The audiovisual structure of much of this *Magic Flute* involves an alternation between sung sections, with a neutral sonic environment usually devoid of sound effects, and spoken sections with a dry environment in which speech is foregrounded and synchronized with visual close-ups. Although the alternating pattern reminds me of a rondo, I hesitate to call it that because the spoken sections are much more critical to the whole than the typically subordinate episodes of a rondo. The alternation of musical and spoken sections describes the structure of the Singspiel, the genre to which Mozart's opera belongs. I am suggesting that Bergman throws substantial weight on the spoken sections and thereby modifies the emphasis of the Singspiel. His dramatic arrangement also results in a particular kind of opera-film: one in which spoken portions assume such a major role that they potentially challenge the primacy of the sung passages. This makes it different from most opera-films, where music is paramount and speech, if present, is subsidiary, and it brings the film into the fold of Bergman's cinema as a whole. That Bergman guided the singers in *Magic Flute* to be such convincing actors in their dialogue is a testament to his skill as a director for cinema and stage.

The spoken sections can be called vococentric, if of an unusual kind. Chion and David Neumeyer each describe vococentrism as an arrangement of the soundtrack where the speaking voice is the main element.[5] Neumeyer goes further: for him, classic film *in general* is vococentric because the spoken voice is the most important aural element. Too often it has ceded its significance to music and noise in the study of the *mise-en-bande*, and Neumeyer wants analysis to return it to its central position. This hierarchy does not apply to films he labels "spectacle," those in which music, dance, or other activity is the focus.[6] Clearly Bergman's *Magic Flute*, like any opera-film, is a spectacle. When one takes the film as a sequential whole, horizontally instead of vertically, the speaking voice predominates in the places in which it appears. This makes for a special sort of vococentrism—the spoken voice is foregrounded in some parts of the film, but not in others. Of course, the voice as singing agent appears in the musical numbers, but I agree with Neumeyer and James Buhler that it is difficult to categorize the singing voice in a larger musical texture.[7] That awaits further study.

I explore the uses of sound in three places in Bergman's film. The first covers the early part of the work, namely, the five numbers and dialogue that make up the second tableau. It foregrounds the juxtaposition of theater and cinema, a characteristic feature of the film, and uses sound as well as image to delineate each mode. It also establishes a link between dry speech and interiority, a psychic state that figures prominently in this *Magic Flute*. The second place is the scene surrounding the turning point of the story, Tamino's spiritual crisis at "O ew'ge Nacht" (Oh, eternal night). An expanded array of effects, which include the *acousmêtre* and reverberation in addition to dryness, depict Tamino's existential state, and highlight one of the key moments of the opera. Finally, we look into Pamina's struggle in the first half of Act II as she undergoes a parental crisis.[8] Like Tamino she experiences a dreamlike state, but hers turns into a nightmare filled with silence as well as sound. Such journeys into the psyche, a hallmark of Bergman's cinema, are one of the ways in which this remarkable auteur fashions a distinctive and highly personal take on Mozart's opera.

Tableau #2

In preparation, a few words on the opening: The movie begins with the visualization of the Overture, the first tableau, through close-ups of audience members in the theater who are fully engaged in the listening process. Of myriad ages and races, the faces form a counterpoint to the music and suggest its universal appeal. The shots start with the expressive face of a girl, full of wonder, who is actually the daughter of Bergman and actress Liv Ullmann. The seriousness of their listening prepares the way for the seriousness of the movie. We are introduced to a visual style of close-ups, sometimes extreme close-ups, one after the other. This intense subjective lens will be a distinctive feature, and it connects *The Magic Flute* with other Bergman films. As Peter Cowie observes, "throughout his career Bergman developed the close-up to startling effect, suggesting the mask-like texture and significance of the human face."[9]

The second tableau—the first vocal number, the Introduction (#1), to the end of the Quintet (#5)—serves as an exposition of the film's sound practices. These practices help to form a contrast between theatrical and cinematic segments, a distinction Bergman thematizes in the film. The duality amounts to a conversation between Bergman's twin loves, theater and film. It is not configured as an argument but as a gentle passing from one to the other that may be barely noticed. In Sweden, Bergman was known principally as a stage director for much of his life, and people were surprised to learn of the international esteem in which his films were held. Bergman loved the theater and working with actors, and this affection comes through in *The Magic Flute.*

The Introduction, a composite number, presents Tamino's struggle with the dragon and the rescue by the Three Ladies. Theater is emphasized with the noisy rise of the curtain,[10] the lurid lighting, and the exaggerated gestures that mock bad stage practices or even the silly events of the plot. In some of the numbers, our perspective is that of a diegetic audience member, placing us squarely in the theater. In most of the Introduction, ambient sound is absent despite the characters' movements. This situation, which can be called "negative sound," applies to most of the musical portions of the film and is typical of opera-films. Sound and theater return at number's end as the audience applauds and the characters flutter offstage.

A big change comes with the entrance of Papageno. The camera goes backstage and shows him, a combination of character and singer, awaken with a start as he hears his musical introduction and realizes he must go on stage. We hear loud clop-clops and other sounds as he dons his gear; they define a real world behind stage and expose the performer's lot. H. Marshall Leicester, notably, has explored the ways in which ambient noise stresses realism in opera-film and opens a space for social commentary.[11] In this *Magic Flute*, the character Papageno is an everyday creature, reactive and elemental, and of low social status. While most of his aria proper lacks noise, his lesser status is expressed in heard footsteps as he moves about the stage.

A new soundscape, dry and stripped of reverberation, emerges in the following dialogue. In this regard it is worth noting that all the spoken passages were captured live during filming, while the musical portions were filmed to playback of the prerecorded score. As opera-films typically rely on playback as the singers lip-sync their music, Bergman's live filming of the dialogue is striking, although not entirely surprising, as there is much more speech in his *Magic Flute* than in most opera-films.[12] We might be tempted to infer that the difference in sound environment between the spoken and sung portions in *The Magic Flute* is due to the different sourcing. But the fact that the spoken passages resemble those found in his other films suggests that the dry speech serves interpretive ends. The absence of reverberation, as Chion notes in an analysis of part of Bergman's *Persona* (1966), "has a tendency to 'dilute' and soften sound contours,"[13] and in *The Magic Flute* the dry words have hard edges with pointed consonants. The impact of this sort of environment can be profound. Once again, Chion explains: "When the voice is heard in sound closeup without reverb, it is likely to be at once the voice the spectator internalizes as his or her own and the voice that takes total possession of the diegetic space. It is both completely internal and invading the entire universe."[14] This captures the power of these passages in *The Magic Flute* and other Bergman films and suggests why we react so viscerally to his work.

The spoken passage after Papageno's aria has two parts and takes us into the serious side of the plot. In the first part, Tamino and Papageno sit together in medium close-up as they chat about the slain dragon. Papageno claims credit, and the Three Ladies insert a padlock over his mouth as punishment. We do not see the women's faces, only their outstretched arms entering the frame: a semi-disembodied aural effect that Bergman uses frequently in the film. In the second section, the camera takes us close-in to Tamino as those semi-disembodied voices attend to him. With a gentle hand on his shoulder they half-whisper, still in a dry environment, "Prince Tamino, be silent!"[15] Another continues, "Our Queen sends you this locket with her daughter's picture." The intimacy of this mystical synchronization point changes the tone of the film. The nonvisibility of the women suggests some greater purpose beyond individuals and the earlier flirtation, as does the solemnity of the half-whispered words. These words could even be imagined by Tamino, suggesting a Bergmanesque technique I will explore later. One starts to lose a sense of theater as the markers of place disappear; a realm of interiority emerges and we enter the domain of cinema as Tamino embarks on a personal journey. It sets up the devotional tone of his aria, "Dies Bildnis," which, not surprisingly, omits ambient noise as befits a noble sentiment of a noble figure. He remains fixed in tight close-up, semi-profile, and saintly lighting. Bergman keeps the focus on the reverential music and Tamino's interiority, with a few breaks as Pamina's face comes alive in the locket. The psychic intimacy also fits with the intimacy of television and the domestic screening space, the conditions for the first showings of the work.

The devotional tone continues in the following dialogue. Now the words are in full whisper as close-ups persist, extending the audiovisual synchronization, and Tamino remains frozen. First we experience a static camera as each Lady passes sideways in and out of the frame and exhorts Tamino to rescue Pamina. Tamino's face replaces theirs, also in full-frontal pose, as he reacts with whispered urgency to their pleas. With their renewed whispers emanating from outside the frame, Tamino is still in close-up and moves slightly. A darkening of face reflects his horror. As he swears to do it, a Lady in tight close-up whispers over his shoulder into his ear, "Do you hear a distant thunder?": the transition to the Queen's aria (see Figure 5.1). Throughout the passage, the emphasis is on Tamino's inner state. In order to hear the sotto voce sounds, the viewer would have to be next to them, an arrangement that negates theater; it would be impossible for the girl in the audience to hear the words. Instead, through sound and image synchronized to foreground interiority, the section indicates an electronically reproduced medium, film.

In these spoken sections, especially those with Tamino and the Ladies, the vocal texture and slow pacing are critical. Neumeyer borrows the concept of "grain" from Roland Barthes to characterize a key component of the spoken voice in film. Neumeyer describes the grain of the voice as "its style and texture,"[16] and he and Buhler assert that it "consists in every material aspect of the voice that is not reducible to the production of meaning, the voice on the sound track that cannot be reduced to script."[17] The "script" aspect falls under "verbocentrism," which refers to what is said rather than how it is said. As is probably evident, the salient element in Bergman's spoken sections is the expressive value of *how* the words are said, not so much *what* is said. Neumeyer and Buhler further observe how a vocal "grain" can become a narrative motif in a film, much in the way that

Figure 5.1: *The Magic Flute (1975)*: Tamino and one of the Three Ladies.

a musical idea can function in a film. This applies to Bergman's *Magic Flute*: the spoken sections, though uttered by different characters, constitute an important narrative element in the arc of the film.

After the psychic journey, the theater returns. An establishing shot of the stage is marked by the noises of moving flats and rising scenery as the Queen descends on a lunar disk. The assertion of place is only temporary, however: the Queen's aria morphs into a horror idiom with ghoulish close-ups as she rages at Tamino. No noise intrudes. When the darkness vanishes Tamino's inner being resurfaces, in extreme close-up, as he half-whispers, "Do I sleep or do I wake?" And as he says in full whisper, "Is this a dream or reality?" he is shown in normal lighting on a rock with a natural setting behind him. Bergman crafted the text here. All in all, we have witnessed clever shifts between two media and the invoking of different mental states. The Quintet (#5) completes the Tableau and foregrounds theater, even emphasizes it, with a deus-ex-machina device and a placard held by the characters. It ends with an establishing shot of the stage and a close-up of the girl in the audience.

The intimacy of *The Magic Flute's* spoken sections is also found in other Bergman films. *Persona* centers on the intimate relationship between two women—an actress who refuses to speak (Liv Ullmann), and a nurse who takes care of her (Bibi Andersson). Considered Bergman's most experimental and psychologically complex movie, *Persona* is filled with facial close-ups, to the point of being a mannerism. In these places, the dialogue, or rather the nurse's monologue, is set in a dry sound environment, and ambient noise is mostly absent. As in the intimate dialogues in *The Magic Flute*, the diegetic world is hermetically sealed and the psyche plumbed to its depths (see Figure 5.2a). *Hour of the Wolf* (1968) offers a similar intimacy in many places. The plot concerns a moody, self-absorbed artist, a painter (Max von Sydow), who moves with his compliant wife (Ullmann) to a remote island in order to work. Fragile and increasingly anxious, he has a mental breakdown. Things come to a head at a dinner at the island's castle where the snobbish guests mock him. These Felliniesque figures are highlighted by close-in

Figure 5.2: (a) *Persona* (1966); (b) *Hour of the Wolf* (1968).

shots of their faces and speech, with little reverb. Perhaps more interesting, the intimate conversations with his wife in their cottage are often in extreme close-up and dry sound environment, exposing deep pain as the world is shut out (see Figure 5.2b).

The journey into psychic angst knows no better example than Bergman's *The Seventh Seal* (1957). Here, a dry sound environment is reserved for interactions between a disillusioned knight just returned from the Crusades (von Sydow) and the figure of Death (Bengt Ekerot). A poignant meeting takes place in the confessional as a close-up shows the Knight and Death next to each other on opposite sides of the grille (see Figure 5.3). Their speech is clipped, closely miked, and extremely intimate, made ironic by the fact that Antonius is not aware he is talking to Death. Like Tamino, Antonius is on a quest for the meaning of life, although in *Seal* the stakes are more explicitly religious. It is interesting that all of the films engage art or the figure of the artist, a common theme in Bergman. In *Persona*, it is an actress; in *Hour of the Wolf*, a visual artist; in *The Seventh Seal*, a painter of religious imagery and an acting troupe that survives the plague; and in *The Magic Flute*, the opera itself, the character Tamino who finds art ("Kunst") in Sarastro's realm, the prominence of the theater, and the figure of Mozart who hovers in the background.[18]

Figure 5.3: *The Seventh Seal* (1958).

Tamino's Crisis

> When Mozart wrote his opera, he was already ill, the spectre of death touching him. In a moment of impatient despair, he cries: "Oh, dark night! When will you vanish? When shall I find light in the darkness?" The chorus responds ambiguously. "Soon, soon or never more." The mortally sick Mozart cries out a question into the darkness. Out of this darkness, he answers his own questions—*or does he receive an answer?*
>
> Then the other question: "Does Pamina still live?" The music translates the text's simple question into the greatest of all questions. "Does Love live? Is Love real?" The answer comes, quivering but hopeful in a strange division of Pamina's name: "Pa-*mi*-na still lives!" It is no longer a matter of the name of an attractive young woman, but a code word for love: "Pa-*mi*-na still lives." Love exists. Love is real in the world of human beings.[19]

This passage from Bergman's autobiography shows his connection with Mozart and the section that begins "O ew'ge Nacht." It actually translates as "O eternal night," but for Bergman the existential despair facing Tamino signals darkness, also expressed in his translation, above, of the third line ("Wann wird das Licht mein Auge finden?"—When will I see [or discover] the light?). Darkness, indeed: Bergman was steeped in *Angst* his entire life. While in-depth biography is beyond the present study, suffice it to say that Bergman spent his later years in isolation on a remote island (like the setting in *Hour of the Wolf*), suffered from personal demons and bouts of depression, feared humiliation above all else, and had a fraught relationship with God that stemmed from his childhood as a minister's son.

These elements coalesce in the astonishing segment where Tamino faces a crisis: the moment where good and evil are confronted and shown to be the opposite of what he thought.[20] The soundscape responds in an imaginative way. Reverberation is heard for the first time, and the *acousmêtre* marks unseen voices whose uncanny presence destabilizes our hero. The section begins well before the critical lines. The Three Boys have transported Tamino to an unknown place and he wonders where he is. His words are uttered as accompanied recitative, a discursive style that forms its own number here and extends through the resolution of the crisis. The longest such stretch in the opera, 121 measures, it also stands out because of its appearance in a finale (of Act I). Instead of constituting an organic whole as in Mozart's opera buffa—the second-act Finale in *The Marriage of Figaro* is a prime example—the finales in singspiel tend to be loose and episodic, and the meandering nature of an accompanied recitative is not out of place. So it is in the Act I Finale of *The Magic Flute*. The freedom allows for quick changes that trace the emotions of the characters and approximates the inflections of speech while using music for expressive ends. Yet the passage is consistent with the traditions of accompanied recitative, namely, a discourse for lofty sentiment by a noble character. That it originated in opera seria underscores the seriousness of this place and Bergman's understanding of the opera.

The accompanied recitative can be divided into six sections. The first is unremarkable with respect to sound and confirms Tamino's high aims. He appears in close-up profile during most of it, and a ritualistic fire fills the left half of the shot. As he recognizes that art and beauty reign here, the music turns diatonic, resolves tonally (to G major), and Tamino addresses us head-on: a Brechtian breach that ruptures his interiority for a moment. With section 2 the situation changes dramatically as the music becomes agitated and wanders tonally, and Tamino walks away with urgency. This is accompanied by a big visual change as a blue filter colors him against a black background. Tamino looks for an entrance, and the first aural accent occurs with the loud reverberation of the metal gate as he tries to turn the handle. The effect is intensified through image as we see Tamino on one side of the grille and then his face in close-up through the grille from the other side. He looks trapped. His musical lines still occur in a neutral sound envelope, although the grille's reverberation suggests a resonant space and bears out Chion's observation that "the more reverberant the sound, the more it tends to express the space that contains it."[21] We almost *hear* the livelier soundscape as a heightened emotional space, and everything points to an uncanny turn. Tamino attempts to go beyond the grille, when a reverberative acousmatic male voice declares "Zurück!" (Stand back!) over a deceptive cadence. Tamino tries another gate, with the sound of his footsteps marking the way, and again the unseen voice intones "Zurück!" now to an authentic cadence. The third point of reverberation has sounded. Undeterred, Tamino wanders to another entrance. As the wooden door creaks open, the music settles into an adagio over sustained notes in the strings, approached through a deceptive cadence to A♭.

This acts as the pivot to the third section: the weighty conversation between Tamino and a Priest, the longest section (53 bars) in the recitative. Edward Dent has likened it to "a dialogue between Bach and Weber. Tamino is youthful and chivalrous, or hot-headed and unreflecting, according [to whether] we regard him from the Queen's point of view or Sarastro's; the [Priest] has learned in years of experience, not only wisdom, but a sympathy with Tamino himself far deeper than Tamino can realize."[22] Bergman brings out the contrast. The Priest sits at a desk stacked with papers in a room stuffed with books, and his wise mien is signaled by flowing white hair and a static pose. A warm palette softens the space. Tamino rushes noisily to sit down and exhibits impatience in the onrush of his thoughts. Some of this is indicated in the score, where a few of Tamino's lines are marked "rasch" (quickly) and a couple of the Priest's "langsam" (slowly). The difference in pacing aligns with the obvious difference in their vocal quality. The

Example 5.1: *The Magic Flute*, transition to fourth section of accompanied recitative in Act I finale.

resonance and weight of the bass voice impart a gravitas to the Priest that forces Tamino to listen, whereas the light-tenor timbre of Tamino, especially that of Josef Köstlinger, is able to negotiate changes with ease. Many musical gestures appear in section three, from pastoral adagio to storm-and-stress agitation. The sound environment remains neutral. What I am calling the fourth section, only a few bars long, is a transition to the climactic fifth section that contains "O ew'ge Nacht." In the brief passage, the Priest has a lyrical line, doubled by cellos, that stands out from everything heard before. Tamino has asked when he will find out about Pamina, and the answer is a memorable phrase in A minor that resembles a cantus firmus or chorale tune (see Example 5.1). Its text is akin to a riddle: "As soon as it is understood that you shall join our brotherhood." The Priest blows out the candle, and all goes dark.

Blackness ushers in section 5. As the strings continue in doleful arioso style, Tamino emerges in close-up in blackened tints and the background is ambiguous. He sings "O ew'ge Nacht! Wann wirst du schwinden? wann wird das Licht mein Auge finden?" (O eternal night! When will you vanish? when will I see [the] light?) (see Figure 5.4a). Sound works empathetically with image, and the passage takes on a *misterioso* quality through reverberation: the first change in Tamino's sung soundscape and his only resonant line. An augmented-sixth chord on "Licht" adds to the intensity. The answer comes as an *acousmêtre*: unseen male voices respond "Soon . . . soon . . . or never!" Tamino does not know their identity and neither do we, although we could assume they are other priests. Yet some elements point toward the uncanny, even a supernatural presence. One is the addition of the trombones, their first appearance since the slow introduction of the Overture. From the time of Monteverdi, trombones in opera were associated with supernatural beings and serious religious matters, such as death. The other suggestive element is the second appearance, now in the cellos with bass support,

Figure 5.4: *The Magic Flute* (1975): (a) Tamino sings "O eternal night"; (b) Tamino's Christlike pose.

of the cantus firmus formerly sung by the Priest. As Tamino listens, his eyes look up: are these heavenly spirits? Religion is affirmed a bar later when he appears in a halo-lit, Christlike pose behind a table that implies the iconography of the Last Supper (see Figure 5.4b). It also prefigures the scene where Sarastro confers with his council. Tamino reacts with frustration: what does "soon or never" mean? In agitated style and neutral sound, reusing the augmented-sixth, he asks "Ihr Unsichtbaren" (you invisible ones) if Pamina is still alive. The oracular response repeats the music and reverberation from before as they intone the syllabified Pa-mi-na and declare that she "lebet noch!" (still lives).

Tamino's elation makes up the final section. Bursts of text reflect his relief, and the lighting brightens as he walks about, shot from above, and takes out his flute. The reverberation tied to the unknown has been dispelled, and the recitative ends with a cadence in C major, the key of the next number. He enters a bright space of nature on the stage of the theater, worlds away from the interiority of film.

It is helpful to reflect on the meaning of the unseen voices, or the *acousmêtre*, for Bergman's film. They originate in Mozart's opera, although the reverberation is the director's addition. According to Chion, the *acousmêtre* is quite different in the theater, for the viewer knows that the source is located in some offstage space in the theater.[23] In film, however, offscreen space is vague and unknowable. Chion further observes that "the acousmatic zone is fluctuating, constantly subject to challenge by what we might see."[24] We form a desire to locate the precise source, to de-acousmaticize the heard voice. In Bergman's *Magic Flute*, this never happens. Instead, Tamino seems to depart from the world, as image and sound take him to an inner place. This suggests that he could be imagining the whole thing: that it is a dream, a fantasy, a hallucination, or, in the early part of the passage, a nightmare. He could be envisioning himself as Christ—as a savior to Pamina, but also as the embodiment of goodness and godliness. He may be a stand-in for Bergman himself, who wrote, "I have struggled all my life with a tormented and joyless relationship with God. . . . God spoke, God said nothing. Do not turn from me Thy face."[25] In a somewhat more sinister vein, Tamino's appearance at Sarastro's position could indicate his desire to replace him. This will happen at the end of the film alongside Pamina, but the possibility of some ulterior motive at this stage cannot be dismissed.

In his films Bergman plumbs the darkness of the mind, to the point that it serves as a distinctive feature of his work. Dreams assume outsize importance and inform his basic view of film: "Film as dream, film as music. No form of art goes beyond ordinary consciousness as film does, straight to our emotions, deep into the twilight room of the soul."[26] We saw this in the second tableau of *The Magic Flute* in some of the dialogue and at Tamino's crisis. Dreams can assume many forms, and in *Hour of the Wolf* they are nightmares populated by demons: the demons that torment Johan's soul. Not only do they keep him up at night but appear as figures he sketches in his diary. Later they materialize as real people. I mentioned the dinner where he and his wife are humiliated, but at film's end the figures become monsters who devour him. At the early encounter he might have been saved, however, and the chance comes by way of "O ew'ge Nacht." The emcee Lindhorst—perhaps a variant of the evil Lindorf in Offenbach's *The Tales of Hoffmann*[27]—assembles the guests for a special event: a puppet-show performance of a scene from Mozart's *The Magic Flute*. As a child Bergman saw two puppet stagings of *The Magic Flute* and was entranced. The scene in *Hour of the Wolf* is "O ew'ge Nacht," and its twelve bars capture Johan's suffering. The room lights are extinguished, the darkness intensified by the black-and-white cinematography, the candles lit in front of the puppet stage, and the recording (in the original German) turned on (see Figure 5.5a). There is no reverberation. The camera follows the spectators in relentless close-ups as they watch transfixed, especially Johan (see Figure 5.5b). Afterward Lindhorst, representing Bergman, calls it "the most shattering music ever written" and essentially says what Bergman does in the quotation that begins this section. The sound environment is dry

Figure 5.5: *Hour of the Wolf* (1968): (a) puppet theater; (b) Johan's reaction.

and stifling, unlike the space-expanding reverberation for Tamino. The respective impact of the scenes is aptly expressed by Richard Hunter: "While Tamino is able to overcome his despair, win Pamina, and with her help defeat the power of Darkness, Johan Borg succumbs to his despair, loses his Pamina (his wife Alma) and, alone, is defeated by darkness and evil."[28]

Pamina's Crisis

While Tamino's crisis involved an amplification of sound, through reverberation, Pamina's struggle engages with its opposite, a decrease in sound, through periods of silence. Tamino struggled with moral questions and the righteous path forward, but for Pamina it is a parental matter: the relationship with her mother and, by Bergman making Sarastro her parent, her father. As Bergman wrote on the film script, "Ever since I was very young, and experienced *The Magic Flute* the first time, I have thought, *Sarastro was once married to the Queen of the Night*. Their daughter was Pamina."[29] They are fighting for control of their daughter, and Pamina's challenge is deciding whom she should follow.[30] This is complicated by the about-face in the opera's plot—the evil Sarastro is now the embodiment of goodness, while the motherly Queen of the Night who brought Pamina to Tamino's attention is now the enemy. In the film, Pamina reckons with these tensions in the first half of Act II. But the resolution, such as it is, deploys a Bergmanesque device that is revealed after the fact: her fears of maternal rejection were only a bad dream. This is told to her by her father. Meanwhile, Pamina experienced a soundscape with silence and dry whispers as well as music, as frightful visions danced in her head.

Pamina's first meeting with Sarastro occurs in a section of the Act I Finale. The soundscape is neutral as the music traces their solemn conversation, using the basset horns for the first time in the opera.[31] As Pamina apologizes for her escape and cites the "evil Moor" as the reason, she expresses pity and love for her mother. Sarastro erupts in anger and declares her mother proud and weak; moreover, "A man you need to guide you, / with counsel fair I can provide you." He does not tell her he is her father. But at the very end of the Act there is a sustained close-up of Pamina as she stares ahead, seemingly at Sarastro, who has the same serious expression. It hints at their special relationship but also suggests dark things to come: an ironic touch against the hymn of praise sounding at the same time.

The nightmare starts about ten minutes into Act II with Pamina asleep in a bed. As Monostatos sings his aria, he runs his hand inches over her body, lusting after her. The racial difference is captured in dual close-up and heightened by a blue filter on his face. Something extraordinary happens after the number: fifteen seconds of silence. Yet the number seems to go on because his face continues the slow movement seen during the fast music, no small irony itself. In other words, the silence does not indicate absence but extends a presence as it replaces the musical envelope that enclosed his actions. It is made more astonishing by the fact that Mozart's music ends abruptly, without a ritard, and Bergman's silent extension succeeds at directing our attention to the seamy actions of Monostatos.

As footsteps mark Monostatos's exit, faces of the Queen's minions appear. The first utterance is by Pamina, seemingly awake, as she whispers in a dry environment, in intense close-up, "Mother . . . Have you come to take me home? . . . Why are you looking at me like that? . . . It makes me frightened. . . . Mother!" The text, written by Bergman, replaces the long dialogue between Pamina and the Queen in which reason and Masonic legend are invoked to get Pamina to do her bidding.[32] Bergman's solution—omitting all speech by the Queen and plunging into her rage aria—heightens the Queen's irrationality and Pamina's fears. Speaking of plunging, this aria, unlike the Queen's other aria, lacks an introduction and starts "venting" immediately, aided by the blue/black palette. In tight close-up, the Queen becomes a ghoul out of a horror film, and unlike the camerawork elsewhere, the montage is lively. At the "B" section, the Queen "yells" in Pamina's ear (see Figure 5.6a). Meanwhile, a cut-away shows Monostatos as he listens. After the dramatic finish there is another stretch of silence, with slow-paced images. Pamina and Monostatos appear in a striking dual close-up (see Figure 5.6b). His creepy whispers amid a dry environment threaten exposure (of the plot against Sarastro) and death if she does not yield to him. More silence follows, this time twenty-three seconds, as Pamina walks slowly, the Queen's dagger in hand, lays it lovingly on her pillow and plops down on the bed. Sarastro appears and awakens Pamina. "Father, do not revenge yourself on my mother." "Revenge? You must have had a nightmare. I'll sit down here until you've calmed down." This dialogue, sotto voce in a dry environment, is almost entirely new.

Pamina calls him Father: how does she know he is her father? We have not seen anyone inform her. Bergman might assume that Pamina senses it by now,

Figure 5.6: *The Magic Flute (1975)*: (a) Pamina and the Queen of the Night; (b) dual close-up of Monostatos and Pamina.

or that her nightmare revealed the truth on a psychological level. We learned it when Sarastro spoke to the priests at the start of Act II. Perhaps the characters know it intuitively or from a time before the film's start, or presumably we sense Sarastro's paternity as surely as the director does. Logic aside, the father has won the war of parental control. Anthropologist L. R. Hiatt sees it in Freudian terms as "a resolution of father-daughter attachment rather than son-mother attachment. Sarastro's incestuous inclination towards his daughter excites his wife's hatred; nevertheless, he organizes Pamina's marriage and, through the symbolism of a phallic gift [the flute], renounces his sexual interest in favour of Tamino."[33]

As we have seen, sound is key to the representation of Pamina's crisis. The dry environment of the spoken passages provides her with a gravitas and inner life as meaningful as those of Tamino. Although this does not happen often with female operatic characters, it is common in Bergman's films. The periods of silence also give her weight. Not only do they direct our attention to her every movement, but they create a sense of atemporality—literally, "timelessness"—that lends an epic quality to the character. While Bergman makes Woman and Mother as personified in the Queen the embodiment of evil,[34] he provides Pamina the interpretive heft to make her a credible counterpart to Tamino in the Perfect Couple.

Conclusion

Bergman's approach to sound in *The Magic Flute* can be characterized as "less is more." Ambient noise is kept to a minimum, even in spoken sections, and few added sounds are heard while the music is playing, conforming to the typical practice in opera-film. The soundscape makes the most of absence through periods of silence, especially for Pamina in Act II, and through a dry sound environment in the vococentric sections that points up the subjectivity of the characters and their psychological state. It is highly effective because it works closely with a minimalist montage and an intense focus on faces: an empathetic relationship that is emblematic of Bergman's cinema. The few times that reverberation or loud noises occur in *The Magic Flute*, they serve specific dramatic ends, for example, the uncanny voices confronting Tamino and his lone resonant reply during the crisis and the loud footsteps of Papageno-the-common-man as he scampers onstage. What is distinctive about Bergman's *Magic Flute* is our entry into the inner world of the characters and sound's prominent role in creating that interpersonal relationship. At the same time, we need to recognize the viewer's pleasure in the film's comic moments and the happy ending, and the persuasive interpretations put forward by Tambling and Joe, respectively. Yet to omit sound and its empathetic relationship with image is to ignore a key element of the film's identity and meaning. Bergman's special take on Mozart's opera depends on his sound-image practices, and it is heartening that sound studies now provide the tools to explore them.

As a coda, let me add a few words on a recent opera-film of *The Magic Flute* that underscores the individuality of the Bergman: In 2006 Kenneth Branagh's film *The Magic Flute* appeared and received generally positive reviews. Updated to World War I and sung in colloquial English, it exploits CGI (computer generated imagery) for the visual content and devises vast expanses of space, many outdoors, to set the plot. The montage is lively and the style obviously cinematic, with nary a trace of theater and its rituals. Intimacy and interiority are strikingly absent, and one can argue that the spectacle threatens to overpower our subjective connections to the characters. Branagh seems to endorse an aesthetic of "more is more," and the large number of effects, both visual and aural, make for a sharp contrast with Bergman's vision of "less is more." But in the final analysis, whatever one's opinion of each film, it is hard to deny that Bergman's version of *The Magic Flute* lingers in memory and encourages us to think deeply about Mozart's great opera.

Notes

1. Jeongwon Joe, "Opera on Film, Film in Opera: Postmodern Implications of the Cinematic Influence on Opera" (PhD diss., Northwestern University, 1998), 88–135.

2. Jeremy Tambling, *Opera, Ideology and Film* (New York: St. Martin's Press, 1987), 126–39.

3. Bergman discusses the film in his monograph, *Images: My Life in Film*, trans. Marianne Ruuth (New York: Arcade Publishing, 2011), 350–59. See also Bergman, *The Magic Lantern: An Autobiography*, trans. Joan Tate (Chicago: University of Chicago Press, 2007), 216–17.

4. See, for example, Michel Chion, *Audio-Vision: Sound on Screen*, trans. Claudia Gorbman (New York: Columbia University Press, 1994), 5, 34.

5. David Neumeyer, *Meaning and Interpretation of Music in Cinema* (Bloomington: Indiana University Press, 2015), especially 3–49; and Chion, *The Voice in Cinema*, trans. Claudia Gorbman (New York: Columbia University Press, 1999), 5–6.

6. Neumeyer, *Meaning and Interpretation of Music in Cinema*, 25.

7. Ibid., 143.

8. Paisley Livingston notes that "each of [Bergman's] works hinges upon a crisis of some sort" and they begin "with the problems of adolescence and marriage" and work their way up to "large-scale social disorders"; *Ingmar Bergman and the Rituals of Art* (Ithaca: Cornell University Press, 1982), 17.

9. Peter Cowie, Narration in Documentary, "Bergman 101," on the DVD of Bergman's *The Seventh Seal* (Criterion Collection, 2009).

10. Bergman wanted to shoot the film in the eighteenth-century Drottningholm Theater but was denied permission. Instead, he built a mock-up that replicated its every detail, including a creaky curtain, wings, and floor.

11. H. Marshall Leicester, "Discourse and the Film Text: Four Readings of *Carmen*," *Cambridge Opera Journal* 6, 3 (1994): 266–79.

12. Another classic of opera-film, Joseph Losey's *Don Giovanni* (1978), recorded the secco recitatives live and faced enormous difficulties controlling acoustics and pitch because of location shooting in cavernous mansions or out-of-doors. See Citron, *Opera on Screen* (New Haven: Yale University Press, 2000), 161–204.

13. Chion, *Audio-Vision*, 207.

14. Ibid., 79–80.

15. In identifying passages, I use the English subtitles in the film or, if well-known, the original German phrase.

16. Neumeyer, *Meaning and Interpretation of Music in Cinema*, 12.

17. Neumeyer and Buhler, "Acoustic Stylization: The Film's Sound World," in Neumeyer, *Meaning and Interpretation of Music in Cinema*, 102, citing Chion, *The Voice in Cinema*, 1.

18. The composer appears through his signature in the title credits and then his portrait three times during the Overture.

19. Bergman, *The Magic Lantern*, 216–17 (emphasis in original).

20. This switch is in Mozart's opera, and much ink has been spilled on the problem. See, for instance, Julian Rushton, "Die Zauberflöte," *New Grove Dictionary of Opera*, vol. 4, ed. Stanley Sadie (London: Macmillan, 1992), 1218.

21. Chion, *Audio-Vision*, 79.

22. Edward Dent, *Mozart's Operas*, 2nd ed. (London: Oxford University Press, 1947), 249.

23. Chion, *The Voice in Cinema*, 22–23. See the chapter on the device, 17–29.

24. Ibid., 22.

25. Bergman, *The Magic Lantern*, 204.

26. Ibid., 73.

27. Bergman reputedly was influenced by the tales of E. T. A. Hoffmann. For other Hoffmannesque characters in *Hour*, see Richard Rosen, "Enslaved by the Queen of the Night: The Relationship of Ingmar Bergman to E. T. A. Hoffmann," *Film Comment* 6 (1970): 26–31.

28. Richard Hunter, "A Meditation on Theatre and Love: Ingmar Bergman's Film of *The Magic Flute*," *Australian Journal of Screen Theory* 7 (1980): 126.

29. The director's emphasis. From Bergman's unpublished film script, "The Making of the *Magic Flute*," 36–37, trans. Mary Sandbach, as quoted in Rose Laub Coser, "The Principle of Patriarchy: The Case of *The Magic Flute*," *Signs: Journal of Women in Culture and Society* 4, no. 2 (1978): 343.

30. For a stimulating discussion of Pamina, see Kristi Brown-Montesano, *Understanding the Women of Mozart's Operas* (Berkeley: University of California Press, 2007), 107–35.

31. The instrument was associated with Freemasonry and appears in several Mozart works connected with the movement.

32. Bergman, notably, omits Freemasonry in his film. While this is more common in recent productions of *Flute*, it was uncommon when the film was made. This helps Bergman to focus on intimacy and psychology as he avoids the spectacle and ritual of Freemasonry.

33. L. R. Hiatt, "Queen of Night, Mother-Right, and Secret Male Cults," *Musicology Australia* 5 (1979): 202.

34. Brown-Montesano argues that the opera's stance against Woman and Mother isolates Pamina, unlike the male companionship the men enjoy; *Understanding the Women of Mozart's Operas*, 114–19.

Chapter 6

Breaking into Soundtrack in 1980s Teen Films

Cari McDonnell

Characters "breaking into soundtrack" are some of the most iconic moments in teen films of the 1980s: Tom Cruise dancing in his underwear in *Risky Business* (1983), Matthew Broderick hijacking a Chicago parade float in *Ferris Bueller's Day Off* (1986), and John Cusack holding his boombox high while blasting a love song toward his girlfriend's bedroom window in *Say Anything*. . . (1989). As emotional energy builds, characters put on a record or cassette tape, turn up the volume, and break into a commercial recording in much the same way that characters break into song and/or dance in traditional film musicals. These performances have become staples in American popular culture and have been copied, re-created, and parodied in commercials, YouTube videos, and late-night television talk shows. They have not, though, enjoyed much attention in critical studies of film or music. Therefore, my task in this essay is to determine what separates breaking into soundtrack from other kinds of musical performance in film (such as the term's namesake, breaking into song), to analyze the audiovisual aesthetics of these performance sequences, and to consider how breaking into soundtrack sequences are involved in the development of character and plot.

Musical Performance and the Teen Film

Though characters do break into soundtrack in films that are not primarily about teens,[1] the practice is most prevalent in teen films; thus, it is useful to set the stage with a short discussion of teen films before we put the performance sequences in the spotlight. The essential nature of teen films is that they are films about teen characters and marketed to teen audiences. This is necessarily a broad definition because teen films appear in a number of traditional film genres such as horror (the *Nightmare on Elm Street* and *Friday the 13th* franchises, for example), science fiction (*The Last Starfighter* [1984], *Weird Science* [1985]), and the western (*Young Guns* [1988]); they range in affect from the lightheartedness of slapstick comedy and misadventure (think *Porky's* [1981] and *Adventures in Babysitting* [1987]) to the seriousness of romantic melodrama and social problem films (*Endless Love* [1981] and *The Outsiders* [1983], for example).

Despite the great variety in the kinds of stories and storytelling styles that appear in teen films, there are some aesthetic elements that bind these films together, and music has consistently been one of the most important. With the emergence of the teen market in the 1950s, these films were initially associated with rock 'n' roll, but in later decades a wide variety of popular music genres appear.[2] As Elissa Nelson points out, the particular style of music is less important than the way that music is used: "Music is an essential way many teens actively express and identify themselves, is fundamental to the world the teens inhabit, and as such, music is a significant part of the narrative construction of these films." Indeed, Nelson argues that, excepting the musical and films about musicians, no other group of films so frequently presents characters who work out and express their identities through popular music.[3]

This musical engagement takes many forms. Teens talk about musical tastes, attend concerts and dances, and, of course, perform music themselves. Prior to the 1980s, musical performances in teen films were generally limited to characters breaking into song in musicals such as *Beach Party* (1963) and *Grease* (1978), or professional musicians entertaining at parties and concerts, such as Bill Haley & the Comets in *Don't Knock the Rock* (1956) and Otis Day & the Knights in *Animal House* (1978). Occasionally a character would sing in voiceover, as Elvis Presley does in *It Happened at the World's Fair* (1963).

In order to differentiate breaking into soundtrack from these and other types of performance, we must make some distinctions. As I mentioned, teen films often depict musicians playing and singing live at concerts and parties. This is a different performance mode from breaking into soundtrack, even when it involves a teen character. When Marty (Michael J. Fox) plays the electric guitar at his parents' prom in *Back to the Future* (1985), he is depicted as playing what we hear on the soundtrack. We can think of this as a live performance mode since the sound is supposed to be emanating from the character and/or the musical instrument and such a performance is understood to be live in the film's diegesis. Such performances do not have to be rehearsed, of professional quality, or in a formal venue like a dance or concert. In *Adventures in Babysitting* (1987), Chris

(Elizabeth Shue) and the kids escape from gangsters by running into the back door of a blues club. They find themselves on stage with Albert Collins, who announces, "Nobody gets out of this place without singing the blues." Chris eventually improvises a twelve-bar blues, with a lot of help from Collins and his band, in an enthusiastic but very amateurish performance.

The live performance mode is fairly easy to recognize when it involves singing and/or playing musical instruments. Dance numbers, though, can be more ambiguous. Dance musicals (sometimes called "dancicals") such as *Flashdance* (1983) and *Breakin'* (1984) have the clearest examples of performances in the live mode. In the former, Alex (Jessica Beal) performs dance numbers for a live audience in both the club where she works and in the audition finale. Though she is not singing or making music, she is performing a planned, rehearsed number for an audience. The dance crews in *Breakin'* perform both choreographed and improvised numbers in public and semiprivate spaces with informal audiences that are often standing within arm's reach of the dancers, but the performances are still coded as live because both the dancers and the onscreen audience understand them to be public exhibitions of work.

Even within dance musicals, however, there are different modes of performance. In addition to live numbers, dance musicals frequently depict rehearsal sequences as characters prepare for some upcoming event. Both *Flashdance* and *Breakin'* contain rehearsal sequences, as do *Footloose* (1984), *Girls Just Want to Have Fun* (1985), and *Dirty Dancing* (1987). These sequences are very similar to one another, so much so that I consider them their own category, the rehearsal mode. This mode is marked by many of the montage editing conventions Carol Vernallis associates with music video.[4] These sequences often avoid continuity editing and obscure the flow of time. Each sequence uses a single song, yet the flow of images is often cut over the course of several days, as indicated by changes in clothing and/or setting. The exact passage of time, though, is often indefinite. The rehearsal montage in *Girls Just Want to Have Fun* ends with the continuation of a scene that occurred early in the sequence, so that the presentation is not strictly chronological. Even the rehearsal sequence in *Flashdance,* which is the only example listed earlier that does not involve clothing and setting changes, is not presented as chronological. Instead, the camera oscillates among shots of Alex running in place, swiveling her hips and head, and stretching in a horizontal plane. The impression is one of repetition and habituation, as though this is Alex's daily routine, rather than excerpts taken from a single, continuous rehearsal session.

Performances in the rehearsal mode also use what Vernallis calls "inappropriate" shots of the body to highlight both the star's body and the progressive nature of the rehearsal sequence.[5] These shots are inappropriate, Vernallis says, in the sense that they do not use the proper proportions of shot composition in the traditional narrative style. Instead, the camera often functions as a wandering eye, hovering over dancing hips, thighs, and torsos, presenting spectators with opportunities to gaze at a star's attractive face and body in intimate close-ups that are uncommon in traditional narrative film, and impossible in real life.

When such shots do not appear, it is often for a specific reason. For example, *Footloose* is the only one of the examples I mentioned that features two young men dancing together, occasionally including children in the scene. All of the others feature a heterosexual couple, individual characters, and/or co-ed groups of dancers. In *Footloose*, when Ren (Kevin Bacon) teaches Willard (Chris Penn) to dance, the camera uses mostly long and medium shots, eschewing suggestiveness or sexiness so as not to complicate the developing buddy relationship between the two teen boys. When Ren and Willard are shown in close-up, it is often to highlight feet, hands, or other parts of the body involved in specific dance moves in order that the montage can document a progression from ineptitude to mastery. This is, of course, another common use of close-up shots in rehearsal sequences.

One of the most important elements of performances in the rehearsal mode is the song. In each of these examples, the recording is sonically foregrounded so that the lyrics assume great prominence on the soundtrack. Diegetic sound is completely muted, though one or two important sound effects or lines of dialogue may be allowed to break through. In every case, the song's lyrics comment on the action, but they do not become a direct expression of a character's feelings. In *Flashdance* and *Footloose*, the song ("Maniac" and "Let's Hear It for the Boy," respectively) speaks about the character onscreen in the third person. Others, such as "Hungry Eyes" in *Dirty Dancing* and "Ain't Nobody" in *Breakin'*, use lyrics in the first person that could speak to a specific character's point of view, but the lyrics are not ascribed to that character in a direct way.

For instance, "Hungry Eyes" seems to speak to Baby's point of view, especially since the title phrase is first sung with a close-up that highlights the flick of Baby's eyes, timed right before the downbeat of the chorus, as she looks up at Johnny with a shy smile. The singer is male, however, suggesting that the song belongs to Johnny, though he spends most of the sequence annoyed and impatient with Baby's mistakes. "Ain't Nobody" in *Breakin'* is equally problematic. Chaka Khan leads the song with first-person lyrics, so the song could speak from Kelly's (Lucinda Dickey) point of view, especially since the song is about the development of romantic feelings. Yet Kelly never appropriates the song in an expressive way. Indeed, she hardly seems aware of the song except as background music for rehearsal. In both *Dirty Dancing* and *Breakin'*, the rehearsal song remains at the level of commentary rather than as a direct expression of a character's romantic feelings.

Most performances in dance musicals are either in live mode or rehearsal mode. But some dance numbers do not fit squarely into either of these categories.

The opening number of *Fame* (1980), for example, starts with a taxi driver blasting the title track from his cab's loudspeakers. As Irene Cara's voice is heard singing about her desire to make it big, students from the performing arts high school that is the basis of the film's narrative flood the street with improvisatory dance, stopping traffic and angering drivers.

In a standard musical, this might be the moment for a communal number, like "June Is Bustin' Out All Over" in *Carousel* (film, 1956). Indeed, the students do offer a more traditional spontaneous song later in the film when they do the "Hot Lunch Jam." But the teenagers in this opening sequence do not sing, and the music is neither supposedly spontaneous nor does it appear from the ether, as is often the case in musicals. Also, the dancing gives no impression of being choreographed or planned, the angry drivers are certainly not a willing audience, and the students are not using the opportunity to rehearse for an upcoming performance. Rather, something about the commercial recording seems to have drawn the teens into dancing. Indeed, they have no other reason to be performing in this scene. The lyrics, which speak of immortality, infinite possibility, and, of course, the desire to become famous, articulate the characters' aspirations as they study and work to prepare themselves for careers in the entertainment industry. The students take the playing of the song as an invitation to convey their hopes and desires to the public, and their dancing unfolds spontaneously and in uninterrupted chronological time. They don't break into song, exactly, but they do break into soundtrack as they appropriate the recording for their own expressive purposes.

Aesthetically speaking, however, the *Fame* performance is not a prototypical example of breaking into soundtrack. The sequence contains several problems from this standpoint. First, music is not the dominant element: the song competes with dialogue and sound effects for prominence as characters shout and honk their horns, refusing to acquiesce to the music. Second, the characters who perform are not narrative focal points in the sequence. The camera does not privilege any single dancer's performance by either focusing on them for an extended period of time or by returning to them more often than to other performers. Instead, Bruno (Lee Curreri) and his father (Eddie Barth) are presented as the most important characters with substantial medium and close-up shots, and though Bruno wrote the song, he does not join the performance. Even Coco (Irene Cara), who recorded the lead vocal track for Bruno, is only shown listening from the school, not dancing in the street. The performers, then, become background elements when important characters take the frame.

Third, the narrative does not halt for the duration of the performance. The dialogue that interrupts the music establishes Bruno and Coco's characters and develops Bruno's story. This may seem like a small interruption, but the more usual way to handle breaking into soundtrack performances is to bookend the narrative, not to have narrative intrude into and interrupt the song. Finally, the performance in *Fame* is visibly and forcibly opposed by other characters in the film. Usually, performers who break into soundtrack either do so in private or are at least tolerated, if not encouraged and appreciated, by any observing characters. The bystanders in *Fame*, by contrast, are mostly confused, annoyed, and even angry to be witnessing the impromptu street dance.

Audiovisual Frameworks for Breaking into Soundtrack

So what does a more typical breaking into soundtrack performance look and sound like? To answer this question, I will focus on eight examples that serve as a corpus for study. These examples are listed in Table 6.1, whose three columns list the film title, the recording featured in the sequence, and the primary characters who perform. The eight sequences are in fact quite varied in both musical style and narrative circumstances, but, while the audiovisual aesthetics are not uniform across all of these films, some conventions do emerge when we look at the group as a whole.

Table 6.1. List of "breaking into soundtrack" sequences

Film (Year)	Song (Recording Artist)	Characters (Actors)
Risky Business (1983)	"Old Time Rock and Roll" (Bob Seger)	Joel Goodson (Tom Cruise)
Footloose (1984)	"Never" (Moving Pictures)	Ren (Kevin Bacon)
The Breakfast Club (1985)	"We Are Not Alone" (Karla DeVito)	Andrew Clark (Emilio Estevez) Brian Johnson (Anthony Michael Hall) John Bender (Judd Nelson) Claire Standish (Molly Ringwald) Allison Reynolds (Ally Sheedy)
Pretty in Pink (1986)	"Try a Little Tenderness" (Otis Redding)	Duckie (Jon Cryer)
Ferris Bueller's Day Off (1986)	"Danke Schoen" (Wayne Newton) "Twist and Shout" (The Beatles)	Ferris Bueller (Matthew Broderick)
Adventures in Babysitting (1987)	"Then He Kissed Me" (The Crystals)	Chris (Elizabeth Shue)
Dirty Dancing (1987)	"Love Is Strange" (Mickey & Sylvia)	Baby Houseman (Jennifer Grey) Johnny Castle (Patrick Swayze)
Say Anything... (1989)	"In Your Eyes" (Peter Gabriel)	Lloyd Dobler (John Cusack)

One of the easiest conventions to identify is that of sound design. At the moment of breaking into soundtrack, the recording usually floods the soundtrack with high-fidelity sound, covering all diegetic sound for the duration of the performance. This is true in *Risky Business, The Breakfast Club,* and *Adventures in Babysitting.* The characters performing are completely immersed in the music, and the soundtrack follows suit by muting all other sounds. Occasionally, a few sounds, such as Duckie's feet stomping in *Pretty in Pink* and Ren's angry banging in *Footloose,* are allowed to bleed through. Though the sonic difference may seem slight, the choice to include diegetic sound is far from inconsequential. The sounds of Duckie's dance—hands banging, feet sliding—ground his performance in the physical space of the record shop and prevent the music from captivating the soundtrack and, presumably, the spectator. Likewise, the onscreen spectators (Andie [Molly Ringwald] and Iona [Annie Potts]) in the shop seem less than enthused with his performance, as Figure 6.1 depicts. The presence of an audience, however small, paired with the sound effects also lends the performance an element of liveness since his body is literally generating sound. Duckie's performance in this scene is memorable, certainly, but it is also ambiguous. The music is loud but not overwhelming, Duckie's dancing is earnest but not skillful, and Andie and Iona are engrossed in his performance but not impressed.

In *Footloose,* Ren's body also generates sound, but with a different effect. Ren goes to the warehouse to vent his anger. After he slams a cassette into his car's tape player and "Never" blasts onto the soundtrack, Ren bangs repeatedly on the steering wheel, slams the car door, throws a beer bottle, and beats on the outside of the car. Other sounds, like the chain rattling when he swings

Figure 6.1: Andie and Iona watch Duckie lip sync in *Pretty in Pink* (1986).

on a pulley from a high catwalk, emphasize Ren's strength and control over the space in which he moves. Whereas Duckie's sound effects are often out of sync with the rhythm of the music and draw attention to his lack of dexterity, Ren's are timed to the beat of the song and carefully curated to showcase his skill. Duckie's performance comes off as passionate but amateurish, while Ren's dancing is athletic and acrobatic.

When a character breaks into soundtrack, dialogue often gives way to lip-syncing, as the *Dirty Dancing* example demonstrates. For the first part of the scene, which takes place in a private rehearsal studio, Baby and Johnny engage in flirtatious dialogue while the instrumental portion of "Love Is Strange," recorded by Mickey & Sylvia, plays on a record player. When Mickey's voice on the recording calls for Sylvia, Johnny switches from dialogue to lip-syncing. When Sylvia answers, Baby lip-syncs the response to Johnny, despite having had her back turned when he started lip-syncing. Without giving each other any cues, they seamlessly change from flirtatious dialogue to flirtatious lip-syncing. The process of breaking into soundtrack in this example is very similar to that of breaking into song in duets like "People Will Say We're in Love" in *Oklahoma!* (1955, film), in which Curly (Gordon MacRae) and Laurey (Shirley Jones) replace dialogue with singing with no segue.

Sometimes the sound design transcends the boundaries of diegetic and nondiegetic in order to render audible the thought processes of the characters. For instance, Bob Seger's recording of "Old Time Rock and Roll" has no crowd sounds on it, but in *Risky Business*, crowd sounds are added at the beginning of the song as Joel slides into the prosceniumlike opening to the living room. One plausible interpretation of these apparently nondiegetic sounds is that the crowd noise comes from Joel's mind as he fantasizes performing the song for a live audience. Indeed, though he does not acknowledge the camera, Joel does perform for a phantom concert audience as he sings into a makeshift microphone and points to members of an invisible crowd. This fantasy is supported by the lack of diegetic sounds that might interfere with Joel's reverie by grounding him in his physical environment.

Say Anything . . . offers another example. When Peter Gabriel's "In Your Eyes" first begins to seep through Diane Court's (Ione Skye) open bedroom window, the music is quiet; but when Lloyd is shown holding his boombox high, the music is much louder. As the sequence continues, the camera alternates between shots of Diane listening and of Lloyd holding the boombox. The volume of the music in Diane's scenes gradually increases until it nearly matches the volume heard during Lloyd's shots, though there is no diegetic motivation for the increase. The volume change is paired with camera zooms that gradually move from long shot to close-up of each character. The sound design and cinematography work together to demonstrate that Lloyd's soundtrack serenade—and thus his emotional message—is getting through to Diane.

Cinematographic conventions in soundtracked performances are a little more diverse than those of sound design. As in the example from *Fame*, most sequences have a performance occurring in a single location and in a continuous, unbroken flow of time. Ellipses of time and space that punctuate most music videos and also the rehearsal performances I discussed earlier are largely absent when characters break into soundtrack. The camera may show the performance from multiple angles, but the impression is one of a single performance rather than multiple fragmented performances.

There are two exceptions to this convention in my example set. The warehouse dance scene in *Footloose* and the library dance in *The Breakfast Club* both contain fragmented editing. In *Footloose*, the sequence begins with flashbacks through the first verse of the song. Once the chorus arrives, the flashbacks end and Ren's aggressive dancing and tumbling take over the image track. The camera shows Ren dancing in various spaces that are all coded as industrial, so that they all seem to belong to the warehouse, but the editing does not visually connect the spaces into a coherent whole. Instead, the montage uses Ren himself to unify diverse and disparate visual fragments. Ren moves across the frame in every possible direction—side to side, corner to corner, top to bottom, background to foreground—while executing an array of gymnastic feats. The shot language is equally varied and stylized, as shown in Figure 6.2. We see Ren in extreme long shots as the camera pans from one side of the warehouse floor to the other, in close-ups as he slides toward the backward-tracking camera, and in medium and long shots as he dances down backlit hallways. Finally, at the end of the sequence, Ren's flying leap into his last tumbling stunt is shown via repeat cut not once or twice, but *six times* from slightly different angles. Clearly by this point in the sequence, the hegemony of continuous time and space has broken down.

The library dance sequence in *The Breakfast Club* also uses montage editing associated with music video, though with less virtuosity than in *Footloose*. When the teens in detention dance to Karla DeVito's "We Are Not Alone," the editing indicates time lapses through a series of jump cuts showing the group dancing in different configurations and at different locations within the library. Each character also has a chance to display his or her own personality in solo shots. As in the *Footloose* sequence, variety, not continuity, seems to be the organizing visual logic.

It is not surprising that both of these sequences use editing reminiscent of music video technique, since they are two of only three examples from my corpus that use a contemporaneous recording for the performance. Peter Gabriel's "In Your Eyes" in *Say Anything . . .*, along with "We Are Not Alone" and "Never," are all songs that derive from the music video era, whereas the recordings used in the other examples predate it. And while the "In Your Eyes" sequence does not use

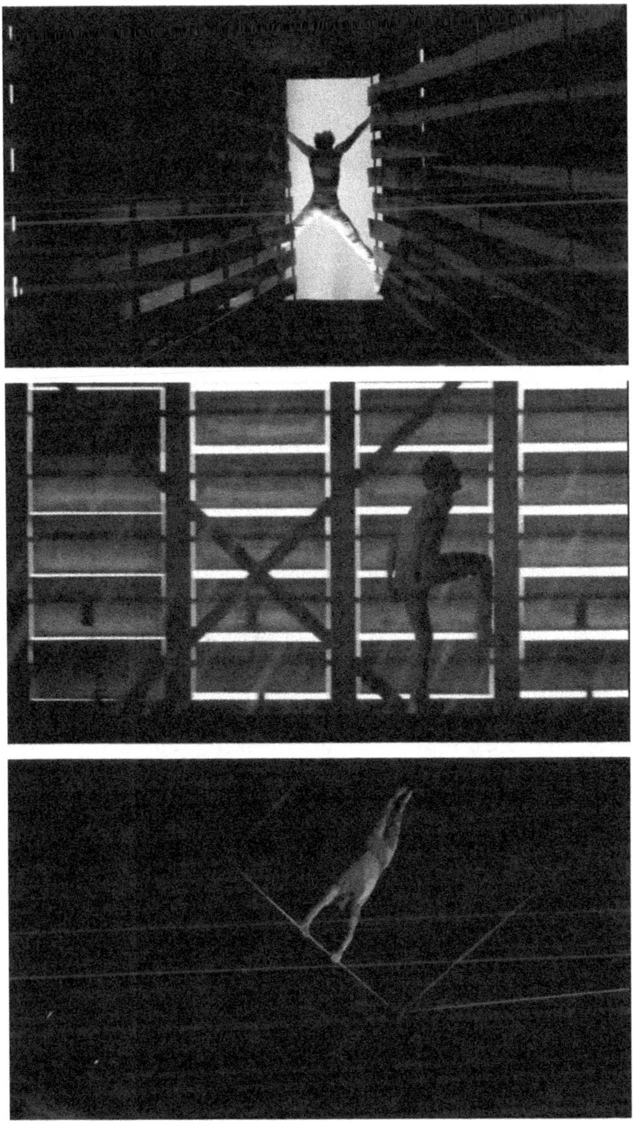

Figure 6.2: Ren is carefully lit and framed as he dances in an industrial warehouse in *Footloose* (1984).

montage, the parallel editing and lack of clear narrative cues are squarely within the music video style.

Whatever shot language and editing style a soundtracked performance sequence may use, two things are notably consistent. First, in contrast with both Hollywood musicals and music videos, performers never look directly into the camera, keeping the so-called fourth wall intact. Instead, the camera continues the traditional voyeuristic practices of narrative film, of observing without being observed and giving the audience viewing positions that would be impossible in either a stage production or real life. This is most remarkable in *Ferris Bueller's Day Off* because Ferris regularly addresses the camera throughout the film; yet during the musical sequence, arguably the most logical time for him to perform directly for the camera, he refrains from doing so. Second, the film's lead character(s) are the performers and, thus, the focal point of the sequence. In most cases, the performance is private, so there are no other characters who can compete for the audience's attention.

These filmmaking strategies work together to present the character in a state of emotional transparency. The spontaneous and often amateur nature of the performance reinforces the sense of transparency and candor. If Ferris addressed the camera during the parade, his lip-syncing might seem calculated or rehearsed, like the orations he delivers to the camera at other points in the film. If Ren got out of his car and immediately launched into the dance, his performance would not flow so organically out of his anger and frustration. The transition from angry outbursts into dancing lends emotional credibility to his stylized dancing and flawless acrobatics. Most of the dancing in these sequences is more amateurish than Ren's, but even in *Dirty Dancing*, with characters who are professional entertainers, Baby and Johnny's dancing during the "Love Is Strange" sequence is informal and improvisatory instead of planned and rehearsed.

When characters break into soundtrack, their song choice is perhaps the most important aesthetic element of the performance, for it is indeed clear at that moment that the character is the curator of the soundtrack. In *Risky Business, Footloose, Breakfast Club, Dirty Dancing,* and *Say Anything . . .*, characters are seen interacting with the stereo or record player that is the onscreen music source. In *Ferris Bueller's Day Off*, Ferris's spoken introduction to "Danke Schoen" indicates that he is choosing the music, and in *Adventures in Babysitting,* Chris's boombox is visible on her dresser. *Pretty in Pink* is an exception in that Iona is the curator of the music which Duckie appropriates for his lip-sync performance, but afterward he explains his connection to the record.

The agency involved in making these musical choices is narratively important. In a section of *Film, a Sound Art* aptly titled "Fate in a Radio," Michel Chion says, "Whenever characters hear song lyrics that they do not then verbalize and appropriate for themselves, we can be quite certain . . . that the song identifies the character's destiny—a destiny that he or she *submits to* rather than actively *forges*."[6] The rehearsal numbers discussed above are good illustrations of this difference. When characters break into soundtrack, though, they do indeed "appropriate for themselves" the song lyrics. Even if they do not lip-sync, they make a clear choice to express themselves with a specific recording. Surely these performances are a sign of agency, of forging ahead toward a destiny chosen by, rather than forced upon, the character. The fate of these characters is in the cassette deck or the record player, not the DJ-controlled radio.

The recordings used for these sequences bear some remarkably consistent characteristics. Every song is sung by an entertainer of the same gender as the primary performer and is sung in first person. The recordings also manage to agree with the number of performers onscreen. "Twist and Shout" in *Ferris Bueller's Day Off* clearly has the other Beatles singing prominent backup vocals with John Lennon. "We Are Not Alone" in *The Breakfast Club* does not have multiple singers, but the song lyrics Karla DeVito sings are in first person plural, not singular, as the song title demonstrates.

The race of the character and the recording artist, however, do not always correspond. All of the protagonists in these films are white, yet many of the singers whose voices they simulate are black. To complicate matters more, in my set of examples, all of the recordings done by black artists are not just used for expressive dancing, but actually lip-synced. Duckie performs to Otis Redding in *Pretty in Pink,* Chris pantomimes to The Crystals in *Adventures in Babysitting,* and Baby and Johnny lip-sync Mickey & Sylvia in *Dirty Dancing.* Of course, white teens enjoying music recorded by artists of color is not inherently problematic; the appropriation of voice that the act of lip-syncing implies is more so. Moreover, this performance convention exemplifies the racial inequity endemic to these teen films. Characters of color are usually entirely absent; they are limited to small feature roles, often musical in nature—like those of Tito Suarez (Charles "Toni" Cole), the band leader in *Dirty Dancing,* and Albert Collins as himself in *Adventures in Babysitting*—or pigeonholed into characters doing service jobs or representing urban city dwellers, like the thieves, gangsters, and prostitutes that populate the Chicago underworld in *Risky Business* and *Adventures in Babysitting. Ferris Bueller's Day Off* exemplifies these conventions by relegating characters of color to service jobs—nurse, delivery man, auto mechanic—and urban Chicagoans who serve as dancing bodies while Ferris lip-syncs the white cover version of song originally recorded by a black trio.[7] As Michael Dwyer points out in his discussion of *Back to the Future,* in using white bodies to represent music recorded by black artists, these seemingly innocuous films can potentially "[rewrite] history" by "relegating the Black musicians and social conditions that actually produced [the music] to the background."[8]

The teen characters choosing the songs seem guided as much by the emotional substance of a particular recording as by the specific lyrics, which may or may not be relevant to the character's life. The characters in *Footloose, The Breakfast Club, Dirty Dancing,* and *Say Anything . . .* all use songs that speak directly to their current situation. Chris in *Adventures in Babysitting* uses "Then He Kissed Me" to act out her desired future, as she hopes her boyfriend will propose marriage. The songs in *Risky Business*, *Ferris Bueller's Day Off*, and *Pretty in Pink* are more general in their lyrical content. In *Risky Business*, Joel seems drawn more to the rock star persona of Bob Seger than to the actual song. Similarly, Ferris appropriates the fervor of Beatlemania and the charisma of John Lennon's vocal performance to whip the parade audience into a dancing frenzy.

In *Pretty in Pink*, Duckie's lip-sync of "Try a Little Tenderness" is more ambiguous than the other examples, largely due to the song's lyrics. Prior to his performance, Duckie struggles to reveal the depth of his affection for Andie. He talks through his feelings when he is alone, discusses the matter with Andie's father, and finally declares his love for her in the record store. Well, sort of. Instead of making a direct statement of love to a potential romantic partner, the song enthusiastically delivers relationship advice to anyone who wants to pursue a young woman. As I discussed earlier, Duckie's presentation, and Otis Redding's singing, is passionate and arresting; but the indirectness of the song renders Duckie unable to compel a response from Andie. The blankness of her expression during the sequence, shown in Figure 6.1, is the visual definition of a nonresponse, and after Duckie's awkward exit, his performance is temporarily open to interpretation. Does Andie know he is declaring his love for her? Is he performing primarily for Andie or for both Andie and Iona? Does Iona have a thing for Duckie? In the argument that follows between him and Andie, Duckie's feelings do become clear, but the ambiguity of his musical performance and Andie's lack of response to it casts a shadow of doubt over their romantic future, which, given the controversy surrounding the film's two different endings, seems like a fatal narrative flaw.[9]

The Self in the Soundtrack

If these teens are consistently breaking into soundtrack at moments and to music of their own choosing, we must ask why. Chion indicates that when characters appropriate a song's lyrics for themselves, they signal ownership over their own destinies. In examining common narrative themes in teen films, Nelson concludes that, broadly speaking, "the genre is about the process of self-discovery and acceptance" rather than maturation.[10] As they navigate this process, these performing teens use commercial recordings to try on an identity—and a potential destiny—like they might try on different styles of clothing at the mall. In Nelson's words, "performance of music becomes a site of performance of self."[11] *Risky Business*, *Adventures in Babysitting*, and *Dirty Dancing* all feature characters who break into soundtrack in order to try out a potential destiny.

In *Risky Business*, Joel starts out anxious about his academic future and his potential for sexual activity. As a response to his uptight demeanor, his friends and even his father encourage him to cut loose and take risks. When his parents leave town for the weekend, Joel decides to take their advice. After leaving his parents at the airport, he partakes of his father's scotch and stereo system. Joel's performance of "Old Time Rock and Roll," then, serves as his initiation into a string of increasingly subversive, high-risk adventures that culminates in sinking his father's sports car into a lake and losing the furnishings of his home to a local pimp. Joel's energetic lip-syncing and erotically charged dancing contrast the sexual paralysis he experienced in both the dream he narrates at the film's opening and the failed romantic encounter he recounted to his friends earlier. From his now-iconic slide into the living room doorway, he is exuberant and uninhibited. Indeed, he is having fun for the first time in the film. In the private spaces of his home and his imagination, then, he is charismatic, confident, and free of the anxieties that hold him back in middle-class society. Bob Seger's dynamic vocal track allows Joel to explore his potential for a more uninhibited life, and by the end of the film, he learns to leverage his newfound confidence toward academic and social success.

In *Adventures in Babysitting*, Chris's opening performance to "Then He Kissed Me" by The Crystals allows her to express youthful energy and sex appeal before she spends most of the film serving in a maternal role and defending her chastity. Her dancing is uninhibited, as she shakes her hips, tosses her hair, and romps all over her bed throughout the course of the song. The vivacious personality Chris displays in this musical performance contrasts greatly with the meekness and conservatism she exhibits in her initial interactions with her boyfriend and her friend Brenda. As she and her babysitting wards experience several misadventures in the seedier sections of Chicago, though, Chris must learn to be assertive and willing to take risks if she is going to bring the kids and her mother's car safely home. Thus, the opening unrestrained performance gives Chris the opportunity to audition her capacity for self-confidence.

The audition pays off when Chris and her charges stumble onto the stage of a blues club, and she is commanded to sing the blues. We, the film audience, know she has the capacity for an energetic performance even if we are not sure if she has the singing voice. The suspense, then, is not based on whether or not she will sing, but on when she will cut loose like she did in her bedroom. Of course, Chris delivers on the promise of the opening sequence, and even uses some of the same basic dance moves in both numbers. And though they seemed skeptical at first, the club audience confirms the success of her performance through their enthusiastic and encouraging responses. In the narrative, the blues number gives Chris and the kids a brief respite from the car thieves who are chasing them and further endears them to Joe Gipp (Calvin Levels), who eventually rescues them from the crime boss. More importantly, Chris begins to take charge of the

Figure 6.3: The student becomes the flirtatious teacher in *Dirty Dancing* (1987).

dangerous situations into which they stumble, going so far as to interrupt a brewing gang brawl with the infamous line, "Don't fuck with the babysitter!"

Dirty Dancing also depicts characters breaking into soundtrack in order to practice in private who they would like to be in public. Baby and Johnny's duet performance to "Love Is Strange" occurs shortly after Baby ignores her father's orders not to associate with the camp's staff and consummates her relationship with Johnny. The performance shows Baby trying out her newfound sexual and emotional confidence—a full reversal of her earlier reserved personality. Instead of being nervous and tongue-tied around Johnny, Baby enjoys a position of power and control as she playfully rebuffs his advances while they practice a cha-cha in a private dance studio. Instead of dancing stiffly and making awkward comments, she moves lithely and sensually, improvising coquettish rebukes using the same dance instructions Johnny gave her earlier in the film, as Figure 6.3 shows.

When Johnny sinks to the floor in exasperation, he begins to lip-sync Mickey's part in the duet. Baby plays along with Sylvia's responses, moving closer to Johnny and affording him access to her body until they are interrupted by the offscreen sound of the door opening. As Neil enters, Baby and Johnny head in opposite directions and she disguises her dancing prowess. Neil condescends by offering to teach her to dance and calling her "kid," undermining the confidence and self-determination she has just demonstrated. At this point in the narrative, her sexual and emotional freedom flourish only in the privacy of her relationship with Johnny and shrink in the presence of others. Yet, as in *Risky Business* and *Adventures in Babysitting*, the performance gives Baby a chance to rehearse greater boldness and independence and foreshadows the public display of both her dancing expertise and her feelings for Johnny at the end of the film.

In addition to offering characters the chance to try out a new identity, the practice of breaking into soundtrack also affords teens the opportunity to express strong and often subversive feelings without negative consequences. Heather Laing's discussion of the emotional function of popular song in traditional musicals is easily applied to 1980s teen films. She takes Rick Altman and Richard Dyer's opposition of narrative diegesis with an interruptive musical number and extends it by describing the narrative as rational and the musical number as emotional, thus establishing a reversed hierarchy of emotional song over rational narrative for the duration of the number. Such a reversal potentially poses the threat of achieving a complete emotional breakdown, Laing says, noting that such performances are often characterized by intense emotional displays, energetic dancing, and camera techniques that bring the audience closer to the performer than would be possible in a live setting—all aesthetic conventions at work in the soundtracked performances we are examining.[12]

These emotional excesses, however, are contained in the predictable structures of popular song. As Laing explains, "While everything else is undergoing radical disruption, the music is at its most contained, formulaic and, by extension, familiar and safe."[13] The lyrics limit emotional expression by making such feelings concrete, and the formal structure of song limits expression by imposing pattern, formula, and temporality on the emotional moment. The emotion, then, is allowed to explode out of the narrative because, Laing says, it can no longer be contained or repressed.[14] The sequences in *Footloose* and *Ferris Bueller's Day Off* will serve as primary examples of such emotional excess at work.

Ren's warehouse dance in *Footloose* is the first musical performance in the film. After arguing with his uncle and storming out of the house, he drives to the warehouse, smoking and drinking, placing the ensuing dance in the context of subversive teen behavior. His whole body is seething with anger as he beats on his car and throws his beer bottle. Clearly this is a moment when Ren's emotions have reached a boiling point, and in a film without musical performances, this would be the moment for Ren's raging monologue. But instead of ranting, he allows a recording to speak (or sing) for him while his angry outbursts become dance moves and acrobatics that manifest the intensity of his feelings. Despite the strength of Ren's movements, though, he is constrained by the music so much that even his violent behavior is subservient to the beat. Just as his performance is expansive but limited to the warehouse interior, so also his emotional expression is powerful but bound by the musical parameters of the recording.

The parade sequence in *Ferris Bueller's Day Off* presents one of the most spectacular examples of breaking into soundtrack. Ferris commandeers a parade float not to express a repressed emotion of his own, but to encourage others, specifically his best friend, Cameron, to blow off some steam. The first song, "Danke Schoen," sets up the scene and confirms Ferris as an effervescent performer. Cameron

Figure 6.4: Ferris is awarded the Grand Marshal's staff for his parade performance in *Ferris Bueller's Day Off* (1986).

and Ferris's girlfriend, Sloane, converse during the performance and reveal their deep-seated anxieties about the future—anxieties Ferris is trying to get them to escape for this one day.

The second number, "Twist and Shout," is Ferris's tour de force stunt in the film (see Figure 6.4). He lip-syncs into a microphone and dances while the parade's marching band plays in a call-and-response style with the singer. The diegetic ambiguity of the brass instruments and crowd noise blurs the line between live and recorded, between lip-sync and sing-along, and instills a sense of magic into the sequence, with Ferris playing the role of conjurer. He is featured in at least every other shot until the instrumental portion of the song, when the camera focuses on the involvement of the crowd and, seemingly, all of downtown Chicago. When the chorus returns, the camera returns to Ferris, affirming him as the stimulus for the community's participation. Everyone succumbs to the musical moment as though they were enchanted, even Cameron and Sloane. This is a moment of joyful anarchy. Like Cinderella's fairy godmother, however, Ferris's magic does not last, and when the song ends, his power over the world begins to unravel as the narrative progresses.

Conclusion

Breaking into soundtrack is a mode of musical performance with aesthetic conventions and narrative functions that are largely consistent across 1980s teen films. These sequences are similar to musical numbers in that characters "perform" popular music in order to express emotions that exceed the limits of ordinary dialogue and diegetic sound. Unlike characters in musicals, though, who sing these songs extemporaneously and with their own voices, characters who break into soundtrack use others' voices—they select and perform to commercial recordings that afford them an emotional outlet, intentionally fusing their own expressions of identity with expressive elements already present in the recording. The result is a mode of performance that explicitly ties the representation of individual identity to the consumption and appropriation of popular music recordings.

Certainly this practice can be critiqued for encouraging teens and other consumers to curate their identities from the options available to them at their local record store. Yet it can also be celebrated for making musical expression more accessible to nonmusicians and nondancers. As Laing concludes, "Music and words together can give the most apparently confusing emotions a clear voice, suggesting that there is nothing which cannot be expressed . . . so that all our feelings can be heard and understood by others."[15] While we may not be able to achieve this kind of clear and uncomplicated expression by bursting into our own original songs as characters in musicals are supposed to do, we might be able to experience a hint of that kind of expression, or the "feeling of utopia," to quote Richard Dyer, when we emulate the teen characters of 1980s films, borrow the voice on a favorite recording, and break into soundtrack.[16]

Notes

1. Two examples are the opening sequence of *Bridget Jones's Diary* (2001), in which the title character performs her loneliness to "All by Myself," and, for a comic reversal of the convention, the dinner sequence in *Beetlejuice* (1988), in which the Deetz family and their dinner guests are supernaturally forced to perform to "The Banana Boat Song."

2. For a thorough discussion of rock 'n' roll's initial attachment to the teen film, see Thomas Doherty, *Teenagers and Teenpics* (Philadelphia: Temple University Press, 2002), 54–82.

3. Elissa Nelson, "Teen Films of the 1980s: Genre, New Hollywood, and Generation X" (PhD diss., The University of Texas at Austin, 2011), 51–252.

4. Carol Vernallis, *Experiencing Music Video: Aesthetics and Cultural Context* (New York: Columbia University Press, 2004), 28–43.

5. Ibid., 32–33.

6. Michel Chion, *Film, a Sound Art*, trans. Claudia Gorbman (New York: Columbia University Press, 2003), 425 (emphasis in original).

7. The dance performed by the group of black teenagers on the steps during the parade sequence is often the subject of much curiosity. It is the iconic dance from Michael Jackson's "Thriller" music video.

8. Michael Dwyer, *Back to the Fifties* (New York: Oxford University Press, 2015), 79–80.

9. In a DVD extra titled "The Lost Dance: The Original Ending," director Howard Deutch and producer Lauren Shuler Donner explain that the film originally ended with Andie and Duckie together. When test audiences responded poorly to this ending, director John Hughes wrote and filmed a new ending.

10. Nelson, "Teen Films of the 1980s," 405–7.

11. Ibid., 253.

12. Heather Laing, "Emotion by Numbers: Music, Song and the Musical," *Musicals—Hollywood and Beyond*, eds. Bill Marshall and Robynn Stilwell (Portland, Ore.: Intellect Books, 2000), 5–13.

13. Ibid., 10.

14. Ibid., 7.

15. Ibid., 12.

16. Richard Dyer, "Entertainment and Utopia," *Genre: The Musical*, ed. Rick Altman (London: Routledge and Kegan Paul, 1981), 177.

Chapter 7

Girls' Voices, Boys' Stories, and Self-Determination in Animated Films since 2012

Robynn J. Stilwell

Since their first animated feature, *Snow White and the Seven Dwarves* (1937), Disney musical films have often centered on the coming-of-age experiences of adolescent girls; however, the reliance on fairy-tale models has often meant a highly conservative structure in which the girl "is won" rather than "wins." But still, the girls are the center of the tales, even if locked within the patriarchal frame: the object of older female jealousy like *Snow White* or *Cinderella* (1950), or the cherished and protected virgin prize, *Sleeping Beauty* (1959).

The modern rebirth of the Disney musical with *The Little Mermaid* (1989), however, prefigures a broader 1990s wave of film stories of girls finding their voices (both literal and metaphorical).[1] In these films, music has a significant narrative role, externalizing an internal process of growth and maturation for the female characters, a process much less active and "cinematic" than the typical male-centered rite-of-passage story. A boy's coming-of-age tale traditionally entails a literal journey and the accomplishment of tasks that result in an elevation of maturity, status, and usually the hand of a conventionally beautiful maiden; her rescue is likely to have been one of those "tasks." Even a feisty female, like most versions of Maid Marian in the Robin Hood tales, will need rescuing, and her eventual pairing with the rescuer is never questioned. Maidenhood (virginity) and girlhood are strongly correlated, and her final state is as trophy/wife.

The mid-1990s films that centered girls' experience were often based on literary sources—for instance, *The Secret Garden* (1993), *A Little Princess* (1995), and *Sense & Sensibility* (1995)—or true stories, *Heavenly Creatures* (1995) and *Grace of*

My Heart (1996). An overarching commonality was that they were period pieces. This historical placement highlighted a narrative arc that was less linear than the traditional boy-story trajectory and more of a spiral: the girl at the center finds her voice—her personality, her sense of self, and her literal voice—suppressed at some point by external forces; during this enforced silence, she discovers inner resources that lead to her maturation and strengthen her sense of self; then the reassertion of her own voice/self is the climax of the story, usually ending with her settled (or resettled) into a relationship, either by the restoration of family or by marriage. Music is commonly the method through which this internal journey is dramatized for the audience.

After the initial wave in the early-to-mid-1990s, this kind of girl-centered film wanes, though a small wavelet of films arises around 2000: *The Virgin Suicides* (1999), *Ghost World* (2001), and *Thirteen* (2003). In these films, that spiraling story-arc is intentionally interrupted or derailed. In *The Virgin Suicides*, for instance, the Lisbon sisters are confined to their rooms by their parents and can communicate only through records played via telephone—a coded communication transmitted technologically and not entirely understood by the neighborhood boys on the other end of the phone; the girls' final means of self-determination is their suicide.[2]

Although a few films—most notably *Whale Rider* and *Spirited Away* (both 2002)—that follow this spiraling storyline appear in the 2000s, it is not until 2012, with the release of *The Hunger Games* and *Brave*, that a new, substantial wave of girl-centered stories emerged; in these films, the girls' spiraling story is wound around the linear story more associated with boys, like a vine around a stake. This doubling provides a satisfying action line for cinematic purposes, with the emotional maturation invested in unusually foregrounded musical processes.[3] Earlier Disney films had gestured toward this narrative strategy: *Mulan* (1998) couched the suppression of the lead's voice in her gender masquerade; *Lilo & Stitch* (2002) divides the girls' development between two sisters, one preadolescent and one in late adolescence; and *Tangled* (2010) notoriously beefed up the role of the male character, Flynn, to appeal to boys who "didn't want to see a movie with 'princess' in the title."[4] But music engages only superficially with the narrative of the girls' maturation in these films.

It was with *Brave* and *Frozen* (2013) that animation began adapting the dual storyline with some finesse and regularity,[5] and the two films represent Disney's two main production strains—*Frozen* was in traditional animation style (blended with some aspects of computer-generated imagery), and *Brave* was the first fairy tale (and female-led film) by computer-generated animation studio Pixar, acquired by Disney in 2006. The year 2012 marked the premiere of the first film in the *Hunger Games* series, the film versions of a popular young-adult novel trilogy that likewise melds a traditionally "boy" story, of an abject character who rises to become the leader of a revolution, with an internal, voice-centered story of personal recovery/discovery and relationship with family and community. This confluence suggests that this narrative strategy captures a zeitgeist and arguably that the films are nurturing that zeitgeist. The dual narrative, with music externalizing the girl's internal journey, is firmly present in a number of animated films since 2012, and in more recent examples from beyond the Disney realm, the dual-narrative strategy is transferred to stories about boys in a move that suggests a greater attention to the emotional maturation of boys.

These animated films comprise the body of study for this essay, though Alfonso Cuarón's 1995 version of *A Little Princess* will first serve as an exemplar of the spiraling "girl" narrative trajectory and its strong resonance with psychologist Carol Gilligan's seminal 1982 study, *In a Different Voice: Psychological Theory and Women's Development.*[6] In critiquing the male-centeredness of psychological theory with its emphasis on individuation, Gilligan's study of girls reveals a distinctly different pattern in their maturation, one that emphasizes relationship. And their voices—a complex of forces that include agency, individual expression, and the voice as an acoustic emanation of the physical body—change significantly as girls develop, a process clearly articulated by the music of *A Little Princess.* This process, twined with the linear "boy" narrative, underpins Disney's *Brave* and *Frozen*; *Inside Out* (2015) and *Moana* (2016) participate in some but not all of the key aspects. Tomm Moore's 2014 film *Song of the Sea* from Cartoon Saloon demonstrates a clear example of the dual narrative, shared between a brother and sister, while Jorge Gutierrez's *Book of Life* from Reel FX in the same year transfers the internal/vocal narrative arc to a boy and differentiates strains of music within a wildly eclectic musical collage. These films suggest the efficacy and power of the dual-narrative strategy disseminating from the mainstream Hollywood model and then turning back toward Hollywood: Disney/Pixar's more classically musicalized *Coco* (2017) bears some significant resemblances to the more playful *Book of Life* and raises some pointed concluding questions about the meaning of transferring an adaptive strategy developed for girls onto a narrative featuring a boy.

Gilligan and *A Little Princess*

Carol Gilligan's *In a Different Voice* made a revolutionary (and in hindsight, obvious) intervention into psychological theory by pointing out its overarching male paradigm; she succinctly states, "Thus a problem in theory became cast as a problem in women's development."[7] Through her study with girls through the 1970s, Gilligan posits a different path for women's development: while the traditional psychological path for boys-to-men was about individuation (separation), for girls, it was about finding one's place in a web of relationships.[8] Gilligan also found that the voice is pivotal as both an agent and symbol of maturation in girls.

Even assertive and independent prepubescent girls will often "lose their voices" in their tween/teen years; they will not only become more withdrawn and speak less, often their voices will shift from a more resonant and embodied chest voice up to a lighter, airier head voice (the provenance of the "airhead" cliché).

In one of the DVD extras of *Inside Out*, story artist Domee Shi relates her own story, offering a classic example of this process:

> I was happy, bubbly, and really talkative up until middle school, and that's when I started developing a stutter, and then I became, like, really closed off and introverted. And that's kind of when I kind of started drawing, trying to find other outlets to express myself, because I figured, like, "I'm just going to give up on talking!"[9]

This shift occurs as girls become more aware of cultural norms and expectations about "femininity": be looked at, but don't take up space in a conversation, or even physically.[10] These cultural norms recognize female maturity in her relationships, rather than the differentiation of the individual expected of the male. Gilligan points out that women often achieve individuation later in life, at a time when men are building relationships, but her more important point is to shift emphasis from individuation to an

> ethics of justice and care, the ideals of human relationship—the vision that self and other will be treated as of equal worth, that despite differences in power, things will be fair; the vision that everyone will be responded to and included, that no one will be left alone and hurt. These disparate visions in their tension reflect the paradoxical truths of human experience—that we know ourselves as separate only insofar as we live in connection with others, and that we experience relationship only insofar as we differentiate other from self.[11]

In Gilligan's formulation, individuation and relationship are deeply intertwined—presaging the relationship of the doubled rites-of-passage narrative—and while they are ideally of equal weight, in practice, this vision of equality shifts more weight than usual to the relational in a culture where individuation is prized most. Still, the relationships in which women are most often positioned have been as wife and mother, associated with a warm, low voice that recovers the lost voice of the girl and settles it back in the throat and chest. That voice resonates lips and tongue and bone and muscle, an embodied sound that Roland Barthes recognizes in his famous essay "The Grain of the Voice": "The 'grain' is that: the materiality of the body."[12] And Barthes also recognizes both individuation and relationship in his encounter with a (singing) voice:

> If I perceive the "grain" in a piece of music and accord this "grain" a theoretical value (the emergence of the text in the work), I inevitably set up a new scheme

> of evaluation which will certainly be individual—I am determined to listen to my relation with the body of the man or woman singing or playing and that relation is erotic—but in no way "subjective" (it is not the psychological "subject" in me who is listening; the climactic pleasure hoped for is not going to reinforce—to express—that subject but, on the contrary, to lose it).[13]

The restoration of the embodied voice thus allows both individuation and relationship within an erotic exchange. The voice is both symbol and agent, physical act and psychological state, a rich complex of being and doing in culture, and for a female, the stakes of maturation are particularly strongly implicated: from unruly child to "lost/silent" adolescent to a reintegration of voice, body, and self in maturity.

This narrative arc is probably exemplified cinematically at its earliest and clearest in *A Little Princess*, directed by Alfonso Cuarón, a director who has demonstrated considerable skill at the coming-of-age film.[14] Because of her father's apparent death in World War I, inveterate storyteller Sara Crewe has been demoted from student to servant in her posh private school, forbidden to speak, and exiled to an attic. One night, speaking to her friend, the servant Rebecca, through the wall that separates the heads of their beds, Sara remembers her happy earlier days in India. A hazy edit takes us to dawn, and the camera tracks over a sleeping Sara as a soft girl's voice sings with the nondiegetic accompaniment of orchestra spiced with the jangle of a sitar. The lyrics ("Kindle My Heart") are words that Sara shared in letters to her father on the front, and the melody (Example 7.1) is an elaboration of the meterless melody associated with India, which for her is "home." A skirl of the sitar blends with a whooshing sound as a gust of wind blows open the French doors of Sara's bare loft room, awakening her. An instrumental verse features the twanging sitar on structural notes that reemphasize the "India" theme as Sara rises from her bed and goes to the window. A trumpet with a slightly distant, military timbre plays a variation of the theme as she sees Ram Dass, the Indian servant in the house next door, in a window opposite. He raises both arms in salutation, and Sara responds; then, with both hands aloft, she begins to spin as the snow swirls around her. The

Example 7.1: "Kindle My Heart" is an elaboration of the theme associated with "India."

girl's voice returns to sing the verse again as Sara spins and then finally stops, and she and Ram Dass bow to each other as the scene and the song end.

This is a pivotal scene, though nothing outwardly happens; however, internally, the silenced and confined Sara pivots from passivity to a refinding of her *self.* The dreamlike musical interlude was created because director Alfonso Cuarón heard composer Patrick Doyle's song and wanted to make a scene around it, stating that *in* the scene, *A Little Princess* (here conflating the movie and the character) found her heart.[15] The slightly distant placement of the girl's voice here in the mix gives a fragility to this new state; the actual voice is that of Abigail Doyle, the composer's daughter, and her chorister's training accentuates the acoustic purity of her head voice.

Sara's voice will eventually recall her father from his war-induced amnesia, and as they, together with Rebecca as newfound adoptive sister/daughter,[16] leave the school at the end of the film, a reprise of "Kindle My Heart" is sung over the credits, this time sung by the actress, Liesel Matthews. Her voice is perhaps less musically proficient but more present in the mix and, most importantly, recognizable as Sara's voice. Placement and plot associate Abigail Doyle's airy, distant voice with Sara, but Liesel Matthews's voice is more embodied and reintegrates her voice and body as she assumes the role of sister/mother in the newly constituted family. It is not yet a mature voice, but it is clearly set on the path of maturation. The relationship (and similarity) between mother and daughter so smoothly elided in *A Little Princess* is forced apart, creating the main point of emotional conflict, in Disney/Pixar's *Brave.*

Brave (2012)

Brave was Pixar's first fairy-tale film and the first with a female lead. Writer-director Brenda Chapman was the first woman to helm a Pixar film and based the story in part on her own relationship with her daughter. Controversially, she was replaced by Mark Andrews in 2010, and although it might be tempting to assume that the dual narrative is an artifact of this creative process, that seems like an essentialist fallacy, unsupported by the original conception as "The Bear and the Bow."

Brave's dual narrative is set out in the prologue with the dual myths of belonging: to the land, and to family. Merida must negotiate both a quest (the vanquishing of the demon black bear Mor'du to restore succession and thus political order) and the finding of her voice within her relationship with her mother, symbolized by the mending of a tapestry that the two of them have made together—Merida under a certain amount of protest. In fact, Princess Merida is at odds with her mother Elinor about voice, tone, and everything else a princess should be.

Brave is less the typical fairy tale, where the female lead is an orphan, motherless, or trapped with a hostile stepmother, and more like Jane Austen's *Sense & Sensibility,* where opposing personalities, mother and daughter rather than sisters, learn from each other.[17] Merida is never as obviously and oppressively silenced as Sara, but her relationship with her mother is fraught as Elinor worries about Merida fulfilling her future role as Queen. In an early scene, Elinor is in the gallery of the throne room, urging Merida to project in her poetic recitation; this launches a montage of scenes where Merida is acting bumptiously—chortling with her father, eating heartily at the table, pulling the pillow back over her head upon being awakened, and being bored in history and music lessons—and at each turn, Elinor has a correction for her increasingly frustrated daughter. Escaping the castle on her horse, Merida takes her bow and rides headlong through the forest, shooting arrows at an obstacle course she has clearly ridden many times and ending by climbing a mountainside and drinking from the "firefalls." The song accompanying this scene is "Touch the Sky," one of two songs in which singer Julie Fowlis provides a nondiegetic representation of Merida's thoughts, much like "Kindle My Heart" had for Sara. Merida celebrates her escape from restraint on the ledge by spinning in the spray of the falls, her arms above her head just as Sara had in the "Kindle My Heart" self-discovery scene (see Figure 7.1). Strikingly, this is a gesture that moves inward (turning toward the body on the spin) and outward (the upward stretch) at the same time.

Unlike earlier Disney princesses, Merida has weight and muscles, some of which strain and rip the silk of the elegant aquamarine silk dress upon which her mother insists for a meeting of the clans, and Merida's riotous red curls are confined by a linen wimple (Merida rebelliously frees one curl over her forehead

Figure 7.1: Sara in the snow in *A Little Princess* (1995); Merida at the firefalls in *Brave* (2012).

each time her mother smooths it back under the wimple).[18] As a princess, however, Merida does have impending responsibilities, and her future includes marriage to an heir of one of the three clans challenging her family for the throne. As the clans gather, an archery tournament is set to determine a winner; as firstborn, Merida enters and wins her own "hand," but succession is not so simple, as shown by parallel scenes of the two women interacting with the fractious menfolk.

In the first, as the throne room descends into chaos among the warring clans (including a tossed sheep), a serene Elinor enters the fray and emerges with each of the four clan chieftains in tow, including her mountainous husband, whom she is pulling by his ear as if he were a toddler. Elinor glides silently across the throne room floor, having cowed the men into submission, and when her husband starts to protest, she fixes him with a cool look. "Yes, dear," he says quickly, subsiding as Elinor takes charge of the negotiations. While playing on comedy based in the "henpecked husband" cliché, this scene also demonstrates the power available to the traditional feminine position—even one that silences her acoustic voice in favor of her queenly agency that derives from an impeccable moral authority and maternal disapproval.

After Merida has turned Elinor into a giant black bear out of adolescent spite, carelessness, and an enchanted cake, the four lords of the land are at each other's throats once more, and Merida must take her mother's place in the fray. She isn't as polished, and she stumbles over her words, almost provoking an outbreak of violence toward her. Like the rebellious adolescent she is, she yells, "Shut it!" with her hands fisted at her sides, and this defiance shocks the chieftains into silence, allowing her to continue her argument (see Figure 7.2).

Figure 7.2: *Brave* (2012). Elinor takes control of the clan chieftains; Merida takes control of the clan chieftains.

Figure 7.3: *Brave* (2012). The tapestries that represent the family: Merida slashing the original tapestry; Merida's quick mending of the damage; and the new tapestry, depicting the mother-daughter relationship through the bear transformation.

As she is about to follow through with the betrothal-as-treaty that convention demands, Elinor (still transformed into a giant black bear and masquerading as one of the stuffed animals in the hall) catches her daughter's attention and mimes the words she wants Merida to say, which are Merida's own desires: to break with tradition and write one's own fate. This trope of writing is one that will be surprisingly common in this latest wave of animated films, and the tale is also told through a tapestry of the family that Merida slashes in anger and must repair to save her mother; at the end, they create a new panel together (see Figure 7.3).

Instead of a single trajectory from childhood to adolescent rebellion/silence to maturity, this film shows Merida and Elinor moving toward each other. Merida speaks for her mother as her silenced mother mimes Merida's thoughts. The political and supernatural elements of the story still must be resolved—and Elinor is in effect reborn, freer if not free of her oppressive sense of responsibility, after her ursine interval. The conclusion of the film recapitulates Merida's first headlong rush into her own fate, on her horse into the wild woods, now with her mother beside her. A different song (Mumford and Sons' "Learn Me Right") gives a similar sense of movement, but the lyrics shift from a solitary celebration of the land to "dance with me," a celebration of relationship with an emphasis on "we." Rather than Sara's reintegration of body and self, we have two women finding themselves in relationship to each other. No longer "just" mother and daughter, Merida and Elinor are shown as friends, even conspirators, as they exchange an impish grin before urging their horses onward. Elinor, normally seen in green, is now wearing blue, Merida's color.

Frozen (2013)

Frozen is loosely based on Hans Christian Andersen's *The Snow Queen*. As in *Brave*, we have two female leads with opposing personalities, but rather than mother and daughter, we meet two sisters. The sister more traditionally coded as feminine, Anna, is the one who embarks on a quest, while the more outwardly powerful sister, the elder Elsa, is forced inward. Elsa is born with the ability to generate ice with a gesture; when she accidentally strikes her younger sister Anna during play, little Anna's memories are rewritten, and Elsa's hands sheathed in gloves by her parents who suppress her power (part of her "voice"). Structurally—like Sleeping Beauty's pricking of her finger on a spindle, or Snow White's eating of the red apple, followed by a deep sleep—this is a symbolic puberty followed by a constraint of sexuality. However, Elsa's gift of ice metaphorically activates not sexual awakening, but frigidity—a fraught complex of failed female sexuality and the paradoxical possibility of power in escaping the confines of a conventional relationship that requires both sexual availability and social probity. The imposition of the gloves attempts to save others from her icy touch, but also isolates *Elsa* from human touch.

By contrast, Anna is defined by nothing more than by her desire for relationship—with her parents, her sister, an ideal mate. When this passionate but continually thwarted desire has her consenting to marry Hans immediately after meeting him at Elsa's coronation, Elsa's refusal of a blessing causes a rift between the sisters. Anna snatches away one of Elsa's gloves in the argument, which escalates until Elsa unleashes winter on her kingdom.

The production of the film was notoriously difficult, including a complete collapse of the original script, which had to be rewritten multiple times. Lyricist Kristen Anderson-Lopez has said that Elsa was the villain throughout the writing process until she and her husband, composer Robert Lopez, wrote "Let It Go" for Elsa's escape from her winterbound kingdom. It was the first song approved for the film, but according to Anderson-Lopez, finding the dramatic key for the song—"we started getting into the head-space of what you'd feel like if you were that isolated"[19]—meant that Elsa could no longer be the villain. While Anderson-Lopez does not state so explicitly, it seems the song evokes too much empathy in audiences, especially girls, for Elsa to remain the villain. It also meant the reconfiguration of the characters from "good" and "evil" to "yin and yang," and making them sisters to emphasize their relation.[20] They can also be read as "extrovert" and "introvert," which lends weight to the building of Elsa's ice "fortress of solitude" in the long subdominant prolongation of the song's bridge. The ambiguous suspension of tonic between the poles of dominant and subdominant in the song gives unusual significance to the subdominant: in addition to the bridge, Elsa's defiant throwaway ("The cold never bothered me anyway") is on the subdominant, which fades into a return to tonic to continue to the verse (giving a false sense of a I-V modulation, echoed in the chorus) and the subdominant is suspended (sus2) at the end of the song. The song thus plays on the polar symmetry between dominant and subdominant around the tonic but subverts the usual strength of "home" by making it the secondary dominant of Elsa's "home" on the subdominant.

"Let It Go" is at the end of the first act, but if we take Elsa as a possible protagonist, this is reclaiming of her power, her voice, and her space—actually creating her space—with a vengeance; she has achieved individuation, but this isn't a resolution available for female characters, or for society, hinting at one of the problems with individuation as an end-goal (however satisfying the act end might be for us introverts).

Although she is otherwise unlike the bumptious and boisterous Merida, Elsa, too, has weight and muscles and palpable physicality. Although her breathing could have been better demonstrated in her core, her shoulders heave, her forearms tense as she makes fists and pulls her elbows in for intensity; these gestures and the fabulous diva-walk toward the camera in the last chorus are reminiscent of the slightly too-physical-to-be-complete glamour of Whitney Houston,[21] a pop princess whose powerful acoustic voice masked a struggle far more complex and real than, but resonant with, Elsa's fantastical struggle for selfhood in a web of relationship where she cannot touch. The act of true love that saves Anna at the end comes from her sister, not a lover, and it is Elsa's recognition of love for others that banishes winter from her kingdom. At the end, Elsa is queen, surrounded by family and subjects; she can now create snow and ice only when she wishes and she can touch Anna without harming her. Which all suggests that had she not been so isolated as a child, much of the plot could have been avoided, a metaphor of child abuse and the dangers of individuation over relationship.

Song of the Sea (2014)

Cartoon Saloon is a collective of filmmakers based in Kilkenny, Ireland. Their leading artist Tomm Moore creates exquisite hand-drawn animations; thus far, his two films *The Secret of Kells* (2009) and *Song of the Sea* (2014) both hinge on the voice of a very young, prepubescent girl. In *The Secret of Kells*, the capricious but fiercely protective wood spirit, Aisling, manifests as a salmon, a white deer, a snow owl, but primarily as a white wolf or a fairly prickly little girl. At a critical juncture, she sings a magical song to turn the white cat Pangur Bàn into a will-o'-the-wisp to unlock the tower and free the lead character, Brendan.

The female voice is even more crucial to *Song of the Sea*, which more closely follows the dual narrative structure, embodied by a brother and sister, sometimes literally tied together so as not to be separated. The film begins with the adult, maternal voice of the pregnant Bronach, who is teaching her son Ben a fairy song (see Example 7.2) as he paints a mural of the myths she has taught him in the nursery for the new baby.

Bronach gives Ben a flute made of a seashell, teaching him the fingering of the tune. When father Brendan joins the family, Ben is excited to show him the newly painted selkies (a mythological creature who resembles both a mermaid and a wereseal). Tucking Ben into bed, Bronach sings the song as a lullaby, and as he falls asleep, she reacts to a pain in her belly and flees their lighthouse home into a storm. After searching for Bronach, Brendan returns to the lighthouse with a newborn girl he calls Saoirse.

Six years later, we discover Saoirse as a child who might be identified as autistic. She cannot, or does not, speak, and Ben resents her sharply for the loss of his mother, while their father has become remote. Their grandmother convinces Brendan that the children will be better off with her in the city, but Saoirse immediately runs away, and a frustrated Ben runs after her. On a bus out of the city, she takes the shell from Ben, who is amazed that she can play the tune their mother taught him. As they make their way back home, encountering a number of fairy

Example 7.2: "The Song," as it is simply called on the commercial soundtrack release. The performance is always *rubato* and metrically fluid, wavering between a dotted and triplet feel.

Figure 7.4: *Song of the Sea* (2014). Saiorse's transformation as she grows ill, hovers near death, responds to Ben's request to sing, floats upward, and regains her health before settling into her mother's arms, relinquishing her selkie coat, and rejoining her human father and brother with her mother's blessing.

folk from Bronach's mythologies, Saoirse becomes increasingly ill, her face and hair greying, and Ben worries about getting her home, his genuine love and care for his sister overcoming his resentment (see Figure 7.4).

As they reach the sea, Saoirse is on the verge of death, and it's Ben who urges her to sing. Her fragile voice takes the melody and grows gradually stronger; her face becomes rosier, her hair darkening once more as she floats upward out of her astonished father's arms. Old gods and mystical beings, who had turned to stone as the song had stopped being sung, awaken.

Her song also recalls her mother from the sea, where she had returned as a selkie. Bronach wraps Saoirse in the fur coat that will allow her to turn into a seal. But Ben pleads with his mother to let Saoirse stay with them, and Bronach says it must be her choice. Saoirse speaks for the first time, a small but definite, "I want to stay," and Bronach helps her out of her fur coat. As Saoirse willingly takes human form, gravity literally reasserts itself on her body, and she settles gracefully on the ground and into the embrace of Brendan and Ben.

The homeward quest, fraught with supernatural danger, is a traditional trope of fantasy. In *Song of the Sea*, Bronach's melody in the voice of her daughter, literally heals the mythological world. And yet the settling of Saoirse's voice into her body asserts her self as a human, separating her forever from her identity as a selkie, and it also reconstitutes her family. Like Sara Crewe in *A Little Princess*, she essentially takes her place as "mother" in the family. Paradoxically, however, Saoirse's journey of individuation also (re)integrates Ben and Brendan into a relationship as a family.

The Book of Life (2014)

The dual narrative strategy is practical—drawing broad audiences—and aesthetic—externalizing the more internal aspects of girls' maturation. We might also argue that, by contrast and as suggested by *Song of the Sea*, the traditional boy narrative often shortchanges the emotional work therein. One of the few boys' stories that is about this *internal* journey is Rob Reiner's *Stand By Me* (1986), based on a Stephen King short story, and it, too, is externalized as a literal quest to see another boy's dead body—in other words, to confront their own mortality; and both King and Reiner use music to help sketch in the outlines of that internal storyline, more peripherally than in girls' stories, but it's still there in the classic records that the boys use as talismans and rituals.

That ventriloquizing effect of records for a boy's experience is a major feature in 2014's *The Book of Life*. The familiar spiraling narrative is complete with the overt suppression of the lead character's voice, but that character is a boy. Manolo is one-third of a trio of childhood friends that also includes Maria (although bookish, Maria is never once in danger of losing her voice), and Joaquin, the orphaned son of a heroic general who is determined to follow in his father's footsteps, in stark contrast to Manolo, who comes from a long line of bullfighters but longs to be a gitarrista.

The musical texture of the film is quite different from more familiar Disney or Pixar offerings, or the dreamlike Cartoon Saloon works. It playfully recapitulates the popular music that formed writer-director Jorge Gutierrez's personal canon while he grew up in Southern California in the 1980s and 1990s, an eclectic mix of both mainstream and Latin music. The quoted songs range from sweetly sincere ("I Can't Help Falling in Love with You," for a candlelight marriage proposal) to rousing (Ennio Morricone's "The Ecstasy of Gold" from *The Good, the Bad, and the Ugly* [1966] in the corrida) to cheeky (the exploits of Joaquin and his "*fabulous*" moustache are accompanied by the churning funk bassline of Kinky's "Más"). A trio of drunken mariachi brothers is complemented by a quartet of nuns who chant religiously, although not always in a religious context. While these often-humorous quotations dominate the run-time of the score, pivotal narrative moments are given over to new songs written by the film's composer Gustavo Santoalalla and songwriter Paul Williams. Thus the song score, too, is doubled, with the most important songs both new and written by the same composer as the emotional underscore.

On the day of Manolo's first corrida, the father and son argue, with his father highlighting his role in continuing the line of great matadors in the family (Grandma, knitting in her wheelchair, adds, "I was a beast in the arena. A *beast*!"). A fragment of a haunting string melody and its accompanying descending tetrachord (a longstanding signifier of lament) underscores Manolo's protestation, "This is not me, this is *you*," as he slings his guitar over his shoulder.

At the corrida, Manolo internalizes the townsfolk's disgust at his refusal to finish the bull with a spirited rendition of Radiohead's "Creep." Later, when he tries to serenade Maria, the Mariachi Brothers suggest Biz Markie's "Just a Friend" and Rod Stewart's "Do Ya Think I'm Sexy." By contrast, Manolo sings an original and very direct song, "I Love You Too Much." Maria is impressed, but as he climbs up the Mariachi Brothers to her balcony, expecting a kiss, she puts her finger to his lips and asks, "You thought it would be that easy?" Tumbling down to the ground in a comically literal downfall, Manolo laments, "I kinda did." Maria rescues the guitar and chuckles affectionately, joining him downstairs nonetheless. Manolo is still too immature for Maria, and even he recognizes it (this is also somewhat parallel to Anna's infatuation with Prince Hans in *Frozen*, where the fairy tale ending is subverted toward something more extended and mature).

In the second act, Manolo follows Maria into the Kingdom of the Dead (only to discover her apparent death was a trick). There he is confronted by the spirit of all the bulls killed by his family. Instead of fighting, Manolo is inspired by the inscription ("Always play from the heart") that Maria had carved into the guitar she had given him as a child, and his weakness becomes his strength. The melody that underscored his dispute with his father returns as a full-blown song in D-dorian over the descending tetrachord, intensifying the trope of lament. Manolo sings "The Apology" for everything he had done to bring pain and death to bulls. The original music underpins not the external, adventure element of the story (the one cluttered, however entertainingly, with familiar songs and musical jokes), but the more internal tale of emotional maturation, engraved in Maria's writing.

This emphasis on relationship—Maria's words kindling Manolo's heart, as it were—literally turns the moment signaling Manolo's maturation from a feat of daring (elsewhere in the film, he has evaded typical adventure tasks through intellect and guile rather than physical strength or agility) to a moment of emotional, relational recognition. The transference of an adaptive strategy from stories about girls to a story about a boy not only suggests the strategy's strength but hints that those boys' stories may have traditionally been lacking in emotional work. When Manolo meets his Great Uncle Jorge, one of a long line of Sanchezes in the Land of the Remembered, he discovers that Jorge had wanted to become an opera singer. They lament their similar fates, chorusing, "Music is not work fit for a Sánchez bullfighter!" with coordinated arm gestures as a flute plays the melody from Bizet's "Toreador Song" from *Carmen* over their little "performance." Shaking his head ruefully, Manolo chuckles and sighs, "Ah, they crushed our dreams. Hi-larious!" Although Manolo does refind his voice with the bull, he has carried the weight of his father's critique as a truth.

Great Uncle Jorge is played by Placido Domingo, whose voice soars in operatic counterpoint to a cover of Us the Duo's celebratory "No Matter Where You Go" in the finale. As they dance at Manolo and Maria's wedding, Manolo and Joaquin (both, in their own ways, overshadowed by their fathers) accept manhood by trading the phrases, "Time to cast our own shadows" and "write our own stories." The last line of the movie is spoken by the Candlemaker, who is the keeper of the book of life and the overseer of mortal lives: breaking the fourth wall, he, in the surprisingly jolly voice of Ice Cube, exhorts the audience, "Hey, write your *own* stories," not as a reprimand but as an encouragement.

Writing Your Own Story, Singing Your Own Song

This newest wave of girls' stories is striking not only for the consistency of the dual narrative and its articulation by the music but for the prominence of this idea of writing, a trope that was present in earlier films—Sara's fantastical storyspinning in *A Little Princess*, the folie à deux Borovnian kingdom of the girls from *Heavenly Creatures*, Edna's songwriting in *Grace of My Heart*—but seems to have become more focused. From diaries and the embroidery-like embellished handwriting featured in *The Virgin Suicides*, to generations of fanfiction, to modern Tumblr curation, the relationship between girls and writing is so culturally familiar that we may not even notice it (Figure 7.5).

Figure 7.5: Some representations of girls' writing: Sara's vivid storytelling from *A Little Princess* (1995); the girls' extravagant Borovnian opera in *Heavenly Creatures* (1994); Edna's songwriting in *Grace of My Heart* (1996); the Lisbon girls' notebook style that pervades the design of *The Virgin Suicides* (1999); Elsa's inscription of the architecture of her palace in the ice; the family tapestry in *Brave* (2012); Bronach's mural records the tales of the fairy folk that her daughter will restore in *Song of the Sea* (2014); Moana uses tapa-cloth to tell her people's history; Maria sends the key message to Manolo on his guitar in *The Book of Life* (2014).

Overtly stated in *The Book of Life* and *Brave*, the idea of writing one's own story is present in so many of the other examples. The story artist from *Inside Out* drew, and that film externalizes the inward quest but is primarily about the preservation (in a digital metaphor of writing) of Riley's memories and thus her own story. Sometimes the idea is filtered through ways of "writing" that are specifically (if not always historically correctly) associated with women, like the tapestry of *Brave* or tapa-cloth of *Moana*. This emphasis on writing the story may be in part because of the history of women being largely *un*written—sometimes unrecognized, erased, or never recorded—and notably, many of these animated stories are about rewriting or restoring stories that have gone wrong or fallen silent.

Silence can be a potent presence, as it is in Elinor's queenly arsenal. Silence is normally cast as a lack, however, and features as such through so many of these girls' stories, echoing the dynamic Gilligan discovered repeatedly in her work with girls that many women may recognize in their own stories. The oppression/suppression of their voices is largely conditioned by cultural expectations of conventional femininity and is (perhaps) in a period of transition now, but its resonance as a narrative trope is clearly powerful. And this period of silence, through contrast, highlights the recovery and reintegration of voice, body, and self in the end.

The relationship between voice, body, and self, as we have seen, is particularly fraught with regard to bodies undergoing development. Animation represents further complication: adult voices fitted to adolescent animated bodies; singing doubles for acting voices—so, sometimes tripling, or quadrupling or even quintupling if there's a preadolescent version of the character who also sings; and the end-credit pop versions of in-story songs pioneered by Disney that bring in new voices singing the words of characters we have come to know (and love). Our association of Broadway-style voices for animation, like Paige O'Hara's for Belle in the 1991 *Beauty and the Beast*, has now for a generation skewed our sense of what Jennifer Fleeger would term a "mismatch."[22] The sylphlike, adolescent Belle occasionally even seems weightless as she dances through the village, but she has the well-developed voice of a 35-year-old Broadway belter. What was once disconcerting has been normalized, resulting in a flurry of widely mixed reactions to Emma Watson's voice in the 2017 live-action film version. While comments about autotuning and the smallness of her voice may be valid, it was striking that many of the criticisms were about the *lack* of a mismatch. That the small voice fit her petite frame (even if, in the opening number, she stomps through the village in boots) and was recognizably *hers* mattered less than the expectations, resulting in calls for dubbing.[23] My point here is less about the musical quality than the psychological effect of the integration of body and voice. Animation has led to calls for the preservation of the mismatch, feeding back into Fleeger's point about the attractions of the constructed, artificial, mismatched woman.

But some of these more recent films do enact a form of voice-body-self integration, despite the animated format. In *Brave*, the duality of mother and daughter and the nondiegetic quality of the music allow the tunes by Julie Fowlis and Mumford and Sons to stand slightly outside the story, functioning as a kind of metadiegetic narration. In *Frozen*, Idina Menzel performs both speaking and singing voices for Elsa,[24] and the strength (and resonance) of "Let It Go," completes her voice-body-self integration arc by the end of Act One, but in a version that stresses individuation; the integration into relationship forms the heart of Act Two, delivering a story that is more conventionally feminine, a mirror image of Anna's progress from indiscriminate relationship to a more moderated maturation. That yin-and-yang itself mirrors their narrative journeys: Elsa's internal search to find herself and Anna's physical journey to find her sister. *Song of the Sea* gives perhaps the most explicit and literal version of the twinned boy-girl narrative, and much of the power of the story comes in its simplicity.

In *The Book of Life*, the story is told by an animated human via puppets who then become sugar-skeletons in the Kingdom of the Dead. Despite those rather insurmountable obstacles in terms of production, the story could conceivably be performed live by its main cast—Diego Luna as Manolo, Zoë Saldana as Maria, and Channing Tatum as Joaquin. The characters are all, to some extent, challenged in their road to maturation—Maria is sent off to school, Joaquin lives in his father's shadow and overcompensates, and, of course, leading character Manolo follows the most elaborated version of the vocal arc that carries him from oppression to self-determination and reintegration of voice, body, and self in the land of the living. But it is always his relationships with Maria and Joaquin that give him direction.

In 2017, Disney/Pixar released *Coco*, a film which is remarkably similar to *The Book of Life*'s narrative, but if anything, assimilates (or possibly appropriates) the girls' trajectory even more thoroughly. Miguel wants to be a singer, like his movie-star idol; an intergenerational ban on music in his family suppresses his voice; imagining that his idol, Ernesto de la Cruz, is his great-great-grandfather, Miguel journeys to the Land of the Remembered in the Kingdom of the Dead; the revelation that Hector, the trickster figure accompanying him on the trip, is his actual progenitor salves the disappointment when his idol is shown to be unworthy of his adoration. Upon return to the land of the living, Miguel's family acquiesces to his desire to be a musician. The recovery of his suppressed voice is united with his recovery of his true family. It's a nearly perfect execution of the Gilligan vocal paradigm with a male subject.

But what if Miguel were Maria? An echo of the more familiar vocal trajectory can be found "on the back of the tapestry," as it were, in the skeletal body of Miguel's great-great-grandmother, Imelda, a woman who had a husband (Hector), a toddler daughter, Coco, and a career she loved as a singer. But when Hector appeared to have deserted her, Imelda suppressed her singing voice (symbolic of her own love of singing, so a large part of herself) in order to provide for her child. She initiated the family ban on music that has stifled Miguel, and even asks him to commit to abandoning music in order to return him to his family in the realm of the living, even after she has sung "La Llorona" to him in order to prove that she does understand his love of music. In the Kingdom of the Dead, the family bands together to avenge the wrong that the "heroic" de la Cruz had done to Hector, and Imelda is thrust onto a stage where she sings "La Llorona" again, torn between the grandstanding de la Cruz and her family, Miguel and Hector, accompanying her. This moment of musical bonding eases Imelda's stance, and she gives Miguel her blessing to return to the land of the living *and,* instead of her earlier injunction against music, to always remember that his family loves him. Thus, Imelda's arc from (self)-suppression to her recovery of music and relationship is the key to sending Miguel back to the living with the memory of his true great-great-grandfather, Hector, and his photograph for the family *ofrenda.*[25]

More pointedly, perhaps, why isn't this story about the title character? Coco is Miguel's great-grandmother, the child who was deserted by her father and is now aged and ailing, never speaking. But her one moment of connection in the film is when Miguel sings the song that his idol had stolen from her father, a song that had been written for her. This stimulates her memory of her father, rescuing him from the Land of the Forgotten within the Kingdom of the Dead. It is the most emotional and fulfilling moment of the film, residing in Miguel's performance, but to a great extent, it is Coco's joining in that creates the climax. Miguel's voice recalls her to herself and across the divide of the living and the dead, she reintegrates her family.[26]

Notes

1. The theoretical underpinnings of this essay also formed the base of a previous essay, "Listen to the Mockingjay: Voice, Identity, and Agency in *The Hunger Games* Trilogy," in *Voicing Girlhood in Popular Music: Performance and Activism,* ed. Jacqueline Warwick and Allison Adrian (New York: Routledge Press, 2016), 258–79.

2. In both *Ghost World* and *Thirteen,* the lack of maturity at the end of the film is part of, or the entire, point of the story.

3. The duality may also be a vestige of the dual-focus narrative of the classic Hollywood musical described by Rick Altman in *The American Film Musical* (Bloomington: Indiana University Press, 1987), especially chapters two and three.

4. See, for instance, Dawn C. Chmielewski, "Disney Wrings the Pink out of 'Rapunzel' | Hero Complex—Movies, Comics, Pop Culture—Los Angeles Times." http://herocomplex.latimes.com/uncategorized/disneys-rapunzel-gets-a-makeover/. March 10, 2010. Accessed May 3, 2018.

5. *Spirited Away* shows an early tendency toward this dual storyline, although the spiraling vocal trajectory is arguably stronger than the journey/quest.

6. Carol Gilligan, *In a Different Voice: Psychological Theory and Women's Development* (Cambridge: Harvard University Press, 1982).

7. Ibid., 7.

8. The two most prominent critiques of Gilligan are that her work is essentialist, rather than about social expectations (something that she herself anticipates and refutes in the introduction) and that her results cannot be duplicated because of the confidentiality of her original clinical work. I would argue that those criticisms do not outweigh the fact that so many stories about girls follow the vocal trajectory Gilligan elucidates, giving it resonance that cannot be easily discounted.

9. "The Women of *Inside Out*." *Inside Out*, directed by Pete Docter and Ronnie del Carmen. (Burbank, Calif.: Buena Vista Home Entertainment, 2015) BluRay.

10. Notably, the photo of Shi shown at this point depicts her tightly curled up on a couch, facing away from the room, her hand to her face as she looks back at the camera. As someone who immigrated to Canada from China with her family as a child, her tale also suggests that this developmental shift happens in most, if not all, patriarchal cultures.

11. Gilligan, *In a Different Voice*, 63.

12. Roland Barthes, *Image-Music-Text* (New York: Hill and Wang, 1977), 182; Barthes maintains that the "grain" is not "merely" timbre (185), but in doing so, seems to cleave timbre from its embodied connotations in order to emphasize language as separate from the singing voice.

13. Ibid., 188.

14. After *A Little Princess* (1995), Cuarón directed a modern-dress version of *Great Expectations* (1998) and *Y Tu Mamá También* (2001), a road trip that foregrounded the coming-of-age of two boys against the background of an adult woman coming to terms with her cancer diagnosis. Cuarón also directed *Harry Potter and the Prisoner of Azkaban* (2001), which takes the central trio through the perilous transition from 12 to 13 years old and a darker turn in the fantasy story.

15. Liner notes, *A Little Princess* Soundtrack CD Varèse Sarabande, 1995.

16. The duality of daughter/mother is accentuated in the film, both in the noted similarity between Sara and her deceased mother, and in actor Liam Cunningham's dual role as Captain Crewe and as the god-king Rama in Sara's romantic fantasies.

17. With the naming of the mother as Elinor, and her voice performance by Emma Thompson, this is probably not a coincidence, as Thompson both wrote and starred as the elder sister Elinor in the 1995 film of *Sense & Sensibility*.

18. This gesture recalls Henry Wadsworth Longfellow's poem about the girl with the curl, right in the middle of her forehead (she was very, very good, unless she was horrid). In comments on the DVD extras, Brenda Chapman relates that she had to argue for keeping the slight curve of Merida's belly in the model, a normal trait that models and fashion photographers try to erase, which only tends to make many young girls even that much more self-conscious, and Chapman was one of the signatories to a petition that protested the "Disneyfication" of Merida in a Disney Princesses campaign. *Brave*, directed by Mark

Andrews, Brenda Chapman, and Steve Purcell (Burbank, Calif.: Walt Disney Studios Home Entertainment, 2012) BluRay.

19. From *The Story of Frozen: Making a Disney Animated Classic* (ABC-TV, 2014). Quoted in Kirsten Acuna, "One Huge Change in the 'Frozen' Storyline Helped Make It a Billion-Dollar Movie," *Business Insider*, September 3, 2014. http://www.businessinsider.com/frozen-elsa-originally-villain-2014–9. Accessed May 13, 2018.

20. Writer-director Jennifer Lee in Charles Solomon, *The Art of Frozen* (San Francisco: Chronicle Books, 2015). Quoted in Acuna, "One Huge Change."

21. The design of the dress she creates along with her castle even bears a strong resemblance to that of Houston's Fairy Godmother in Disney's 1997 remake of Rodgers and Hammerstein's *Cinderella*, with ice blue replacing the champagne color scheme.

22. Jennifer Fleeger, *Mismatched Women: The Siren's Song through the Machine* (New York: Oxford University Press, 2014). The turn to more pop-oriented voices in a more recent Disney film still retains voices (Mandy Moore, Julie Fowlis, Kristen Bell, and particularly Idina Menzel) with a mixed/belting delivery.

23. See, for instance, Jackson McHenry, "If We're Going to Cast Movie Stars in Musicals, It's Time to Bring Back Dubbing," *Vulture*. http://www.vulture.com/2017/03/beauty-and-the-beast-proves-its-time-to-bring-back-dubbing.html. Accessed May 11, 2018; and Megan Bianco, "When Actors Can't Sing," *Times of San Diego*. https://timesofsandiego.com/arts/2017/03/26/when-actors-cant-sing-beauty-the-beast-shows-value-of-dubbing/. Accessed May 11, 2018).

24. Fourteen-year-old Auli'i Cravalho is an astonishing double for her animated counterpart, Moana, despite the fact she was cast after the character was designed. Still, the large, strong voice is itself disconcerting coming from someone so young, a dichotomy that has recurred fairly frequently in popular culture, with performers like Judy Garland, Deanna Durbin, Brenda Lee, and Charlotte Church.

25. An *ofrenda* is the altar prepared in memory of passed loved ones for the Day of the Dead celebrations in Mexico. It includes photographs of the dead and offerings for their journey in the Kingdom of the Dead.

26. Rebecca Fülöp has explored the stakes of older women singing in Disney films, and in *Coco* in particular in her paper, "La Llorona: Music and Old Women in Disney/Pixar's *Coco*," presented at the Music and the Moving Image Conference 2019.

Part Three

The "Auteuristic" Voice of the Soundtrack

Chapter 8

The Trouble with Onscreen Orchestrators

Progeny and Compositional Crisis in the Four Daughters *Films*

Nathan Platte

In Richard Dehmel's poem, "Transfigured Night" (Verklärte Nacht), a woman tells her male companion that she is carrying another's child. "I walk in sin beside you," she confesses. Her partner responds: "May the child you conceived/ be no trouble to your soul . . . a peculiar warmth glimmers from you to me, and then from me to you. Thus is transfigured the child of another man. You will bear it for me, as my own."[1] Dehmel's poem contemplates the relationships that enable and sustain procreation—not only the physiological, but also the interpersonal and spiritual. The woman and man, in a sense, confront and resolve a crisis of authorship. Whose work is this? Who decides? And to whom will it have meaning?

I did not have Dehmel's (or Schoenberg's) "Verklärte Nacht" in mind when I encountered *Four Daughters* (1938) and its sequel film, *Four Wives* (1939), but the poem's relevance to the films' themes was raised by Erik Heine and Alison Altstatt when they heard earlier versions of this research. And indeed, the issues the poem raises are apropos for a story preoccupied with authorial and procreative anxiety, as mediated by a cheerful composer, his sullen orchestrator, and a pregnant woman prized by both. Investigation of the film's production history reveals that these concerns extended offscreen, and that the making of the film was riven with authorial apprehensions, clashes, and gendered power dynamics.

It is this particular synergy between story, production, and music that makes spending more time with the *Four Daughters* films worthwhile. The films raise a host of issues specific to voice and cinema, including the depiction of musicians and music-making in film, gendered relationships to musical experiences, the collaborative construction of scripts and scores, and the inevitable conflicts over credit and control. Concerns over authorial voice are a recurring theme in the films and their production, such as when screenwriter Lenore Coffee added an orchestrator to the tale and had to defend her contribution against a male colleague claiming the story as his alone. Such concerns over shared voice echo in the film's music, with onscreen composer and orchestrator openly acknowledging their blending of compositional voices while offscreen musicians initially concealed collaborative efforts so as to elevate the first film's lone-credited composer, Max Steiner. Drawing on scores from the Max Steiner Collection at Brigham Young University as well as scripts and production documents from the Warner Bros. Archives at the University of Southern California, this chapter shows how battles over narrative and musical voice were waged through the conception and onscreen depiction of a composition that became an unlikely vessel for anxieties over Hollywood's intensely collaborative methods.

The film *Four Daughters* began as an adaptation of Fannie Hurst's short story, "Sister Act," which was published in *Cosmopolitan* in 1937.[2] Fannie Hurst's appeal to Hollywood was well established: her stories "Imitation of Life" and "Humoresque" were each adapted for film before *Four Daughters,* and they would be adapted again afterward.[3] She had also written the story for RKO's *Symphony of Six Million* (1932), a film for which Max Steiner provided a foundational score. Hurst's "Sister Act" centers around four young women whose widowed father works at a music foundation in a quaint suburb. Their lodger, a young composer who teaches orchestration at the foundation, receives a good deal of interest from the sisters. Hurst sold the film rights for "Sister Act" to Warner Bros. The studio's screenwriters overhauled the narrative, and "Sister Act" became "Four Sisters," then "Women Courageous," then "Daughters Courageous," and, finally, *Four Daughters.*[4] Because of the film's musically inclined characters, the production required greater involvement from the music department. Max Steiner led the effort, but he ceded key tasks to others. When *Four Daughters* became a critical and popular success, the studio planned multiple sequels, including *Four Wives.*

Authorial Polyphony: Discerning Authors' Voices from Story to Screenplay

Both films chart the lives of the sisters as they transition from living with their father to finding husbands and having daughters of their own.[5] This chapter focuses on the films' central love triangle. The composer, Felix Dietz, falls in love with Ann; she returns his affections. Felix's orchestrator, Mickey Borden, is musically talented but lacks Felix's accomplishments and confidence. In a draft of the film's script, Mickey is described as: "An orchestrator. Careless in dress. His humor is ironic. His demeanor sardonic. He doesn't think well of himself or of the world. Poverty has done the trick."[6] A case in point is Mickey's own composition—a melancholy, incomplete melody that he is unable to finish. Ann pities Mickey and devotes herself to improving his spirits. Felix and Ann plan to marry, but when Mickey professes his love to Ann and explains that her sister, Emma, also loves Felix, Ann leaves Felix at the altar to elope with Mickey. After several months of scraping by with Ann in an urban tenement, Mickey succumbs to guilt. At the end of *Four Daughters,* he deliberately crashes a car and dies, allowing Ann to reunite with Felix. At the start of *Four Wives,* we learn that Mickey left more than an unfinished melody; he also left Ann with child. Felix proposes to the expectant mother, but Ann remains haunted by Mickey's memory and resists committing to Felix. In an effort to redeem Mickey and help Ann, Felix completes and orchestrates Mickey's unfinished opus. Just before the composer conducts his new arrangement of Mickey's theme, the child is born. If the films' intertwined creative and procreative crises receive pat onscreen resolutions, study of the film's production reveals a less tidy struggle. In multiple ways, the two films present simulacra of offscreen events concerning the writing of the screenplay, casting, the construction of the film's score, and subsequent reception.

To begin with, Fannie Hurst's version for *Cosmopolitan* differs from the film synopsis just provided. In Hurst's original story, there is no orchestrator for Ann to marry. Instead, she marries a Welsh contortionist. They have a child, but the contortionist dies unexpectedly. Then Ann dies. Emma marries Felix, and they adopt the orphaned child. One of the writers at Warner Bros. wrote a "brief outline" that proposed removing the baby but keeping the contortionist—who still dies. Ann marries Felix, but in this version, the film ends with Emma—still in love with Felix—crying in the film's last scene.[7] A subsequent outline transformed Ann into a party girl who throws herself at Felix. Meanwhile Emma loves from afar and helps Felix with his compositions. At a major premiere of his work, Felix tells the audience that Emma was the co-composer, an acknowledgment "that assures her fame in the music world."[8] Felix marries Emma. This latter scenario, in which a man and woman compose collaboratively and the woman's contributions are recognized publicly, represents an attractive alternative to the male-composer/female-muse binary that dominates so many musician narratives of this era, including the final version of *Four Daughters.*[9]

Neither scenario passed muster with the studio, although each informed the version that followed. Instead of Emma helping Felix with his music, Felix employs pianist Mickey Borden to orchestrate a composition he will submit to a competition. In the film, curiosity over Mickey is sown before he is seen. Felix, currently lodging with Ann's family, is working on his competition composition at the living room piano. His playing is interrupted by Ann's father, Adam Lemp, a music school director whose tastes are incorrigibly conservative. When Felix explains that he's waiting to meet Mickey Borden, an out-of-work pianist who will be orchestrating the piece, Adam rejoins that orchestrating this "collection of catcalls" is "one step lower than being out of work." Adam asks when Mickey will arrive:

> **Felix:** He's an hour late now, but he may not be here for a week. In fact, he may not get here at all.
> **Adam:** I was under the impression that only trombone players drank.
> **Felix:** Oh, Mickey doesn't drink. He's just a little, well, unpredictable.
> **Adam:** Well, I'm glad to hear it. No completely sane person could do a good job on it.

Through a humorous pivot, Felix's use of an orchestrator is quietly normalized. Adam doesn't ask why Felix, a composer of concert music, requires an orchestrator. Instead, emphasis is placed on Mickey's mysterious qualities.

Adding an orchestrator to the film was the brainchild of writer Lenore Coffee. Coffee, who had worked in films since the 1920s, excelled as a script doctor, detecting stories' vulnerabilities and devising compelling alternatives. It was a skill that she likened to "having an ear for music."[10] Coffee's invention of Mickey is known because Coffee's partner on the script, Julius Epstein, tried to claim her voice as his. Unlike the fictional Felix, whose virtues included freely acknowledging his assistants, Epstein felt Coffee did not merit screen credit on *Four Daughters.* Coffee submitted a seven-page rebuttal detailing her contributions: "Because the story chiefly concerns itself with Ann, Felix, and 'Mickey' (the new character I created) it was necessary to make the third corner of the triangle an interesting and convincing personality to replace the unbelievable and grotesque contortionist in the novel."[11] Coffee's name went into the credits, and the script received an Oscar nomination—a first for both Coffee and Epstein. (Epstein would later serve as cowriter with his brother on the screenplay for *Casablanca* [1942].)

If Coffee's creation of Mickey gave the story an inspired musical twist, the casting of John Garfield in his screen debut brought another stroke of good fortune to the production. When Mickey finally arrives—ringing the bell and entering the house before Felix can answer the door—he does not disappoint. Taking in the tidy living room, he mocks its middle-class trappings: "Hmmm. Rug on the floor, smell of cooking from the kitchen, piano, flowers. It's homes like these that are the backbone of the nation. Where's the spinning wheel?" Mickey's hat, cocked at the back of his head, stays on until he sits at the piano and begins playing Felix's composition. After exchanging insolent remarks with the sisters' Aunt Etta (who gives as good as she gets), Mickey meets Ann. As she regards Mickey, he begins playing a new melody and asks Ann for a cigarette. After she places it in his mouth and lights it—Mickey's hands are occupied with the piano—she asks if the melody is Felix's. "Something of my own," Mickey replies.

> **Ann**: It's beautiful.
> **Mickey**: (after a beat) It stinks.
> **Ann**: You're probably right, I was only making conversation. (Listens closely.) Still, I hope you're not entering it in the competition. You know, around these parts we want Felix to win.
> **Mickey**: I couldn't enter it if I wanted. It's only got a middle.
> **Ann**: You only wrote a middle?
> **Mickey**: Just a middle.
> **Ann**: No beginning, no end? Do you think it's right to leave a song dangling in midair, with no face, no feet?

When Ann observes that a "full-bodied composition" might win first prize, Mickey assures her that she is wrong. "The fates" are steadfastly against him: they gave him no family, no education, no money, no prospects.

Mickey's outsider status is by now established on all fronts: he comes from the city (not the suburb), he is shabbily dressed and ill-mannered, and his musical pedigree is vague. Whereas Ann's father's classical training is beyond reproach—the film's opening shot lingers on his diploma—and the smartly dressed Felix teaches at the music school, Mickey depends on the pity of friends. In her commentary on the film, Catherine Jurca observes that even Garfield's acting style, which reflects his work with the Group Theater, moves in a slower and more self-conscious manner than the rest of the cast.[12] But some of Mickey's distinguishing traits also played to another facet of his character: that of the romanticized, misunderstood genius. He is misanthropic; he has an unhealthy relationship with fate; and his music, unlike Felix's, visibly moves Ann. Indeed, Ann's anthropomorphic response to his theme, which references a face and feet, foreshadows what is to come. Their dialogue all but proposes that Mickey is in sore need of a muse, and that Ann may be able to help him create, if not a composition, then something with a face and feet. Composition and procreation had both been individual concerns in Hurst's original story and the earlier adaptations; Coffee's critical change was to link them together, making them the films' narrative and thematic hinge.

Vocal Support: Constructing Composers' Voices, on and off the Screen

Felix and Mickey's fictional compositions had to be written by real-life musicians. One irony of the *Four Daughters* production is that the sole credited composer, Max Steiner, wrote neither. Felix's piece—which is only heard in part during scenes of Felix and Mickey at the piano—was written by Heinz Roemheld, a prolific film composer who later assisted Steiner on *Gone with the Wind* (1939).[13] Roemheld's stylistic direction came from the script. One draft describes Dietz as "a composer of music of the Gershwin type. Possessor of a personality that makes it perfectly feasible that all four sisters should fall in love with him."[14] Roemheld provided a 44-measure piano piece aptly titled "Rhapsody."[15] A swooning legato line opens the work and is highly reminiscent of the so-called "love theme" from Gershwin's *Rhapsody in Blue*, both of which feature a plunging downward leap of an octave. (See Examples 8.1 and 8.2.) Roemheld also incorporates blue notes, colorful harmonic substitutions, and swung rhythms in the accompaniment to make the work redolent of Gershwin's jazz gestures in his symphonic works. Although Roemheld wrote a contrasting scherzolike section for Felix's "Rhapsody," it is not used in the film. The opening idea, however, plays throughout the film's main titles. When the sequel films reused this theme in their main title sequences, the melody became the calling card of the *Four Daughters* series.

Mickey's "middle" was composed by pianist Max Rabinowitsch.[16] Hailed by critic Isabel Morse Jones as an "accompanying genius" who "adds distinction to the music life of Los Angeles," Rabinowitsch had played in recitals with singer Fyodor Chaliapin, violinist Nathan Milstein, and actress Doris Kenyon.[17] He also regularly performed in studio orchestras for films. For *Four Daughters*, Rabinowitsch helped train the actors to mimic performances on musical instruments and arranged music recordings for on-set playback during production.[18] Rabinowitsch playfully dedicated Mickey's "middle" to "Hula Boy Max Steiner," who, in a rare departure from his workaholic regime, had indulged in a vacation to Hawaii.[19] In his annotated copy of the script, Rabinowitsch evinces pride for his contribution to the film's original music. At the moment in the script where Rabinowitsch planned to have Mickey play the piece that captures Ann's interest, Rabinowitsch writes in the margin "He

Example 8.1: The opening measures of Heinz Roemheld's "Rhapsody," which plays during the *Four Daughters* (1938) main title and is later identified as Felix's competition composition.

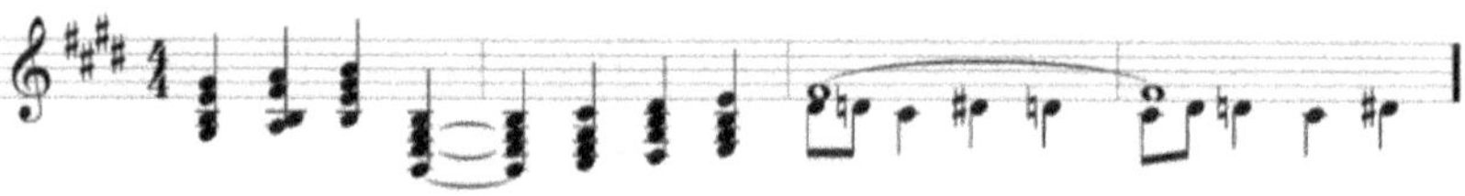

Example 8.2: The opening of Gershwin's "love theme" from the *Rhapsody in Blue* (mm. 324–27). Its opening ascent and plunging octave are incorporated in Roemheld's "Rhapsody."

starts to play my composition."[20] Rabinowitsch's opus is only 21 measures long and offers two varied repetitions of a six-measure idea. The spirit of Gershwin may be detected in this theme as well. There are again resemblances to the love theme from *Rhapsody in Blue* (including a shared key), although Rabinowitsch's model is appropriately the "middle" of that theme.[21] Not surprisingly, Rabinowitsch's full piece sounds incomplete. (See Examples 8.3 and 8.4.)

Steiner, for his part, wrote the film's underscore, interwove his colleagues' melodies, and contributed two additional themes for Emma's character and the sisters. Although Steiner regularly relied on orchestrators for his film scores and occasionally had others ghostwrite individual passages for his films, *Four Daughters* is unusual in that Steiner commissioned colleagues to supply original themes that he then arranged. Steiner may have felt the film's unusual narrative, which featured two fictional works on solo piano by two different characters, merited the strategy. Even so, the credits for *Four Daughters* make no acknowledgment of Roemheld's or Rabinowitsch's contributions. Felix's repeated mentions of Mickey's assistance in the film makes Steiner, his offscreen counterpart, look bad.

Example 8.3: The opening of Mickey's theme by Max Rabinowitsch. The sustained, melodic half-step motion in measures 3–5 from G♯ to F𝄪 to G♯ recalls a similar passage from Gershwin's *Rhapsody* (shown below, set as G♯ and G♮). Both feature triplet-inflected counterlines set against sustained chords.

Example 8.4: The interior passage of the "love theme" from Gershwin's *Rhapsody in Blue* (mm. 342–46).

In building a musically laced story of four sisters' coming of age and finding husbands, *Four Daughters* resembles Louisa May Alcott's *Little Women*. *Four Wives*, in contrast, points to Dehmel's "Verklärte Nacht" through tensions concerning procreation and paternity. At the start of the film, Emma, now recently married, learns she is unable to become pregnant. Emma worries about her husband, who has had his hopes pinned on fatherhood. Her married sister, Thea, is reluctant to carry a child and makes plans to adopt, a decision that initially disappoints her husband, who worries what men at his club might say. Ann, meanwhile, discovers that she is pregnant with the deceased Mickey's child. Although Felix immediately accepts Ann's pregnancy as part of their restored romance, Ann's feelings over Mickey's desperate suicide become inflamed, further complicating her relationship with Felix. The notion that she might find happiness with Felix as they raise Mickey's child perturbs her. Would it be wrong if Mickey's only legacy were claimed by his romantic (and musical) rival? These narrative tensions not only extended the *Four Daughters* storyline, they also responded to problems arising from the first film's success.

Made on a modest budget with no major stars in its cast, *Four Daughters'* sentimental depiction of middle-class, middlebrow family life had struck a powerful chord in 1938, with the film performing well at the box office and garnering four Academy Award nominations, including one for Best Picture and Best Screenplay. John Garfield, whose disaffected character complemented the film's otherwise cheerful crew, received a nomination for Best Supporting Actor. Thrilled by his initial work, Warner Bros. had already begun casting him as a star in new productions.[22] With audiences clamoring for more of both Garfield and the "Four Daughters," the studio had to reckon with Mickey's fiscally imprudent death. One solution was to film the same cast in a different story. In *Daughters Courageous* (1939), the studio reused the entire starring cast of *Four Daughters*, allowing Garfield to again pair up with Priscilla Lane, the actress who had played Ann. Although they were obliged to play different characters in *Daughters Courageous*, their bad-boy/good-girl chemistry continued.[23] When the studio decided to extend the *Four Daughters* storyline, the writers had to be especially creative to keep their new star, Garfield, attached to the production. Mickey's "middle," that tune lacking face and feet, was the lynchpin that would summon Mickey from the underworld and put the fears of fatherhood to rest. Inspired in part by fan mail inquiring about Mickey's theme, the studio decided that Mickey's unfinished opus would become a key twist in the film's plot.[24] Work on Mickey's piece also entailed reuniting the behind-the-screen musicians from *Four Daughters*. Now that Mickey and his theme were famous, Steiner would need to work closely with Rabinowitsch on fashioning a lengthier composition.

Vocal Blend: Narrative Dissonance and Authorial Resolution in *Four Wives*

For much of *Four Wives*, Ann is a soul divided between the perceived desires of two men—her dead husband and her living fiancé. Mickey's haunting presence is reflected through the entrances of Rabinowitsch's melody for Mickey in the underscore, which serves as explanation for Ann's recurring despondence. Pointing to films like *Rebecca* (1940) and *Laura* (1944), David Neumeyer observes that "music [in such situations] represents the structuring presence of an absence: the force of the dead on the living."[25] In *The Gendered Score: Music in 1940s Melodrama and the Woman's Film*, Heather Laing describes another phenomenon of later films that is already present in *Four Wives*:

> The designation of the woman as the muse-like influence on the man's diegetic music only compounds the powerless circularity of her dependence upon him. The male musician meanwhile becomes tantamount to an unwitting voice-over narrator, inflecting scenes, characters and trajectories with his emotional/psychological point of view. . . . The strength of the woman's emotional response to this influence comes from her romanticization of the music's meaning in relation to the musician.[26]

This affiliation of Mickey's theme with Ann's thoughts is made explicit when Ann plays his theme at the piano. (See Figure 8.1.) Her performance invokes his ghost—not only does Mickey's voice narrate over her playing, but his ghostly hands are shown playing the keyboard; Ann's are shown resting. Ann's performance unlocks his voice and presence, which effectively eclipse hers. Laing notes that the linking of a female listener's subjectivity with a musical theme from a male musician may produce a psychological vertigo, in which the woman's feelings for the man are confused with—one might say silenced by—the man's feelings for the woman. But in this scene the dependency is mutual. Mickey the musician is no longer capable of "speaking" for himself; his ghostly aura must be roused by Ann, and although his dialogue is essentially a paraphrase from the first movie, changes in his words and delivery suggest the distortions of Ann's memory.

Anxious about marrying Felix in a large wedding that had been denied to Mickey, Ann decides to elope again—this time with Felix. But Mickey's music remains in her mind, and Ann finally pushes her new husband away, telling Felix to focus on his career and forget about her and the baby. When Felix does leave, Ann's distress induces labor. A baby girl is born prematurely and saved by blood transfusion from Felix, who hustles off to conduct a concert. Unaware of Felix's life-giving gesture, Ann recuperates in a hospital room. While listening to the radio, she is surprised by a live broadcast of *Symphonie Moderne*, a composition by Mickey that was completed—unbeknownst to Ann—by Felix. For the next

Figure 8.1: Ann's performance of Mickey's piece at the piano invokes his ghost in *Four Wives* (1939).

six minutes of the film, the symphony becomes an aural axis around which the film's characters and visuals are plotted.

The sequence is by far the film's most visually and musically complex, and it required heightened coordination among studio personnel. In August of 1939, an orchestra of 90 musicians recorded *Symphonie Moderne* with studio music director Leo Forbstein conducting.[27] Director Michael Curtiz and his staff attended the session to begin planning possible shots of the number. (Curtiz proposed placing the entire orchestra on a rotating turntable; producer Hal Wallis objected.) Two conferences with Curtiz, Steiner, Rabinowitsch, and members of the sound and cinematography departments allowed them to draft a detailed plan of how individual shots would align with specific measures of music from the composition. (See Figure 8.2.) Working with an enlarged orchestra of 110 musicians, Curtiz directed the sequence over two days on the same stage on which Forbstein had recorded the previous month. The resulting scene is spectacular, overwrought, and transformative. The most transfigured character, of course, is Ann. Close-ups of Ann and her new daughter nuzzling in a hospital bed are intercut with shots of Felix bravely directing the enormous orchestra. Ann's family, who listens to the broadcast from the family home, are also integrated into the concert montage. Towards the end of the piece, the ghost of Mickey appears in the orchestra, seated at the piano, where he delivers a short solo with evident satisfaction. Although the

"FOUR WIVES"

Curtiz

#284
9/25/39

ROUTINE FOR SHOOTING SYMPHONIC ARRANGEMENT OF "MICKEY'S THEME".

	Bars	
AA.		Two Camera (long shots) of the complete number.
1.	1 to 9	A shot starting on radio in hospital with the announcer coming thru and going to a close up of Ann in bed.
2.	10 to 14	Stationary shot of Felix.
3.	15 to 30	A shot starting on cellos past Felix back and going to a long shot ending in Mixing Booth.
4.	31 to 32	Close shot of Ann in bed.
5.	33 to 34	Group shot - favoring violas.
6.	35 to 38	Group shot - favoring violins with violas in background.
7.	39 to 42	A shot of all string instruments without Felix.
8.	43 to 50	Full long shot of orchestra passing Felix and ending on group of trombones (solo).
9.	51 to 52	Close shot of Ann.
10.	53 to 62	A shot starting on WOODWIND AND CELESTE and panning to violins and continuing the pan to end up on FELIX conducting.
11.	63 to 64	Quick cut of horns.

Figure 8.2: A production document outlines the synchronization of visual editing with specific measure counts from the concert work, USC Warner Bros. Archives.

scale, sound, and expense for this sequence are out of proportion to the rest of the film, this imbalance is deliberate. It marks the scale of achievement accomplished through the *Four Daughters* series, including the birth, death, and resurrection of its brightest star, John Garfield.

Depicted as a performance that traverses time, space, and the hereafter, the concert scene is best appraised through multiple lenses. First, there is the screenplay, which details the concert's effect on listeners but precedes Steiner's actual writing of any music. The emotional consequences of the composition—no matter its actual sound—are predetermined by this document. And yet in the film world, the character's responses must correlate with the aural experience of this specific performance, not a hypothetical piece described in a screenplay. Second, as a composition, *Symphonie Moderne* was beholden to both the expectations of mainstream classical cinema and the external expectations of symphonic art music. This put considerable, if not conflicting, constraints on the work's length and musical language. Third, music across this scene—while all belonging to *Symphonie Moderne*—shifts in its dominant function, at times representing "itself" as a live, orchestral broadcast, at other times, functioning more as underscore for the montage that plays out during its performance. Although all three levels are interrelated, they will be treated individually here.

If one were reading this scene in script form without hearing any music or seeing the visuals, narrative circumstances alone show that the orchestral performance functions redemptively and therapeutically. Felix's setting of Mickey's piece, like his giving of blood to Mickey's child, assures Mickey's legacy by repaying Mickey's service. "I just finished Mickey's piece as he did mine," admits Felix after the performance. Addressing the newborn, he informs her and her mother that he'll perform Mickey's composition in every city on his tour: "Can you imagine: Mickey Borden right between Beethoven and Bach?" Ann's ready acceptance of Felix after hearing the piece show that the experience has amended her understanding of Mickey's life and death. Listening to Mickey's piece appears to transfigure Ann's perception of her late husband. "Seeing" the ghost of Mickey perform with the orchestra suggests that Mickey is now a posthumously contented musician.

Contemplating *Symphonie Moderne* as sounding music—as opposed to the abstract idea of a piece written into a script—reveals other facets. Drawing on the monumental registers of Strauss, Wagner, Rachmaninoff, Puccini, and Gershwin, Max Steiner has Rabinowitsch's theme saturate the entire work. The theme's distinctive four-note descent fuels ostinati, sequences, retrograde variations, and, through rhythmic diminution, counterpoint with itself. The piece adamantly insists that Mickey's motive has engendered a resplendent whole. Finally, Mickey's middle has a face and feet. Ironically, this notion of wholeness—so significant to Mickey's posthumous fulfillment—was challenged when some preview audiences and critics expressed impatience over the concert piece's length.[28] Although the film shows Felix and Mickey's *Symphonie Moderne* performed in its entirety, the middle of Steiner and Rabinowitsch's *Symphonie Moderne* is cut, abbreviating their full work by about a minute.[29]

Steiner also had to accommodate within the six-minute symphony a prominent part for piano, as the script specified that the pianist's body would be replaced by a vision of Mickey playing his own work. For the mandatory piano solo, Steiner handed the compositional reins to the theme's author. In his arrangement, Steiner

Figure 8.3: Max Rabinowitsch plays solo piano in the onscreen orchestra for *Four Wives* (1939).

specified that Rabinowitsch would play the exposed passage for the recording session, adding in his manuscript that Rabinowitsch should "work out a good piano part that fits!!!"[30] By giving the solo's performance and finer details to Rabinowitsch, Steiner honored the script's deference to Mickey's authorial presence. With Rabinowitsch playing on the film's soundtrack, the filmmakers decided to bring Rabinowitsch onscreen: he is the pianist whose body anticipates the appearance of Mickey's.[31] It is hard to imagine a more thorough conflation of film narrative and music production practices. (See Figure 8.3.)

This, in turn, introduces the third layer: how *Symphonie Moderne* functions as film music. Instead of only listening to a piece of concert music alongside fictional characters, the spectator watches (and listens to) the listeners within the film. In his thoughtful study, *Music, Performance, and the Realities of Film: Shared Concert Experiences in Screen Fiction,* Ben Winters notes that the reflexivity of such sequences "openly reveal[s] and celebrate[s] many of the functions of film music, drawing our attention to its ability to provide the appropriate register for moments of high drama. . . . This is something that cannot be simply forgotten when the scene finishes, and the music is returned to the underscore."[32] As detailed earlier, director Curtiz and the music department worked at length over this sequence and structured the visual editing around the composition's sections and timing. Consequently, punctuating gestures in the music sync with dramatic cross-cutting from urban concert hall to suburban living room to hospital. In this way, the film toggles between the spectacle of the sound—loud passages show instrumentalists and conductor laboring mightily—and the interiority of the listening experience. One abrupt shift to a softer, lyrical passage cues a slow pan of Ann's family listening to the broadcast, each bearing contemplative expressions. (See Figures 8.4a and b.) Meanwhile, the soft-focus scenes of a dewy-eyed Ann gazing into

Figure 8.4: (a) The French horn players in the onscreen orchestra raise their bells to visually signal a bombastic passage; (b) Ann's family listens thoughtfully to the performance via a radio broadcast.

the distance from her hospital bed illustrates what Michael Long has described as the "aesthetic sublime": "the trope usually involves a concert performance, with the camera focused on the transfixed, immobile face of a central character as she becomes lost in a sometimes sexually tinged 'aesthetic moment.'"[33] Here, Ann's epiphany is both complicated and extended by Mickey and Felix's shared efforts as composers and performers. While this sequence seems to assure the reconciliation of Ann's torn emotions between the two men, Heather Laing's observations on male musicians and female listeners could not be more salient. Ann's emotions, it seems, are decided by the men who desire her. Shown in a supine position and radiant from childbirth, her "transfiguration" comprises an acceptance of their feelings for her as her feelings for them.

Whose brave idea was it to bring *Four Wives* to this thrumming climax? An initial outline for the sequel film by Maurice Hanline has no such scene, in part because in that version Felix resents Mickey's child.[34] Although no treatment from Coffee has been found, studio records strongly suggest that Coffee gave the story its present arc. Story department head Walter MacEwen reported to producer Hal Wallis that, after Hanline's outline, "what the story now needs is LENORE COFFEE rather than the Epsteins, in my opinion. She is available. Would you like to have her read the outline? The Epsteins would probably be more valuable later after she had done a thorough job of construction."[35] Several weeks later, MacEwen reported that Coffee was finishing a fifty-page treatment: "she really feels that she has to give her all to this treatment and that it will hit the spot."[36] Assuming that Coffee created the opportunity for this performance, she succeeded in bringing closure to the relationship between Ann and Mickey that had been foreshadowed in their first dialogue from *Four Daughters*. Yet, in what appears to be an astonishing irony of authorial misappropriation, the screen credits for *Four Wives* list only Hanline and the Epsteins.

Whereas it seems Coffee's name was unjustly sidelined from the credits, Coffee's orchestrator—whose disruptive presence in the first film largely enabled the plot for the second—may have motivated some changes in music credits. With Mickey's theme occupying the film's high point, Rabinowitsch now received screen credit for this lone theme. The film's two orchestrators also receive credit. Publicity documents encouraged audiences to savor the remarkable parallel between Mickey and Felix's collaborative composition and the behind-the-scenes relationship between Steiner and Rabinowitsch.[37] In the *Los Angeles Times*, Edwin Schallert devotes the first paragraph of his review to the film's music and "tips his hat" to Rabinowitsch, Steiner, orchestrators Hugo Friedhofer and Ray Heindorf, and even studio music director Leo Forbstein.[38] It is unusual for film music to get such prime exposure in a review, but even more extraordinary is Schallert's celebration of musical collaboration, a gesture enabled by the film's story.

Conclusion

The musical drama of the *Four Daughters* films did not end with *Four Wives.* For the last installment, *Four Mothers,* Steiner passed the baton to Heinz Roemheld, the composer whose theme had been featured in the opening title of the three previous films. For the first time, Roemheld receives screen credit for his "Rhapsody" theme. Following *Four Wives,* Warner Bros.' writers devised more films ending in culminating symphonic works. The 1940 film *City for Conquest* concludes similarly with another Gershwinesque concert piece ("Magic Isle Symphony"), composed by one character to honor the aspirations of his brother.[39] Max Steiner provided the music. *Humoresque* (1946) ends with John Garfield playing violin alongside pianist Oscar Levant and a symphony orchestra as Joan Crawford listens to the radio broadcast from her beach house.[40] Both films use radio to show the expanse of music's reach and cinema's unique capability of depicting both performers and distant listeners through cross-cutting. In the 1950s, Warner Bros. brought back the *Four Daughters* story in a remake titled *Young at Heart* (1955), which starred Frank Sinatra in Garfield's old role. Authorial anxieties reared their head yet again. Sinatra objected to the death of his character and had the story changed. Sinatra's arranger survives his car crash, living to see his new child and his first compositional success as a songwriter. Offscreen drama also continued. Ray Heindorf, who had served as an orchestrator on *Four Wives,* was by now director of the Warner Bros. music department and worked closely on *Young at Heart,* even writing an original song. (He also created a new adaptation of Mendelssohn's "On Wings of Song," performed earlier in the opening of *Four Daughters.*) After Warner Bros. and Heindorf tussled over the appropriate credit—Heindorf wanted the common title of "musical director" but the studio resisted—the print shown in theaters withheld Heindorf's name entirely.[41]

In terms of authorial control, filmmaking is inevitably messy: Ideas are voiced, circulated, adapted, replaced, and transformed. Those who make films or make music for films understand these as part of the business and, sometimes, part of the fun. Fairly assigning credit where credit is due can be difficult, and issues of professional status, gender, race, and social networks place pressure on how such decisions are made. Writer Lenore Coffee, who adapted *Four Daughters* and *Four Wives* but received screen credit for only the first, seems to have felt these issues keenly. By fashioning an alternative tale from Hurst's original, Coffee envisioned a creative collaboration through music that is not only freely acknowledged but becomes a powerful means for resolving the similarly fraught collaborations of couples and the lives they make together. It is a beautiful idea, even if the musicians and writers working behind the camera failed sometimes to hear it.

Notes

The author gratefully acknowledges Alison Altstatt, Robynn Stilwell, Erik Heine, and David Neumeyer, whose insights and suggestions on earlier presentations of this material have been incorporated here. A hearty thank you is also extended to Brett Service of the USC Warner Bros. Archives and the helpful staff of the University of Iowa Special Collections. This article would not be possible without the people who preserve these archival documents and help researchers access them.

1. Richard Dehmel, "Verklärte Nacht (Transfigured Night, 1896)," translated by Scott Horton in "Dehmel's 'Transfigured Night,'" *Harper's Blog*, January 25, 2008. https://harpers.org/blog/2008/01/dehmels-transfigured-night/. Accessed December 12, 2017.

2. Fannie Hurst, "Sister Act," *Cosmopolitan* (March 1937): 20–25, 110ff.

3. Film adaptations of "Imitation of Life" were released in 1934 and 1959; films of "Humoresque" were released in 1920 and 1946.

4. Another working title for the production was "Because of a Man." See Robert Nott, *He Ran All the Way: The Life of John Garfield* (New York: Limelight Editions, 2003), 81.

5. Three of the four sisters in the film were real-life siblings from Indianola, Iowa: Priscilla, Rosemary, and Lola Lane. Although there was a fourth Lane sister in show business, Leota Lane was not cast. Instead, Gale Page played the fourth sister in the film.

6. Julie Epstein and Lenore Coffee, "Four Sisters, Rev. Temp. Script," February 12, 1938, Robert Blees Papers, The University of Iowa Libraries, Iowa City, Iowa, 29.

7. Lawrence Kimble, "Four Sisters—Brief Outline," July 29, 1937, *Four Daughters*, Warner Bros. Archive, University of Southern California, Los Angeles, California, box 2, folder 2244 (Hereafter, WBA, 2:2244).

8. Walter MacEwen to Hal Wallis, with attached outline by Henry Blanke and Lawrence Kimble for "Four Sisters," August 3, 1937, *Four Daughters*, WBA, 2:2244, 2.

9. Films of the era in which a female character serves a muselike role for a male composer or performer include *Intermezzo* (1939), *The Constant Nymph* (1943), *Song of Russia* (1944), *Deception* (1946), *Escape Me Never* (1947), *Humoresque* (1946), and *The Red Shoes* (1948). Heather Laing's *The Gendered Score: Music in 1940s Melodrama and the Woman's Film* (Burlington, Vt.: Ashgate, 2007) treats this topic at length.

10. Coffee quoted in Patrick McGilligan, *Backstory: Interviews with Screenwriters of Hollywood's Golden Age* (Berkeley: University of California Press, 1986), 142.

11. Coffee's reference to the grotesque is likely a response to the contortionist's sudden death from an untreated spinal fracture. The typed letter is unsigned and undated, although its contents make it clear that Lenore Coffee is its author. "Sister Act" is penciled at the top of the first page, and the letter begins: "Mr. Epstein's original script had some delightful and some charming sequences in its earlier development, but it had an impossible middle and a lame and frustrated ending" (*Four Daughters*, WBA 2:2244). Coffee's letter is dense with detail, and claims many key plot details, including the composition competition (that necessitates Felix's need for an orchestrator). Coffee identifies Mickey as her own literary progeny:

> I re-named him "Mickey Borden," I made him an orchestrator, a slick New York boy of dubious background who was brought into the story through Felix. *Every step* of the Mickey Borden–Ann story is identical with my script, even to the point of when Felix proposes to Ann she holds him off . . . and then her surprise announcement later in the evening, prompted by her reaction to Mickey.

These assertions are in turn supported by the surviving production documents. Mickey's character is absent from initial outlines, but later scripts with Coffee's name feature the character.

12. Catherine Jurca, *Hollywood 1938: Motion Pictures' Greatest Year* (Berkeley: University of California Press, 2012), 145–46.

13. Nathan Platte, *Making Music in Selznick's Hollywood* (New York: Oxford University Press, 2018), 164–67.

14. Julius Epstein and Lenore Coffee, "Four Sisters, Rev. Temp. Script," February 12, 1938, Robert Blees Papers, The University of Iowa Libraries, Iowa City, Iowa, 29.

15. Heinz Roemheld's manuscript sketch of "Rhapsody" is in *Four Daughters*, WBA 7:1261. The same piece is also preserved in the hand of a copyist in MSS 1547, The Max Steiner Collection, Film Music Archives, L. Tom Perry Special Collections, Harold B. Lee Library, Brigham Young University, Provo, Utah, Volume 64. Hereafter, this collection is referred to as MSS 1547, LTPSC.

16. There are several variants of Rabinowitsch's name printed in newspapers, sheet music, and film credits: Rabinowitsh (the spelling used in the credits for *Four Wives*) and Rabinowitz are both common.

17. Isabel Morse Jones, "Actress Hit in New Field," *Los Angeles Times*, January 14, 1932, 6.

18. Indications of Rabinowitsch's duties are evident in his personally annotated copy of the shooting script, which make reference to recordings and other musical facets (such as when a character's hands are visible). "Because of a Man: Sister Act; Final Title: 'Four Daughters,'" March 18, 1938, script annotated by Max Rabinowitsch, Special Collections, The University of Iowa Libraries, Iowa City, Iowa.

19. Many thanks to Steven C. Smith, whose knowledge about Steiner's vacation clarified this humorous dedication. Smith's forthcoming biography of Steiner is tentatively titled: *Music by Max Steiner: The Epic Life of Hollywood's Most Influential Composer*.

20. "Because of a Man: Sister Act; Final Title: 'Four Daughters,'" 66.

21. Rabinowitsch's "Mickey's Theme" is also preserved in MSS 1547, LTPSC, Volume 64.

22. "WB Starring Garfield," *Variety*, August 3, 1938, 3.

23. For more on the unusual status of *Daughters Courageous* as a sequel in which cast members and their respective character types remained intact while names and narrative changed, see Jennifer Forrest, "Of 'True' Sequels: The *Four Daughters* Movies, or the Series That Wasn't," in *Second Takes: Critical Approaches to the Film Sequel*, eds. Carolyn Jess-Cooke and Constantine Verevis (Albany: State University of New York Press, 2010), 31–44.

24. Studio press kits often indulge in exaggeration. Even so, an item identified as a "Special to the Music Editor" in the *Four Wives* pressbook suggests that the storyline was partly shaped by audience demand:

> During the year since *Four Daughters* was released, thousands of letters have poured in to the studio asking about that "middle" [Mickey's theme]. Many of the writers have asked where they could obtain the music. Others have inquired from what published work it was an excerpt. Far more have demanded that it be given a beginning and an end and that they be allowed to hear it in finished form. That last demand is being answered in *Four Wives*. (*Four Wives*, WBA 2:688)

25. David Neumeyer, *Meaning and Interpretation of Music in Cinema* (Bloomington: Indiana University Press, 2015), 83.

26. Laing, *The Gendered Score*, 97.

27. The details relayed in this paragraph are all drawn from daily production reports drafted by Frank Mattison and relayed to TC Wright, *Four Wives*, WBA 2:1485.

28. *Box Office Digest* reported that "one of the highlights of the picture is a performance of Michael's symphony . . ., which the music critics will probably hail with joy. It is given full length. To your reviewer, who must be a lowbrow, it only accentuated the fact that the audience was beginning to grow restless" (November 22, 1939). The *Hollywood Reporter* also complained of the film being "quite long in its showing." But this critic liked Mickey's composition and found the cinematography in this sequence "inspired and its direction won merited applause by the preview audience" (November 21, 1939).

29. Forbstein petitioned Hal Wallis for the reinstatement of the excised passage, but to no avail:

> Dear Hal: I wish you would reconsider leaving the Symphony intact. I honestly feel with all the cuts you have made in the picture and the additional cuts of last night, that it would not hurt to put back the extra minute that was taken out, on account of the construction of Mickey's Theme which is supposed to run throughout the Symphony.
>
> . . . I honestly and sincerely believe with the amount of publicity that we will get out of this symphony it is worthwhile leaving it intact. (Leo Forbstein to Hal Wallis (and copied to Jack Warner), November 29, 1939. *Four Wives*, WBA 2:1899)

30. Unsigned but in Max Steiner's hand, "Tone Poem [*Symphonie Moderne*]," *Four Wives*, MSS 1547, LTPSC, volume 65, 20.

31. "By the time we get to Bar 139 we are ON RABINOWITZ [*sic*]—SPOTLLIGHT ON HIM while playing piano solo." "Musical Number," undated, *Four Wives*, WBA 2:1899.

32. Ben Winters, *Music, Performance, and the Realities of Film: Shared Concert Experiences in Screen Fiction* (New York: Routledge, 2014), 13.

33. Michael Long, *Beautiful Monsters: Imagining the Classic in Musical Media* (Berkeley: University of California Press, 2008), 61.

34. Maurice Hanline, "Four Wives," undated, *Four Wives*, WBA 2:2709. In many other ways, this original version is almost unrecognizable from the shooting script.

35. Walter MacEwen to Hal Wallis, December 5, 1938, *Four Wives*, WBA 2:1899.

36. Walter MacEwen to Hal Wallis, December 29, 1938, *Four Wives*, WBA 2:1899.

37. Advance Publicity Pressbook, *Four Wives*, WBA 2:688. *Symphonie Moderne* was published and sold by Remick Music Corporation. Remick printed the orchestral version as well as arrangements for one and two pianos. The cover for the solo piano version reads:

"On a theme by Max Rabinowitsch; Symphonic Adaptation [by] Max Steiner; Transcribed for Piano Solo [by] Albert Sirmay."

38. Edwin Schallert, "Music and Comedy Best Facets of *Four Wives*," *Los Angeles Times*, November 21, 1939, A16.

39. Ben Winters notes that this work's presentation has much in common with *Four Wives*, including use of superimposed images to suggest the ghostly presence of characters brought forth by the thematic material in the music. In *Four Wives*, this is Mickey; in *City for Conquest*, it is the composer's brother. See Winters, *Music, Performance, and the Realities of Film*, 115–16.

40. This casting of Garfield and Levant was particularly significant, as Garfield had modeled his performance as Mickey after Levant. See Sam Kashner and Nancy Schoenberger, *A Talent for Genius: The Life and Times of Oscar Levant* (Los Angeles: Silman-James Press, 1994), 206.

41. Thomas Pryor, "Music Chief Sues Director's Guild," *New York Times*, October 20, 1954, 33.

Chapter 9

Some Thoughts on Genre, the Vococentric Cinema, and "Stella by Starlight"

David Neumeyer

Within the field of soundtrack studies, the term *voice* alone gathers a wide variety of phenomena and interpretative approaches, ranging from my very narrow conception of character voice as dominating the system of the integrated soundtrack[1] to voice as representing a remarkable series of modes of agential sound, out to and including the place where "voice" and "soundtrack" blend into one another, and even beyond to the broadly metaphorical (as if the voice of the cinema).

Film sound can be understood as system and analyzed as such, but "voice" is always agential. In *Meaning and Interpretation of Music in Cinema,* my adoption of Michel Chion's notion of the vococentric cinema—"the first thing people hear is the voice"; "the voice hierarchizes everything around it"—was intended to facilitate a hermeneutics of system, that is, to permit but also to situate (to interpret) close descriptions of soundtrack events by means of the hierarchy of a soundtrack that is integrated, constructed, and stylistically plural.[2] James Buhler and I try to underline the pragmatic nature of the model by saying that "vococentrism does not intervene in [the] hermeneutic impulse but simply insists that any conjunction be considered from the standpoint of how it affects the placement of the voice in the field of meaning."[3]

In what follows, I intend to allow that "hermeneutical impulse" free rein in constructing a reading of music's somewhat unusual narrative functions in *The Uninvited* (Paramount, 1944), while also respecting the vococentric constraint by framing the work as "Stella and the Voice" through discussion of themes and their topical associations in conjunction with a focus on those places where the main musical theme is heard and on the interaction of soundtrack elements in those moments. As we will see, *The Uninvited* was deliberately crafted—and marketed—in imitation of Hitchcock's *Rebecca* (1940) and is of interest for the parallelisms that arise from that. More directly relevant to my purpose here, however, is the historical significance of the film not only as the source of the jazz standard, "Stella by Starlight," but also as an early and influential entry in the distinct genre of the female Gothic, which, like the horror genre in general, relied heavily on the uncanny doublings common in Romantic literature.

Music is implicated in the film's generic doublings from the first moments. The problems that arise in reading the music with respect to clarity of placement versus ambiguities in character association are what I take as my key opening into interpretation. In brief, if we consider typical treatments of music, Stella's theme isn't Stella's own: initially, it is a man's, briefly it *is* hers, but then it becomes awkwardly placed between two relationships, of Stella with the man and of Stella with her mother—all this being consistent with the genre and gender bending that critics and scholars have found of interest in this film.

"Stella by Starlight" in *The Uninvited*

Table 9.1 shows the six appearances of the main theme during the course of *The Uninvited*.[4] An additional item in the table is a cue (3C) written for a deleted scene. The film was intended as an A-level feature, the first directorial effort of Lewis Allen, who later became known especially for his work in television; it stars veterans Ray Milland and Ruth Hussey, along with newcomer Gail Russell and veteran character actors Donald Crisp, Alan Napier, and Barbara Everest. Stage actor and writer Cornelia Otis Skinner also appears in a special role. The theme and all of the underscore were written by Paramount music department head and principal composer, Victor Young. With the exception of the fact that the studio announced the upcoming film immediately on securing film rights for the novel on which it is based, nearly a year before the film's release,[5] its history is unremarkable: Paramount production number 1362 was budgeted at about $1,500,000—typical for the studio's A pictures—when it was registered in April 1943 and shooting began. Despite a hiatus in June for some script rewrites, the film was "in the can" by July. Lithographs of the first piano/conductor fair copies are dated August 3, and music was finished and recorded before the end of that month. The film was previewed in New York on December 30 and then put into general release for first-run theaters in early February 1944. Grosses were good, but *The Uninvited* couldn't match the appeal of Paramount's homefront comedy *Miracle at Morgan's Creek*, a Preston Sturges farce starring Betty Hutton. A *Variety* writer who saw the New York preview said presciently that the unusual subject

Table 9.1. "Serenade to Stella by Starlight": Cues in *The Uninvited* (1944)

Reel	Title	In @	Out @	Note(s)	Placement
1A	Prelude	0:36	1:45		Main title sequence
3C	Piano Solo No. 1	Not used	—	Note at beginning: *Pam:—"Oh Lizzie etc."* At :21 *Diss:—Rick playing piano*	Meant to be at about 23:00? After kitchen scene, dissolve to drawing room
3D	Piano Solo No. 2	25:35	25:52	Note at beginning: *Rick plays piano (after his line—"you can't help it")*	In the drawing room scene. Rick and Pam talk, then he walks to the piano.
5D	Piano Solo No. 3	43:15	43:50		In the studio, Rick plays the piano for Stella, names the theme.
5E	The Cliff	44:23	46:14	Main theme restarts as in 5D; then broken up or submerged as dramatic music overlaps	Continues the studio scene. Stella becomes agitated.
6B	Stubborn Ghost	52:36	56:47	At 54:47: main theme, finished before 55:56. Theme starts over at 57:10; out at 57:40	Stella at window, dawn; she talks about the ghost as her mother. Theme repeats in next scene as she and Rick argue.
10D	Finale	98:32	99:21	[Main theme at 98:43]	Brief final scene and "End."

Reel numbers (column 1), cue titles (column 2), and quoted text in column 5 are taken from the piano/conductor score in the Victor Young Collection, Brandeis University.

matter of the ghost story was likely to dampen *The Uninvited*'s chances for the largest box office returns.[6] Nevertheless, the film was popular: it "did business approaching [that of] top Paramount releases" and was lauded particularly for its serious treatment of the ghost story and of the supernatural more generally.[7]

We first hear "Stella by Starlight" (cue 1A) under the main title sequence, with the piano figuring prominently in the second phrase. The effect is to hint at a piano concerto of the type becoming popular in Hollywood at the time. The trend started in Europe with Richard Addinsell's "Warsaw Concerto" for *Dangerous Moonlight* (1940) and Hubert Bath's "Cornish Rhapsody" for *Love Story* (1944), and eventually included—among others—Miklós Rózsa's "Spellbound" Concerto (1945), Franz Waxman's Rhapsody for *The Paradine Case* (1947), and Leith Steven's Concerto in C Minor for *Night Song* (1948). In all but *Spellbound*, a main character is either a pianist or a composer serving to anchor the prominence of the piano diegetically. The stylistic ancestors of most of these pieces are Sergei Rachmaninoff's concertos, whose dramatic main theme sections and richly lyrical second themes provided excellent expressive resources for a film composer and whose ambiguously modern-but-Romantic character was popular with both audiences and record buyers.[8] In fact, Young's first spin-off from *The Uninvited* was not a song: he recorded an orchestral arrangement with piano that was released in early 1945. At a bit over three minutes, Young's miniature "Stella" concerto fits easily on one side of a Decca 10-inch 78-rpm record. A three-sentence review in

Billboard correctly says that "*Stella by Starlight* is a wistful serenade serving to spotlight Ray Turner's concertizing at the Steinway." A helpful summary of the recording's jukebox potential follows: "strictly class music for class locations." It is important to note, however, that the lead on this recording does not go to "Stella," which is on the B-side, but to an arrangement of Young's theme for *Love Letters*; that *was* a commercial tie-in because *Love Letters* had just been released.[9]

Although known for many decades now as the jazz standard, "Stella by Starlight," the theme was originally titled "Serenade to Stella by Starlight," a fact we learn during the studio scene that includes cues 5D and 5E. The connection to the piano comes from Milland's character Roderick (Rick) Fitzgerald, who is a composer. At two points in the film he plays the instrument. The first is during the drawing room scene in which he inadvertently reveals his romantic interest in Gail Russell's Stella Meredith (cue 3D; the scene would also have included the deleted cue 3C). The second is later when he names the piece after Stella asks about the music during their visit to her painter-father's studio. The theme reappears in the underscore—as cue 6B "The Stubborn Ghost"—during a pair of scenes in which it becomes apparent that the haunting of the house is intimately connected to Stella herself. The last appearance is in the film's final minute (cue 10D).

I have grouped the scenes and their cues as (1) the frame (main title and finale), (2) the two drawing room cues, (3) the studio and the cliff, and (4) the singleton of the "stubborn ghost." In the following sections, I discuss each group in turn.

Main Title Sequence (cue 1A) and Finale (cue 10D)

Consider the main title sequence and first scene in *The Uninvited*. The Prelude, which covers almost all of the main title sequence, includes a very nearly complete version of the 32-bar theme in D major. Three bars of introduction over the Paramount logo—a wash of orchestral color but static on the tonic-add6 chord—precede the theme, which enters with the main title card. Its design is somewhat unusual for a song in that era: thirty-two bars, yes, but the four phrases are ABCA', not the stereotypical AABA or binary ABAB. The latter two may be found throughout Young's published songs, including those written for or derived from films. I have found no other with the same design as "Stella." The theme's final tonic chord is cut off, replaced by a stinger chord, D♭^{7} over a C-natural bass, that is not only a harsh dissonance but a dramatic undermining of the main key. By the time the cue ends ten seconds later, the dissonance has become even sharper: Dmin^{13} with a raised 7.

The abrupt dissonance is the first significant hint that the film's genre is suspense or possibly even horror.[10] Earlier, at the moment the title card appears, we see "The Uninvited" in bold letters against a background that suggests a cloud (or a sheet) with shadows near the edges. Although this image may faintly suggest suspense, the suggestion is flatly contradicted by the broadly lyrical theme and even more so by the piano's solo phrase B. In saying this—and in the description later—I am assuming a particular kind of viewer: one who was experienced at filmgoing but who had not read the novel on which *The Uninvited* is based. Obviously, the expectations and reaction of the novel readers would differ, but I suspect that Young's theme and its luxuriant orchestration would catch their attention in a way that was not dissimilar.

The genre the music points to is the women's film, the concerto topic even implying an upper-class urban setting of the sort that would have been familiar to audiences from, among others, Warner's well-established series starring Bette Davis (one of its earlier entries is *The Great Lie* [1941], which stars Davis but also features Mary Astor as a concert pianist; in these films, also, the homes and apartments of the well-to-do invariably have a grand piano in a modern-style case). It is only with the cut to a landscape shot and long slow pan over a rocky seashore with Ray Milland's voiceover narration that we begin to suspect the genre is properly the ghost story, as he talks about "haunted shores," "mists," and "eerie stories"—although his point is rather undercut by what is too obviously bright California sunlight on rocks and water. This contrast provokes a question for the viewer very like that of the opening music against the main title card, and, similarly, it has implications for the film. Rick's description is heard against an image that runs contrary to appearances, and, despite his first mention of them, its "haunted shores" and mention of ghosts will be taken over by narration, not for the benefit of his hopes of romance with Stella but to support the ghost story that threatens to envelop and suppress that romance.

In his monologue, Rick even mentions Devon and Cornwall, so that one might wonder if the film was meant to imitate the recently developed hybrid form "female Gothic" or "Gothic romance," of which Hitchcock's *Rebecca* (1940) is generally considered the initial gesture.[11] This indeed was the case. Dorothy Macardle's novel *Uneasy Freehold* was a best-seller in the later months of 1942, and it was frankly understood to imitate Daphne du Maurier's 1938 novel in a number of important respects. Paramount fully exploited the similarity: text repeated on posters and other publicity documents, for example, declared "From the most popular mystery romance since 'Rebecca'!" The distinctive elements in Macardle's novel, however, were also essential to the film's success: the appearance of ghosts (rather than the suffocating memory of the malevolent Rebecca) and a sympathetic treatment of spiritualism.[12]

A substantial counter to the genre label at this early point in the film is that the voiceover is delivered by a man, not a woman. Rhona J. Berenstein compares this recitation with *Rebecca,* where the opening voiceover is delivered by Joan Fontaine: "This difference in narrational gender should not fool the reader into believing that *The Uninvited* is, unlike *Rebecca,* a tale of male desire. Whereas [the] novel is narrated entirely in first person by Rick, the movie drops his voiceover after the opening sequence and positions him among a group of women, some living, some undead. Rick's desire may be a force in this film, but it does not drive the story."[13] As we will see, much the same happens to Rick's ownership of the "Stella" theme. In the near term, however, his words are obviously privileged. Music has dropped off sharply, offering no more than a bit of tuneless upper-register murmuring. Furthermore, though we see plenty of waves, we hear no sound from them, even when they are mentioned. In this moment, at least, the voice carries the entire burden of meaning.

An extreme long shot of a house near a cliffside with small figures climbing is followed by a 180° shift, the camera viewing from the lawn as a small dog and then the two people—Rick and his sister Pamela (Ruth Hussey)—emerge from the top of the cliff. The dog barks, conversation begins, and music continues at a low dynamic level with a more pronounced pastoral tune (see Example 9.1; cue 1C is titled "The Garden" but I will refer to it as the "House theme"). This melody, however, is interrupted by a lengthy comic cue—with volume higher in the music—as the dog chases a squirrel into the elegant but abandoned house and the couple follows. This scene is accompanied by the first, if still limited, effects sounds, which, however, are easily overridden by the music and the nearly constant dialogue interchange—often shouted—between Pamela and Rick.

Example 9.1: The pastoral themes and their variants: (a) "House theme," heard during the first visit to Windward by Pamela (Ruth Hussey) and Rick (Ray Milland); (b) "House theme" variant, heard three times (bedtime scene, the sobbing ghost, and after the second ghost is exorcised); (c) "Nursery theme."

At this point, music drops out as the two tour the house and debate buying it. Thus, overall, music begins the film, but it leads before very long to the voice, which initiates the story albeit from a curious, decentering point of view for the genre. Moreover, despite this characteristic progress of an establishing sequence from music, titles, and setting into narrative, over the course of five minutes the genre clues remain a jumble: women's film at first, then ghost/horror, then domestic comedy. What might reasonably be seen as the most awkward element—the introduction of the comedic tone—was in fact understood as positive by early reviewers. The *New York Times* principal film reviewer, Bosley Crowther, regarded "Milland's comic persona [not] as out of place within the film, but rather as contributing to its effect. He and Ruth Hussey . . . are 'sufficiently humorous in spots to seem plausibly real' while the way in which the film's horrors crack his 'diligently light hearted' facade only emphasizes the magnitude of the threat."[14]

At the outset, then, the musical theme evokes the women's film (certainly not the female Gothic), but the influence of the women's film quickly fades, and the oscillation between ghost story (which moves more and more toward the female Gothic in the second half) and domestic comedy (which morphs easily into romantic comedy) ends up dictating the generic terms of the film as a whole. The genre is not a hybrid, but a doubling. The moments of female Gothic and romantic comedy do not merge: they are kept largely separate, in alternating scenes or interrupting one another by uncanny intrusion—the romance through the sudden emergence of an obstacle related to Stella's past, the Gothic through a joke by Rick. As Jacob Mertens observes, "*The Uninvited* thrives on a contrast between a gothic mood and the warm affection of a Hollywood romance." In particular, "a supernatural murk finds its way into the carefree moments of the film and drags the characters back down again."[15] The female Gothic aspect of the doubled genre remains somewhat unstable through at least the first half of the film, in that the burden of the story falls not on the confrontation of Stella and a ghostly woman but on attempts by others to shield Stella from it (early on, for example, her grandfather forbids her to go to the haunted house or even to socialize with the new owners). On the two occasions when she does encounter a ghost, on the other hand, the female Gothic mode promptly shifts into high gear: Stella collapses emotionally, in the first instance trying to kill herself by running off the cliff near the house, in the second by fainting. She is also hopelessly outmatched in her one confrontation with a powerful female character: Miss Holloway (Cornelia Otis Skinner), in whose sanatorium Stella is briefly imprisoned through her grandfather's request and who only releases Stella as part of a subterfuge whose true aim is to allow Stella to succeed in suicide.[16]

Another way to look at the problem of genre in the main title sequence is in relation to the studio's positioning of the film; that is, not in terms of genre identification but in terms of exhibition status. Paramount made a special effort to market *The Uninvited* as a prestige film, which was unusual for a ghost story at the time. The studio was helped along by marketing of the novel: as Michael Bronski notes, the novel "was considered highbrow reading—the July 26, 1942, *New York Times* review treated it as a literary, not genre, work."[17] And the film's reviewers also contributed to establishing the film as high class. One of them wrote: "This is no catch-penny fabrication of thrills and chills concocted for the horror-picture trade. On the contrary, it's a piece of distinguished product, rich in the values that count for entertainment."[18] This quote suggests a reason behind the studio's efforts to distinguish *The Uninvited*: ghost films as a genre belonged to "the horror-picture trade," B-films that truly did rely on "thrills and chills," the best known being Universal's well-established and very successful series beginning with *Frankenstein* in 1931 and spawning multiple films and sequels by the early to mid-1940s. Ghosts also figure in comedies, especially those verging on the screwball type, such as *Topper* (1937) and its sequels. Although these latter films generally had higher production values than the B-level horror films, Paramount still had an interest in keeping *The Uninvited* at a distance from them, as well: it "was explicitly marketed as 'the first serious story of spirit influence' and 'the first serious ghost story in which the hauntings are never explained on natural grounds.'" Once again, the reviewers fell in line, emphasizing these as the film's most outstanding features.[19]

All this being the case, it is reasonable to conclude that the generic ambiguity of the main title sequence and its music was quite deliberate. The starkness of the image background offers a hint of the ghost or horror genre, but the elegant music speaks to—indeed, insists on—both seriousness and high production values. And, of course, the lyrical theme and its rich orchestration broadly echo Franz Waxman's music for the opening of *Rebecca*. Beyond that allusion, Young's adoption of the piano concerto *topos* was another inspired choice.

The doubling, not merging, of genres persists even into the film's final minute. Earlier we learned that there were *two* ghosts: Carmel, Stella's natural mother and Mr. Meredith's studio model, and Mary Meredith, the painter's jealous wife. The film, in turn, has both an emotional climax and a dramatic one. In the former, Carmel's ghost retires in peace once she is recognized as Stella's true mother. In the latter, the vengeful Mary is driven away after Rick challenges and mocks her. This second ghost finally being exorcised, the dreadful night is over, the shutters on the outer doors of Windward House open to the morning sun, the "Serenade" is briefly heard again (cue 10D), and two newly formed couples are framed in the light: Stella with Rick, and Pamela with the attending Dr. Scott (Alan Napier). Thus, in its framing function—and of course through the device of a night/morning opposition—the finale revives the real world and confirms the romantic expressive potential of the theme from its first presentation at the film's opening. Rick offhandedly confirms the point by making a rather poor joke—the last speech in the film—about his having escaped the ghost's becoming his mother-in-law: the theme only breaks off just after this for the stereotypical "up-and-out" closing cadence with "The End."

The Drawing Room Scene (cues 3C and 3D)

Once Stella's grandfather agrees to sell Windward, Rick departs for London to finish projects there, and Pam stays behind to work on furnishing the house. When Rick returns with their longtime maid, Lizzie, who was originally their nanny, he and Pam engage in a brief after-dinner conversation in their large drawing room. We encountered Stella earlier—she and Rick even share a morning sailing adventure—but it is only in this scene that an association is finally drawn between her and the musical theme. Rick awkwardly inquires about Stella, Pamela realizes he is interested in her and teases him, and he retreats to the piano. The theme has not been heard since the main title sequence, and here it is unmistakably attached to Stella, as Rick talks about her while he plays: "You can't help it. There's a kind of sleeping beauty magic about the kid" (Figure 9.1). The music breaks off in the tenth bar, or just into the second phrase (B), although the written cue 3D extends several more bars to the end of that phrase.

Figure 9.1: "A sleeping beauty magic about the kid": Rick (Ray Milland) speaks as he plays during the drawing room scene. Screen still.

Example 9.2: Pastoral themes and their variants: (a) Stella Meredith's theme (cue 1E); (b) variant of Stella Meredith's theme for Windward House (cue 2C1).

There is a catch, however. The theme may be linked to Stella, but less directly than it might seem: here, she is a musical image, "Stella in Rick's imagination"; that is, she is a love interest to be sure but remains at an odd distance. In Figure 9.1, it is Rick the musician we see, after all, not Stella, nor previously has there been any kind of connection at all made between her and the theme. In fact, against her first appearance, when Pamela and Rick arrive to make inquiries about Windward, a vaguely English pastoral tune sounds (Example 9.2a)—the cue that introduces it is even titled "Stella" in the music score. The melody is similar to the "House theme" that we hear when the siblings and their dog emerge from the cliffside in the opening scene (compare Examples 9.1a and 9.2a), but now in triple meter. This other "Stella" tune of Example 9.2a *does* establish an association with her: it is heard again shortly after, when she pleads with her grandfather to be allowed to visit Windward (in cue 2B), and a variant—or at least a very closely related melody—sounds when she does (cue 2C1; see Example 9.2b). In all cases, orchestration is almost identical: pastoral woodwinds and strings.

Furthermore, the volume level of the music for the drawing-room scene is noticeably lower than would be plausible for the acoustics of the room given the framing: the adjustments to the mix suggest the point of the scene is the conversation, Rick's revelation of his feelings in speech, not associations established by this reprise of the theme. Playing the piano (which Milland barely even bothers to try faking, by the way) is just a diegetic necessity. This scene acquires significance only retroactively, when the connection of the theme to Stella is more firmly made in the studio scene, but as we shall see even there Rick's role as composer can be interpreted as equal to the music's "naming" function.

The scene might have been more effective—or at least clearer in its intent—had it not been edited down, work that the awkwardness of the initial dissolve suggests and that the piano/conductor score confirms. Annotations in the deleted cue 3C show that the "Stella" main theme was to begin in the orchestral background and continue over a dissolve to Rick playing the piano—a reverse audio dissolve, in other words. Only after he stops would he and Pamela have walked across the room and conversed—that is where the scene now begins. Not only would the theme have been given more attention, but the scene overall would have been given greater weight in relation to the comic tones that end it: Lizzie's exaggeratedly formal entrance and announcement, Rick's flipping off a couple notes on the piano and then fiddling with the gas lamp.

Here again, in this scene sound effects are almost entirely absent. A microphone over the doorway behind Rick does catch very faint sounds: swish of cloth as Rick sits down, Lizzie's footsteps as she enters, Pamela's as she leaves. The suppression of effects is typical of classical Hollywood practice, to be sure, but in this particular instance not surprising given the limited action and strong focus on dialogue and diegetic music.

The Studio Scene (cues 5D and 5E)

Outside of the appearances of Mary Meredith's ghost, the most often cited sequence in *The Uninvited* begins nearly twenty minutes after the drawing room scene and prominently features "Stella by Starlight." Pamela and Rick try to settle into their new home, even after she realizes that it is haunted, and Stella comes to visit, defying her grandfather, who then calls Miss Holloway for help. During Stella's visit, she and Rick walk into the former nursery, and she evinces fond memories as we hear a sentimental melody closely related to the "House theme" (see again Example 9.1c). She then asks to see the studio, and they go upstairs. As soon as they enter—see Figure 9.2a—the music changes to a now well-established "eerie" mode with unstable (often whole-tone) harmonies, and scales, tremolos, and plaintive solo violin figures. In the midst of this, the nursery melody returns briefly, twice, the second instance being just before he sits down and starts playing.

All of this happens within the first two shots. Pacing throughout the scene is leisurely. Here is the complete shot list:[20]

1. 41:50, they enter the room and talk.
2. 42:22, medium two-shot; they talk about Carmel. Pan with Rick to the piano and he lights candles. Stella walks into the frame.
3. 43:15. *"Stella," phrase A*. He's at the piano, she's close looking down at an angle at the music. *"Stella," phrase B*: she turns and walks away toward the window.
4. 43:41, at about the fifth or sixth bar of phrase B, medium shot of her; she turns to look at him (see Figure 9.2b). *"Stella," phrase C*: medium shot continues; she turns toward the window, but then he stops in bar 2.

5. 43:52, medium shot of him at the piano writing, she in the background. She walks in close again. During the ensuing dialogue, he names the theme—see Figure 9.2c.
6. 44:19, medium close-up of the two seen from over the piano. The brace of candles lies between Stella and the camera. She says "please go on," and Rick starts over. *"Stella," phrase A*: she is on the piano bench next to him; he talks while playing (see Figure 9.2d). Sound level of the music track is lower than it was previously. *"Stella," phrase B*: by bar 4, things go dark, the orchestra enters, and the music is distorted; they are still at the piano. After the air clears, a return to the beginning of phrase B, piano and orchestra now. The piano drops out in the second half of B, after she stands (the camera follows her as she does so; he is cut out of the frame with the short pan to the left).
7. 45:09, cut back to him; then he moves into the frame with her (as at the end of shot 6). This continues through all of phrase C (in at 45:18). *"Stella," phrase A'*: the theme immediately breaks down into motivic figures. She runs as this begins (see Figure 9.2e).
8. 45:35, cut to her running down the stairs.

Here, there can be no doubt about the association. Not only does Rick name the theme, but Stella immediately drives the point home with a question, while pointing to herself: "You mean, *this* Stella?" Furthermore, cue 5D, which is virtually identical to the one we heard in the drawing room scene, is at a higher volume level. When he starts in again from the beginning (cue 5E), the volume level is reduced as conversation ensues.

Nevertheless, I would argue that, despite all this effort, "Stella by Starlight" is not an effective associative theme, like a leitmotif. Instead, it persists as a free-floating signifier, whose shifting allegiances and dramatic changes over the course of this scene are the key to its narrative functions in the film as a whole. At the beginning, the theme is set up as associative—Rick plays while she walks away and stands near the window; then in shot 4 we see only her and hear only the theme (Figure 9.2b). That association, surprisingly, is not very secure: it has to be forced on us when he says the title and she responds with her question, the latter suggesting that, even at this point, she does not recognize herself in the music. Both Stella and Rick are in the frame at this point, and attention goes equally to him as composer (Figure 9.2c): he may have written it for Stella, but it's Rick's music and Rick's musical image. She had already asked "Did *you* write that?" but now the association with her largely collapses when she blurts out, "Why, you must be brilliant!" and Rick makes a silly joke that draws attention onto himself. I have already noted that, when she sits on the piano bench and he starts the music over, she is partially masked by the brace of candles (Figure 9.2d), a further, visual weakening of the association attempted in shot 4. When things go dark and the orchestral distortions begin, it is clear that

Figure 9.2: The studio scene: (a) as Stella (Gail Russell) and Rick enter; (b) "Stella by Starlight" visually connected to Stella's person; (c) when he names the "Serenade"; (d) she sits with him at the piano; (e) she rushes from the room, heading toward the cliff. Screen stills.

both she and Rick have lost control of the music, an effect made more disconcerting by its diegetic origin (the two even look up briefly, as if seeking a source for the intrusion). He tries to start again, but gets only halfway through phrase B before she jumps up, speaking with both regret and fear about having returned to Windward, as it would harm "her" (that is to say, the ghost of her mother). We never do hear the reprise of phrase A, as it promptly breaks down amid Stella's rush from the room and the house toward the cliff (Figure 9.2e).

The theme laboriously attached to Stella at the beginning of the scene is not entirely detached from its musician author. At the same time, although it is fair to hear it as associated with an awakening romantic relationship—certainly in shots 4 through the early part of shot 6—that trajectory is undercut by age discrepancy, most obvious when they sit together at the piano (also recall that Rick referred to Stella as "the kid" during the drawing room scene).[21] In any case, immediately thereafter, the theme is wrestled away from both of them through the orchestral distortions, not to become the comments of an extradiegetic narrator but rather to come under the power of the ghost. As Stella then speaks over the righted version of phrase B, she links the theme not to her relationship with Rick but to that with her presumed mother, Mary Meredith, a connection we will see denied and corrected in the music's subsequent appearance.

Finally, it is worth noting that, although the film is only about halfway through, Rick never plays the piano again.

The "Stubborn Ghost" (cue 6B)

As Rick and Pamela bring Stella back from the cliffside, their housekeeper Lizzie screams. She has seen the ghost and refuses to stay in the house overnight. In this flurry of activity they forget Stella, who has gone to the studio again and fainted. The doctor arrives and the three watch while she sleeps, talking and playing cards as they wait for the ghost to appear just before dawn.

Scene 1

Shots 1.-15. The scene in the room, as above. At 52:36, a medium close up of Pamela as she smells a mimosa scent (a marker of Carmel); an "eerie" cue (6B) starts. In subsequent shots, they go into the bedroom, find the bed empty and then see Stella behind window curtains, looking outside. Rick approaches her; the others enter the frame, and Stella speaks at some length about having a sense of being comforted and loved, not frightened. Near the end of her speech, at 54:47, *"Stella," phrase A* enters.

16.-21. Phrase A continues across a dissolve to the outside as the doctor takes Stella away. At 55:04 *"Stella," phrase B* begins on the cut to a medium shot of Pamela and Rick at the doorway and *"Stella," phrase C* as they turn to go inside. They talk in the foyer. *"Stella," phrase A'* starts as Pamela says "suppose we haven't a ghost anymore." The two start up the stairs to see if the studio is now quiet. The "Stella" theme finishes at the top of the stairs, with the final chord extended until they open the door to the studio. "Eerie" music returns. At 56:45 fade to black, after Rick says, "now we have *two* ghosts."

Scene 2

Begins at 56:48, later in the morning, Rick comes to the door of the Commander's house; he goes inside. At 57:10 Stella comes down the stairs: *"Stella," phrase A. "Stella," phrase B* enters as they walk across the foyer. They go into another room; he talks about moving to London with her; he kisses her but she rejects him, speaking angrily about not leaving her mother. The scene ends at 58:36 with a cut to the doctor's office, where Pamela is reunited with her dog, who had wandered off and was taken in by the doctor.

In the dawn scene, we hear "Stella by Starlight" in its entirety for the only time in the film. The work it is doing is not immediately obvious; the layers are worth unpacking. A slow but firm resolution to the tonic, acting as introduction, occurs just before 54:47, when Stella says "I tell you my mother would never hurt me." After she leaves with the doctor, Rick says (we are now in phrase B): "I wonder what I've done to her. . . . That look in her eyes, that terrible happiness." Pamela mentions "happiness" again shortly thereafter, and their search for confirmation in the studio proceeds. It is perhaps no coincidence that the theme ends just before they enter the room and are disappointed. Indeed, I argue exactly that it is no coincidence: the suggestion from earlier that the theme represents love interest, the Stella theme as Stella-and-Rick, is brushed aside vigorously here, replaced by the theme as Stella-reconciled, found by the ghost of her mother. "That terrible happiness" is powerfully present in the theme with its new, equally luxuriant orchestration for strings. This time there is no piano—in other words, there is no Rick. Ghost or no ghost, what we have reached at this point is a generic standard: the emotional connections made explicit in the music are as recognizable and as strong as they would be in any women's film of the era.

Unfortunately, the clarity achieved in this moment is undermined in the subsequent scene at the Commander's house. Stella is alone in the frame when the music starts—it reprises cue 6B in the same recording—and her joyful mood is due to her assumption that Rick has come to take her back to Windward, in which she experienced the warm connection to her true mother, but which she had nevertheless been warned against visiting again. For a brief moment or two, we understand the theme as directly recalling the earlier situation of Stella's happiness. Rick, however, dashes her hopes and then goes beyond that to urge her to move away with him. If the underscore attempts to propose that the theme is now Stella-and-Rick again, that connection is surely forced and unconvincing, all the more so as they begin to argue. In my view, it would have worked better without the repetition of two phrases from cue 6B—in fact, the entire scene, which reveals obstacles to their desire for both Stella and Rick, might have done better without any palliative effects of music. The most charitable interpretation of the theme's presence and prominence is the emotion of desire during the couple's argument, but the music seems oddly oblivious to that conflict as its two phrases simply flow along, as they had done—and for an opposing purpose—in the previous scene.[22]

Looking back at the six "Stella by Starlight" cues, then, we can say that the simple model of the associative theme is redrawn by the voice (in every case, if we allow the text of the main title card to stand in for speech). The formal functions in the Prelude and the brief finale are unmistakable, though in the former there is dissonance between the main title itself and the character of the melody and its musical setting. In the drawing room scene, the theme as presented in the low-volume piano version would simply be Rick-as-musician-playing except that he explicitly mentions Stella, thus suggesting some kind of modest link between her and this particular music ("modest" because we have heard a different associative theme for her earlier). In the studio scene, each of the elements is amped up, so to speak: Stella is frozen in a one-shot while the music plays—the classic method of establishing association; Rick names the piece, thus reconfirming himself as a composer, while she asks if the music is for her; they sit at the piano together as he starts over, but the theme as representing love interest, or Stella-and-Rick, is quickly and mysteriously undermined as they express their dismay. Later, the theme reappears with an aura of pastoral richness and calm as Stella speaks to the others about her experience with the ghost who visited her in the predawn hours; and, finally, the theme in that same orchestration is caught between the two as they argue.

Conclusion

From elegant theme for a women's film (as we initially suppose) to an associative theme for love interest, then to its most emotionally expressive utterance, connecting a child to her ghostly mother and then out into the world as recorded instrumental, as popular song, and finally as jazz standard, the "Serenade to Stella by Starlight" took a historical path not unlike its chronological path within *The Uninvited* itself: at the simplest level, it started as one thing but became another. The potential for this in the film is present already in the establishing sequence: it is the shrill disruption of the theme's cadence that announces the ghost story, and thus it is music—there is no hint in the imagetrack—that offers up the first of the genre's typical doublings: the "everyday" life and social expectations of the women's film or romantic comedy against the disconcerting and irrational supernatural. The immediate follow-up confirms this mundane/supernatural binary: we have not seen Rick yet—for the moment he is a disembodied narrator, with the narrative control we allow such entities—but when the first scene follows with Pamela, Rick, and their dog emerging from the cliffside, by making a joke Rick loses that control, and he never regains it.[23] Indeed, before long Rick finds himself among those who are most frightened by the haunting: their housekeeper Lizzie, her cat, and the dog.

The "Stella" theme is thus oddly compromised: try as he might, Rick cannot confirm and hold it as Rick-and-Stella, the most obvious indicator of that inability being the distortions as he plays the theme during the studio scene. The agent of those distortions is Mary Meredith's ghost, who is resident in the studio, a fitting place for her to seethe in anger against her artist-spouse and his model. Through Mary, the supernatural acquires a voice as mode of action—it is physical, not literally vocal: the studio is repeatedly described as cold or "icy cold," a bouquet of flowers wilts in seconds, Stella faints by simply going back into the room, candlelight wavers or goes out. Even in the final moments, when the ghost materializes and Rick challenges her, she makes no sound, though a few brief treble-register instrumental figures might be mistaken for it. Mary, in other words, is a classic apparition. Carmel, on the other hand, *has* a sounding voice: she is the "sobbing ghost," a voice that can be stilled only when she is able to reach Stella. And thus we can speak of a doubling-within-a-doubling: Carmel, through comforting her daughter, becomes the symbol of the normal, while Mary, through her unquenched jealous rage, is fully revealed as the uncanny. Remarkably, this is the good sister/bad sister pair that was a staple of the women's film, but now transposed to the ghost story, a striking, additional narrative layer that was without doubt one factor in the general view that the film treated the supernatural seriously.

The main theme of *The Uninvited* sounds secure, genuine, only in cue 6B. "Stella by Starlight," then, is not Rick's serenade in the studio's shadows with backlighting from its windows, nor is it the statue on a pedestal, as in the lyrics for the published song. It is Gail Russell's character, with radiant eyes, looking out the window in a predawn hour, having made contact with her true mother.

Notes

1. This is the central argument in my *Meaning and Interpretation of Music in Cinema* (Bloomington: Indiana University Press, 2015).

2. Michel Chion, *Audiovision: Sound on Screen*, trans. Claudia Gorbman (New York: Columbia University Press, 1994), 6.

3. Neumeyer, *Meaning and Interpretation*, 142.

4. I would like to acknowledge the help of Chloe Morse-Harding and Anne Woodrum of Brandeis University's Archives and Special Collections, where the Victor Young Collection is housed.

5. Michael Brunas, "*The Uninvited*," *Scarlet Street* 12 (1993): 29. Thomas Schatz explains that such gaps were common during the war years 1942–1945, when film attendance increased dramatically and studios were able to stockpile films (delay release) while getting maximum

revenue from prolonged first runs (Thomas Schatz, *Boom and Bust: American Cinema in the 1940s*, [Berkeley: University of California Press, 1999], 170–73).

6. Unsigned review, *Variety*, January 5, 1944, 16.

7. Tim Snelson, "World War II, Popular Occultism and Hollywood's 'Serious' Ghost Films," *Media History* 17, 1 (2011): 26.

8. Artur Rubenstein's 1946 recording of Rachmaninoff's second concerto was at or near the top of the *Billboard* classical albums chart from the time of its release. In mid-May 1947, it was at number 1 and had been among the top five for thirty-five weeks (n.a., "Retail Record Sales: Best-Selling Record Albums by Classical Artists," *The Billboard*, May 17, 1947, 29).

9. M. H. Orodenker, "Record Reviews," *The Billboard*, December 15, 1945, 80. It is telling that the reviewer does not connect "Stella" to a film: "*Love Letters* is the picture theme and *Stella by Starlight* is a wistful serenade."

10. The low brass attacks in the lead-up to the cadence are rather emphatic, but audiences would have been accustomed to such orchestral overreach as the conclusion of the main title sequence approached.

11. For an extended study of this film, see David Neumeyer and Nathan Platte, *Franz Waxman's "Rebecca": A Film Study Guide* (Lanham, Md.: Scarecrow Press, 2012).

12. Snelson, "World War II," 22. See also the comparison of *Rebecca* and *The Uninvited* in Patricia White, *Uninvited: Classical Hollywood Cinema and Lesbian Representability* (Bloomington: Indiana University Press, 1999), 68–79. To this we might add that Ray Milland mentions Devon, Cornwall, and Ireland in his voiceover. Macardle's novel is set in named towns and on the shoreline of North Devon, some distance from Cornwall; adding the latter to Milland's list was another obvious attempt to link *The Uninvited* to *Rebecca*.

13. Rhona J. Berenstein, "Adaptation, Censorship, and Audiences of Questionable Type: Lesbian Sightings in *Rebecca* (1940) and *The Uninvited* (1944)," *Cinema Journal* 37, 3 (1998): 19.

14. Mark Jancovich, "Victims and Villains: Psychological Themes, Male Stars and Horror Films in the 1940s," in *Popular Media Cultures: Fans, Audiences and Paratexts*, ed. Lincoln Geraghty (Basingstoke, U.K.: Palgrave Macmillan, 2015), 94. The quotes are from Crowther's review of *The Uninvited* titled "Whooooooo!," *New York Times*, February 21, 1944, 19. Another factor of interest is that the genre definition of horror was quite broad in the 1940s: according to Jancovich, many films "are no longer associated with the genre, although they were understood as horror films at the time of their original release" (91).

15. Jacob Mertens, "Criterion Core: The Balance between Light and Dark," *Film International* 12, 1 (2014): 126.

16. In the feminist literature, *The Uninvited* is often discussed because of the lesbian context of Miss Holloway's devotion to Mary Meredith, obviously an expansion on the relationship of Mrs. Danvers and the title character in *Rebecca*. See especially Berenstein, "Adaptation, Censorship"; White, *Uninvited*, 68–79; and Michael Bronski, "The Uninvited," *Cineaste* 39, 2 (2014): 50. While I certainly agree with the barely concealed lesbian context, I would argue that the two films are hardly in the same class on those terms. In *Rebecca*, the relationship is central to the plot and appears early on, as it drives Mrs. Danvers's persecution of "the second Mrs. DeWinter" from the moment the latter arrives at Manderley, whereas in *The*

Uninvited Miss Holloway's relationship with Mary Meredith—revealed only two-thirds of the way into the film—certainly enriches the story but is not necessary to explain the vengeful ghost's attempts to kill her rival's daughter.

17. Bronski, "The Uninvited," 49.

18. William R. Weaver, "Review: The Uninvited," *Motion Picture Daily*, January 4, 1944. Quoted in Berenstein, "Adaptation, Censorship," 20. See also several similar opinions from other reviews: pp. 34–35, n18.

19. Snelson, "World War II," 22. The internal quotes are from Paramount promotional materials.

20. Timings are from the Criterion Collection DVD/Blu-ray edition (2013).

21. Patricia White notes that "Stella is if anything more childlike than the heroine of *Rebecca*, an impression reinforced by Rick and Pam as the protagonist couple whose interest in her reads as parental" (*Uninvited*, 69).

22. A simpler, practical explanation in terms of music production would be that Young had no other opportunities to reprise "Stella by Starlight" because the ghost story completely takes over the narrative for the remainder of the film, up to the final minute.

23. Rick's challenge of Mary Meredith's ghost certainly counts as courageous, but shortly after Stella breaks the mood by saying, "Why, you're still shaking."

Chapter 10

Listening to Soundscapes in Kurosawa's *Dersu Uzala* (1975)

Brooke McCorkle

Despite the triumph that Kurosawa Akira's *Dersu Uzala* garnered at the 1976 Academy Awards as Best Foreign Language Film,[1] most critics of Japanese film have typically either ignored or disparaged the director's Soviet-sponsored work.[2] To date, none has considered the film's sound design, its sonic depictions of environments or soundscapes, and its reflection on listening and the voice. Doing so allows for a reevaluation of *Dersu Uzala*'s place in Kurosawa's output and in modern Japanese cultural history.

Although the story is set in late imperial Russia, I read the film as a presentation of Kurosawa's attitude toward nature vis-à-vis environmental degradation in Japan. This environmental critique suited Soviet Russia's anticapitalist philosophies and was certainly helpful in getting the film made, but the critique derived from Kurosawa's own strongly held beliefs, and in this essay I show how these beliefs affected his choices for music and sound design. In particular, I want to consider the ways the soundtrack challenges traditional vococentrism and deconstructs the idea of the well-integrated soundtrack in service of the film's environmentalist/anti-industrialist message. The paucity of dialogue in *Dersu Uzala* affords a broader understanding of voice in cinema, an understanding that includes sound design and music emphasizing nature's "voice," the soundscape.

To illustrate this point, after providing a brief background on the making of the film and its narrative, I turn to the soundtrack and analyze a few specific moments in the film. Although many moments in the film exemplify the phenomenon of interaction between humans' and nature's voices, four instances in particular capture this idea: the scenes of male choral singing, the first meeting between Arseniev and Dersu, the blizzard sequence, and their final parting. These moments effectively convey the men's relationship and contrast the natural and urban environments.

Throughout *Dersu Uzala*, the film's sound design, completed by O. Burkova under Kurosawa's guidance, clearly demarcates rural and urban environments. For the film, Kurosawa used six-track stereophonic sound, its enveloping effect an aural corollary to the 70mm film he shot on. Ambient sounds evocative of nature are prominent in the effects track and contribute to the establishment of differentiated soundscapes in the film. In regards to the concept of soundscapes, I am primarily drawing on R. Murray Schafer's eponymous 1977 work. Like Kurosawa, Schafer laments the distortion and destruction of natural acoustic environments, a distortion spurred by humanity's encroachment on nature.[3] The conception of soundscapes as heard rather than seen environments is at the core of Schafer's argument.[4] Because of this, I suggest that the act of listening to soundscapes is a political one; attending to sound is an act that values the intangible, ephemeral qualities of the natural world over a materialistic epistemology.

Background and Synopsis of Film

Immediately prior to *Dersu Uzala*, Kurosawa faced several personal crises, among which was the fiasco of *Tora! Tora! Tora!* (1970) that resulted in Kurosawa's being asked to leave the set after two weeks of filming due to his irascible behavior.[5] Following the disaster was the poor reception of his 1970 film *Dodesukaden*, which sent Kurosawa into a depression that culminated in a suicide attempt the following year.[6] These troubling outbursts and episodes contributed to Kurosawa's reputation for being difficult and unreliable. As a result, he could not acquire Japanese funding for a new production. Thus, when the Soviet company Mosfilm approached him, Kurosawa, who already had a fondness for Russian culture, accepted their offer.

As early as the 1940s, Kurosawa had wanted to make a film based on the memoir of explorer and cartographer Captain Vladimir Arseniev.[7] Now with the backing of Mosfilm and the conglomerate investor Nippon-Herald, he was able to reignite this dream, creating a movie that follows the relationship between the Russian Vladimir Arseniev (Yuri Solomin) and a local Asian hunter from the Mongolian Goldi tribe named Dersu Uzala (played by Tuvan actor Maxim Munzuk). The movie begins in 1910 with Arseniev attempting to locate Dersu's grave, now erased by a rapidly growing settlement on the outskirts of a forest. The rest of the film occurs in flashback and is split into two parts. The first depicts Dersu and Arseniev's initial meeting in 1902 and their growing camaraderie fueled by their shared hardships of exploring and mapping the Siberian wilderness along the Russia-China border. The second shows the two reconvening in 1907. As the year progresses, Dersu gradually becomes blind and unable to hunt. Arseniev invites Dersu to abandon forest life and join him and his family in Khaborovsk. Dersu finally accepts his friend's offer but is miserable. He cannot fathom urban social laws and paying money for natural resources like water and wood. After some social mishaps, Dersu decides that he must leave the city even if it means his death. As a parting gift, Arseniev gives him a new rifle. Within a day, Dersu's body is discovered, the rifle missing. The police surmise that he was murdered for the gun. The film ends with Arseniev mourning his friend and a closing shot that lingers on Dersu's grave. The film never returns to the "present day" of 1910. This trick endows the movie with a sense of temporal suspension and a kind of timelessness that throughout the narrative is associated with nature and, by extension, Dersu.

Dersu becomes a kind of symbolic archetype in Arseniev's imagination. Dersu is the Rousseauian ideal of a natural man, a "noble savage." Multiple voiceovers by Arseniev wonder at Dersu's abilities to thrive in the forest and his good nature. Dersu leaves matches, firewood, and salt in a small hut for future travelers, sees signs along the path others miss, and helps Arseniev and his men survive the devastating Siberian winter. Dersu is also untainted by "civilized society," which is characterized by capitalist exchange of labor for goods or money. For example, multiple times in the film, Dersu fails to comprehend capitalist exchange of goods for money. He refuses payment from Arseniev, is swindled by traders, and later cannot function in the city. Dersu does not understand alienation from labor because it is beyond his life experience. This portrayal underscores the Marxist concept that capitalism is unnatural and corrupt, a portrayal that Mosfilm would have encouraged. Alienation from nature in the context of the film soundtrack is reflected by either silence or by the music of the petit bourgeoisie, characterized by banal piano music discussed later.

It is also crucial to note that while Arseniev is ostensibly sympathetic, he is not an innocent subject, whereas Dersu is. He cannot understand Dersu's need to live in the forest instead of settling in the city. Moreover, Areseniev's job as cartographer systemically injures nature and Dersu's way of life more generally. Arseniev's maps transform the Siberian wilderness into a legible guide for Russians that facilitates the mining of natural resources and the establishment of settlements. Arseniev's maps are the means by which nature is commoditized. So despite Arseniev's well-meaning admiration and even love for Dersu, he contributes to the imperial mission and, by default, to the destruction of the native hunter's world.

The film's sound design, rich with effects mimicking nature and long shots of Siberian landscapes, creates an audiovisual narrative that interweaves an ecological critique into a humanist story focused on Dersu. Like the film as a whole, the moments examined later in this essay depict contemporary environmental hopes and fears, fears that were as relevant to Japan of the 1970s as they are to the world today.

The Environmental Movement in Japan

Kurosawa began working on *Dersu Uzala* in 1972, a time when Japan was experiencing the ecological repercussions of rapid postwar economic growth.[8] Problems with pollution emerged throughout the 1950s and 1960s, the most infamous case being a high-profile industrial poisoning in Minamata that led to illness, birth defects, and multiple deaths.[9] By the 1970s, industrial pollution was affecting Japan's fishing industry and poisoning consumers. Air quality also reached untenably poor levels. Tokyo suffered particularly bad smog in the summer of 1970, which gained the attention of the national government and awakened a populist environmental movement.

Kurosawa's *Dersu Uzala* participated in an emerging national and international discourse on environmental awareness and interrogation of economic expansion. Additionally, by means of its narrative and audiovisual elements, the film advocated a turn from single-issue, victim-oriented movements toward one of more general ecological protection and conservation. Kurosawa was certainly conscious of these issues. In an interview about *Dersu Uzala,* he stated:

> The relationship between human beings and nature is getting worse and worse. . . . I wanted to have people all over the world know about this Soviet Asian character who lived in harmony with nature. . . . I think people should be more humble toward nature because we are part of it and we must become harmonized with it. If nature is destroyed, human beings are destroyed too. So we can learn a lot from Dersu.[10]

From this declaration, it is evident that *Dersu Uzala,* rather than being an anomaly in Kurosawa's career, is actually in keeping with Kurosawa's penchant for embedding political messages in his works.[11] Such examples include everything from *No Regrets for Our Youth* (1946), which dramatized the death of a prewar Marxist pacifist; *Drunken Angel* (1948), which subtly critiqued the American occupation; the concerns over nuclear arms proliferation highlighted in *I Live in Fear*

(1955); and *The Bad Sleep Well* (1960), which dealt with corporate corruption. Even the aforementioned *Dodesukaden* tackled issues of poverty and homelessness in a Japan that increasingly ignored those in need. Yet *Dersu Uzala* is more than political commentary with a humanist bent. It addresses not only humans' relationships with nature, but also the ideological underpinnings of imperial exploration and exploitation.

The cinematography of *Dersu Uzala* underlines the relationship between nature and society emphasized by the narrative and the sound design. Many of the shots are naturalistic, as opposed to the preceding *Dodesukaden*, with many of its scenes shot on a soundstage filled with gestures toward impressionism. In contrast, Kurosawa shot much of *Dersu Uzala* on-site in Siberia, using 70mm stock to richly capture the landscape. The numerous scenes of the Russian company walking through the forest are reminiscent of the famous forest scenes of *Rashōmon* (1950). In the case of *Dersu Uzala*, the forest is in many ways just as fantastic a location; it is a place apart from the rules of civilized society.

Beyond the symbolic function of the forest, though, are the several long takes and long shots of natural scenes in the film. For example, a scene early on features a striking mid-shot of Dersu and Arseniev's silhouettes from behind (23:32). Both the moon and the sun hang in the sky, which comprises almost the entire frame (Figure 10.1).[12] In other shots, such as when the pair becomes lost on the taiga, the men are almost always shown at a distance, the vast plains overwhelming their small figures (41:16–47:00). Kurosawa lingers on these shots so long that they transform into something more akin to a moving painting, or a scroll. Yet as Mitsuhiro Yoshimoto points out, the camera does not objectify nature; Kurosawa eschews panoramic or aerial shots of Siberia. Rather, most of the shots are at eye level, as if aligning the audience with the human characters Arseniev and Dersu.[13] Kurosawa uses similar shots for the scenes in Arseniev's home, resulting in a sense

Figure 10.1: Dersu and Arseniev's bodies appear as silhouettes; the sun sinks and the moon rises.

of confinement that encourages empathy with Dersu. The shots underscore the difference of space in a semi-subjective sense. Collectively, the visuals indicate that the ailments of modern life are symptomatic of a rupture with nature. The sound design does likewise.

Soundscapes and Soundtrack Elements

Soundscapes are as vital as visuals in a Kurosawa film. One cannot think of *Rashōmon* or *Seven Samurai* (1954) without recalling the use of rain as an impressive and even oppressive component in the soundtrack. Works set in the modern era such as *Drunken Angel* and *Stray Dog* (1949) rely on the construction of urban soundscapes via diegetic jazz and popular music in addition to sound effects of cars and trains. While much work remains to be done on sound design in Kurosawa's films, it is evident that from early in his career he was concerned with sound as much as cinema's visual elements.[14] *Dersu Uzala* maintains this conscious aesthetic of soundscape construction evident in the earlier Kurosawa films while laying an acoustic foundation that links nature with nostalgia, a theme prominent in Kurosawa's late pieces like *Dreams, Rhapsody in August,* and *Madadayo.*

However, it is not only natural sounds that are of narrative concern in the film. While the soundscape's keynote sounds are a definitive component in the soundtrack, a few other effects stand out: the train whistle and the rifle gun shot. Both sounds represent manmade technology, though the train is portrayed as the greater evil of the two. The whistle of the train appears both at the beginning of the film, with Arseniev unable to locate Dersu's grave, and at the conclusion. Yet Kurosawa never provides a shot of the train itself; rather it looms in the offscreen space. This decision better enables a consideration of the psychological implication of the sound. This aural bookending works to associate the train with the destruction of nature in general and Dersu and his way of life in particular.[15]

The gunshot receives a more generous portrayal in the soundtrack. Though a manmade tool, the sound of the gunshot is closely associated with Dersu and his relationship to the world. The gun is itself a means of survival for the men, and Dersu's prowess with it in a shooting contest earns him the Russian soldiers' admiration. As he makes the prize shot, the burst of sounds echoes through the forest, aurally signifying his status as a master hunter in the natural world. The gunshot later on becomes a means of communication between the lost Dersu and Arseniev and the men searching for them as they call and respond with gunfire to indicate their locations. The gun enables Dersu to more efficiently survive outside of society, but it also is his physical connection to the world of Arseniev, and by extension, modernity. This quality is what makes the film's conclusion so tragic; Dersu is ultimately destroyed by that relationship, as symbolized by the new rifle Arseniev presents to him. Like the train whistle that physically warns of an oncoming engine, the symbol of modernity, the gun and its indexed sound, too, warn of danger.

Diegetic dialogue in the film is sparse; this decision allows for greater attention to sound design and its relationship to music and voice. The twenty-three voiceovers by Arseniev are the most notable incursion of language into the soundtrack. The voiceover, as Doane puts it, endows Arseniev with "the privileged mark of interiority."[16] He is the only character with an inner life; we never learn of others' inner thoughts and feelings so directly, even Dersu's, beyond how they are expressed to and through Arseniev. Dersu does have an extensive inner life too; his accounts of his dreams to Arseniev hint at this. But they are always to Arseniev, and thus the captain again serves as a mediator through which we understand Dersu.

In the plentiful voiceovers, Arseniev typically comments on the environment or Dersu, and most of them are actual excerpts from Arseniev's memoirs, the source material for the film. One voiceover near the opening sets the tone for them all; in it Arseniev relates, "Sometimes the mountains and forests look cheerful and attractive. At other times they seem wild and sullen." Arseniev is uncertain how to reconcile the natural world's uncaring attitude toward humans, and thus he regularly couches it in oppositional terms. For example, when he beholds the frozen Lake Khanka he observes, "Some menace to humans was lurking in this silence" and later he opines, "man is very small before the face of nature." Arseniev, like Dersu, anthropomorphizes nature, yet always in terms of struggle instead of simply being.

The pervasive use of Arseniev's voiceovers encourages the audience to empathize with him and his personal growth in relation to nature. However, the voiceovers also denote something more ominous. Arseniev's voiceovers assume a narrative omnipotence; they assert a control over the soundtrack, just as his cartographic creations assert dominance over the environment. Yet, the sound design works to show Arseniev's transformation via his relationship with Dersu. He strives to "see" and "hear" from Dersu's position, though he never fully accomplishes the kind of synthesis with nature that Dersu possesses.

Dersu Uzala and Music

Nondiegetic music is sparse in the soundtrack, although a few cues written by Soviet composer Isaac Schwartz appear in the film. There are two styles of orchestral underscoring in *Dersu Uzala*. Both appear in connection with shots of landscapes and have an atmospheric rather than narrative function. Sometimes, as with the opening credits shot of the title card and autumnal treetops, the nondiegetic cues evoke a late-nineteenth-century Russian musical style reminiscent of the "Mighty Handful" composers, particularly Rimsky-Korsakov. This cue begins with a drone in the low strings punctuated by shimmering celeste. Following this, an oboe enters with a plaintive, folklike melody in the minor mode. This music and several other moments of nondiegetic underscore convey a sense of mystery and awe at the natural world. In other sequences, experimental harmonies and textures interrupt this recurring cue. These appear during moments emphasizing nature's dangerous supremacy, such as a blizzard sequence discussed later in this chapter.

Diegetic music also occurs in the film, usually as a men's chorus.[17] These choruses bookmark the film's two sections set in 1903 and 1907, respectively, and demarcate the beginning, middle, and conclusion. The diegetic male chorus has a long history in cinema and opera before it as a symbol of masculine camaraderie, particularly in a pastoral setting.[18] Kurosawa draws on this topic via a call and response tune sung by Arseniev's men as they tromp through the forest. They are loud and jovial as they sing of a luckless hunter who heads to the warm waters of the seashore. Aside from their captain, the men are deaf to the sound world of the forest. The lyrics do not seem to reference or foreshadow Dersu; instead, the tune works more as a reference to past traditions of the male chorus, as its appearance in the first minutes of *Dersu Uzala* quickly establishes the film's focus on the homosocial bonds between men in a natural setting. Yet it also works to instantly set Arseniev apart. He leads the men through the forest, looking and listening, but does not join the singing. He is already marked as separate from the group and more aware of his surroundings; it is this quality established early on that enables his close friendship with Dersu. The Russian soldiers take up this song again at the end of the first expedition; though they have just observed that Dersu is a "fine fellow," aside from Arseniev the Russians are little changed by their interaction with the Goldi hunter.

At the beginning of the film's second part, when Dersu and Arseniev reconvene after years apart, another male chorus appears in the soundtrack. Here, as well, the male chorus is diegetic, the music sung by Arseniev's men while he and Dersu catch up around a campfire. This song, referred to as "The Eagle's Song," is a folklike tune in E♭ major (Example 10.1). The melody spans an octave and mostly moves in stepwise motion, as befitting a folk idiom, though according to the soundtrack release, the music is an original composition by the film's composer Isaac Schwartz. The lyrics speak of an eagle flying high in the great sky above the mountains; in combination with the occasional leaps of a fifth, the tune expresses a sense of unrestrained freedom associated with Dersu as a man of nature who exists outside society.

The song appears nondiegetically in a bumptious folk music incarnation during a montage of photographs of Arseniev's "fondest memories of Dersu" during

Example 10.1: Melody for "The Eagle's Song."

the fall of 1907. This use of the melody with the montage of old-fashioned photographs (apparently from Arseniev's collection) solidifies the song as one that simultaneously represents Arseniev's nostalgia for his friend and the concretizing of memory via technology (Figure 10.2).

At the film's conclusion, "The Eagle's Song" reappears in the soundtrack, accompanying a shot of Dersu's grave and the end credits. In this closing appearance, the song is nondiegetic and elegiac. The men's chorus first intones the melody without words with orchestral accompaniment, establishing a churchlike solemnity before entering with the lyrics proper with full-blown homophonic chorale texture. A reverberation effect complements this arrangement's religious airs. However, the manipulation of the song is at odds with what the character Dersu represents. While the song seems to be an homage to the Goldi hunter, its prominence at the film's end in a more formalized musical style than the rowdy diegetic chorus at the film's opening and midway point echoes the triumph of the imperialist mission. The maudlin orchestration of the tune at the film's conclusion implies that "The Eagle's Song" is *not* Dersu's music but rather Arseniev and the other Russians' imagining of Dersu. Instead, the "music" empathetic to Dersu is the sound of the natural world.

Figure 10.2: Arseniev's "fondest memories of Dersu" captured by photography.

The First Meeting

The austere soundtrack emphasizes these natural sounds. The scantiness of dialogue and nondiegetic underscore in the film provides room for several "aural close-ups" of the effects track. What Schafer refers to as keynote sounds define the movie's depiction of the natural environment; bird calls and the sounds of fire, wind, and water all prevail in the film's numerous static long takes. Dersu repeatedly refers to the elements as well as animals as "men" and the sound design's emphasis on the keynote sounds strengthens this anthropomorphization. This is evident in the first scene I examine, in which Dersu and Arseniev first meet.

Dersu and Arseniev encounter each other early in the film (7:40–13:17). Arseniev and his men have set up camp in a gloomy valley. In voiceover, the captain compares the setting to Walpurgisnacht. A nondiegetic orchestral cue similar to that of the opening credits conveys Arseniev's assessment of the valley as a place of the fantastic but also dangerous. The music cuts off abruptly, acting as a kind of silent stinger as a loud rustling noise emits from the darkness. The moment marks a transition from the Russians' world of fabricated music to the "authentic" sound of the natural world. Sound effects that were heretofore almost inaudible rise to prominence in the mix. The campfire crackles while offscreen bird twitters and cricket chirps provide a low drone. Dersu cries out, "Please don't shoot, me people!" His voice is briefly acousmatic, and by extension, uncanny, until he slowly emerges from the darkness. The Russians, who had mistaken Dersu for a bear, laugh at their folly and return to bed. Arseniev and his second-in-command sit at the campfire, eyeing Dersu bemusedly. As Dersu lights his pipe, Arseniev initiates conversation, inviting Dersu to join the troop and offering food. A bird caws in the distance as Dersu eats. Eventually, the second-in-command asks Dersu about his life in the forest, teasing him about a missed shot on a stag. Dersu retorts, "You great hunter, shoot all beasts. We don't have anything to eat."

Arseniev chuckles at Dersu's candor, and soon after this, the sound of crackling fire rises to a noticeably louder volume. Speaking to the fire, Dersu orders, "Hey you! Enough babble!" The fire ignores him. "Well, well," Dersu concedes and he pokes the fire with a branch. "Here, now you can babble," he chuckles, returning to his food. Arseniev, entranced by Dersu, speaks slowly, introducing himself. Dersu returns the gesture in kind.

From his entrance on, Dersu acts as an ecological messenger, critiquing the Russian troop, here a metaphor for civilization, for its intrusion and wasteful consumption of resources. When the crackling fire rises in the mix, Dersu engages with sound as if it were dialogue.[19] This "conversation" instantly signals Dersu's ontology, one vastly different from the Russians', in which natural elements are imbued with human attributes and afforded respect. Dersu maintains this attitude throughout the film, claiming the sun, moon, water, wind, and fire are all "men." The effects track, saturated with keynote sounds, supports his worldview.

For example, soon after their meeting and Dersu's agreement to serve as a guide, the men are caught in a rainstorm. The deluge seems relentless as the group huddles in a flimsy lean-to. Dersu tells them the rain will soon stop and the sun will emerge. The Russians laugh at the impossibility of Dersu's prediction, though they are quickly silenced when his prediction comes true a few minutes later. Astounded, they ask how Dersu knew the rain would end. He relates that he heard birdsong. Logically, if the bird had decided to exit its hollow it meant it knew the rain would soon let up. Its song alerted Dersu to the same information. While this scene may seem inconsequential to the film's general narrative, it solidifies what Arseniev is already discovering: Dersu has the capacity to listen to nature and to interpret both its aural and visual signs. He carries an internal map within him that enables him to read these signs. Like Arseniev, Dersu has established a means of navigating the land, but unlike Arseniev's maps, Dersu's knowledge is not easily commodified and distributed for mass knowledge.

The Blizzard

Dersu's knowledge and ability to "read" nature is crucial to his and Arseniev's survival during a blizzard. Kurosawa slowly builds up to the blizzard sequence, spending almost ten minutes depicting a lost Dersu and Arseniev wandering across the frozen Lake Khanka to the Siberian plains. Arseniev attempts to contact the rest of the men by shooting his gun, but to no avail. Dersu realizes they must work fast if they are to spend the night on the plains. He orders Arseniev to quickly cut down as much tall grass as possible (47:41). For almost a minute and a half, Kurosawa shows the men cutting in silence, with only their heavy breathing and the crackling sound of the reeds in the soundtrack. In such a tension-filled moment, one might expect an orchestral cue. The decision to limit the sound to effects, though, is effective in that it conveys a kind of realism rather than heroic romanticization. The dire scene, in combination with the realistic (though elevated in volume) sound, envelops the audience in a sonorous wash of effects. It is a different path to empathization, but it works nonetheless. The sound effects give the scene a vitality that music could not.

Eventually nondiegetic music does enter (49:24), but initially it is very low in the mix, underneath the aforementioned sound effects. The music functions here more as a rendering of natural effects than as an emotionally imbued cue. As the daylight fades, the music becomes more prominent. It is the same cue from the opening of the film, with oboe, strings, and celeste. This revelation indicates that the music, from the beginning, has a certain relation to nature. Yet soon this cue dissolves into something more sinister. Trilling flutes and upper strings pierce the texture (50:15).[20] A woodblock punctuates moments of orchestral respite. A high-pitched chime interjects in synchronization with moments of lens flare in the shot in a shrewd gesture toward mickey-mousing. The pointillistic strikes emphasize the waning sun as if the music itself is urging the men to hurry with their task. An atonal brass line enters concomitant with a shot of the horizon and setting sun (51:30). The sound of wind rises in the mix as the celeste tinkles; soon, only the wind remains, transforming into a blizzard (52:09). The elision of music and sound, the diegetic and nondiegetic, implies something about the natural world. Nature is both mundane and fantastic. Coming to this realization of locating the wonder in the everyday is the true wisdom Dersu embodies.

The Final Parting

It is only in the film's final act, set in Khabarovsk, that the soundtrack undermines the natural world; the absence of the nature-based sounds signifies the rupture between nature and urban life. Kurosawa employs church bells and dog barks to aurally stamp the establishing shot of Khabarovsk seen from the rooftops. The rest of the act takes place inside Arseniev's bourgeois home, its closed walls visually conveying Dersu's anxious sense of confinement.

Here, too, the sound design supports this, with multiple scenes portraying an auditory domestication of the hunter. For example, early in the Khabarovsk sequences, Arseniev's son Vova, who idolizes Dersu, records the hunter's voice with a phonograph. At his wife's behest, Arseniev listens to the recording (which is at a quality higher than any true turn-of-the-century phonograph could accomplish) (Figure 10.3). In it, Dersu bemoans his inability to contribute to the household in any meaningful way. The phonographic technology mediates Dersu's melancholy, his voice captured in waxy grooves as the closed environment envelops his body and ensnares his spirit. The recording is an auditory version of Arseniev's maps. Dersu's voice has been abstracted from his body. Once a part of the Siberian landscape and soundscape, Dersu is now neither. The mediation of phonography makes his depression all the more poignant. It is as if Dersu has already died and all that remains of him is the audio artifact.

Dersu's unease comes to a climax when he insists he must depart despite his failing eyesight. During this scene, Arseniev reads the newspaper and his wife knits in the austere parlor. Dersu is huddled in a corner, sitting on the floor near the fire, like an aged hound (Figure 10.4). Across the room, Vova practices Ferdinand Beyer's *Vorschule im Klavierspiel* No. 59 from Op. 101 on an incredibly out-of-tune piano.[21] Uncertain pauses lend an air of sincere preciousness to the

Figure 10.3: Arseniev listens to the recording of Dersu's voice.

music. Juxtaposed against this diegetic music is a depressed Dersu huddled in the corner. The Beyer etude acts as a moment of what Michel Chion terms *anempathy*, a technique Kurosawa was famously fond of.[22] The piano music is the sound of domestic banality, a world at odds with nature. It is not sinister, but it is oblivious and naïve. Its out-of-tuneness intones bourgeoisie society's dissonance with the natural world. Dersu stands feebly, a thin blanket sliding off his hunched shoulders. He begs Arseniev to allow him to leave the city, despite his physical afflictions. Vova accidentally hits a dissonant cluster of notes as Dersu finishes his plea. This "accidental music" denotes a point of sound that is empathetic both to Dersu's urban experience and to the family's distress at his decision to leave. The pause following these sour notes emphasizes the moment. The lack of a nondiegetic underscore heightens the emotional weight of Dersu's plea and his pain at being separated from nature. "Silence" expresses deeper authenticity than any underscore could achieve.

Figure 10.4: A depressed Dersu in Arseniev's bourgeois parlor.

Listening in *Dersu Uzala*

In the preceding pages, I have outlined some of the ways we as informed auditor-spectators might hear *Dersu Uzala*. By means of a conclusion, I want to ponder the ways the film engages with listening and voice on multiple levels. Because listening is such a crucial component to the film's ultimately tragic narrative, it is worth considering the auricular palimpsest embedded in the film.

As stated earlier, this picture is Kurosawa's only one shot entirely in a language other than Japanese. Thus, the most international of the Japanese auteur directors created a film that in many ways instantly distanced viewers in his home country. What happens when an audience is unable to comprehend the meaning of words in a vococentric cinema? When we watch a film in a foreign language, is it natural for sound to take a more prominent role since we are unable to do linguistic listening? Michel Chion explored this question at length, writing,

> Subtitling entails a bizarre paradox: it supplies written language in limited time, ephemeral text we must read in a hurry—whereas normally, writing is the way we *fix* language so that it is not subject to temporal constraints, allowing the reader to assimilate the text at a speed he or she chooses. . . . Because of the way it gives access to meaning, subtitling kills language. It short-circuits the issues of comprehension and translation, which it appears to do "in real time," even though it actually translates nothing but the skeleton of meaning (and this happens even with excellent subtitling). Through this short-circuiting, subtitling separates the sound of language from language itself. It *kills the signifier*, and in killing the signifier it reduces language to sound.[23]

While the subtitles' text captures "the skeleton of meaning," as Chion puts it, the subtitles also open up our ears to listen not for intelligibility of dialogue but for sound more broadly. We still attend to the human voice, but in this case, the voice more readily dissolves into the sound effects. In this, the Russian language's distancing effect for nonnative speakers is an effective tool for conveying the film's didactic message. The human voice steps down from its hierarchical peak within the soundtrack and draws closer to sound effects and the natural world. The established classical hierarchy of privileging voice over sound effects and music crumbles.

The significance of listening is also evident in *Dersu Uzala*'s narrative. Throughout the film, Kurosawa endows the act of listening and interpreting what one hears with a moral weightiness. The Russian troop doesn't listen to the world of nature; they sing loudly as they stomp through the forest. Ignorant of their surroundings, they are unable to observe nature as anything more than an object to be harnessed for man. Dersu scolds them for this: "You like children; eyes not see." Implicit (because it is obvious by their boisterous singing and loud voices) is the corollary: the Russians' ears do not hear. Later in the film, Dersu explains to them his animistic worldview in which all natural elements are "man." Dersu hears and sees what the Russian soldiers do not and perhaps cannot. Even Arseniev, despite his love and admiration for Dersu, cannot unravel this vastly foreign, sensorial epistemology.

Dersu's ability to listen to nature and to interpret its "voice" is a key to his competence as a hunter and guide for the Russian troop. If the introduction between Dersu and Arseniev at the campfire fire scene was a quaint depiction of an animistic Goldi hunter, the rain scene solidifies Dersu as a capable human being in a natural world foreign to the Russians.

In contrast, the Russians are producers of sound, but rarely listeners. They fill the natural world with sound whether it is the sound of hammers hard at work of the beginning of the film, the soldiers singing, or the train whistling. Even when Arseniev's son Vova practices piano, none of the characters seem to really listen or encourage him in his playing. A rare moment when Russian characters *do* listen is at the specific moment of technological mediation of the voice, when Arseniev listens to Vova's recording of Dersu's voice. But despite Arseniev's attentive listening here, he does not process the meaning of Dersu's words. Despite his wife's warning that Dersu is unhappy, Arseniev listens to neither her nor Dersu. Instead he brushes it off, saying, "Never mind, he'll get used to it." That the Arseniev family can only listen to Dersu mediated by the phonograph is significant. It is only by extrapolating his voice from his body that the Russian characters heed his voice. The technology of the phonograph metaphorically disembodies Dersu, just as the technology of the rifle literally destroys Dersu's life. Dersu, in the end, is treated like nature—that is, as a thing, an object instead of a human being. In not listening, Arseniev is complicit in Dersu's destruction.

Dersu Uzala, though not a rousing samurai epic or modern morality play, exists on a cusp of two different periods in Kurosawa's legacy. If we accept Kurosawa as an auteur, then it is his voice that is perhaps most present in the film.[24] *Dersu Uzala* is a Janus-faced piece that meditates on humanism and environmental issues while gesturing to a diminished optimism and Zenlike reconciliation with existence associated with Kurosawa's late style. And while *Dersu Uzala,* like many of Kurosawa's works, is visually stunning, it is the sound design that validates it as a significant artwork. In *Dersu Uzala,* Kurosawa and his team harnessed sound effects to generate a poignant commentary that rejected an imperialist vision of man's dominance over nature. The porous boundary between nature and human as embodied in the character of Dersu is mirrored in the sound design, in which sound effects become musical and vice versa. Overall, the movie implies that the exploitation of the natural world, no matter how benign the intentions, ultimately ends in destruction. It behooves us as thoughtful auditor-spectators to consider elements beyond the "brotherhood of man" relationship between Arseniev and Dersu.

It is not the crux of the film.

Instead, in *Dersu Uzala,* Kurosawa wielded audiovisual elements in service of a plea. We must do more than listen to Dersu. We must listen *like* Dersu.

Notes

1. The Japanese government recently proclaimed that Western texts should follow the Japanese custom of placing the surname prior to the given name, and I have observed this practice for names except when an author published in English.

2. For example, Japanese film scholar Donald Richie assesses the movie in his seminal overview of the director's oeuvre, writing "with *Dersu Uzala* the decline in Kurosawa's powers truly becomes apparent. . . . Style had become an end in itself. . . . And in abandoning a dynamic sense of character, Kurosawa has produced for the first time in his long and outstanding career a rather lifeless film" (Donald Richie, *The Films of Akira Kurosawa,* 3rd ed. [Berkeley: University of California Press, 1996], 197). Mitsuhiro Yoshimoto ponders *Dersu Uzala* briefly in his more recent work but does not consider the soundtrack. See Mitsuhiro Yoshimoto, *Kurosawa: Film Studies and Japanese Cinema* (Durham: Duke University Press, 2000), 344–47.

3. R. Murray Schafer, *The Soundscape: Our Sonic Environment and the Tuning of the World* (Rochester, Vt.: Destiny Books, 1994), 7.

4. Ibid., 8.

5. Richie, *Films of Akira Kurosawa,* 196.

6. Ibid., 195.

7. Ibid., 197. The memoir itself has been translated into English. See V. K. Arseniev, *Dersu the Trapper,* trans. Malcolm Burr (Kingston, N.Y.: McPherson, 1996).

8. The push for economic growth in the 1950s and 1960s under the Yoshida Doctrine enabled Japan to attain incredible growth in GDP but at a great cost to the environment. See Sean Rhoads and Brooke McCorkle, *Japan's Green Monsters: Environmental Commentary in Kaijū Cinema* (Jefferson, N.C.: McFarland and Company, 2018), 105–6.

9. Ibid., 106–10.

10. Richie, *Films of Akira Kurosawa,* 199.

11. Ibid., 241–43. These critiques are generally within the purview of Kurosawa's overall humanist angle.

12. *Dersu Uzala,* dir. Kurosawa Akira (1975; New York City: Kino Video, 2000), DVD.

13. Yoshimoto, *Kurosawa,* 345–46.

14. For more on this, see Michael W. Harris, "Hayasaka Fumio, Ronin Composer: Analysis and Commentary of Five Film Scores" (PhD diss., University of Colorado–Boulder, 2013).

15. Richie reveals that the script characterizes the train as a symbol of "the separation between the primitive and civilized worlds." See Richie, *Films of Akira Kurosawa,* 201.

16. Mary Ann Doane, "The Voice in the Cinema: The Articulations of Body and Space," *Yale French Studies,* 60 (1980): 41.

17. Female characters and voices are practically absent from the film; the only female role with dialogue is Arseniev's wife, who appears in the final portion of the movie. This serves to inform the "masculine" space of the natural world and the homosocial relationships formed within it. This itself is an interesting inversion of the stereotypical connection between woman and nature and fantasy in Hollywood cinema. For more on this, see Claudia Gorbman, *Unheard Melodies: Narrative Film Music* (Bloomington: Indiana University Press, 1987), 79–82.

18. Carl Maria von Weber's Huntsmen's Chorus from *Der Freischütz* comes to mind. Similar moments could include the Richard Wagner's Sailors' Chorus from *Der fliegende Holländer* and Pilgrims' Chorus from *Tannhäuser*. In film, the trope of male singing and wartime goes hand in hand thanks to the military cadence calls, as exemplified in Stanley Kubrick's *Full Metal Jacket* (1987).

19. The fire in some form appears in every shot in this sequence.

20. The sound of the underscore here is reminiscent of Béla Bartók's *Music for Strings, Percussion, and Celeste* (1936).

21. Many thanks to Kunio Hara for identifying this piece.

22. Kurosawa frequently employed audiovisual counterpoint. *Drunken Angel* (1948) depicts the extremely ill protagonist stumbling through a black market to the strains of gleeful "Cuckoo Waltz." *Stray Dog* (1949) shows two men exhausted from grappling collapse to the ground as school children pass by, singing but not noticing them. Even *Dodesukaden* gestures toward this technique, with a tinkling line in the celeste akin to a music box appearing in the underscore while a starving boy begs for scraps.

23. Michel Chion, "The Audio-Logo-Visual and the Sound of Languages in Recent Film" in *The Oxford Handbook of New Audiovisual Aesthetics*, eds. John Richardson, Claudia Gorbman, and Carol Vernallis (New York: Oxford University Press, 2013), 81 (emphasis in original).

24. For a deeper interrogation into the reception of Kurosawa as an auteur, see Yoshimoto, *Kurosawa*, 53–68.

Chapter 11

Peter Weir and the Piano Concerto

Erik Heine

Australian director Peter Weir is often classed as an auteur, although he rejects the label, stating, "I've tried, to some extent to disassemble my style, to fight against my own signature."[1] Weir typically takes several years off between projects, and does not seek out large-budget films that are largely based on spectacle, instead preferring to "be unpredictable and just look for good stories."[2] Weir is recognized for his deft handling of music, which has a significant presence in his films, and he draws especially on preexisting music. Table 11.1 provides a list of classical music used in Weir's films. His choices run from early Baroque to contemporary, using music by Albinoni, Bach, Mozart, Beethoven, Chopin, Vaughan Williams, Glass, and Górecki, among others. This is a varied set of composers, and Weir seems to take special care in selecting works that fit his films.

One genre, the piano concerto, is used especially effectively in Weir's films. The second movement of Beethoven's Piano Concerto No. 5, "Emperor," appears in two films, *Picnic at Hanging Rock* (1975) and *Dead Poets Society* (1989), and the second movement of Chopin's Piano Concerto No. 1 is found in *The Truman Show* (1998). The canny use of these two movements displays keen insight into the cultural resonances of the slow, second movement of these concertos, and the peculiar way the soloist in these movements engages with the orchestra parallels the narrative paths of the primary characters in each of the three films: Miranda, Neil, and Truman. Just as the soloist in these movements never breaks free of the orchestra to offer a cadenza, so, too, the protagonists of the films are unable to escape the social repression of their respective scenarios. Moreover,

Table 11.1. Films Directed by Peter Weir and the Use of Classical/Art Music

Title	Year	List of Works
The Cars That Eat People	1974	None
Picnic at Hanging Rock	1975	Bach—Prelude in C Major, *Well-Tempered Clavier*, Book I
		Beethoven—Piano Concerto no. 5, "Emperor," II
		Mozart—*Eine kleine Nachtmusik*, K. 525, II
		Tchaikovsky—String Quartet no. 1 in D major, II
The Last Wave	1977	None
Gallipoli	1981	Albinoni—*Adagio in G minor* for Strings and Organ
		Bizet—"The Pearl Fishers' Duet" from *Les pêcheurs de perles*
		Paganini—*Centone di Sonata, no. 3*
		Johann Strauss II—*Roses from the South*
		Strauss II—*Tales from the Vienna Woods*
The Year of Living Dangerously	1982	Richard Strauss—"Beim Schlafengehn" from *Vier letzte Lieder*
Witness	1985	None
The Mosquito Coast	1986	None
Dead Poets Society	1989	Beethoven—Piano Concerto no. 5, "Emperor," II
		Beethoven—Symphony no. 9 in D minor, IV
		Handel—*Water Music Suite no. 2*, Overture (Allegro)
Green Card	1990	Mozart—Concerto for Flute no. 1, K. 313, II and III
		Mozart—Concerto for Flute and Harp, K. 299, II
		Mozart—Concerto for Clarinet in A major, K. 622, II
Fearless	1993	Beethoven—Piano Concerto no. 5, "Emperor," III
		Beethoven—*Für Elise*
		Górecki—Symphony no. 3, "Symphony of Sorrowful Songs," I
		Penderecki—*Polymorphia*
The Truman Show	1998	Brahms—*Wiegenlied* (Lullaby)
		Chopin—Piano Concerto no. 1 in E minor, II
		Glass—"Anthem—Part 2" from *Powaqqatsi*
		Glass—"The Beginning" from *Anima Mundi*
		Glass—"Living Waters" from *Anima Mundi*
		Glass—"Opening" from *Mishima*
		Kilar—"Father Kolbe's Preaching" from *Leben für Leben*
		Mozart—Piano Sonata in A major, K. 331, III
		Mozart—Concerto for Horn in D major, no. 1, K. 412, I
Master and Commander: The Far Side of the World	2003	Bach—Suite no. 1 for Violoncello in G major, BWV 1007, Prelude
		Boccherini—*Musica notturna delle strade di Madrid*, op. 30, no. 6, V. Passa Calle
		Corelli—Concerto grosso in G minor, op. 6, no. 8, *Christmas Concerto*, III: Adagio
		Mozart—Violin Concerto no. 3, K. 216, III
		Vaughan Williams—*Fantasia on a Theme by Thomas Tallis*
The Way Back	2010	None

both movements lack conclusive endings in the films, and Weir leaves the fate of these characters in various stages of ambiguity. In addition, the musical soloist acts as a seeming "voice of innocence" to each of these characters. This is a voice that characters cannot speak themselves since they do not recognize the deep repression inherent in the situation, but they also have not themselves been corrupted, so the voice of innocence can still speak, as it were, on their behalf. This musical voice protests the repressive structures that these characters confront, and the play between soloist and orchestra in these slow movements serves as a particularly apt musical metaphor for their highly regimented lives and their dreams of escaping the control.

The slow movement of the "Emperor" Concerto is an especially interesting example because it is evidently semantically cool. For instance, the movement has attracted little interest from theorists of musical topics.[3] Others have noted that it eschews dramatic interpretation. Leon Plantinga claims that the movement "is mainly flat, virtually devoid of development or drama of its own," and that "it is a moment of nostalgic reflection, of pathos that gives pause to the scenes of unbounded energy and struggle developing around it."[4] Plantinga essentially reads the movement in terms of lack and so its nostalgic reflection is for an absolute music that has escaped the struggle for meaning that evidently rages in the outer movements. In any event, it suggests a refuge, a space apart.

This sense of respite gives the movement something of the feeling of a nocturne, and that association in turn suggests an implicit narrative.[5] Byron Almén identifies nine types of interaction between musical topic and narrative, and this movement most closely aligns with his "Type II: Narrative within a single, overarching topic (topic as frame)."[6] The movement never really leaves its nocturne style, so the movement lacks stylistic oppositions. And its lack of clear associative meanings—its semantic coolness—gives it a peculiar quality: the movement is, we might say, seemingly innocent of meaning. This innocence makes it entirely fitting for the use Weir makes of it in both *Picnic at Hanging Rock* and *Dead Poets Society*, since both films concern characters attuned to the voice of innocence. And David Neumeyer has stated explicitly that in *Picnic at Hanging Rock*, Beethoven's music represents "innocence and purity."[7]

The slow movement of Chopin's Piano Concerto No. 1 resembles that of the "Emperor" Concerto in being set apart from the rest of the concerto. Indeed, Chopin thought the movement presented a memory, a dream, thus also a nostalgic reflection. "It is not meant to create a powerful effect; it is rather a Romance, calm and melancholy, giving the impression of someone looking gently towards a spot that calls to mind a thousand happy memories. It is a kind of reverie in the moonlight on a beautiful spring evening."[8] If the scholarly literature is any guide, Chopin's movement carries significantly more semantic heat than the slow movement of the "Emperor" Concerto, and John Rink, for instance, devotes a small portion of his book on Chopin's concertos to the "narrative" of the movement, providing a detailed description at the phrase and tonal levels. "After the portentous bassoon and horn announcement of bar 63, idyllic lyricism gives way to anguish and agitation . . . [the re-entry of b_2 in bar 80] exudes a sense of rediscovery after a brief but emotional journey."[9] Rink sees the movement governed by a play between idyll and agitation, the idyll representing a kind of inward emotional journey, which is answered by anguish as the idyllic vision collapses into a state of general, worldly agitation.

Weir in fact uses this moment most effectively in *The Truman Show*, where it serves to underscore a portion of the flashback to Truman's fateful romance with Lauren (Natascha McElhone). Just as Weir draws on the slow movement of the "Emperor" Concerto to become the voice of innocence denied to the protagonists of *Picnic at Hanging Rock* and *Dead Poets Society*, so too the idyllic portion of Chopin's slow movement marks the innocent romance denied Truman. In all three of these films, then, the slow movement of a piano concerto serves to give voice to an innocence that is denied to the character by large repressive social forces.

The theme of innocence is found across Weir's directorial career, for instance in the films *The Mosquito Coast* (1986) and *Fearless* (1993). But innocence features most strongly in *Picnic at Hanging Rock*, *Dead Poets Society*, and *The Truman Show*. In the remainder of the essay, I will consider each of these films in more detail.

The Piano Concerto in *Picnic at Hanging Rock*

The plot of *Picnic at Hanging Rock* is both straightforward and mysterious. The students at an all-girls school in Australia take a day trip to Hanging Rock on Valentine's Day in 1900. On that trip, three girls, Miranda, Marion, and Irma, and one teacher, Miss McCraw, disappear. A week later, two boys, Michael and Albert, who originally saw the girls ascending to the top of the rock, find Irma, but she has no memory of what happened to her. The others are never found, and no explanation for their disappearance is ever offered. The film is considered to be one of the first Australian art house films.

Marek Haltof identifies a number of oppositions present in *Picnic at Hanging Rock*, such as culture versus nature, familiar versus mysterious, and British versus Australian,[10] and the music plays a significant role in highlighting these oppositions. Bruce Smeaton's original score usually accompanies events near the titular Hanging Rock, and it is nonmelodic, emphasizing low synthesized rumblings and other mysterious sounds that serve to present the rock as mysterious and natural, specifically belonging to Australia. Gheorge Zamfir's panpipe music, by contrast, usually appears with shots of the rock itself, although it is also used in the opening sequence as the female students of Appleyard College share their sentiments regarding St. Valentine's Day. The classical music that Weir chooses—Bach, Mozart, Beethoven, and Tchaikovsky—accompanies scenes away from the rock, where it underscores the oppositions of culture versus nature and familiar versus mysterious.

A further opposition is articulated by the perpetual motion of Bach's C Major Prelude from the *Well-Tempered Clavier*—a musical embodiment of the drive of a mechanically applied social rule—and the middle movement of Beethoven's "Emperor" Concerto, which, as noted earlier, seems to give voice to the innocence foreclosed by the application of those repressive social rules. Bach's music is thus heard as Mrs. Appleyard, the school's head mistress, delivers detailed instructions reinforcing the school's "rules" before the girls depart for the rock (0:09:19–0:11:07). These rules serve to enforce a particular social order: the girls are told to dress a certain way, to sit a certain way, and to speak at a specific volume; they are being trained to become "ladies" in the "proper" English tradition. Bach's music is precise and unwavering—qualities that Mrs. Appleyard wants her girls to possess. In her mind, the girls should not be curious or idealists. Instead, they should learn how to take orders, and they should always behave in a proper Victorian manner.

Weir uses Beethoven's "Emperor" Concerto to represent an escape from the repressive regime of Appleyard College, and the lyrical, romantic qualities of this slow movement stand in sharp contrast to the regimented order of the Bach prelude. Indeed, Jonathan Rayner states that Beethoven's music "conveys more of an elegiac tone for Victorian society's vulnerable state. . . . It suggests that the stalwart values are in retreat, and the final pensive scenes indicate the capitulation of a social construct soon to pass into history."[11] Beethoven's music appears only after the picnic, where the missing girls "broke the rules."

The other classical music—the slow movements of Mozart's *Eine kleine Nachtmusik* and Tchaikovsky's first string quartet—is heard during the garden party scene at Michael's family estate, and the comparative neutrality of this music allows it to represent something like the full Victorian ideal. The Bach prelude then embodies the drive of social pedagogy, the music at the garden party the social ideal that that pedagogy seeks to produce, and the Beethoven concerto a kind of decadent synthesis (combining, as it were, the individual "social subject" at the keyboard and the collective "society" of the orchestra) that points to a hidden social truth: namely, the rigid terms of social exclusion and indeed structural amnesia (the silencing of the voice of innocence) that makes this society possible. The concerto is both symptom and fantasy of an underlying social pathology stemming from the cultural logic of colonialization. At least this is the interpretation of David Neumeyer: "Beethoven becomes the mediator between the Victorian European white world that white Australians are shown as being at great pains to develop and sustain, and the natural or Aboriginal world of the continent they have colonized."[12] This is how the music functions in the film—as a mediator—but not necessarily what it means in itself but how it comes to mean in the context of the other music in the film. As Neumeyer notes, the slow movement of the "Emperor" Concerto "acquires strong narrative significance, as its nondiegetic cues are balanced against the diegetic string quartet performances of Mozart, on the one hand, and Gheorge Zamfir's pan flute music, on the other hand."[13] In turn, Zamfir's pan flute music becomes the call of the Aboriginal world that is being overwritten by the pedagogy of places like Appleyard College. In its role as mediator, Beethoven's music, because it gives voice to innocence, in a sense also remembers this call.

Beethoven's music is heard on four separate occasions in the film; and all four occasions are nondiegetic. Table 11.2 provides timings used in the film as well as measure numbers of the music. The music first appears after the girls—Miranda, Marion, Irma (who is later found), and their teacher, Miss McCraw—have gone missing. Sergeant Bumpher, as he grabs a garment of Miranda's, says to Sara, "One last go . . . for the bloodhound." The music begins after he says, "One last go" (0:46:59–0:48:12).

As Sara pines for the missing Miranda, the protagonist of the film, the music enters with the orchestral ritornello at the start of the movement, appropriately without the soloist, given this music will accompany the search for Miranda and the other girls. However, the girls have completely vanished, and the group has no idea where to look, so they are also waiting for the girls to reappear. Similarly, Sara is not actively searching for Miranda and is waiting for her to return home. This situation suits the conventions of the concerto—those who recognize the music will know we await the arrival of the soloist while we hear the ritornello. But the tune is a strong one and can stand on its own without the soloist, so in the context of a film it is by no means clear at first that the soloist will ever appear. In this respect, the music in this scene is in line with Weir's unclear narrative and lack of explanation for the disappearance of the girls. The music allows the ambiguity of the presence and absence of the soloist, continuing to blur the plot.

Table 11.2. Formal Outline of Beethoven's Piano Concerto no. 5 in E-flat major, "Emperor," II (Concerto Ternary Form)

Measures	Formal Section	Comments
1–16	Orchestral Ritornello	BM; deceptive cadence (DC) in m. 10; PAC in 13; cadential extension with ♭6 in mm. 13–14
16–28	Part I	BM → F#M (m. 22)—PAC in m. 24; cadential extension in mm. 24–26; transition to Part II in mm. 26–28 with modulation from F#M to DM
28–44	Part II	DM → BM (m. 44); PAC prepared in mm. 35–39, but never reached; solo passage in thirds in mm. 35–38; chromatic sequence (*monte*) in mm. 39–43
45–60	Part III	BM; DC in m. 54 (parallel place to m. 10); PAC in m. 60
60–79	Coda	Roughly a repetition of Part III; BM; DC in m. 69 (again, parallel place); PAC prepared in mm. 70–71, but does not arrive in m. 72; cadential extension now expansion with ♭6
80–82	Transition	EM; Transition *attacca* to movement III

The second occurrence presents mm. 13–46, and it accompanies Irma as she recovers and is examined by a doctor (1:11:08–1:13:48). Here, the tonal rupture from the closely related dominant key of F♯ major to D major clearly indicates that an extraordinary event has occurred, both the initial disappearance and the singular return of Irma, who, as the only girl to return, assumes Miranda's place as the soloist, the protagonist. The solo piano takes flight, allowing the doctor's theory of what happened to the girls to gain traction. In the ascending sequential passage, mm. 39–42, the doctor comments on the strange absence of shoes or stockings, but as he reaches the end of his hypothesis, which fails to truly explain anything, he announces that she is "quite intact," that she has not been sexually violated, as though nothing really happened to her. At this moment the music returns to the movement's home key of B major, as though it agrees with the doctor that nothing really happened. The music here seems to confirm Irma's nonviolated innocence and purity, although this confirmation is in line with the Victorian-era prudishness, confirmed by failing to acknowledge that anything occurred. We soon learn, however, that Irma has been radically affected by her disappearance, most notably through her choice of clothing and its colors. The music has left the home key and returned, and although it appears, on the surface, to be unchanged, it is not; nor is Irma.

When Beethoven's music sounds for the third time (1:23:50–1:26:34), as searchers pose for photos for the newspaper, it begins with mm. $13–15_2$, a cadential extension that emphasizes the lowered sixth scale-degree; then it restarts, using mm. $1–32_1$. The appearance of the minor-inflected scale degree introduces a melancholy affect that seems appropriate for the fruitless search since the lowered scale-degree occurs only in the orchestra and is not essential to the phrase structure. Indeed, the soloist uses only the diatonic scale degree, which suggests that the soloist and orchestra are not fully in accord and perhaps indicates that the police are seeking the wrong thing in the wrong place. The music then jumps from beat 2 of m. 15 to beat 1 of m. 1 as the scene cuts to Mademoiselle de Poitiers talking to a now-awake Irma. When asked about the incident, Irma cries out, "I remember nothing," as m. 15 is reached. The absence of the soloist here seems to figure Irma's amnesia as a loss of self.

The scene then changes to Michael, who has become obsessed with finding Miranda, believing that he sees Miranda in the distance. A white swan appears with the entrance of the soloist in m. 16. Though the swan plausibly serves as Michael's fantasy projection of Miranda, the displacement resists a straightforward sexual interpretation, as it encompasses Michael's perception of Miranda's basic innocence and perhaps also his repressed desire (for either Miranda or for the innocence she stands for). Michael is from a wealthy English family, so his social standing and class are higher than Miranda's native Australian class, making her an inappropriate match by the terms of society. Accompanying the scene, the music plays out an implicit social drama. Although Michael only observes the swan and does not approach it, the swan ultimately takes flight from his gaze. The music similarly resists closure, and the soloist resists being contained by the orchestra. So, too, Michael is associated with classical music—the string quartet music played at a garden party at his family's estate—but despite his social and class status he cannot appropriate Beethoven's music; or, rather, the soloist in this movement is constantly taking flight, refusing the terms offered by the orchestra.

In the final occurrence (1:43:43–1:47:10), the music begins with the entrance of the soloist. As Mrs. Appleyard sits in her office, the clock stops, the image becomes still, and a voiceover narration begins, stating that the girls' disappearance remains a mystery to this day. When the music reaches m. 18_3, the film cuts to a slow-motion "remembrance" of the picnic, using the same shots as earlier in the film. Curiously, at the modulation to D major in mm. 27–28, Miss McCraw is shown; she is the only person present at the picnic who is not in white. The soloist's sixteenth-note passage in m. 35 coincides with a cut showing Miranda waving goodbye to Mademoiselle de Poitiers, and at the end of the passage in m. 39, the film fades to black, with the credits beginning in m. 41. Beethoven's music continues without interruption during the credits and ends at m. 56, on a dominant seventh chord in the home key of B major. This ending is similar to the Bach prelude heard on the carriage ride to the rock, which also abruptly ends in the midst of the final dominant prolongation. The music's lack of conclusion in the film is indicative of the fact that the mystery of the missing girls was never solved; we don't know how it ends.[14] According to Miranda, "Everything begins and ends at exactly the right time and place."

As the music is almost exclusively associated with the slow-motion flashback in this final instance, and the visual element ultimately focuses on Miranda in its final shot, the piano soloist becomes explicitly linked to her in this sequence. The enduring image of the film becomes Miranda waving farewell to Mademoiselle de Poitiers; as Miranda turns, the image freezes, and then fades to black. The music fails to reach a satisfactory cadence at its conclusion. The lack of narrative ending, combined with the dreamlike nature of the slow-motion flashback, and the music's enigmatic continuation into the credits, leave the audience hanging as to what really happened on the picnic.

In a comment following a presentation of an earlier version of this essay, Marcia Citron noted that the second movement of Beethoven's "Emperor" Concerto is "not goal oriented" and that, like the rock in the film, the "movement is 'hanging,'"[15] meaning that the music seems to float, being more interested in prolonging harmonic functions than in realizing cadential gestures. The lack of goal direction in the movement is indeed significant because it allows longer stretches of music to be heard without cadences, and when cadences are heard, their significance, combined with the onscreen action and image, is that much more punctuated. The absence of goal direction also plays into the dreamlike nature of the film's narrative, echoing the opening words, spoken by Miranda, "What we are and what we seem are but a dream, a dream within a dream." Just as dreams are not commonly goal-oriented, Beethoven's concerto movement aligns with the absence of clearly defined musical goals.

Picnic at Hanging Rock resists a number of narrative conventions, including a clearly defined plot and an explanation for the disappearance of the girls and their teacher. The tension present in the music—Bach, Mozart, and Beethoven—gives a voice to repression, social standing, and innocence, respectively. The soloist in the "Emperor" Concerto signifies Miranda, and just as the soloist never ends with a cadence, leaving the music incomplete, so too does the film remain incomplete, open to further interpretation. Once the girls embark on their journey to Hanging Rock, accompanied by Bach's music, they have escaped the repressive confines of the school, free to allow their innocence and naïveté to rule them. In escaping repression, the girls ultimately remain missing, with the exception of one, Irma, who, upon her return to classes, is dressed differently than her peers, indicating that she had been transformed through her experience, that she cannot go back to the way she was before the trip to Hanging Rock, nor can the music.

The Piano Concerto in *Dead Poets Society*

Almost fifteen years after *Picnic at Hanging Rock,* Weir revisited the boarding school genre. *Dead Poets Society* is another period film, set at all-male Welton Academy in Vermont in 1959. The main character is Neil Perry (Robert Sean Leonard), who at the insistence of his father intends to go to medical school. When he takes John Keating's (Robin Williams) poetry course, he is changed, wanting to immerse himself in poetry and acting instead of medicine. When Neil's father (Kurtwood Smith) finds out, he orders Neil to leave Welton, give up acting, and become a doctor. Neil's dreams are shattered and he commits suicide; the Perrys and Welton hold Mr. Keating responsible.

As a student at Welton Academy, Neil Perry's education is imposed upon him. Creativity and original thought have no place in the school. Poetry is evaluated with a mathematical equation. His father has already chosen medicine as his career, whether Neil wants that life or not. The students of Welton are asked to recite the four pillars on command: Tradition, Honor, Discipline, Excellence. Neil's desire to become an actor is repressed, both by the school and by his father, but it is not just his career desires that are repressed. His ability to think for himself, his emotions, and his need to feel a part of something larger are also kept out of reach. Michael Bliss writes, "The conflict between the repression that seems an integral part of the schooling at Welton and what goes on in the natural world is made manifest in Weir's shots of the landscape."[16] Even the natural environment is in conflict with the school. Keating's classroom teaching persona, beliefs regarding poetry, and passion for English represent the escape from his father and his prescribed path to medical school that Neil so desperately wants. To Neil, Mr. Keating represents everything that Welton is not: creativity, excitement, curiosity, and humor. Neil's innocent academic explorations with Keating allow him to make his own decisions but they cannot be permanent due to the predetermined path and overbearing presence of his father.

The single presentation of the Beethoven concerto movement, which is stylistically different from the other diegetic classical music Weir opts for throughout the film, occurs at the beginning of the film's third act. Neil's father learns that Neil has lied to him and taken a role in a production of *A Midsummer Night's Dream*; he demands that Neil quit, even though the performance is the following evening. Neil enters Mr. Keating's office one evening to ask advice on how to speak to his father and to tell him that he wants to be an actor, not a doctor. Neil is desperately searching for a way to appease his father while still satisfying his own desire to act, to be creative, to live. He wants a means of reconciling these two paths.

The excerpt begins in m. 16, as the solo piano enters, implying that Keating has been listening to the music as he has been composing a letter. He is writing to a woman with whom he (presumably) has a relationship. The love that Keating has for his female recipient cannot be physically realized, as the relationship is a transatlantic one. When asked by Neil how he can stand being apart from her, Keating declares that he loves teaching and that there is no place that he would rather be than Welton. In this way, Keating is repressing one need of adulthood, a romantic relationship, and replacing it with another need of adulthood, the need to have a productive career. His presence at Welton allows him to substitute his romantic relationship with a mentoring relationship, but the presence of the photograph on his desk indicates that something is still absent in his life. For Keating, this music perhaps represents his romantic attachment, and the fact that we do not hear the poignant lyrical statement of the theme by the orchestra figures in its own way her absence as he finds his way as soloist. For Neil, this music—specifically the solo pianist—voices his basic innocence and strong passion to embark on his own journey, not out of spite toward his father, but out of a need to fulfill his own desires, the soloist refusing the terms proffered by the orchestra, however lovely. Beethoven's movement thus becomes an analysis of Neil's two worlds and signals that he will ultimately follow the path of his desire, acting.

But the music is mere suggestion, and Citron's comment regarding the movement's lack of goal orientation is appropriate here. Keating is serving as a mentor, guiding Neil, and not telling him specifically what to do. Life has no clearly stated goal, and the music supports this lack of finality. Of course, as it is heard in the film, the music doesn't end with the conclusion of the movement, and part of the suspended quality of the movement that Citron notes is that Beethoven doesn't end it properly but dissolves *attaca* into the finale. The idea that the music "hangs" in the air is also significant. Keating is between two worlds—his love for a woman and his love of teaching. He is not operating with a specific goal in mind; his teaching style also appears to lack clear pedagogical direction. Neil is also between two worlds, but clearly desiring a life of acting. His father keeps pulling him back to medicine, allowing Neil's life to hang between the worlds of science and performing arts, never really reaching either one. The suspended quality of the music may also provide insight into Weir's aesthetic and narrative objectives, in that neither film has a satisfactory resolution, and neither of the protagonists, Miranda or Neil, remains alive at the conclusion of the film. Even at the end of *Dead Poets Society*, with a cue titled "Keating's Triumph," Keating has lost his job. While some students may see him as a hero, he is not victorious. The ending of the film is not narratively closed. Instead, it remains open for interpretation, hanging like the music.

Keating's office is likely the only location on campus, outside from a specifically designated classroom, where music would be played. It was already a different place from the austere classrooms and setting of the rest of the school, but the presence of music sets it even further apart from everywhere else. By itself, however, the presence of music doesn't make the office an enchanted space, free from repression. Instead, the fact that the student has entered the domain of the professor imbues the physical space with this sense of enchantment, which is confirmed by the coincidence of the music and Neil's arrival in the office. Neil and Keating also form a complementary relationship: Neil is seeking an escape from his repressive home and school lives, while Keating, who represses certain needs of adulthood, actually fulfills the role of an adult through the presence of Neil. With its emphasis on the piano soloist, which here refuses to elaborate on the ritornello, this excerpt provides a model that helps both characters break out of their accustomed roles: Keating can be a proper adult, a character he has been repressing, and Neil can lead a life of both scholarly and artistic pursuits, if his father permits it. However, it is only in Keating's office that this voice of innocence can speak. When Neil attempts to articulate his desires to his father, he cannot. Neil's voice falls silent in the face of repression.

Beethoven's piano concerto movement voices innocence and an escape from social constraint in *Dead Poets Society*, much as it does in *Picnic at Hanging Rock*.

In both cases, the innocence of the students is represented by the concerto. Earlier in *Dead Poets Society*, the first movement of Handel's *Water Music Suite No. 3* plays as the students line up, recite various lines of poetry, and then kick a ball into a soccer goal. While the scene contains music, it is somewhat mechanical, as every boy does the same thing, even if the poetic lines are different. The music also does not feature soloists in the style of the concerto; instead all the boys are individuals. Later, music from the fourth movement of Beethoven's Ninth Symphony, including the sung words, "Alle Menchen werden Brüder," is used to accompany a victory in a soccer match, after which the boys pick up Keating in a celebratory fashion. This scene shows the unity between the boys in Keating's class, but the figure of the soloist is still not present. The musical soloist appears only when Neil enters Keating's office. In both *Picnic at Hanging Rock* and *Dead Poets Society*, individual students, Miranda and Neil, respectively, are trying to break free from various forms of repression embodied in the codes of society. These characters are associated with the soloist in the movement, while the orchestra represents the social institution—the school itself or, in Neil's case, his overbearing father. In both films, this concerto movement is a stylistic outlier from other music, allowing it to function differently from the rest of the music. After using the second movement of Beethoven's "Emperor" Concerto twice, both times in films about boarding schools, Weir turned to a new piece that could function the same way.

The Piano Concerto in *The Truman Show*

The Truman Show stars Jim Carrey as Truman Burbank, the unwitting star of a reality show that never goes off the air. Truman was adopted by a network and has been on camera his entire life. His parents on the show are actors, his best friend is an actor, and his actions are guided by the creator of the show, Christof (Ed Harris). Music plays a significant role in *The Truman Show*. Philip Glass's music, which consists of specific cues from other original film scores, complements Burkhard Dallwitz's original score for the film.[17] In the liner notes to the soundtrack recording, Weir writes:

> In the case of *The Truman Show*, since it is the story of a live television program, I was also determining the music that the show's creator, Christof, would have chosen. The tracks that seemed to be drawing the most out of the images for me (and presumably Christof) were those of Philip Glass. Due to the round-the-clock nature of the show, I determined that Christof would play either pre-recorded music (as a DJ might do) or . . . improvise with one of the musicians who work in several shifts. . . . The use of music in this film is as unusual as the concept of the movie itself. Sometimes the music is Christof's choice, sometimes it's mine![18]

Since the bulk of the television show is unscripted, having musicians improvise in a style similar to Glass's minimalism would be appropriate. But during flashbacks, montages, or other times, such as when Truman is asleep, music that could be preselected would seem to be most convenient.

The way the music functions in the film raises issues regarding *whose* diegesis, and for whom is the music diegetic or nondiegetic. Very little of the music heard in the film is diegetic to Truman or to his audience. One piece that is diegetic, and prominently so, is Mozart's "Rondo alla Turca" from his *Piano Sonata in A major*, K. 331, which plays every morning on the radio as Truman drives to work. It is clearly part of Truman's routine, but as Rebecca Doran Eaton notes, this music is also "anempathetic, indifferent to Truman and his internally agitated state."[19] In general, however, the implied audience watching "The Truman Show" would hear typical film music gestures to enhance emotions or to underscore flashbacks as nondiegetic. However, the audience watching *The Truman Show* has a quite different sense of the nondiegetic, because the musical performers for "The Truman Show" are frequently shown on screen. Even when musicians are not shown playing for a particular scene of "The Truman Show," we suspect that somewhere musicians for the show are performing it, or the music has been selected by someone for the show.[20] The one exception to that is Wojciech Kilar's music near the end, which could potentially not be grounded in "The Truman Show" and so function as nondiegetic to the audience of *The Truman Show*.

Beyond the stylistically minimal music, Chopin's concerto movement also occupies an unusual location within the diegesis. The music is not played (or performed) during the live feed; it is, instead, part of an edited flashback sequence where Truman's "lost love" is shown. Since the music cuts in and out, there's no way that it could have been used in the original live feed, and thus, while it is used in "The Truman Show," the music is not really part of "The Truman Show." Chopin's music is nondiegetic to "The Truman Show," as Truman, of course, does not hear it, but the audience watching the show does. Christof has edited this flashback and specifically selected this music to maximize its manipulative effect on his audience, making them sympathetic to Truman's love interest so that his wife can be phased out of the show. But, is Christof making this choice, or is Weir? As the audience of *The Truman Show*, we are already rooting for Truman to escape Seahaven, so we don't need to be manipulated into cheering for Truman's controls to be lessened. The metadiegetic placement of Chopin's music in this flashback raises the issue of who, character or director, is making the musical decision.

Eaton notes that Mozart's Turkish Rondo has a curiously anempathetic effect in the film because it lacks the agitation that Truman feels. Her choice of "agitated" is particularly pertinent, as Rink uses the same word when discussing the move to C♯ minor in the Chopin concerto. Truman has been in a perpetually agitated state since his love was taken from him in college. Christof determined whom he wanted Truman to date while in college, the woman who ultimately played his wife, Meryl (Laura Linney). Truman, however, fell in love with someone else, a woman named Lauren (Natascha McElhone). When Lauren tried to tell Truman that his life was a TV show, she was banned from the set and written out of the story. But years later, Truman is clearly still infatuated with her, as he goes through magazines to create a collage of her face. During the flashback sequence showing his budding relationship with Lauren, Weir uses Chopin's First Piano Concerto, second movement: Romance-Larghetto, mm. 1–48 and mm. 63–88 after the interruption. As noted earlier, this music is similar to the second movement of Beethoven's "Emperor" Concerto, as it has a similar suspended quality.

The flashback scene lasts just over ten minutes, and Chopin's music, which is interrupted, underscores just under six minutes of the flashback (0:22:44–0:29:33). The gap between these excerpts does not have music. During this flashback, Truman is young and idealistic, and Chopin's music makes Truman's infatuation with Lauren seem very charming and innocent. Truman first sees her outside of the football stadium as the marching band is presumably warming up prior to a football game. Truman is later shown studying in the library. When his best friend Marlon (Noah Emmerich) and his assigned girlfriend Meryl leave, he peers around the study carrel and finds Lauren there. Chopin's music enters with Truman's recognition of Lauren's bracelet.

When Truman says Lauren's name out loud, his (unscripted) words are nearly synchronized with the entrance of the solo piano. After a brief flirtation, they abscond from campus to the beach, with Lauren attempting to elude the cameras, and as they cross the university boundary, Chopin's music cadences in F♯ major, the major supertonic key relative to the home key of E major. At this point, having reached the idealized physical space of the beach, the right hand of the solo piano plays in thirds, and Lauren tells Truman that they have very little time. He responds, "Then don't talk," and kisses her. The kiss is synchronized to m. 45 in the music, a magical piano embellishment of the cadential dominant harmony in the upper register just before the arrival of the perfect authentic cadence in B major. However, fifteen seconds after this moment, a vehicle arrives to take Lauren away, and Chopin's music quickly ends through a very short fade-out. Lauren tries to tell Truman about the falseness of his world, the absence of music reinforcing reality, not Truman's reality, but reality to the rest of the world watching "The Truman Show."

Chopin's music resumes seventy seconds after it ended, skipping ahead fifteen measures, and is in C♯ minor, the first instance that Chopin's music has been in a minor key. This section is where Rink referenced the "idyllic lyricism" turning to "anguish and agitation." When learning that she is being taken to "Fiji," Truman begins a lifelong obsession with attempting to travel to Fiji, only to be thwarted at every attempt. His reaction to Lauren's forcible removal is certainly fraught with longing and despair. We then learn that Truman married Meryl on the rebound. Truman takes out a photo of Meryl; underneath is a collage that he works on to make Lauren's face, and the music moves to G♯ major. Truman has built this facial collage over the years and is looking for the right pair of eyes in an attempt to recreate Lauren's face. This moment corresponds to Rink's narrative of "rediscovery" and is quite literally realized on screen, as Truman "rediscovers" Lauren's face.[21] As he finds the correct set of eyes, the piano recalls the music for their kiss and concludes just after that with a perfect authentic cadence in D♯ major in m. 87, a key distantly related to the movement's home key. The flashback ends, and Chopin's music is interrupted by the scene change to Truman's drive to work once again, the following day.

The music present in the flashback resides primarily in the major mode, using the tonal areas of E major (the home key), B major, F♯ major, C♯ minor, G♯ major, and D♯ major. The only minor tonal area, C♯ minor, is heard when the music restarts, after Lauren is taken away, representing Truman's frustration and turn to Meryl, in whom he is not particularly interested. As he works on his collage of Lauren, the music returns to the major mode, and acts as a transposition of the music heard earlier in the flashback when they were on the beach, the transposition suggesting that, while the memory can be recalled, the moment will never return. The flashback sequence ends with the parallel musical moment to the beach kiss, perhaps indicating that finding Lauren has been Truman's objective since she was forcibly removed from his life.

While Truman Burbank believes that he is fully in control of his life, many of his decisions, most notably his relationship with Meryl, are shaped and guided by Christof, the Godlike showrunner of "The Truman Show." In an interview, Christof states that he is hoping to broadcast the world's first on-air conception, not because he believes that Truman and Meryl would be the best parents, but because of the exceptionally high ratings the "episode" would receive. Christof has manipulated Truman's emotions and life, even created an early childhood trauma to exploit so that Truman does not desire to leave Seahaven. Eaton writes: "Conceivably, Christof's use of minimal, entrapment music over Truman's bids to escape is yet another means to interpret Truman's actions—suggesting that he does not really want to escape."[22] Despite Christof's efforts, however, Truman yearns to break free from the life Christof has created for him, a life exemplified by hearing the same piece at the same time every day on the drive to work and the show's minimalist style score. Eaton notes, "Perhaps Weir did not intend for minimalism to signify escape, but rather Truman's impotence to escape. From this perspective, minimalism underlines Christof's entrapment and control of Truman's life."[23] While Christof works to repress Truman's true desires of escape and for Lauren, a more appropriate way to describe Truman is "trapped."

In the flashback sequence, Truman finds one escape from his life of surveillance, and that refuge is entirely in his head, a place that no one can see and no one can alter. At the film's climax, Truman says, "You never had a camera in my head," implying that Christof could never really know Truman's thoughts, desires, and wants. Truman's flashback, his ability to relive the one relationship that he wanted, even if it was denied to him, allows him to escape from the repetitive, redundant, and repressed nature of his daily life. And because it occurs in a flashback, this music does not clearly belong to the music of the real-time "The Truman Show." Moreover, the style of Chopin's music clearly differentiates it from Glass's minimalism. The nature of the soloist represents Truman as the solo protagonist in the television show and in the film. The piano soloist longs for autonomy from the orchestra, though it is fleeting, in the way that Truman longs to escape his life in Seahaven. When Truman kisses Lauren during the flashback, the piano part contains one of its most florid moments in the movement, a passage that is transposed and heard again at the end of the flashback. Most importantly, the music presents the aural signifier of Truman's love, his reason for continuing, the ultimate escape from his repressed life.

As this flashback sequence is the only time that Truman is demonstrably shown thinking about Lauren, it is the only time that the piano concerto movement is heard in the film. Stylistically, the only other music that is outside of Mozart's "Alla Turca" and Glass's minimalism is Wojciech Kilar's "Father Kolbe's Preaching," used during the climactic finale, where Truman speaks with "God"/Christof. Kilar's piece, which sounds hymnlike, sets it apart from the earlier music, but Eaton makes the claim that it functions similarly to the overt minimal cues—as a control to keep Truman in place. She writes,

> Because of its repetition and the tonic static drone, a persuasive argument could be made for calling this cue minimalist; but even if it is not, it has the same function within the film. Perhaps this music was not simply intended to give religious weight to Truman's final escape but was chosen by Weir to highlight another ploy by Christof to control Truman, to try to get him to stay.[24]

Taking Eaton's assessment into account, Chopin's music is the only music outside of the minimalist style in the film, thus giving the audience insight into Truman's thoughts. More sinisterly, though, the presence of Chopin's concerto could be Christof manipulating the television audience (and Weir manipulating the film audience) into seeing and hearing what he wants concerning Truman, since Christof sees Truman pining for his lost love as preparation for Meryl's leaving Truman.

Christof could be using Chopin's music to raise expectations of the audience of "The Truman Show" that Truman will get together with Lauren, even though Christof will not allow that to occur. Truman's voice of innocence, articulated through the flashback music, remains true, even if Kilar's music allowed him to verbally speak truth to the repressor. While we see Lauren (whose real name is Sylvia) rushing down a flight of stairs at the end of the film, presumably to meet Truman when he exits the studio, we don't learn if they will ultimately be together, or if her interest in him is also manipulative. After all, their moment of cadence was in D♯ major, not the home key of E major. We do not know how it will end.

Conclusion

Weir's use of remarkable slow movements from two piano concertos shows how each character with whom this music is associated—Miranda, Neil, and Truman—is innocent while simultaneously comparing that character to the soloist trying to achieve a measure of autonomy from the orchestra. Weir's films rarely provide satisfactory conclusions, even if the narrative is clear. Megan Abbott writes, "At an industry screening of [*Picnic at Hanging Rock*], Weir recalled in an interview, one distributor, 'threw his coffee cup at the screen at the end . . . because he'd wasted two hours of his life—a mystery without a solution.'"[25] The film leaves the girls' mysterious disappearance in *Picnic at Hanging Rock* unexplained. In *Dead Poets Society*, Neil's story is concluded, as he kills himself, but what happens to Mr. Keating when he is fired from Welton Academy goes unanswered. In *The Truman Show*, we see Truman exiting the studio and Lauren racing down the stairs of her apartment to meet him, but the film withholds an image of their embrace. Additionally, once the signal from the show goes dark, we actually see viewers attempt to find something else to watch on television. The film ends as two security guards change the channel, and the end credits begin.

The repressive structures of the three films—Appleyard College, Welton Academy, and Christof's Seahaven—silence the voice of innocence and prevent the protagonists/soloists from speaking, living, even recognizing their desires. Truman is consistently thwarted from leaving and finds what little peace he can in his memories. Neil's desire to pursue a career in acting is crushed by his father, and he takes his own life. Miranda's desires are unclear, other than her statement that, "Everything begins and ends at exactly the right time and place." Perhaps this statement is enough to allow the escape from repression that she finds at Hanging Rock. In all these cases, the slow movement of a piano concerto gives voice to the innocence that the characters cannot verbalize. But, however much the soloists of these concerto movements work to articulate a different path, they are ultimately subsumed into the society of the orchestra. Within the musical structure, the individual has moments of outward expression, but ultimately returns to the larger whole of the tutti, if not in the slow movement then in the finale; the orchestra absorbs the soloist, and if the concerto does not precisely give representation to repression, it offers a musical structure that plays the individual soloist off against the collective orchestra, the musical genre acting as a metaphor that is legible but remains ambiguous. Weir's concept of the protagonist as one who attempts to break free of repression never clearly ends conclusively, and the audience is left to interpret beyond the image and soundtrack.

Notes

1. John C. Tibbetts, "Introduction: 'Unmet Friends': Encounters with Peter Weir," in *Peter Weir: Interviews*, ed. John C. Tibbets (Jackson: The University Press of Mississippi, 2014), xx.

2. Nancy Griffin, "Poetry Man: *Dead Poets Society*," in *Peter Weir: Interviews*, 177.

3. For instance, Robert Hatten's *Musical Meaning in Beethoven* (Bloomington: Indiana University Press, 1994) does not address any of the three movements of the work, nor does *The Oxford Handbook of Topic Theory*, ed. Dinuta Mirka (New York: Oxford University Press, 2014).

4. Leon Plantinga, *Beethoven's Concertos* (New York: W. W. Norton and Company, Inc., 1999), 267.

5. I am indebted to my colleague Dave Easley for hearing this interpretation. Other interpretations may exist, but none have been published.

6. Byron Almén, *A Theory of Musical Narrative* (Bloomington: Indiana University Press, 2008), 79.

7. David Neumeyer, "Music Analysis and the Audiovisual: Problems and Prospects," Keynote Lecture given at KeeleMAC, July 6–8, 2015.

8. Chopin, in a letter to Tytus Woyciechowski, May 30, 1830 (written in Warsaw), in *Selected Correspondence of Fryderyk Chopin*, collected and annotated by Bronislaw Edward Sydow (London: William Heinemann, Ltd., 1962), 44.

9. John Rink, *Chopin: The Piano Concertos* (Cambridge: Cambridge University Press, 1977), 77.

10. Marek Haltof, *Peter Weir: When Cultures Collide* (New York: Twayne Publishers, 1996), 25.

11. Jonathan Rayner, *The Films of Peter Weir*, 2nd ed. (New York: Continuum, 2003), 80.

12. David Neumeyer, *Meaning and Interpretation of Music in Cinema* (Bloomington: Indiana University Press, 2015), 241.

13. Ibid.

14. This same approach to music occurs in *Fearless* (1993) with the first movement of Górecki's *Symphony No. 3*, as the music begins during the conclusion of the film and simply continues into the credits.

15. Citron's comments followed my presentation at the Voicing the Soundtrack Conference, April 15–16, 2016, held at the University of Texas at Austin. The word choice of *hanging* was a coy reference to *Picnic at Hanging Rock*.

16. Michael Bliss, *Dreams within a Dream: The Films of Peter Weir* (Carbondale: Southern Illinois Press, 2000), 142.

17. A composer is always in the control room for the television show, and in one scene, Philip Glass plays the composer.

18. Peter Weir, liner notes to *The Truman Show*.

19. Rebecca Doran Eaton, "Unheard Minimalisms" (PhD diss., The University of Texas at Austin, 2008), 190–216.

20. Eaton discusses the nondiegetic/diegetic/metadiegetic levels of narration in "Unheard Minimalisms," 192–97.

21. Of course, this music is quasi-recapitulatory, which makes the idea of "rediscovery" a bit less germane since that is most commonly how music is structured.

22. Eaton, "Unheard Minimalisms," 207.

23. Ibid., 205.

24. Ibid., 214.

25. Megan Abbott, "What We See and What We Seem," Reference booklet in Criterion Collection Blu-Ray/DVD Edition of *Picnic at Hanging Rock*, (CC2360BDDVD, 2014), 7.

Part Four

Narrative and Vococentrism

Chapter 12

Monocentrism, or Soundtracks in Space

Rediscovering Forbidden Planet*'s Multi-Speaker Release*

Eric Dienstfrey

In the Fall of 1955, Metro-Goldwyn-Mayer (MGM) chief Dory Schary accomplished what no studio chief had ever accomplished before: he signed New York musicians Bebe and Louis Barron to compose a fully electronic score for the studio's forthcoming science-fiction thriller, *Forbidden Planet* (1956).[1] At the time, the married composers were known for their *musique concrète* as well as their collaborations with John Cage, Anaïs Nin, and other artists with a penchant for acoustical experimentation. The Barrons' music for *Forbidden Planet* ultimately became an extension of their established avant-garde techniques. In lieu of traditional orchestrations, the score boasted synthetic buzzes, sirens, and thwamps. To no surprise, the soundtrack received considerable attention by critics.[2] These "electronic tonalities," as they were called in the opening titles, even prompted the Academy of Motion Picture Arts and Sciences to nominate *Forbidden Planet* for Best Special Effects. There was just one problem: Bebe and Louis Barron were not mentioned in the list of nominees. Instead, the awards announcement listed only MGM sound director Wesley Miller as the creator of the movie's iconic soundscapes.[3]

Forbidden Planet was not the first motion picture to see its sound effects—or "audibles"—recognized by the industry in the Special Effects category. *Portrait of Jennie* (1948), for instance, was nominated for the same award for its use of surround sound during the picture's climactic storm sequence. Though unlike *Forbidden Planet*, the designer of *Jennie*'s signature wind noises, James G. Stewart, was listed among the film's special effects team.[4] The Academy's decision to overlook the Barrons for similar acoustical labor was thus not taken lightly. The two composers immediately asked the courts to issue an injunction to stop the industry from announcing the award at its upcoming ceremony.[5] They also sued Schary and MGM for breach of contract, specifically for letting the Academy exclude their names from the list of key sound personnel.[6] According to the lawsuit, the Barrons designed the film's musical accompaniment as well as its innovative sound effects, whereas Miller merely dubbed these effects into the final mix. Such arguments nevertheless fell on deaf ears. The lawsuit was quickly dismissed, and the Academy's ceremony went ahead as scheduled.[7]

This short-lived legal battle was presumably understood to be no more than a simple disagreement over the dramatic value of the Barrons' electronic tonalities. After all, their narrative functions were, and still remain, ambiguous throughout the movie. At first glance, the sounds seem diegetic, not unlike the audibles nominated in years past. They add physical presence and believability to many of the low-budget set pieces, and they resemble the space-age noises later associated with science-fiction titles like *Star Wars* (1977) and *Tron* (1982). Yet as Rebecca Leydon and James Wierzbicki detail, the iconic blurps and thwamps also adhere to the conventions of nondiegetic accompaniment, wherein each character receives a unique leitmotif that repeats and develops over the course of the film.[8] As Bebe and Louis Barron acknowledged: "In *Forbidden Planet*—as in all of our work—we created individual cybernetic circuits for particular themes and leit motifs."[9] With this in mind, the Academy perhaps saw the Barrons' strange sounds merely as extensions of MGM's other musical experiments, such as the twelve-tone serialism featured in *East of Eden* (1954) and *The Cobweb* (1955).[10] By classifying the electronic noises as music, there was then no reason to also recognize the two composers in the category of Special Effects.

But was the legal dustup simply a disagreement over the ontology of the tonalities? In the pages that follow, I address this question by considering an overlooked piece of *Forbidden Planet*'s history: its stereophonic sound design. In so doing, I argue that MGM's engineers knowingly treated the Barrons' score as diegetic effects when mixing the film for multi-speaker playback. To explain this conclusion, I introduce an aesthetic concept that I call "monocentrism." The concept builds upon Michel Chion's theory of vococentrism, particularly David Neumeyer's expansion of this theory, which states that classically structured films prioritize the voice above music and effects, and that mixers often lower the volume of nonvocal elements in order to maintain the audibility and clarity of spoken dialogue.[11] My concept of monocentrism extends Neumeyer's observations to stereo and surround sound. Rather than altering the volume of individual sounds, I contend that mixers routinely move dialogue, music, and effects to separate loudspeaker locations in order to preserve the primacy of the voice. In most instances, dialogue plays exclusively through a sound system's center speaker, much as it would in mono theaters. I detail such acoustical designs through a brief analysis of *The Martian* (2015), one of many contemporary blockbusters influenced by *Forbidden Planet*'s soundscapes.

Following this analysis, I chronicle monocentric practices during the 1950s, with particular attention given to the stereo technology used during *Forbidden Planet*'s theatrical release. I then reconstruct *Forbidden Planet*'s multi-speaker design in relation to these stereophonic practices. Through this analysis, I explain how the film's treatment of the musical score broke from conventional mixing techniques. The electronic tonalities specifically panned from speaker to speaker in concert with onscreen action. These acoustical effects invited audiences to interpret the musical score not as nondiegetic accompaniment but as diegetic noises. In other words, Bebe Barron, Louis Barron, and MGM were likely in agreement as to the dramatic function of the film's electronic tonalities; they were special diegetic effects. I thus end my analysis by offering an alternative explanation for why the two composers were presumably snubbed by the Academy.

Monocentrism: Vococentrism in Stereo

As Neumeyer argues, Hollywood films are vococentric.[12] Their soundtracks are constructed into unified systems wherein dialogue, music, and effects collectively provide narrative clarity and aesthetic coherence to each motion picture. And as the term indicates, these soundtrack systems manifest an internal hierarchy that prioritizes the voice over all other sonic elements. To achieve this hierarchy, rerecording engineers generally move music and effects out of the way when mixing scenes with dialogue, particularly when the dialogue conveys important story information. For example, a party might begin with source music blasting from the soundtrack, but once characters begin talking, the music lowers in volume in order to bolster the dialogue's intelligibility. If the music failed to move out of the way, and instead lingered in the soundtrack at a relatively loud volume, the soundtrack might call attention to itself and invite filmgoers to find meaning in this acoustical decision. (It could be presumed that the music was meant to be noticed because it enhances the film's broader themes or expresses a character's subjectivity.) In this regard, vococentrism is more than a storytelling aesthetic that prioritizes clarity and speech; it is also a system of norms and variations that filmmakers abide by in order to arouse an audience's interpretative instincts.

For much of the studio era, vococentrism was a defining feature of Hollywood filmmaking, and it remains a dominant trait of contemporary cinema as well, even for an acoustically adventurous surround sound release like *The Martian* (2015). During the film's climactic sequence, for instance, American astronaut

Mark Watney (Matt Damon) launches himself into Mars's stratosphere in hopes of reuniting with his former crew members who concurrently orbit the desolate planet. The sequence contains a number of conversations between Watney and Commander Melissa Lewis (Jessica Chastain) as they attempt to connect at breakneck speeds, and between Lewis and her crew as they improvise ways to decelerate their spaceship. And to accentuate the obstacles that these astronauts face, the volume of the music and effects often overpowers their dialogue. When Lewis tethers herself to the spaceship and propels toward Watney, the underscore at times plays approximately twelve decibels louder than the voice of Beth Johanssen (Kata Mara), who updates Lewis about her distance from Watney. Similarly, the film adds loud "whooshes" as the astronauts fly toward each other, details that are humorous given an absence of wind (or sound) in outer space. Such creative decisions embody what historian Jeff Smith terms the "sound of intensified continuity," an aesthetic that favors wider dynamic ranges and densely layered effects—even nondiegetic effects—in order to highlight the affective, sensory, and phenomenological dimensions of a film.[13] In *The Martian*, this aesthetic accentuates acoustical flourishes that call attention to the astronaut's life-threatening predicament. Consequently, the dialogue at times seems to take a proverbial back seat to the scene's other noises.

The scene's vocal performances, however, never lose their perceptual salience within the soundtrack. In keeping with vococentric principles, the rerecording engineers—led by Paul Massey—utilized an alternative means of privileging dialogue in theaters, one that allowed the musical gestures and effects to play at loud volumes without completely masking spoken information.[14] Massey and his sound team mixed voices to play from one loudspeaker, and they directed competing sounds to play from other loudspeakers. Lewis's communications with her crew, for instance, play through the loudspeaker at the center of the screen, as does Watley's wry commentary. However, there are a few exceptions. When Watley learns the spaceship will miss his intercept by 312 meters, Watley retorts, "Great, I'll wave at you guys as I go by." He delivers this line while rotating across the screen, and to punctuate his precarity, his voice pans horizontally from the left speakers to the right speakers. Similarly, when the rescue mission succeeds and Johanssen tells NASA "We got him," her voice plays through the center loudspeaker and echoes in the sides. Though the film's stereo design prioritizes important acoustical information by directing nearly all dialogue to the middle of the screen, it deviates from this norm for dramatic emphasis, as is common in vococentric soundtracks.

In contrast, the scene's music and effects play almost exclusively from offscreen locations. The roar of the rocket that propels Watley into space, as well as the controlled detonation of the crew's makeshift bomb, blast from the side speakers and reverberate through the rears, a design that situates the explosions within the space of the movie theater. Likewise, the bursts of air that propel Lewis and Watley toward each other pan from speaker to speaker in concert with the on-screen action. Conversely, the music does not move around the theater. Rather, it radiates loudly through the sides and quietly through the center. This design allows the score to remain forceful throughout the sequence, and to even rise to peak levels during suspenseful moments without masking the dialogue. In sum, the spatial separation of sound allows engineers to sequester music and effects to the film's background—at times behind the audience—so characters can deliver their lines unobstructed at the front of the theater.

I call this spatial organization of sound monocentrism, both a reference to vococentrism and to Hollywood's earlier acoustical practices. During the transition to sound, talking pictures were monaural. They were distributed to theaters on a single channel of audio—either a record's groove or a narrow optical track. The sounds in this channel would then play from a single loudspeaker or from a group of speakers arranged around the center of the screen. When studios began releasing films with multiple audio channels, such as the two-track premieres for *Hell's Angels* (1930), they continued to adhere to monaural aesthetics.[15] Dialogue played from the center of the screen while the side speakers were reserved for gunfire, jet engines, and other background noises. Because these screenings required multiple tracks of sound, they were not technically monaural. Rather, they were monocentric. They stored dialogue and other important narrative information in the center channel, while the sides played details that smaller venues could jettison if they lacked space for extra speakers.

Despite the many innovations to stereophonic technology following the transition to talking pictures, multitrack films have remained primarily monocentric, as heard throughout six-track roadshows of the 1960s, Dolby Stereo releases of the 1970s and 1980s, and—as *The Martian* illustrates—the digital surround sound titles that shake today's multiplexes.[16] There are several reasons for this longevity. First, centric practices are common, if not inherent, to all forms of art. As theorist Rudolph Arnheim contends in his essay, *The Power of the Center* (1982), the concentricity of circles and the eccentricity of grid lines are integral to the way humans express themselves aesthetically and, in turn, have become structural components of artistic representation.[17] Cinematic representation is no exception. Although Arnheim famously dismissed talking pictures for their apparent "violation" of basic aesthetic laws, film's audiovisual appeal nevertheless derives from its adherence to long-held principles of clarity, simplicity, and balance, as well as the norms of centrism that Arnheim details throughout history.[18] Monocentric soundtrack designs merely extend these aesthetic norms into the realm of stereophonic storytelling.

Similarly, monocentrism strengthens cinematic absorption. Films are roughly two hours in length, and sound technicians generally want audiences to focus on the story the entire time. By keeping dialogue in the center channel, filmgoers are likewise encouraged to keep their eyes on the screen. If engineers routinely send dialogue to the rear channels, audiences might turn their heads away from the image to locate the person talking—an occurrence that many mixers fear would undermine a film's dramatic impact.[19] In this context, monocentric sound designs became a practical means to control the attention of moviegoers, and as such they continue to be produced by Hollywood.

Monocentrism's greatest value to filmmakers, however, resides in the way it standardizes motion picture playback. Like many other Hollywood releases, *The Martian* is designed to play through a wide variety of sound systems, from 64-channel Dolby Atmos for the industry's largest screens, to traditional configurations for the home. Though these loudspeaker variations could interfere with the way audiences experience stories like *The Martian*, the film's spatial acoustics nevertheless remain constant from theater to theater because each stereo system can be partitioned into (a) the center channel, and (b) its surrounding channels. In large and small theaters alike, dialogue plays front and center while music and effects become an acoustical frame that encircles the voice and bolsters its prominence. The most important element of the soundtrack, the voice, therefore never loses its perceptual salience, even in cinemas that surround audiences with subwoofers and other sensory attractions. In effect, monocentrism preserves the principles of vococentrism in any theater regardless of its loudspeaker arrangement.

Monocentrism in the 1950s

Although most films adhere to monocentric principles, and have done so since the introduction of sound, technicians routinely disagree as to what constitutes a proper monocentric soundtrack. For instance, during action sequences with offscreen gunfire and explosions, some mixers send key effects to only the side speakers, while others routinely pan these sounds to the rear speakers.[20] Some technicians even mix music into specially installed ceiling channels, as demonstrated by the premiere showings for *Ben Hur* (1959) and *Man of Steel* (2013).[21] Such aesthetic debates also pertain to the reproduction of dialogue. Whereas a film like *The Martian* reproduces voices generally through the center channel, other monocentric films throughout history have been far more adventurous when it comes to panning dialogue across the front loudspeakers.

These stereo effects were especially common in the 1950s. As scholars note, it was during this decade that 20th Century Fox introduced the popular CinemaScope format, a technology that promised filmgoers new kinds of audiovisual sensations.[22] Each 35mm CinemaScope print stored an image that was nearly twice as wide as the standard 1.37-to-1 picture ratio. And this expansive canvas was further enhanced by an equally immersive stereo system. In place of a single optical track, CinemaScope prints housed four separate tracks of magnetically encoded audio, each corresponding to a different playback channel. The left, center, and right tracks contained information for the three loudspeakers behind the screen, and the fourth track contained effects that played through the banks of speakers located on the rear and side walls of the auditorium.[23]

To highlight the technology's sensory possibilities, Fox initially recorded its CinemaScope productions onto three separate microphone tracks. Actors located on the left side of the sound stage would speak into the left microphone at the loudest volume, whereas actors at the other end of the stage would speak into the right microphone.[24] These stereo effects were extraordinarily noticeable when they played in theaters. For instance, during theatrical screenings of *River of No Return* (1954), when Matt Calder (Robert Mitchum) and Kay Weston (Marilyn Monroe) converse from opposite sides of the frame—a common staging throughout the feature—their voices bounced between the left and right sides of the auditorium, as their voices were recorded on the set by the left and right microphones.[25] These multi-mike techniques became an inventive way for engineers to accentuate onscreen dialogue without straying too far from vococentric principles.

Such techniques, however, were quite demanding of filmmakers. The use of additional microphone tracks increased equipment and labor costs, and—as Fox engineer Lorin Grignon documented in detail—it created a host of obstacles when staging scenes for multiple camera angles and, later, when editing together the different sound perspectives in postproduction.[26] As a result, many studios continued recording production sound onto only one audio track. Their stereo effects were then generated with special rerecording equipment, such as Westrex's line of RA-1500 mixing consoles.[27] This equipment enabled rerecording technicians to keep production recordings in the center speaker for most scenes, and it allowed them to open up the dialogue to the side channel during voice-offs and climactic moments. The flexibility therefore made it easy for engineers to adhere to monocentric norms when mixing their single-track recordings into four-track stereo release prints.

It was during this time that many studios also began experimenting with Perspecta, a playback format that could reproduce stereo effects without special release prints.[28] Like the industry's monaural films, Perspecta soundtracks were encoded as single optical soundtracks and distributed onto standard 35mm filmstrips. The core difference between a standard release and a Perspecta release was that a Perspecta soundtrack contained three low-frequency control tones at

30Hz, 35Hz, and 40Hz—tones that fell below the standard playback range for optical sound systems. The sub-audible tones would increase and decrease in volume, and these shifts in intensity directed the soundtrack to the left, center, or right loudspeakers during select sequences.[29] Thus, if a rerecording engineer wanted a gunshot to emanate from the left side of the auditorium, he would raise the volume of only the 30Hz tone when mixing that sound for the release print. Theaters with special Perspecta integrators would then decode this tone and play the gunshot through the left loudspeaker. Thus, the technology produced stereo effects without requiring studios or theaters to fully invest in expensive multitrack equipment.

Perspecta was the invention of C. Robert Fine, a seasoned audio engineer known for high-quality music reproductions. While at Reeves Sound Studios in New York, Fine famously cut the disks for several prominent symphonic recordings, including Virgil Thomson's score to *Louisiana Story* (1948).[30] And with his wife, Wilma Cozart, Fine similarly oversaw the acoustical design of the popular "Living Presence" series for Mercury Records.[31] Fine's reputation in the music industry added prestige to his new theatrical format. Consequently, many in Hollywood jumped at the chance to apply Fine's invention to dozens of motion pictures. By the mid-1950s, MGM, Paramount, Warners, and Columbia were all releasing pictures in Perspecta stereo, including *Seven Brides for Seven Brothers* (1954), *A Star is Born* (1954), *White Christmas* (1954), *Bad Day at Black Rock* (1955), *The Man Who Knew Too Much* (1956), *Forbidden Planet*, and even the 1954 rerelease of *Gone with the Wind* (1939).[32]

Exhibitors showed admiration for Fine's invention as well. Whereas installing Fox's four-track system cost roughly $15,000 per screen, Perspecta's installation rates were reportedly as low as $850.[33] The price encouraged a number of smaller theaters to install the system. In October 1954, *Motion Picture Daily* reported that nearly 700 screens were wired with Perspecta integrators, and by the end of 1955 this number quadrupled to nearly 2,800 screens worldwide.[34] Hundreds of thousands of filmgoers therefore were listening to Perspecta sound designs throughout the 1950s, perhaps even unknowingly. Indeed, when Fred Astaire sings about "Stereophonic Sound" in the middle of *Silk Stockings* (1957), some audiences would have heard the number's acoustical effects resound not through traditional stereo technology—to which the lyrics referred—but through Fine's single-track format. And it is doubtful that many filmgoers noticed.

Perspecta's invisibility was no accident. Fine wanted his format's acoustical effects to sound indistinguishable from those of four-track stereo. For instance, throughout the Perspecta mix of *The Barefoot Contessa* (1954)—a mix encoded at Fine's New York studio—the onscreen dialogue between Harry Dawes (Humphrey Bogart) and Maria Vargas (Ava Gardner) often vacillates between the left and right loudspeakers, similar to the movement of Mitchum's and Monroe's voices during four-track screenings of *River of No Return*.[35] As historians note, such stereo effects were hallmarks of Perspecta soundtracks in general.[36] But they rarely occurred when onscreen conversations were accompanied by nondiegetic score. During those scenes, if the dialogue panned between the side speakers, so too would the musical accompaniment. Since nondiegetic scores were expected to remain stationary during a movie, these stereo effects would have surely confused audiences. Many dialogue sequences were thus cautiously mixed. Their sounds emanated from the center loudspeaker, while the side channels played the same audio roughly eight to ten decibels lower.[37] Perspecta films, in turn, illustrated a unique variation of monocentrism, one in which the soundtrack mostly played through the center channel, while the localization effects that defined stereo releases were largely reserved for dramatic sequences.

Forbidden Planet in Perspecta

The 1956 theatrical release of *Forbidden Planet* was thus historically significant. Rather than adhere to industry norms, its Perspecta mix deviated from monocentric principles, particularly in regard to the spatial design of its electronic score. Whereas *Barefoot Contessa*, *River of No Return*, and even *The Martian* relegate their musical accompaniment to the soundtrack's background, *Forbidden Planet* routinely pans the Barrons' score between the theater's loudspeakers. In effect, the film's construction treats the music as if it were diegetic information.

Such departures from Hollywood's soundtrack conventions were undoubtedly motivated by the film's eccentric story. It follows a team of astronauts, led by Commander J. J. Adams (Leslie Nielsen), as they attempt to rescue scientists stranded on the distant planet of Altair-4. After landing on the planet, however, the astronauts endure a series of attacks from a species of invisible monsters. Adams soon learns that these monsters are controlled by the thoughts of the chief scientist, Doctor Morbius (Walter Pidgeon). Morbius had uncovered an ancient technology that inadvertently causes his subconscious desires to manifest themselves as violent creatures. And due to his displeasure at seeing the astronauts court his daughter Alta (Anne Francis), these "monsters of the id" attack the crew and sabotage their mission.

The film was loosely inspired by Shakespeare's *The Tempest*, with the play's Mediterranean locale transformed into Altair-4, and with the titular storms reimagined as invisible villains.[38] The narration thus centers around the monsters' attacks, and the sound design for each of these sequences adds to the mysterious nature of the antagonists. For instance, roughly one hour into the film, audiences witness an invisible creature sneak into the docked spaceship. First, its footprints appear to walk along the planet's soil, then the steps of the ship's large metal staircase bend one-by-one as the monster boards the cabin. The scene consists of a single shot, and to complement this simplicity the Barrons' sonic accompaniment remains eerily sparse. The upper registers contain pulsations of a single electrical tone, while the lower registers play thwamps in synchrony with the footsteps. As Rebecca Leydon details, the Barrons achieved such sounds by eschewing traditional instrumentation in favor of homemade equipment, including vacuum-tube oscillators and extensive feedback paths. Noises from these oscillators were then recorded onto magnetic tapes and manipulated by speed changes, splices, and other studio techniques.[39] The resultant pulses and thwamps—sounds that one critic called "skin-prickling"—presumably stood out to typical filmgoers.[40]

To further enhance the salience of the music, MGM's rerecording mixers peppered the score with stereo effects that steered the noises around many of the industry's theaters, specifically those wired for Perspecta technology. Today, however, such experimental effects are nearly impossible to hear. Exhibitors have long since discarded the integrator equipment that once enabled *Forbidden Planet* to play with a Perspecta stereo design. Additionally, most home video releases of the film are remastered for digital formats like 5.1 and 2.0, neither of which provides a faithful representation of 1950s stereo aesthetics. One can only study *Forbidden Planet*'s original multi-speaker mix by recovering the three low-frequency control tones embedded in unrestored versions of its soundtrack. Interestingly, these tones remain intact in the film's French language dub available on the 2010 Blu ray release, as this dub appears to be a digitization of the optical track that played in European theaters during the 1950s.[41]

To excavate the Perspecta mix from these control tones, I uploaded the French soundtrack into Sonic Visualizer, software that provides detailed spectrograms for every bit of data on any given audio track, including low-frequency metadata.[42] The software allowed me to generate a clear picture of how MGM's engineers used the Perspecta system when mixing *Forbidden Planet*. During the famous footsteps scene specifically, the high-frequency pulses and low-frequency thwamps play from the center speaker, they move to the right speaker as the monster's footsteps move right, and they return to the center speaker when the camera repositions the footsteps back in the center of the frame. Thus, during the film's original theatrical run, the sounds would have panned from speaker to speaker in correspondence with the movement of the monster.

Such stereophonic designs are not entirely foreign to motion picture soundtracks. During the Dolby Atmos release of *Gravity* (2013), for instance, Steven Price's score regularly pans throughout the back, side, and ceiling channels—an effect that, as Miguel Mera argues, frees the music from its traditional sound stage spatialization.[43] That being said, these kinds of stereo experiments have never been common in Hollywood. Indeed, the unique acoustical effects heard during *Forbidden Planet*'s

Perspecta mix would have been a noticeable departure from the norms of musical accompaniment at the time of the film's release.

One might conclude that such localization effects were simply a mistake, a consequence of MGM's attempts to turn a single-track release into a multichannel soundscape. Film critic Rick Mitchell argued as much after hearing *Forbidden Planet* play in its original Perspecta stereo design:

> On the whole the presentation resembled the results of putting a mono track through a good stereo synthesizer, however in dialog scenes where attempts were made to position the dialog on the screen with the actor speaking it, rather incongruously the entire track, including production effects and ambience would also jump from speaker to speaker![44]

Mitchell's comments were in reference to several sequences, such as when Robbie the Robot humorously delivers sixty gallons of bourbon to the cook, or when Adams, Alta, and Morbius all hide from the invisible creatures in the engine room. Both scenes combine dialogue with musical accompaniment, and like Mitchell describes, as the voices of the characters pan between the left and right loudspeakers, so do the Barrons' electronic tonalities. These types of movements were a byproduct of Perspecta's methods of compression. Because the system required dialogue, music, and effects to share the same soundtrack on release prints, whenever engineers would direct dialogue to the left loudspeaker, all other elements on the soundtrack, including the music, were forced to play from this loudspeaker as well.

But not every instance of musical panning contains dialogue. Indeed, as the aforementioned id monster slowly approaches the spaceship, the Barrons' tonalities are the only elements on the soundtrack. The movement of the music was therefore not tied to any concurrent movement of voices. Even more interesting, the score does not simply pan back and forth between the center and right speaker. The stereo design is instead far more intricate. For every low-frequency thwamp, the control tones shift their volumes in a manner that quickly sends these noises back and forth between the center and right loudspeakers, and briefly to the left speaker, too. This complex soundscape suggests that the thwamps are reverberating in space. Perhaps the monsters are so large that their footsteps shake the ground as they walk, and these tonalities are the noises that emanate from each footstep and that continue to radiate throughout the setting. Moreover, this audiovisual effect happens repeatedly throughout the scene, an indication that the panning of the score was not a one-off mistake, but an intentional effect designed to invite audiences to pay greater attention to the music.

Interestingly, this listening activity is built into the soundtrack's larger narrative structure. By the time the monster boards the spaceship, the film has repeatedly asked audiences to consider the diegetic possibilities of the electronic tonalities.

As James Wierzbicki argues, "throughout *Forbidden Planet* the audience member is made to wonder, especially at the onset of a cue, about the source of what is being heard."[45] In the opening scene, for example, Adams orders his crew to prepare for the ship's deceleration from light speed. They then briefly turn into green beams of light that protect the men from injury during these powerful changes in velocity. The score for this sequence consists of beeps and buzzes as well as various electrical tones that rise and fall in pitch. Being that these noises resemble many of the musical effects heard previously during the film's opening titles, audiences might presume that the beeps and buzzes are also nondiegetic accompaniment. Yet the rising and falling of each sound's pitch also aligns with the spaceship's changes in velocity, and this audiovisual correspondence encourages filmgoers to read the electronic tonalities as the noises made by the spaceship. As this sequence demonstrates, the exact source of the electronic score is often ambiguous. In response, audiences were guided to pay greater attention to the soundtrack, as if the sounds could provide explanations for the mysterious phenomena that define the story world.

By the end of the film, however, these acoustical ambiguities all but disappear from the broader stereo design. The electronic tonalities become synchronized to footsteps and other onscreen actions, and they move freely through the theater in concert with these actions. Audiences accustomed to Hollywood's stylistic conventions were unlikely to have interpreted these roving sounds simply as nondiegetic accompaniment, for such localization of music was rare, if not completely unheard of, at the time of the film's release. Rather, those who heard the film play in Perspecta were invited to interpret these buzzes, beeps, blurps, and thwamps as the physical presence of an invisible entity that could not be represented through traditional visual techniques. The history of monocentrism therefore explains why the Barrons' allegations against MGM were misdirected. Contrary to the composers' accusations, the studio's sound department did more than simply set the decibel levels of the musical accompaniment. MGM performed a creative feat that was necessary given the visual limitations of the story. When the score passed through the studio's mixing consoles, Wesley Miller and his team of rerecording engineers changed each cue's ontological value. They turned the Barrons' nondiegetic tonalities into elements of the film's diegesis.

Conclusion

As this chapter demonstrates, stereo complicates vococentric practices by adding a spatial dimension to the soundtrack. The concept of monocentrism clarifies this spatial transformation by defining the aesthetic principles that govern how dialogue, music, and effects are traditionally mixed for multi-speaker soundscapes.

Forbidden Planet serves as an unusual case study for how monocentrism functions, for instead of abiding by the industry's mixing norms, MGM's engineers deviated from these conventions in ways that enhanced the film's narration. When the Barrons' music moved through the space of the theater, it signaled to audiences that the electronic tonalities were no longer mere background accompaniment, but a conduit for diegetic information. In turn, the music became a special stereo effect, much like the Oscar-nominated winds that shrieked to the sides of audiences during *Portrait of Jennie* several years prior.

It therefore remains curious that MGM and the Academy failed to add the names of Bebe and Louis Barron to the list of personnel responsible for creating the film's audible effects. We can speculate that there may have been animosity between Dore Schary and the two composers, or that MGM routinely prevented contract employees from receiving nominations for their creative labor. However, it seems more likely that the Barrons misunderstood the kinds of acoustical sensations that the Academy intended to recognize. Instead of commending the tonalities themselves, the Special Effects category celebrated the ways that MGM's Wesley Miller fit these tonalities into the film's multichannel soundscapes. When the science-fiction thriller was released, such localization effects were a novelty. Filmmakers generally adhered to conceptions of proper fidelity, wherein music was to remain motionless in the space of the theater, much like a concert stage.[46] *Forbidden Planet* was different. The movement of the music challenged these ideals by giving life to story elements that lacked physical, pro-filmic referents. In nominating Miller, the Academy was recognizing his departure from the industry's monocentric ideals. Though Hollywood valued these ideals for their storytelling efficiency, those who successfully strayed from such conventions were praised for their ingenuity as well.

Forbidden Planet would not be the last time that principal sound workers were overlooked by the Academy. Wendy Carlos's and Frank Serafine's acoustical contributions to *Tron* were conspicuously neglected when the film's mix was nominated, and when *Stars Wars* won the Oscar for Best Sound the Academy omitted Ben Burtt's name from the list of nominees (the famed sound designer would instead receive a Special Achievement award during the ceremony).[47] Bebe and Louis Barron's exclusion from the Special Effects category was thus not a unique event. Rather, it was a harbinger of the Academy's difficulties when recognizing all unionized and nonunionized personnel who contribute to a movie's soundtrack. Though in many ways, the Barrons did not need the nomination in order to win accolades for their time in Hollywood. The score for *Forbidden Planet* helped the two composers secure a series of high-profile theater and television commissions in the decades that followed.[48] Today, the film is routinely heralded by scholars and sound technicians as one of the more innovative and influential pieces of music ever written for the screen.

In contrast, Wesley Miller's contributions to the science-fiction thriller are trumpeted at a far softer volume. The film's audible effects failed to win the Academy Award; the prize instead went to *The Ten Commandments* (1956).[49] And in recent restorations of *Forbidden Planet*, Miller's spatial effects have been replaced with an entirely new 5.1 stereo design, one that is more typical of monocentric practices. Indeed, despite his Oscar nomination, Miller and his sonic achievements have become merely a footnote in history. The Barrons thus presumably misunderstood the actual value of a nomination. For if the two composers knew that they would one day be championed, while Miller would be all but forgotten, it is doubtful that they would have taken legal action against the very producers who could have hired them to compose more electronic music for the cinema.

Notes

1. Donald John Long, "*Forbidden* Film Score: The Life, Death and Rebirth of Music for a '50s Sci-Fi Classic," *Film Score Monthly* 9, 4 (Apr. 2004): 23–25.

2. For instance, see Philip K. Scheuer, "Wail of Tortured Electrons Provides Eerie Film Score," *Los Angeles Times*, Feb. 26, 1956: D2; "Eerie New 'Plastic Sound,'" *New York Herald Tribune*, Apr. 15, 1956: D4.

3. Edwin Schallert, "Surprises Mark Selections for 29th Academy Awards," *Los Angeles Times*, Feb. 19, 1957: 2.

4. "Nominations Made for Oscar Honors," *Los Angeles Times*, Feb. 11, 1949: 4.

5. Thomas M. Pryor, "2 Ask Injunction to Bar Film Prize," *New York Times*, Mar. 27, 1957: 27.

6. "Suit Seeks to Block Oscar Movie Nominee," *Los Angeles Times*, Mar. 27, 1957: B2.

7. "Writ Denied to Halt Sound Effects Oscar," *Los Angeles Times*, Mar. 28, 1957: 2.

8. Rebecca Leydon, "*Forbidden Planet*: Effects and Affects in the Electro Avant Garde," in *Off the Planet: Music, Sounds and Science Fiction Cinema*, ed. Philip Hayward (Eastleigh, U.K.: John Libbey, 2004), 61–76; James Wierzbicki, *Louis and Bebe Barron's* Forbidden Planet*: A Film Score Guide* (Lanham, Md.: Scarecrow Press, 2005), 99–153.

9. Quoted in Timothy D. Taylor, *Strange Sounds: Music, Technology & Culture* (New York: Routledge, 2001), 94.

10. Sabine M. Feisst, "Arnold Schoenberg and Cinematic Art," *The Musical Quarterly* 83, 2 (Spring 1999): 106.

11. Michel Chion, *The Voice in Cinema*, trans. Claudia Gorbman (New York: Columbia University Press, 1999), 1–6; David Neumeyer, *Meaning and Interpretation of Music in Cinema* (Bloomington: Indiana University Press, 2015), 3–49.

12. Neumeyer, *Meaning and Interpretation of Music in Cinema*, 3–49.

13. Jeff Smith, "The Sound of Intensified Continuity," in *The Oxford Handbook of New Audiovisual Aesthetics*, ed. John Richardson, Claudia Gorbman, and Carol Vernallis (New York: Oxford University Press, 2013), 331–56.

14. For additional discussion of the Massey's creative decisions, see "The Sound of The Martian with Re-recording Mixer Paul Massey," *Soundworks Collection*, Dec. 27, 2015. https://sound

cloud.com/soundworkscollection/the-sound-of-the-martian-with-re-recording-mixer-paul -massey. Accessed August 3, 2018.

15. Donald Crafton, *The Talkies: American Cinema's Transition to Sound, 1926–1931* (Berkeley: University of California Press, 1999), 349–50.

16. James Corcoran and Douglas Williams, "The Recording and Re-Recording of Stereophonic Sound for Wide-Screen Motion Pictures," *Journal of the SMPTE* 77, 12 (Dec. 1968): 1292–94; Jay Beck, *Designing Sound: Audiovisual Aesthetics in 1970s American Cinema* (New Brunswick, N.J.: Rutgers University Press, 2016), 169.

17. Rudolf Arnheim, *The Power of the Center* (Berkeley: University of California Press, 1982).

18. Rudolf Arnheim, *Film as Art* (Berkeley: University of California Press, 1957), 199–230.

19. Smith, "The Sound of Intensified Continuity," 342.

20. Mark Kerins, *Beyond Dolby (Stereo): Cinema in the Digital Sound Age* (Bloomington: Indiana University Press, 2010).

21. Milo Lory, interview with Irene Atkins, in *American Film Institute/Louis B. Mayer Oral History Collection* (Glen Rock, N.J.: Microfilming Corporation of America, 1975), 105–9; Benjamin Wright, "Atmos Now: Dolby Laboratories, Mixing Ideology and Hollywood Sound Production," *Living Stereo: Histories and Cultures of Multichannel Sound*, ed. Paul Théberge, Kyle Devine, and Tom Everrett (New York: Bloomsbury Academic, 2015), 241–42.

22. For examples, see John Belton, *Widescreen Cinema* (Cambridge: Harvard University Press, 1992), 113–57; Ariel Rogers, *Cinematic Appeals: The Experience of New Movie Technologies* (New York: Columbia University Press, 2013), 61–90.

23. E. I. Sponable, H. E. Bragg, and L. D. Grignon, "Design Considerations of CinemaScope Film," *Journal of the SMPTE* 63, 1 (July 1954): 1–4.

24. Matthew Malsky, "The Grandeur(s) of CinemaScope: Early Experiments in Cinematic Stereophony," in *Living Stereo*, 207–25.

25. The film's original four-track mix can be accessed via the 4.0 audio option on *River of No Return*, directed by Otto Preminger (1954; Beverly Hills: 20th Century Fox, 2012), Blu-ray.

26. Lorin Grignon, "Experiment in Stereophonic Sound," *Journal of the SMPTE* 61, 3 (Sept. 1953): 364–79.

27. J. G. Frayne and E. W. Templin, "Stereophonic Recording and Reproducing Equipment," *Journal of the SMPTE* 61, 3 (Sept. 1953): 395–407.

28. Nathan Platte, "Postwar Hollywood, 1947–1967," in *Sound: Dialogue, Music, and Effects*, ed. Kathryn Kalinak (Piscataway, N.J.: Rutgers University Press, 2015), 67–73.

29. Robert Fine, "Perspecta—the All-Purpose Recording and Reproducing Sound System," *International Projectionist* (July 1954): 32–33, 41–42; Norman H. Crowhurst, "Advantages, Scope and Limitations of the Perspecta Stereophonic System," *Journal of the SMPTE* 64, 4 (Apr. 1955): 184–89.

30. Thomas Fine, "Less Is More: The Mercury Living Presence Recording Technique," *Tape Op* (July/Aug. 2012): 22–32.

31. Robert Baird, "A Fine Art," *Stereophile* (July 2012): 57–61.

32. "Pictures Here and on the Way with Perspecta," *Motion Picture Daily*, Oct. 27, 1954: 8, 12; "Feature Index," *BoxOffice Barometer*, Feb. 9, 1957: 131; Jean-Pierre Verscheure, "The

Challenge of Sound Restoration from 1927 to Digital," *Film History* 7, 3 (Autumn 1995): 264–76.

33. "Exhibs Resist Costly 'Sound,'" *Variety*, Oct. 21, 1953: 11, 22; "Magnetic vs. Perspecta Sound Poses Foreign Contrast to Situation in U.S.," *Variety*, Mar. 24, 1954: 15.

34. Sherwin Kane, "Tradewise . . .," *Motion Picture Daily*, Oct. 27, 1954: 1; Lloyd Thompson, "Progress Committee Report," *Journal of the SMPTE* 65, 5 (May 1956): 256.

35. George Schutz, "Full-Scale Sound for the Wide-Screen Techniques," *Motion Picture Daily*, Oct. 27, 1954: 6. The film's original Perspecta mix can be accessed via the 3.0 audio option on *The Barefoot Contessa*, directed by Joseph L. Mankiewicz (1954; Glendale, Calif.: Twilight Time, 2016), Blu-ray.

36. Verscheure, "The Challenge of Sound Restoration," 269–74; Platte, "Postwar Hollywood, 1947–1967," 70.

37. Charles R. Daily, "Progress Committee Report," *Journal of the SMPTE* 64, 5 (May 1955): 234.

38. Bradley Schaeur, *Escape Velocity: American Science Fiction Film, 1950–1982* (Middletown, Conn.: Wesleyan University Press, 2017), 57.

39. Leydon, "*Forbidden Planet*," 62. See also Ted Greenwald, "The Self-Destructing Modules behind the Revolutionary 1956 Soundtrack of *Forbidden Planet*," *Keyboard Magazine* (Feb. 1986): 54–65.

40. "Eerie New 'Plastic Sound,'" D4.

41. *Forbidden Planet*, directed by Fred Wilcox (1956; Beverly Hills: 20th Century Fox, 2010), Blu ray.

42. The control tones are a few cycles off from their original frequencies. This indicates that the audio track weathered significant transcoding over time. It was likely ported to digital tape as well as converted between European (PAL) and North American (NTSC) video standards. During these conversions, its frame-rate would have shifted, causing the three tones to move to a slightly different frequency range.

43. Miguel Mera, "Towards 3-D Sound: Spatial Presence and the Space Vacuum," in *The Palgrave Handbook of Sound Design and Music in Screen Media: Integrated Soundtracks*, ed. Liz Greene and Danijela Kulezic-Wilson (London: Palgrave Macmillan, 2016), 91–111.

44. Rick Mitchell, "More History of 4-Track: 35mm 4-Track Magnetic Stereo: The Undocumented Years," in *Hollywood Sound Design and Moviesound Newsletter: A Case Study of the End of the Analog Age*, ed. David E. Stone with Vanessa Theme Ament (New York: Routledge, 2017), 96.

45. Wierzbicki, *Louis and Bebe Barron's* Forbidden Planet, 152.

46. For more discussion on this fixed sound stage aesthetic, see Mera, "Towards 3-D Sound," 102–3.

47. "The Oscar Nominations," *Screen International*, Feb. 27, 1983: 8; "Winners of Academy Awards for 1977," *BoxOffice*, Apr. 10, 1978: 3.

48. Wierzbicki, *Louis and Bebe Barron's* Forbidden Planet, 14–15.

49. "Oscar Winners," *American Cinematographer* 38, 4 (Apr. 1957): 228–30.

Chapter 13

Sound and the Comic/Horror Romance Film

Formula, Affect, and Inflection

Janet Staiger

Occasionally, I have taught the horror film, and, thus, when *Zombieland* (2009), directed by Ruben Fleischer appeared, I dutifully watched it. Almost immediately, however, I eliminated it from my collection of horror cinema. True enough: it has lots of zombies and a particularly horrific opening with plenty of blood and gore and a few occasions of the startle effect to make spectators jump. Indeed, the film is littered with classic horror music and sound tropes. But within five minutes, its tone was obviously that of a comedy, and within twenty minutes, with the arrival of a male buddy, Tallahassee (Woody Harrelson), to accompany our hero, Columbus (Jesse Eisenberg), and two young women, Wichita (Emma Stone) and Little Rock (Abigail Breslin), one of whom was just the age of Columbus, who is traveling mostly to find companionship, it was obvious where the plot was headed. Somehow Columbus would hook up with Wichita after the zombies provided some trials and tribulations. Boy meets girl, loses girl, regains her. Moreover, the romance obstacles are not really the zombies, of course, but rather character flaws: in him, his rule-making; in her, lack of trust.

Additionally, *Zombieland* did not enact the horror formula of equilibrium, disequilibrium caused by possibly unnatural events, explanation of the phenomenon, actions to avert the tribulation, and temporary cessation of the threat. No narrative question arises about the cause of the horror since the zombie problem is a given from the first (great) scenes of zombie attacks, and the problems of the zombie crisis are completely "given." Instead, *Zombieland*'s narrative questions are: Where is the protagonist headed? How does the girl he meets fit in? And, how will they resolve their differences? Finally, *Zombieland* uses the classical romance road journey plot with catastrophes along the trip to unite the couple, a plot that goes back at least to Frank Capra's 1934 masterpiece *It Happened One Night.*

So why did the film seem to be a horror film anyway? The title was one reason.[1] Others were the film's publicity which employed the words "action," "comedy," and "horror"—but not "romance"—and images and sounds in the trailer which, in retrospect, probably should have cautioned a potential filmgoer to be suspicious. Moreover, the poster for *Zombieland* emphasizes action, not romance (Figure 13.1).

However, even after watching the film, it appears that typical audiences did not scoff at the horror genre label. The first eleven reviewers on the Internet Movie Database (IMDb) all call *Zombieland* a "horror comedy" or "zombie comedy" or, even, a "zomedy."[2] Only one person even mentions the word "romance" when "Jaypugh" writes, "A little romance is thrown into the mix when Columbus and Tallahassee come up on Wichita . . . and Little Rock. . . . For a zombie comedy I thought [actors] Eisenberg and Stone actually had decent chemistry. Not much time is dedicated to romance but what is there comes across as sincere."[3]

So, audiences seemed to have perceived the film to be a comic horror movie. While I respect reception matters, here I want to remove that critical hat and put on my film analysis cap. Since the film is so obviously to me a romance, how did the studio manage to disguise it so successfully? It goes nearly without saying

Figure 13.1: Poster for *Zombieland* (2009).

why the producers might want to do this given long-standing stereotypes about male adolescent audiences and the genre category of romance; recall the IMDb writer's comment. In thinking this through, my answer turns to matters of genre analysis, specifically the venerable discussions of how to group films on the basis of their form and subject matter. This essay argues—from a critical perspective as an academic analysis of texts and not as a historical study of reception—that media scholars may be able to make useful comparative analyses of texts by employing a multidimensional approach to grouping. Furthermore, this analytical approach will contribute to explaining how the studio was able to disguise this film as a horror film rather than reveal that it is a romance. After describing the multidimensional approach and then applying the approach to horror films—particularly in connection with sound and music—the essay will conclude with further thoughts about how the multidimensional approach facilitates positioning and comparing texts and the functions of sound and music within that process.

The Multidimensional Approach to Genre Analysis

This multi-dimensional approach to genre analysis involves three formal and subject matter aspects of texts: (1) plot formulas, (2) affects, and (3) inflections. The first term, *formulas*, should be fairly transparent in meaning. Formulas are the sorts of plot events that scholars associate with the major action segments of a narrative. Hopefully, the rough description of the romance plot formula above seemed reasonable. A more sophisticated version of it is from Jackie Stacey and Lynne Pearce in which they describe the romance narrative as composed of four movements. The initial movement is the "first sighting," which ignites the chemistry between the two future lovers. Second is a series of obstacles that function as barriers to the couple. These may be obstacles that are basically out of the couple's control, such as race, geographical distance, class, or the existence of another lover or spouse; or the obstacles may be "an initial clash of personalities." For the seasoned reader of such narratives, the question is not whether the couple will pair but how. This question is answered in the third movement, which is a transformation based on new information or actual character change, in the latter case usually occurring for *both* characters. Finally is resolution, which may be happy or tragic.[4] Horror narrative formulas, as described above, also contain a few broad movements involving the appearance of potentially supernatural events, the exploration of causes, and the triumph (or not) over the disruption. Detective narrative formulas require the appearance of a mystery, and so forth. It is the case that romance is ubiquitous in movies; for the initial purposes of categorizing genre for comparison, the question is, what is the primary narrative structure? Then, an analyst might consider subplot formulas which may reinforce (or not) the primary plot.[5]

The second dimension in this multidimensional approach to genre analysis is *affect*. As Steve Neale writes, genres are a "set of expectations."[6] A major expectation is the affects spectators will experience in engaging with the text. Associated with traditional narrative formulas are affects such as (1) thrills and excitement for the action/adventure formula that underlies the western, a lot of science fiction, disaster, war, and other such movies; (2) desire for social or moral justice for social problem, crime, detective, gangster, war, and cop films; (3) inspiration and admonition for biography pictures, epics, and historical dramas; (4) romantic fantasy and contentment for romances and erotica; (5) fright, fear, anxiety, or gross-out for horror cinema; (6) sorrow or happiness for drama and melodrama; and (7) laughter or amusement for comedy. Few texts remain within only one of these affective registers so charting out the dominant and supporting affects as for formulas is important. Noting certain affinities among affects is also valuable. For instance, the horror formula traditionally and habitually utilizes humor.

The third dimension is *inflections*. Inflections are the other sorts of variables that authors use to create different sorts of stories. Examples of such variables are time, place/space, claims of verisimilitude (strong to weak), tone (serious to satirical), use of music and sound, mise-en-scène style, spectacle, target audience, taste (high to low), performance style, and narrational manner.[7] For instance, film scholars have pointed out that *Star Wars* (1977) uses a plot formula suggestive of the western. However, because *Star Wars* is not set in the U.S. West between 1860 and 1900 (a typical requirement for being a "western"), the film is traditionally treated as science fiction. What the multidimensional approach would illuminate are the similarities of the plot formula and affect to the traditional action/adventure formula of the western but the inflectional variations of time and place.

Another example of inflections, one involving tone and taste, occurs as a joke in the 1933 Ernst Lubitsch film, *Design for Living*, written by Noël Coward and Ben Hecht. George (Gary Cooper) comes home to discover that his girlfriend, Gilda (Miriam Hopkins), has slept with his best friend Tom (Fredric March). A crash occurs offscreen. The philandering friend, Tom, says:

> Well, that's one way of meeting the situation. Shipping clerk comes home; finds Mrs. with boarder. He breaks dishes. Pure burlesque. Then there's another way. Intelligent party returns home unexpectedly; finds treacherous friends. Both discuss the pros and cons of the situation in grown up dialogue. High-class comedy, enjoyed by everybody.
>
> **George**: And there's a third way. I'll kick your teeth out, tear your head off, and beat some decency into you.
>
> **Tom**: Cheap melodrama. Very dull.
>
> George socks Tom.

If these sorts of narrative, narrational, and stylistic options are considered as inflectional variations for plot formulas rather than as definitional criteria for a genre, certain anomalies in genre categorizing might be resolved and connections among films can be more easily perceived and described. For example, take the vexed generic category of the musical. Scholars have tended to describe the musical based on Hollywood films created between 1930 and 1960. During this period, most musicals use a standard romance plot formula and vary the space and time to form several common so-called "subgenres." I would argue that in the 1960s, filmmakers begin to turn to other plot formulas such as the male quest story—see *Tommy* (1975), for instance—or the fallen-man melodrama in *All That Jazz* (1979) and *Pennies from Heaven* (1981). What the musical "is" is inflecting a formula with a particular musical treatment—bursting into song or dance not provoked by a reasonably motivated diegetic event such as a nightclub act. Such an inflection of musical treatment could be applied to any narrative formula and has been. See, for instance, *Sweeney Todd: The Demon Barber of Fleet Street* (2007).[8]

Later, this essay considers further the relationships of formula and affect, drawing from Alistair Fowler's 1982 work in distinguishing between "kind" (another word for genre) and "mode." Fowler argues that "kinds"/genres are structural whereas "modes" modify. For Fowler, Jane Austin's *Emma* is a "comic novel" while Henry Fielding's *Tom Jones* is a "comic epic."[9] In this case example, *Zombieland* employs a romance formula that makes use of two affects. One is fright, fear, and gross-out; the other, comedy. The horror affect is occasional and not fully "structured"—to use Fowler's terminology—while the formula of romance is complete and configures the action, with the affect of laughter and amusement sustained throughout. Thus, what is here in critical analysis terms is a "comic/horror romance."

Inflections of Music, Sounds, and Voice

Focusing on inflections, specifically the use of music, sounds, and voice, will illustrate the critical value of this approach for grouping and comparing texts. Undoubtedly, one of the major reasons to move quickly away from describing *Zombieland* as having a horror formula is that its music and sound effects are "wrong" for that formula with horror's typical affects of fright, fear, anxiety, or gross-out. Moreover, actor Jesse Eisenberg's voiceover narration, besides having amusing content, is intoned in a mock-serious manner that seems significantly at odds with creating terror, as is usually associated with a traditional horror movie. As David Neumeyer emphasizes, vococentrism means that the voice (including its grain) is granted priority in interpreting the soundtrack, and in classical films this gives great weight to audible voiceovers as conveyers of meaning.[10] It is not so much what the protagonist says (which is funny enough) but *how* he says it that immediately sets *Zombieland* apart from a standard horror film.

What, then, are the characteristics of music, sounds, and voice for a traditional horror film? As Anahid Kassabian reminds us, different genres have their soundtrack conventions. She notes Kathryn Kalinak's very detailed description of how composers for classical Hollywood films typically scored the "fallen woman" and "virtuous wife": "dotted rhythms, increased chromaticism, and saxes, often in jazz or blues styles" versus the "virtuous wife's violins and flutes [that] sweep upward melodically in even rhythms and lush but simple harmonic language."[11] Likewise, the horror film has a set of strategies for the soundtrack. While Julie Brown notes, "Watch a horror movie and there is a good chance you will hear an organ, probably a pipe organ"[12] and James Buhler remarks on the prevalence of synthesizer music which contrasts with instruments in "normative society,"[13] both writers go on to discuss that it is not so much the instruments that matter as the methods of their deployment. In an extended passage on music and sound in horror film, K. J. Donnelly provides an excellent list of characteristics: a blurring of the line between diegetic and nondiegetic sound or music (whether from real or supernatural sources); brooding lines of "deeply pitched strings"; drones to create anticipation; "unresolved dissonance"; certain associated instrumental sounds (like the organ); tremolos; and sparing use of melodic or song forms, although Donnelly does note that some melodic, "empathetic or romantic" music is often used for contrast.[14] Joe Tompkins summarizes the soundtrack of horror films as filled with "licensed transgressions"; for instance, normally music should be inaudible as in "scarcely noticed" and subordinated to the action. Not so in horror.[15] Thus, the use of "dissonance, atonality, and unusual configurations of instruments to signify all sorts of anomalous, paranormal activity" (199) call attention to the out-of-whack world.

It is not just the types of sound, music, and voice that change but the intensity of their deployment. Val Lewton's use in *Cat People* (1942) of the sound of the arrival of an everyday object, a bus, with a simultaneous explosive, quite amplified, sound to climax a tense scene—the stinger—invests an ordinary object with what seems like occult power and has become almost a requirement for horror films.[16] So intensity of sound is a tool in the genre. In summarizing "sound design" for horror films, William Whittington argues that it is akin to surrealism through its tactics of offering "challenges to the hierarchy through the collision of scale" (such as in the startle effect), "amplified perception" (sounds are louder than they would normally be), "disjunction" (putting sounds in unusual places to create "the sonic grotesque"), and "cognitive dissonance" (such as a sound that "mimics madness").[17]

Remarks by Neil Lerner, Janet Halfyard, Lloyd Whitesell, and Isabel Pinedo augment and amplify the *affective* purposes of these strategies. Lerner points out that "horror film's repetitious drones, clashing dissonances, and stingers (those assaultive [*sic*] blasts that coincide with shock or revelation) affect us at a primal level."[18] Halfyard focuses on unsettling atonal and dissonant harmonies and, particularly, the demonic tritone.[19] In discussing *The Sixth Sense* (1999) and *The*

Others (2001), Whitesell points out that "both scores make skillful use of spine-chilling effects (amorphous textures and pitch continua, percussive shocks, disturbing timbres and registers, increasing tension, distorted allusions to religious music) in line with horror conventions."[20] Pinedo explains Carl Plantinga's "auditory entrainment" as "the process by which the human pulse synchronizes with music, or beats at equal time intervals to an external rhythm" to argue that horror music is often composed for "generating emotional intensity in the viewer."[21] So, it is not merely that horror sound design is composed to tell spectators what is going on—something weird—but to make them *feel* it as well.

Tompkins nicely summarizes what horror music usually does, which is to "dutifully adhere (through rhythm, tone, phrasing, timbre) to the perceived feelings of the characters—most often the emotional state of a victim caught in tumultuous throes of fright, shock, anxiety, or pain."[22] Tompkins does note that the history of horror music and sound has periods of variation. Generally, the musical practice of horror film has pushed the boundaries of ordinary tonal practice without overturning it, but, of all the standard film genres, horror is the most likely to make use of avant-garde and modernist techniques. As well, Donnelly notes that horror films, especially Hammer studio movies, have been using popular music from the 1970s with horror directors commissioning rock groups to do soundtracks.[23] Still, these music/soundtracks follow the "mutually" reinforcing dictum for most Hollywood movies that images and sounds should be in sync with the narrative content, and, as Neumeyer would emphasize, voice and dialogue remain centered even if they have a tendency to devolve into screams.[24] Tompkins does discuss the atypical *The Last House on the Left* (1972), which features an unusual pop music track that often seems quite at odds with the actions occurring in the story. I would hasten to add that the composition of the track has similarities to some of the indie cinema of the 1960s, specifically films by Robert Downey Sr., Brian De Palma, and Martin Scorsese.[25] Still *Last House* is an anomaly in its musical choices from a great horror director, Wes Craven.

Tompkins's counter-example does raise a question worth further research about music for horror films. Although critics describe the horror soundtrack as in sync with characters' emotions (feelings) and the events being represented (action), a better description would often situate the feeling with the audience: at times sound and music seem to cue the spectators' emotional reactions, signaling more what the audience should be feeling (tense, suspenseful) than what the character is feeling. An example here might be from a fairly mediocre horror film *Prince of Darkness* (1987). The director John Carpenter is listed as composer along with Alan Howarth, and he is known for having produced several memorable film soundtracks such as for *Halloween* (1978). The music for *Prince of Darkness* consists of short, repeated themes of rhythmic percussive sounds, which do not reflect the activities or feelings of the characters so much as mark the potential for something to happen that will surprise or scare the spectator. When this does happen, the soundtrack elevates in volume, producing an effect akin to a classical stinger. It may well be that the soundtrack is composed to prime a particular affect in the audience as much as to convey narrative information about characters and events.

In contrast with musical or sonic attempts to create or reinforce affects of fright, fear, anxiety, or gross-out, *Zombieland*'s primary affect is comedy, supporting the pleasures of the romantic coupling to come, and the opening credit and first sequences immediately establish that through the soundtrack. As I noted above, the rather flat-toned voice of Columbus, expertly spoken by Eisenberg, brings spectators up to date about the zombie apocalypse. The first shot is of the U.S. flag upside down on a wrecked car while a Jimi Hendrix–style version of "The Star-Spangled Banner" plays. The credit sequence unfolds over a series of humorous, if bloody, images of zombies attacking people while Columbus explains his survival rules: cardio, seat belts, "double-taps" (shoot zombies twice), and wariness of bathrooms. During this voiceover narration, driving hard rock music plays. The soundtrack features many hard rock and heavy metal bands such as Metallica, Sea Wolf, Band of Horses, Metric, The Velvet Underground, Doves, Blue Oyster Cult, The Black Keys, and The Raconteurs, and the trailer uses Van Halen's "Everybody Wants Some." Additionally, mixed in is music from pop, country western, and even classical genres.

It is not so much the presence of hard rock per se that deserves attention, however, as the way the loudness of the music especially is used to construct a dissonance from the "normal" world of the United States. Though loud, in other words, the hard rock is not necessarily screechy and threatening in the typical manner of music in horror films. Compare, for example, the opening of Tobe Hooper's *The Texas Chain Saw Massacre* (1974) in which squealing violins, drones, and percussive sound effects produce a weird, avant-garde ambiance. Or consider the effect of Nine Inch Nails' performance of "She's Gone Away" in David Lynch's *Twin Peaks* (2017, episode 8) to open a twenty-six-minute montage of the Trinity bomb blast and evil entering the world. In *Zombieland*, with slow motion images making zombie violence comic (and less threatening) and the delivery of Columbus's commentary, the rock music synchronizes to the action in a way that exaggerates, following the dictum that images and music/sound should be in affective sync—in this case, comedically.

Is music for zombies different from other horror monsters? The theme song for *The Walking Dead* (2010–) is a series of repeated, intense, and incomplete string phrases. The film *28 Days Later* (2002), important in a new cycle of zombie output, has screechy sounds with long sustained chords over its opening scene of video footage of mass panic. Its second scene of an emptied hospital only has some diegetic sounds with the silence—no people and no cars—providing an eeriness that then drifts into melancholy music transitioning to dissonant rock and roll. Marilyn Manson and Marco Beltrami composed the music for *Resident Evil* (2002). Even the titular ur-, founder-text of zombies, George A. Romero's *Night of the Living Dead* (1968), opens with music in a minor key and an other-worldly vibrato as the brother and sister drive into the scary cemetery. While certainly some serious zombie movie might not conform to horror sound conventions, it would seem from this spotty sampling that sound and music composers treat zombies fairly similarly to other sorts of horror monsters.[26]

Thus, that *Zombieland* pulls back from most of the horror film music/sound characteristics—no drones, no melodic themes with strings shifting to unresolved dissonance, no tremolos, no scary screechy instruments in moments of great tension—indicates that the filmmakers want scenes with romantic action and certainly the mode of comedy and that sustaining affects of fright, fear, anxiety, and gross-out are a very low priority. Additionally, as the romance formula develops, some songs with romantic lyrics play, and "happy" transition music appears.[27] Again, as in horror, music exists to reinforce narrative action or for gestures of proposed spectators' affective response. For example, in a rather clichéd choice, Mozart's *The Marriage of Figaro* is used while the main characters enjoy trashing a tourist shop. Even in the big action finale—a fight-out in an amusement park—the music is not classic horror with suspenseful dissonant phrases, but the sound track is instead inundated with hard rock.

Formula and Affect

Fowler's distinction between genre and mode has much analytical value, and Fowler's additional remarks about the behavior of both genres and modes are helpful. For one thing, Fowler notes that "modes have always an incomplete repertoire, a selection only of the corresponding kind's [genre's] features, and one from which overall external structure is absent." He further notes, "normally, a modal term will imply that some of the nonstructural features of a kind are extended to modify another kind" (107). In other words, the adjective form of comedy—comic—modifies the genre to which it is attached.[28] Although he does not express it this way, it seems to me that modes are creators of, or indicators of, proposed affects. To modify a genre so that it is melodramatic implies the association of melodramatic affects such as happiness or sadness. Making something "horrible" hopes to create affects of fright and fear.

Just as Fowler wants to distinguish between the kind/genre and the mode and to point out that modifying a kind/genre via a mode is significant in analyzing the features and historical developments of literary texts, I am claiming that examining plot formulas as modified by affects can help scholars appreciate, compare, and group films.[29] For example, in Table 13.1, I posit ten major formulas and their commonly associated affects.

Table 13.1. Formulas and Affects

FORMULA	FORMULA DESCRIPTION	MAJOR INFLECTIONS	SUB-FORMULAS	PRIMARY AFFECTS
ADVENTURE/ ACTION/ THRILLER	hero or group faces and overcomes obstacles to accomplish mission	Spectacle	Caper/heist	Excitement
			Conspiracy	Suspense
			Disaster	
			Quest	
			Rags to riches	
			Rebirth	
			Road	
			Thriller	
			War	
			Voyage and Return	
			TV Game Shows	
			Reality TV	
			Sports	
			Place/time	Jungle/safari
				Sea
				Swashbuckler
				Western
			Verisimilitude	Fantasy
				Science Fiction*
				*also in Horror and Social Issue
BIO PIC	"birth," trials, big break, results; based on a "real" person			Admiration
				Reproach
COMEDY	people are confused in a humorous and nonthreatening situation; revelations dispel confusion and/or person changes			Laughter
				Happiness

FORMULA	FORMULA DESCRIPTION	MAJOR INFLECTIONS	SUB-FORMULAS	PRIMARY AFFECTS
CRIME	1. Start with criminals: person frustrated or impatient (greedy) with status quo; breaks law; becomes excessive to point of social or legal rejection; stopped		Gangster	Disgust Suspense Relief
	2. Start with "law": people realize crimes are being committed; search out, and stop; "law" may be imperfect (corrupt, excessively violent)		Cop/do-gooder	
EROTICA	stimulation and satisfaction of sexual or sensual pleasure			Pleasure Arousal
HORROR	equilibrium, premonition of horror, disruption, semi-resolution	Spectacle	Complex discovery Over-reacher Shock Gore	Fright, fear, dread, revulsion Surprise Anxiety
(MELO)DRAMA	story about good and evil; temptation, decisions, revelations, outcome	Narration	Fallen woman Fallen man (often film noir)	Sadness Happiness
MYSTERY	investigation and discovery of hidden secret (such as a murder or other crime)		Amateur Professional	Curiosity Intellectual pleasure
ROMANCE	couple with obstacles must overcome to unite; types of obstacles with an associated sub-formula:		Mystery: gothic or "gaslight" Crazy behavior: screwball comedy Sex vs. love: sex comedy Death: one-true-love melodrama	Hope, happiness
SOCIAL ISSUE	social problem to be examined and resolved; may have hero or not			Anger Moral indignation Resolution to fix

In this case, I am arguing that *Zombieland* employs a romance formula that presents two types of affects. One type offers fright, fear, anxiety, and gross-out. This affect is occasional and not fully "structured"—to use Fowler's terminology—while the plot formula of romance and dominance of the other type of affect—comedy—configure the action. That is why I perceive *Zombieland* as in the romance and not horror genre. While *Zombieland*'s secondary affect is fright, fear, anxiety, and gross-out, its primary affect is laughter and amusement, a common combination of affects for romance films but in which, for the horror formula, horror affects would overwhelm the comedic moments.

Returning now to the basic question of how the studio managed to disguise the romance formula so pervasively, I need to detour slightly once more. The title of this essay describes *Zombieland* as a "romantic horror" film. In part, that phrasing creates a parallel with the very common term "romantic comedy." However, if I apply Fowler's analysis to this situation, I would want to reverse the terms. Fowler places the genre in the noun's place (it is the structure) and the mode in the adjective's modifying location so as to produce the "comic epic" or the "comic novel." I am making a similar equation: the formula (the narrative structure) should be in the noun's position; the affect (or mode) should appear in the adjectival location. Thus, what *Zombieland* "really" *is* is not "comic horror film" but "comic/horror romance." In fact, recent scholars of romantic comedy suggest that it *is* the romance that defines the grouping of these sorts of films. Tamar Jeffers McDonald in *Romantic Comedy: Boy Meets Girl Meets Genre* states: "A romantic comedy is a film which has as its central narrative motor a quest for love, which portrays this quest in a light-hearted way and almost always to a successful conclusion."[30] Geoff King in *Film Comedy* declares: "[Romantic comedy] is a format in which romance is the main and foregrounded element of the narrative. . . . Second, the romance is generally treated lightly."[31] In equivalence, then, to the comic romance would be the horror romance, if one exists.

It is significant that the "romantic comedy" has not become widely labeled "comic romance." Returning to the adage that male adolescents only barely tolerate their female dates' desire to see "chick flicks," saying that they are heading to a comedy is a far cry from going to a romance movie. Similarly, seeing a horror film is "manly" stuff.

The success of this labeling strategy—calling these comedies or horror films—has produced a collection of movies that would not otherwise probably have been so successful. *Dead Alive* (1992), *Shaun of the Dead* (2004), *Warm Bodies* (2013), and *Pride and Prejudice and Zombies* (2016) are among the films in this group. McDonald has also pointed out that recently "a man instead of a woman [is positioned] as the center of the narrative,"[32] also working to cover up the romance foundations, which is the case not only for *Zombieland* but also *Dead Alive, Shaun of the Dead,* and *Warm Bodies*. *Warm Bodies*, following *Zombieland*'s success, indulges in romance tropes: the meet-cute occurs when the zombie protagonist "R" (Nicholas Hoult) sees the human girl Julie (Teresa Palmer) while he is out marauding for flesh, but he protects her by teaching her to act like a zombie. Their zombie-human differences need to be overcome. Once the zombies start to change into nonthreatening life forms, a happy ending can be achieved, accompanied by familiar standard pop music.[33] None of these comic/horror romance films indulges in typical horror music or sound despite their populations of zombies. Moreover, it might be noted that the *inflection* of giving priority to one sex (male) over the other (female) permits seeing more similarities and differences among these romances.

Finally, turning then to considering the place of affects and inflections within analysis of genre, I have no desire to try to correct the popular categorizing of these films. Rather, I offer this multidimensional approach for the value it may have in helping scholars compare and associate films in order to understand the films' operations and their appeals to audiences. Certainly music, sounds, and voices are highly significant, perhaps at times even pivotal, in cueing modes, which reinforce (or contradict) the formulas. Much of the pleasure of romance and horror films are the recognizable formulas, affects, and inflections conveyed both visually and aurally *and* the pleasures of the variations. Having a method to describe these similarities and differences may allow seeing more complexities and tracing their historical variations.

Notes

For their helpful remarks on drafts of these materials, I thank the University of Texas Film Faculty group, the 2011 Society for Cinema and Media Studies conference audience, the 2016 "Voicing the Cinema" conference, and Peter Staiger.

1. Alistair Fowler, who will be discussed further later, argues that one of the major signals of genre is the text's title; *Kinds of Literature: An Introduction to the Theory of Genres and Modes* (Cambridge: Harvard University Press, 1982), 88–105.

2. User comments, *Zombieland*, IMDb, www.imdb.com/title/tt1156398/usercomments, accessed June 14, 2010; "Coolvin91," "Solid Zombie Comedy," September 28, 2009, User comments, *Zombieland*, IMDb, accessed June 14, 2010.

3. "Jaypugh," "Brilliantly Crafted with Laughs from Beginning to End," September 21, 2009, User comments, *Zombieland*, IMDb, accessed June 14, 2010.

4. Jackie Stacey and Lynn Pearce, "The Heart of the Matter: Feminists Revisit Romance," in *Romance Revisited*, ed. Lynne Pearce and Jackie Stacey (London: Lawrence Wishart, 1995), 11–45.

5. Hollywood films are notorious for utilizing multiple plot lines; the question is dominance and subordination. See Janet Staiger, "Hybrid or Inbred: The Purity Hypothesis and Hollywood Genre History," *Film Criticism* 22, 1 (Fall 1997): 5–20.

6. Steve Neale, *Genre and Hollywood* (London: Routledge, 2000), 23.

7. As David Prindle and Herbert Eagle have pointed out to me, perhaps we have four or five or more dimensions; for the introduction of this model of genre analysis, however, I am grouping all of these inflectional possibilities together.

8. Another example of how inflections can help us sort through these variables is recognizing how certain stylistic treatments might disguise what is happening. See Janet Staiger, "*Film Noir* as Male Melodrama: The Politics of Film Genre Labeling," in *The Shifting Definitions of Genre: Essays on Labeling Films, Television Shows and Media,* ed. Lincoln Geraghty and Mark Jancovich (Jefferson, N.C.: McFarland and Company, 2008), 71–91.

9. Fowler, *Kinds of Literature,* 106. Rick Altman, in applying Fowler's approach to film, believes that Fowler "fails to note the importance of adjective-to-noun progression in the creation of genres." *Film/Genre* (London: BFI Publishing, 1999), 51.

10. David Neumeyer, *Meaning and Interpretation of Music in Cinema* (Bloomington: Indiana University Press, 2005), 12–13.

11. Anahid Kassabian, *Hearing Film: Tracking Identifications in Contemporary Hollywood Film Music* (New York: Routledge, 2001), 17–18.

12. Julie Brown, "*Carnival of Souls* and the Organs of Horror," in *Music in the Horror Film: Listening to Fear,* ed. Neil Lerner (New York: Routledge, 2010), 1.

13. James Buhler, "Music and the Adult Ideal in *A Nightmare on Elm Street,*" in *Music in the Horror Film,* ed. Lerner, 180.

14. K. J. Donnelly, *The Spectre of Sound: Music in Film and Television* (London: BFI, 2005), 90–91, 100.

15. Joe Tompkins, "Mellifluous Terror: The Discourse of Music and Horror Films," in *A Companion to the Horror Film,* ed. Harry M. Benshoff (Chichester, U.K.: John Wiley and Sons, Inc., 2014), 188–90.

16. Michael Lee, "Sound and Uncertainty in the Horror Films of the Lewton Unit," in *Music, Sound and Filmmakers: Sonic Style in Cinema,* ed. James Wierzbicki (New York: Routledge, 2012), 110–11.

17. William Whittington, "Horror Sound Design," in *A Companion to the Horror Film,* ed. Benshoff, 180–82.

18. Neil Lerner, "Preface: Listening to Fear/Listening with Fear," in *Music in the Horror Film,* ed. Lerner, ix.

19. Janet Halfyard, "Mischief Afoot: Supernatural Horror-comedies and the *Diabolus in Musica,*" in *Music in the Horror Film,* ed. Lerner, 21–23.

20. Lloyd Whitesell, "Quieting the Ghosts in *The Sixth Sense* and *The Others,*" in *Music in the Horror Film,* ed. Lerner, 207. Also see Mervyn Cooke, *A History of Film Music* (Cambridge, U.K.: Cambridge University Press, 2008), 98–99; also 70, 115, 253–56, 375, 381–82, 394, and 498.

21. Isabel C. Pinedo, "Torture Porn: 21st Century Horror," in *A Companion to the Horror Film,* ed. Benshoff, 354.

22. Joe Tompkins, "Pop Goes the Horror Score: Left Alone in *The Last House on the Left,*" in *Music in the Horror Film,* ed. Lerner, 07.

23. Donnelly, *Spectre of Sound,* 101.

24. Halfyard, "Mischief Afoot," 25.

25. See, particularly, Brian De Palma's *Murder a la Mode* (1968), Robert Downey's *Putney Swope* (1969), and De Palma's *Hi! Mom* (1970). On 1960s indie cinema, see Janet Staiger, "Proto-Indie: 1960s 'Half-Way' Cinema," in *A Companion to American Indie Cinema*, ed. Geoff King (Oxford, U.K.: Wiley-Blackwell, 2017), 209–32.

26. This does have to be reinforced. Comic zombie movies, which are usually romances like *Zombieland*, conform to *Zombieland*'s avoidance of horror film sounds and music.

27. Granted, this occurs in horror films if a subplot of a romance is included.

28. It is important to distinguish between "comedy" as a plot formula and, hence, a genre, and "comic" as a mode. Discussed later.

29. Fowler, *Kinds of Literature*, 107.

30. Tamar Jeffers McDonald, *Romantic Comedy: Boy Meets Girl Meets Genre* (London: Wallflower, 2007), 9.

31. Geoff King, *Film Comedy* (London: Wallflower, 2002), 51.

32. McDonald, *Romantic Comedy*, 106.

33. *Warm Bodies*'s zombie male protagonist "R" also serves as the film's narrator in voiceover as did Columbus for *Zombieland*.

Chapter 14

Once More into the Breach

Interrogating Ben Winters's Nondiegetic Fallacy

Jeff Smith

The difference between a story world and the cinematic elements used to communicate information about that world is a foundational element in film narratology. Although this distinction is largely a settled matter among film scholars working in other areas, it remains a contentious topic within theories and analyses of film music. Claudia Gorbman introduced the terms *diegetic* and *nondiegetic* to film music studies more than four decades ago, but several newer books and essays have sought to refine, recast, and revise the way these two ideas circulate within film music scholarship.[1] Inspired by Robynn Stilwell's proposal of a "fantastical gap" that acts as a space dividing more clearly demarcated instances of diegetic and nondiegetic music, these scholars seek to explore the dynamics by which a cue seems to migrate from one side of this gap to the other or even eliminate these categories altogether.[2]

Stilwell's "fantastical gap" gave the field of film music studies a serious jolt, encouraging scholars in both film studies and musicology to reconsider the foundational premises of the distinction between diegetic and nondiegetic. David Neumeyer, Giorgio Biancorosso, and I all contributed to the ongoing debate in separate articles published within a few months of each other.[3] Each of us addressed issues raised by Stilwell's essay on the "fantastical gap," but arrived at subtly different conclusions.

Moreover, interest in this topic shows no signs of letting up. In 2013, Anahid Kassabian revised and updated a position she had previously articulated in her book, *Hearing Film*.[4] Musicologist Guido Heldt resituated the diegetic/

nondiegetic split within Edward Branigan's multileveled theory of film narration.[5] More recently, *Music and the Moving Image* has published two more essays reevaluating these categories.[6]

All of this literature made important contributions to a field still coming to grips with its basic nomenclature. Ben Winters, though, provided the most influential challenge to conventional wisdom about music and cinematic space by rather provocatively characterizing the entire problem as the "nondiegetic fallacy." Winters explores the issue both in his 2010 essay of the same name and in his recent book, *Music, Performance, and the Realities of Film*.[7] Winters's initial foray into the debate has been cited more than 110 times. His critique struck a chord with scholars who felt that our existing conception of sound and narrative space was hopelessly old-fashioned and needed to be replaced with something else.

Winters builds his critique of the diegetic/nondiegetic distinction on the well-established premise that any filmic universe operates according to its own rules, systems of belief, characters, and settings. Citing Etienne Souriau's claim that diegesis indicates the existence of a unique filmic universe, peculiar to each movie, Winters argues that film musicologists have been too hasty in assuming that what we conventionally take to be nondiegetic music does not belong to the fictional universe of the film. Such a notion is incontrovertible, especially within the conventions of certain genres, like musicals, science fiction, and fantasy. But Winters goes further in suggesting that such deviations also pervade realist films that adhere to their own logics and conventions.

Indeed, Winters identifies Ron Howard's historical film, *Apollo 13* (1995), as just such an example where a scientist's explanation of free-return trajectory to other NASA personnel or the sound of a rocket's thrusters in the vacuum of space cannot be justified on realistic grounds. Given that such unrealistic elements are found in the vast majority of fictional films, Winters claims that there is no reason a priori why music with no evident source should be automatically excluded from the fictional worlds they present. As Winters puts it, "Might we better understand such music not as a narrating voice but as the product of narration, belonging to the same narrative space as the characters and their world?" In such instances, the music usually thought of as belonging to a register external to the diegesis would have an ontological existence in the film's own peculiar universe irrespective of whether the characters within that world can hear it.

From a purely philosophical perspective, Winters's argument seems absolutely irrefutable. Insofar as all fictional films depart from aspects of our everyday reality, it then follows that any aspect of cinematic discourse could be construed to belong to this imagined world rather than existing in a register separate from the narrative. Yet, if we reframe the question to address the issue of how viewers actually respond to narrative cues, then it seems equally clear to me that Winters's model is a wildly improbable account of viewers' behavior, one that would make it impossible to make sense of any story, much less the mainstream Hollywood films that facilitate the easy uptake of narratively salient information.

In what follows, I counter Winters's "nondiegetic fallacy," not on ontological grounds, but rather by demonstrating ways in which his critique fails to account for the normal inferential processes involved in spectators' comprehension of a film. I will first outline what I take to be the chief premises of Winters's argument. In doing so, I elucidate some problems that Winters inherits from the extant literature he cites. Then I show how Winters's neglect of what narratologists call the "principle of minimal departure" proves to be a fatal flaw in his model. By abandoning all grounds for understanding fictional worlds according to terms drawn from everyday experience, Winters opens up our interpretive schema to a seemingly endless succession of questions regarding the "rules" by which any particular fictional world operates. Finally, I also argue for the usefulness of the diegetic/nondiegetic distinction by analyzing instances where viewers could not make sense of a film without tacitly construing the sonic phenomena they hear as belonging to different registers of narration. Drawing upon David Neumeyer's conception of "vococentrism," I argue that Winters's characterization of a nondiegetic fallacy for music in film would equally apply to all other elements of the soundtrack, thereby rendering other ways of conceiving of sound's relation to narrative space entirely moot.

Thinking about "Film Thinking": "Filmosophy" Meets Natural Philosophy

The question Winters asks is an important one insofar as it sheds light on a common aspect of film spectatorship, namely our suspension of disbelief when we encounter aspects of a fictional world that depart from real-world experience. Lurking within Winters's espousal of a "nondiegetic fallacy," however, is a more fundamental question: how do viewers distinguish elements of a film's diegesis that are realistically motivated from those that aren't? In other words, in a medium that typically deviates from real-world experience, are there any firm epistemological grounds by which a viewer could exclude an element of film narration from its diegesis?

In critiquing the concept of nondiegetic music, Winters endorses Annahid Kassabian's argument that music cannot be separated from the diegesis insofar as it participates in the construction or articulation of the diegesis.[8] That is, if music helps to create the story world, it ipso facto necessarily must be a part of it. Intuitively, the logic supporting this premise seems sound. After all, one can enumerate many different objects in which a specific element of a substance helps bring it into being. An egg, for example, is an ingredient in a quiche, and its inclusion in the making of the quiche means that eggs are necessarily a part of the whole. The same could be said for glass in a window, sand in an hourglass, or hydrogen and oxygen as elements in water.

Yet, if you probe the premise a little more fully, it seems clear that Winters and Kassabian must define music as an ingredient or natural element for the argument to work. This conclusion is simply assumed without any reasoning or evidence to support it. Music's role in constructing the diegesis would be envisioned in a quite different way if one categorizes it as a communicative tool for narrative information. One can just as easily enumerate cases where something serves as a tool in the creation of an object but does not become part of it. A blueprint is necessary for the construction of a building, but it does not physically become a part of the structure. Likewise, a bowl and a whisk might be used to mix the eggs with other ingredients in the preparation of the aforementioned quiche. But that does not entail that the bowl and whisk become a part of the quiche.

Rephrasing the argument such that music "articulates" the diegesis does not fare much better insofar as it is prone to a similar type of illogic. For example, imagine that I read the story "Jack and the Beanstalk" to my nephew. In reciting the narrative, I have articulated the fictional world of Jack and the beanstalk such that my nephew is able to identify: (a) Jack as a goal-oriented protagonist, (b) the Giant as an antagonist that blocks Jack's progress toward achieving those goals, and (c) several causal connections that link the story events together, including the significance of the magic beans that cause the beanstalk to sprout outside of Jack's house. Yet, even though I have articulated the fictional world of Jack and the beanstalk, it would be nonsensical to believe that I have become a part of that diegetic space. No matter how many times I tell my nephew this story, I am never going to meet Jack, be chased by a giant, or climb a beanstalk to reach a magic kingdom within the clouds.

What this means for Winters's and Kassabian's arguments is that music need not be seen as an element of diegetic space for it to contribute to the construction or articulation of a fictional world. If Winters truly believes that music's role in the production, construction, or articulation of the diegesis makes it part of the story's fictional space, then the burden of proof falls on him to demonstrate that music always becomes a part of the diegesis by virtue of that process rather than simply being a tool used to communicate narrative information.

If Winters's uncritical acceptance of Kassabian's work creates one set of problems, his citation of Daniel Frampton's concept of film-worlds and filminds produces another. Frampton's *filmosophy* outlines the basic precepts of the filmind as a means of explaining the myriad and particular ways in which film fictions depart from real-world knowledge and experience. For Frampton, film-worlds are created by filminds that are immanent to them. Consequently, a film-world is not the product of a collective creative endeavor that synthesizes the various inputs of screenwriters, directors, cinematographers, costumers, set decorators, et al. Nor is it the intersubjective experience of viewers cued to construct a fictional world from the information communicated to them through the film's plot and discourse. Rather, Frampton's film-worlds are something else entirely insofar as each film-world is a unique expression of its filmind. According to Frampton:

> Filmosophy conceptualizes film as an organic intelligence: a "film being" thinking about the characters and subjects in the film. Yet the concepts of the filmind and film-thinking are not intended to be replacements for the concepts of a "narrator" and "narration," but are simply proposals that reflect the limits of the idea of "the narrator" and the restrictive and literary nature of theories of "narration." . . . The filmind is not an "external" force, nor is it a mystical being or invisible other, it is "in" the film itself, it is *the film* that is steering its own (dis)course. The filmind is "the film itself."[9]

Frampton's theory, which purports to provide "a radically new way of understanding cinema," is counterintuitive to say the least. As social beings, viewers commonsensically understand a film to be the product of human agents, whether it is designed to be an artwork or a commodity. Indeed, every time someone buys a ticket at the box office, one is reminded of film's status as a consumer good bought and sold on the open market.

Yet Frampton seems to be aiming at something deeper here, an understanding of cinema beyond its place within social relations, a grasp of its most basic state of being. Still, Frampton's formulation of the problem risks being a tautology. If the filmind is the film itself, it is not clear what is gained by positing a filmind as the immanent source of a film-world. For example, why not simply adopt the position of the New Critics, who conceptualized the artwork as a set of formal relations immanent to it? For Frampton, the answer to the last question is fairly straightforward: a formalist or technicist explanation of cinema doesn't capture our phenomenological experience of it.

Such phenomenological experience usually involves beings, creatures, objects, and actions that are literally impossible in the real world, as when the title character of *Amélie* (2001) turns from flesh and blood to water. Frampton argues that such a conceptualization of the relation between filminds and film-worlds not only accounts for the latter's uniqueness and particularity, but it also reveals a fluidity inherent in film thinking.

Still, Frampton is careful to point out that the prereflective side of a filmind entails a basic belief in a film-world that resembles our everyday experience in several important respects. Frampton writes, "In this unstudied natural intention, the film-world obeys normal and natural laws. . . . In this natural attitude we simply see objects as neutrally as possible. The base creation is a simple likeness of the real world we know, with gravity and shadow and people and buildings."[10] If, however, Frampton is willing to grant such continuities between film-worlds and the real world, then it begs an important question about where one draws the line between that which obeys the dictates of natural laws and that which is subject to the fluidity of film-thinking. More importantly, though, it also begs additional questions about Winters's citation of Frampton's work. If the laws of gravity and optics operate within the base creation of a film-world, then shouldn't we also assume that the natural laws governing acoustics are also in force? If film-worlds contain objects and spaces that have real-world acoustic properties, then can music really be just "in the air" with no apparent physical cause?

Winters does not address this apparent contradiction—or at least, tension—between natural philosophy and the properties specific to a film-world that are immanent to a filmind. Yet the failure to do so puts him on the horns of a dilemma. If Winters doesn't believe that acoustics fall under the natural laws that Frampton identifies as part and parcel of the viewer's prereflective state, then he has cited a theory of cinematic ontology to which he doesn't fully subscribe. If, on the other hand, Winters is willing to grant that acoustics are part of the natural laws that govern most fictional worlds, then he would need to explain why he has exempted the production of musical sounds from the "base creation" outlined by Frampton. In other words, although Winters enumerates the three types of thinking that Frampton locates in the filmind (basic, formal, fluid), he doesn't do anything more than simply list them. To genuinely support his case, Winters needs to justify the position of music in the formal or fluid categories of thinking rather than the basic.

To be fair, no matter how Winters resolved this dilemma, it would not negate the basic premise of his argument, which he expresses thusly: "To imagine the film-world of *Star Wars* created by the filmind as one saturated with the 'sound' of music (whether or not the characters hear it as 'sound') seems perfectly acceptable to me as a filmgoer."[11] To the extent that cinema presents an art of the possible, its unrealistic elements always will entail the prospect that the fictional universe onscreen is "saturated with the 'sound' of music." Such opportunities seem especially strong in fantasy and science fiction films, which differentiate themselves from other genres through their creation of unusual creatures, make-believe settings, and futuristic technologies.

The problems with Winters's delineation of the nondiegetic fallacy become more evident, though, if we shift the terms of debate from ontological to epistemological grounds. The more pertinent issue here is not whether music "in the air" is part of a film-world, but rather how viewers process the narrative information communicated to them. Unless viewers share exactly the same sorts of knowledge about film-worlds as the filminds that imagined them, then one wonders how spectators could *know* that these fictional universes possess these special properties.

Making Sense of "Make Believe," or Why Does a Fictional World Still Have Gravity?

Is there a way to bridge the divide opened up between Frampton's "base creation" and Winters's "what if" scenarios regarding fictional cinematic soundscapes? There is, but as I mentioned earlier, it requires a shift away from ontological questions about what is possible within fictional universes to the pragmatics of narrative comprehension. It is my contention that viewers must make use of some degree of real-world knowledge in order to understand the narrative information given to them. That is, if we had to "bracket" our knowledge in a phenomenological sense and thereby entertain every possible permutation or property of a fictional world, then even the most basic and common character actions would seem opaque to us insofar as they might mean something else entirely to the filmind that imagined them.

Consider, for example, a brief scene from Krzysztof Kieslowski's *Three Colors: Red* (1994). A narrative description of the scene couldn't be simpler: while driving through Geneva, Valentine stops at a traffic light. If we bracket everything we know about the real world in watching this scene, among the hundreds of questions we could ask include:

- Do red lights mean the same thing in Valentine's world as they do in our own?
- Is Valentine's hometown of Geneva located in a fictional version of Switzerland that fought for the Axis powers during World War II?
- Does Valentine's car have an internal combustion engine that burns gasoline? Or does she have superhuman strength that enables her to power her vehicle with her feet, à la Fred Flintstone?

I am deliberately being facetious here, but my point is clear. If Winters is right about the peculiarities of filmic universes, we would have to mentally catalog every possible way in which it might differ from the real world in order to understand even the simplest events of a story.

Narratologists refer to this tendency to leverage our real-world knowledge in such circumstances by a number of names. Marie Laure-Ryan calls it the "principle of minimal departure" (PMD). Noel Carroll refers to it as the "realistic heuristic." David Bordwell calls it the "Philip Marlowe has lungs" hypothesis. All of them describe the same phenomenon, though. As Ryan puts it, PMD "states that we reconstrue the world of a fiction and of a counterfactual as being the closest possible to the reality we know. This means that we will project upon the world of the statement everything we know about the real world, and that we will make only those adjustments which we cannot avoid."[12] That is, in the absence of specific descriptions of Philip Marlowe's physiology, we assume that he has a heart, lungs, and other internal organs, and further that he is not invulnerable to bullets fired by an assailant's gun. Indeed, our understanding of the character's actions and psychology would make little sense otherwise. If bullets bounced off Marlowe's chest like they do Superman's, then his failure to intervene when Lash Canino poisons Harry Jones in *The Big Sleep* (1946) would seem exceptionally callous and cruel.

PMD, thus, explains one of the reasons why we tend to automatically exclude unsourced music from the fictional space depicted as part of the diegesis. The suspension of disbelief does not entail that we suspend all of our beliefs when we engage with fictional texts. Moreover, just as I do not expect orchestral accompaniment in the real world when I spontaneously burst into song, I do not expect music to be a part of the vast majority of fictional worlds depicted onscreen. The conventions associated with integrated numbers in musicals are learned, and I do not apply them unless specifically cued to do so.

You might well be thinking that I've stacked the deck in my favor by comparing two genres—the detective film and the Hollywood musical—that exist on opposite ends of the realism/fantasy spectrum. Yet I contend that the PMD is fully operational even in cases where the ontological status of an element of the fictional universe of a film is fully in doubt. Take, for example, *Harvey* (1950), a film that gives the viewer inconsistent cues about whether or not its titular character is real. The film's central conceit is that its protagonist, Elwood P. Dowd, claims he can see a six-foot rabbit that remains invisible to other characters. Dowd's belief in Harvey as a pooka, a Celtic fairy visible only to rumpots and crackpots, is established in his first scene. As Dowd approaches the gate of his family's home, he opens it for his unseen companion and even pauses to allow Harvey to pass through.

Despite the fact that Dowd talks to Harvey and even has a painted portrait of the two together, the viewer is encouraged to see the rabbit as a figment of Dowd's imagination. Because of Dowd's habitual tippling, the viewer weighs the probabilities that Harvey is real, and infers that Dowd's belief in him is more than likely the result of alcohol-induced hallucinations. Given Winters's emphasis on film as an antirealist medium, there is no reason to exclude the possibility that Harvey genuinely inhabits the film's diegesis as an unseen entity. (After all, ghosts enjoy such ontological status in many horror films.) Yet, because the narrative primes us with a more plausible alternative (i.e., the frequent early references to Dowd's fondness for drink), I can't imagine any viewer initially believes that Harvey is real.

I say this, in part, because our construal of various characters' motivations would make little sense without some appeal to PMD. If viewers, for example, believed that Harvey was real from the film's first frame, then Veta's attempts to exclude Elwood from a family social function would seem petty and mean. However, if our initial default favors a judgment of Elwood as likely being delusional, then Veta's machinations seem forgivable insofar as she seeks to find a suitable romantic partner for her daughter, Myrtle Mae.

More important perhaps, PMD also tacitly supports the viewer's understanding of the film's mood and tone. That is, if we immediately accept Harvey's reality as an ontological premise of much fantasy cinema, and further of the particular filmind that imagined him, then the scenes of Elwood's commitment to the local sanitarium would play less as light comedy and more like the crusading melodrama of *The Snake Pit* (1948) or *Changeling* (2008). Our sense of injustice regarding this plot development is sharpened if we assume Elwood to be a gifted seer rather than a besotted fool. Here again, because our sympathies rest with Veta, her concern for Elwood's psychological condition seems justified. Rather than seeing *Harvey* as a Foucauldian critique of institutional definitions of madness, one likely recognizes Dowd's passive acceptance of his commitment as a reasonable response under the circumstances presented.

Finally, without the PMD, there would be no surprise when the narration's alignment shifts to Dr. Chumley and we see that Harvey also has enchanted the sanitarium's medical director. Chumley has gotten roaring drunk at Dowd's favorite watering hole and during his return to the sanitarium, the doctor shows visible signs of distress, apparently pursued by an unseen assailant. Chumley's behavior arouses the viewer's curiosity momentarily, but his actions suddenly become more explicable when doors and windows suddenly begin to open themselves. What is the putative cause of these strange occurrences, which violate the natural laws we'd previously believed were in force? Harvey, who turns out to be a real being in the film's fictional universe.

This plot revelation is not unmotivated, though. The unlikely possibility that Harvey is real was previously established by Wilson's perusal of the dictionary definition of a pooka as a being visible to rumpots. Moreover, since Chumley acknowledges that he is not a habitual imbiber, his unexpected inebriation explains why he suddenly can see Harvey when he wasn't able to do so before. Following the logic of PMD as a particular heuristic, viewers come to accept the reality of an invisible, six-foot rabbit only when it becomes an adjustment of real-world expectations that we cannot avoid.

In the case of *Harvey*, the narrational processes that produce curiosity, suspense, and surprise depend upon PMD and the set of default assumptions that viewers bring to the fictional world depicted. These assumptions are not entailed by the ontological conditions we associate with fictionality. Rather they provide the conceptual framework for the viewer's comprehension of film narratives, which are guided more by pragmatics than philosophical premises. In sum, although I cannot disprove the *filmosophical* conception of spectatorship endorsed by Winters, the notion that viewers must a priori entertain every possible variance and permutation of real-world experience strikes me as wildly improbable.

As a heuristic device, though, the PMD is far from foolproof. Indeed, filmmakers sometimes use our tendency toward "quick and dirty" assumptions against us when they suddenly reveal that a peculiar filmic universe does not operate according to real-world rules. This is the case with both Giorgio Biancorosso's "harpist in the closet" from *Bananas* (1971) and Mel Brooks's famous placement of Count Basie's orchestra in the middle of a desert in *Blazing Saddles* (1974). Still the fact that we can be fooled attests to the general reliability of the realistic heuristic as a guide for the viewer's inferences. Woody Allen could not break the "rules" for the conceptual divide between diegetic and nondiegetic music if those rules were not in force in the first place. And the joke would fall flat if such situations were the norm for the types of situations in which diegetic music is motivated.

Theory out of Sync: The "Nondiegetic Fallacy" and the Integrated Soundtrack

Perhaps the most troubling aspect of Winters's "nondiegetic fallacy" is that he fails to consider his theory's implications for other elements of a film's soundtrack. More specifically, in laying out the case for believing that music could be "in the air" of a film's fictional world, Winters never considers the fact that dialogue and sound effects would seem equally indeterminate. In their discussion of the spatial dimension of sound in *Film Art: An Introduction*, David Bordwell and Kristin Thompson locate the distinction between diegetic and nondiegetic in relation to other conceptual divisions, such as those distinguishing onscreen sound from offscreen and internal sounds from external. Winters does not address these other categories per se, but the same denial of realistic motivation that undergirds his critique of the "nondiegetic fallacy" also vitiates our ability to make conceptual distinctions for other types of sound. If every film operates according to the peculiar rules of its own filmic universe, then there is no reason to automatically assume that vocal sounds or noises would function as they do in the real world. If this is the case, the same logic that produces the "nondiegetic fallacy" for music also makes it impossible to discern onscreen sound from offscreen or internal sounds from external.

Here, as was the case with *Harvey*, the inability to make such category distinctions would make certain films almost literally incomprehensible in that characters' actions and motivations would make little sense. Indeed, our ability to understand the subjective experience of sound proves absolutely essential in stories where the representation of a character's mental activities is vital to a film's unfolding plot. An especially instructive instance of this phenomenon is the 1943 John Garfield espionage thriller, *The Fallen Sparrow*, where our understanding of the protagonist's actions and motivations hinges on our ability to discern the differences between internal and external sounds.

Early in the film, Kit, a former POW during the Spanish civil war, describes being systematically tortured by his Fascist captors. After characterizing his captivity as akin to being stuffed into a bottle with the cork then put in, Kit describes the conditions thusly: "It was dark. Hot. You lived mostly by sounds." He adds that his most vivid memories of these sounds included the screams of other prisoners down the corridor, the squeaky hinge of the jail door, and a faucet drip. The latter served as particular psychological torment as prisoners were given very little water to drink. To underscore the gravity of this revelation, composer Roy Webb mimics the sound of dripping water with a steady, repeated plunk of a xylophone.

Yet the sound that haunted Kit the most was "the drag of that foot," which presaged the guards taking prisoners out of their cell for bouts of physical abuse. As before, to represent Kit's memory of this sound, Webb uses a repeated two-note figure to imitate the sound of the lead interrogator's hobbling gait. Kit adds, "I never saw him, the one that limped. The others would come down and take me upstairs. And go to work on me."

In subsequent scenes, however, *The Fallen Sparrow* shifts its representational strategies regarding Kit's subjectivity. This change is signaled in a scene where Kit discovers an old letter he had written to his longtime friend, Louis Lepetino. An insert shows the text of the letter, which reads: "I can't stand it much longer, sometimes I think I've lost my reason." When the film cuts back to a close-up of Kit, Webb's now familiar "foot-dragging" musical motif returns. In a gesture of narrative redundancy, Webb's score is joined on the soundtrack by an aural flashback of the dragged foot's actual sound. The scrape and thump have obvious affinities to Webb's two-note motif. But the soundtrack's design differentiates Kit's auditory recall from its musical representation by giving the former a slightly slower tempo than the latter. As the shot lingers on Kit's face, the sounds of the dragged foot are gradually replaced by Webb's "water dripping" motif. When the expression of Kit's face changes to one of puzzlement, Webb's score fades out only to be replaced by the sounds of actual water drops. Kit rises from his chair and makes a beeline for the next room where he locates the source of those sounds in the kitchen faucet.

Kit shuts off the tap and goes back to the living room. Although the dripping sound has ceased, the imagined sound of the dragged foot returns. Kit's growing psychological distress is cued both by the reprise of Webb's musical motif and the now familiar rhythm of the foot's scrape and thump. In an effort to drown out the sounds in his head, Kit begins opening windows to let in the sounds of traffic and car horns from the street below. Just before the scene fades out, Kit sits down at the piano and begins pounding the keyboard wildly with his fists. The scene ends with a close-up of Kit, a sick smile pasted over his sweaty visage.

The apparent tension between objective and subjective sounds is finally dispelled in a scene where Kit confronts his previous tormentor. The camera de-acousmatizes the sound, initially showing us a medium close-up of the killer's labored walk before ultimately tilting up to reveal his identity. The culprit turns out to be Dr. Christian Skaas, a suspect overlooked by police since he appeared to be confined to a wheelchair. Skaas's feigned handicap turns out to be a ruse intended to hide his telltale limp.

I've described *The Fallen Sparrow* at some length in order to illustrate the way that its dense weave of offscreen, internal, and nondiegetic sounds provide insight into its hero's troubled psychology. Indeed, viewers could scarcely follow *The Fallen Sparrow*'s story if they were incapable of distinguishing each sound's relation to narrative space and its place within different levels of film narration. Yet it is precisely this ability to make reliable inferences about a fictional soundscape that is denied by Winters's model. The same epistemological grounds that led Winters to reject nondiegetic music as a category would also seem to impair our ability to distinguish between internal and external sounds. In a medium that is inherently unrealistic, who's to say that Kit's internal monologues aren't some special form of ventriloquism specific to its fictional world? Similarly, if a "filmind creates a film-world in which music exists 'in the air,'" isn't it also possible that *The Fallen Sparrow*'s sound of a dragging foot has the same liminal status? In fact, if we assume that sounds in a fictional world need not follow real-world rules of physics or acoustics, then any offscreen sound can attach to any possible source or even no source at all. Maybe the "filmind" that imagined *The Fallen Sparrow* has created a world in which sound we take to be music is really the sound of a dragging foot and the sound we think is the dragging foot is really its music? Indeed, since they are frequently heard together and since a film-world has no necessary connection with reality, there would seem to be no reason to prefer one reading of these sounds over the other.

Perhaps the most significant problem with Winters's theory, though, is its failure to account for the classical soundtrack's vococentrism. The notion that the cinema is vococentric can be traced back to the work of Michel Chion, who analogizes the centrality of the voice in film sound design to Alfred Hitchcock's remark that "the position of the face determines the shot composition."[13] More recently, David Neumeyer productively enlarges Chion's concept in *Meaning and Interpretation of Music in Cinema*. Early in the book, Neumeyer establishes the importance of vococentrism by asserting that it is one of two overriding principles of the analyses that follow, the other being the primacy of the integrated soundtrack. For Neumeyer, these two ideas give rise to three general principles, the second of which "acknowledges that the sound track is constructed—the overriding priority in the classical system being narrative clarity, not acoustic fidelity—and it is hierarchical, with the voice (speech, dialogue) at the top, music and sound effects below."[14]

Neumeyer's description of vococentrism underscores a serious problem with Winters's model, namely its glaring lack of historicism. There is, of course, a very obvious explanation of this specific deviation from real-world experience. As sound technology was being implemented, the desire for clarity led to the development of norms for sound mixing that privileged the voice over other elements. But such an explanation requires an appeal to extrafictional factors of the type that lie completely outside the scope of Frampton's filmosophy. Indeed, Neumeyer's emphasis on vococentrism yields the kind of technicist description of film that Frampton characterizes as uninteresting.[15]

Because Frampton and Winters are so concerned with specific deviations from real-world experience, they overlook the fact that the particular representational strategies used to present narrative information are governed by norms and conventions extrinsic to the stories they tell. More important, these norms and conventions play an important role in guiding spectatorial comprehension in ways that function independently of the narrative material they communicate. Unlike the laws of nature, which govern our real-world experience, conventions do not have the force of necessity. Instead, as Todd Berliner points out, conventions of all types enhance the viewer's processing fluency by facilitating the efficient uptake of information.[16] But conventions can be tweaked, manipulated, and played with according to broad schema and revision principles. Sound mixing conventions, thus, explain why music's volume rises and falls in relation to the presence of dialogue in so many fictional universes. But it also explains much more divergent practices, including conventions regarding the presence of sounds in outer space settings in science fiction films. Schema and revision principles not only account for the audibility of spaceship sounds in *Star Wars* (1977) and *Apollo 13* but also the unnerving silence that characterizes the environments of *2001: A Space Odyssey* (1967) and *Gravity* (2013).

The appearance of music in films operates according to such conventions, which together comprise a vococentric approach to sound design. More importantly, these conventions also cue viewers to infer music's relation to narrative space in particular ways. In a much earlier essay on Hollywood practitioners' distinction between source music and background music, Neumeyer offered a list of ten interactive pairs of musical codes that, when used as analytical tools, provide richer, more nuanced readings of music's role in cinematic discourse.[17]

Diegetic/nondiegetic (or source/background)
Onscreen/offscreen
Vocal/instrumental (performative forces)
Rerecording: synchronized/not-synchronized
Sound levels: realistic/unrealistic (for diegetic music)
Musically continuous/discontinuous
Musically closed/open
Thematic/motivic referentiality
Formal interaction of cutting and music: yes/no
Motivation, or narrative plausibility: yes/no

Neumeyer has since distanced himself from this earlier formulation, feeling that he demoted the status of the diegetic/nondiegetic pair by grouping it with the others on the list. However, I contend that Neumeyer's list still has enormous heuristic value in that the clustering of some codes tends to favor the inference that a piece of music is either diegetic or nondiegetic. All things being equal, a cue that is musically continuous, musically closed, and presented at a realistic sound level is likely to be construed as diegetic. In contrast, music that is formally discontinuous, open, interacts with the film's editing, has thematic or motivic referentiality, and lacks a plausible source will be construed as nondiegetic. Because of the conventional nature of these musical properties, certain combinations furnish a "quick and dirty" guide to music's place within the film's discursive patterning.

As before, these conventions guide the viewer's inferential processes, but are far from foolproof. For example, *Baby Driver*'s (2017) use of the Button Down Brass's recording of "Tequila" disrupts most of our conventional expectations for diegetic music. Although the song is motivated as something heard through the ear buds of Baby's iPod, its sound level increases so as to evoke the protagonist's point of audition; it is musically continuous and closed in its formal patterning; and it not only is synchronized with the character's physical actions and the film's cutting, but its rhythms also match up precisely with the gunfire exchanged by the film's characters.

Yet *Baby Driver* is also an extremely *unconventional* film in its treatment of music as part of the film's overall sound design. Much of the pleasure of watching the film comes from its quirky soundtrack, even as it embraces nearly all of the usual moves of the contemporary action film.[18] More important, the fact that *Baby Driver* is an acknowledged outlier is tacit recognition that these conventions are fully operative in countless other instances of music in film. These more standard usages are utterly uninteresting when compared with *Baby Driver*. But the far-reaching typicality of such music is also what enables viewers to reliably infer their status in relation to the diegesis.

At the end of the day, Winters's nondiegetic fallacy fails to recognize the force of cinematic conventions as the grounds for viewers' expectations about how narrative information will be communicated. If one begins with the assumption that every film creates its own filmic universe and further that these filmic universes are the products of film-thinking by filminds, then it becomes much harder to explain why particular patterns of cinematic discourse occur across specific groups of films. These corpora can be quite small, such as the eight narrative features in Terrence Malick's filmography, or quite large, encompassing the thousands of titles that make up the classical Hollywood cinema. Yet the conventions within them offer powerful indicators of a film's formal design, including the deviations from real-world knowledge that Winters finds so troubling.

Conclusion

As I've argued throughout this essay, most of the problems I see with Winters's nondiegetic fallacy come from approaching the issue from a philosophical perspective rather than from the viewpoint of the spectator's narrative comprehension. The crux of the issue is not the kinds of departures from everyday experience of which film-worlds are capable, but rather how viewers could process any story information without some tacit application of real-world knowledge. Implicit in Winters's model is the notion that viewers are folk philosophers, who comprehend film-worlds on the basis on their own unique ontologies. We aren't and we don't. Viewers display the same mix of "fast" and "slow" thinking that Daniel Kahneman identifies with normal cognitive functioning. And just as we do in the real world, viewers employ heuristics, like the principle of minimal departure, to understand the details of the cinematic worlds they see. Such a heuristic may not be logically necessary to any theory of film narrative, but it retains extraordinary value by checking the infinite variations of fictive space, time, and causality made possible without it. The principle acknowledges the ways in which fictional worlds differ from the real world but highlights the degree to which these differences are quite limited and specifiable.

Yet if we accept that this principle has heuristic value and further that we likely could not comprehend any film narrative without it, then we can see why the presence of music "in the air" of a fictional world is a problem. Since that premise represents a major departure from our everyday experience, it seems quite unlikely that viewers would default to the position that musical underscore exists in the same fictional space as the characters. The categories of diegetic and nondiegetic sounds are imperfect ones, precisely because their boundaries are permeable and can be manipulated to quite dramatic effect. But they also seem necessary, despite these imperfections, to any systematic explanation of the way music functions as a tool of cinematic narration. To avoid the traps and pitfalls I've outlined here, any theory attempting to explain music's relation to narrative space should display the following features.

1. Each category must be centered around prototypical instances even as we acknowledge they are likely to have fuzzy boundaries and clear borderline cases. All too often those who seek to revise or even dismiss our concepts of diegetic and nondiegetic music develop their theories around outlying examples, a strategy that almost always pushes the conversation in unproductive directions. Prototypes usually aren't very interesting. For example, chihuahuas, Irish wolfhounds, mastiffs, and dachshunds are much more interesting dog breeds than the humble Labrador or German Shepherd. But the latter are prototypes and thus more fundamental to our understanding of dogs as a particular genus of mammals. The same is true of the most normative cases of diegetic and nondiegetic music.
2. Attempts to define diegetic and nondiegetic music should avoid treating the film score as having properties distinct from the techniques and devices found in film's other formal systems. As an aspect of film narration, music does certain things more efficiently than other techniques, but most all of its functions, from conveying characters' emotional states to providing continuity to criterial prefocusing, can all be achieved by other means. The tendency among musicologists to see the film score as a unique aspect of film narration always begs questions about why we construe film music's status in one way and the status of all other discursive elements in another. If we believe it is possible for music to just be "in the air" as it were, do we believe the same thing of superimposed titles, like those that introduce Blondie, Angel Eyes, and Tuco as "the good," "the bad," and "the ugly," respectively? Is this also true of the sounds produced by heterodiegetic voiceover narration, like that found in *The Magnificent Ambersons* (1942), *Dogville* (2003), or *Little Children* (2006)?
3. Cinematic conventions, both narrative and stylistic, account for many of the ways film-worlds deviate from real-world experience. Music in film is no exception to this very basic principle. Conventions, though, are not rule-bound and instead operate according to established, extrinsic norms. Like other types of conventional film practice, the norms associated with sound design create a horizon of expectations for viewers that, in turn, enable them to make inferences about any particular sound's relation to

> the narrative. This remains true even for sounds whose status is ambiguous. Instead of positing, though, that a music cue actually somehow transforms its status from diegetic to nondiegetic (or vice versa), I believe we are better served by an analytic approach that focuses first on the way it violates conventional norms and thereby disrupts our normal conceptual schemas.

To my mind, the categories of diegetic and nondiegetic sound, including music, capture the features of the phenomena and fulfill the above three criteria better than any rival concept that's been proposed. To paraphrase Winston Churchill's famous dictum about democracy, diegetic and nondiegetic might be the worst way to conceive of sound's relation to narrative space save for all those others that have been tried from time to time.

Notes

1. For Gorbman's earliest use of this terminology, see "Narrative Film Music," *Yale French Studies* 60 (1980): 183–203.

2. See Robynn J. Stilwell, "The Fantastical Gap between Diegetic and Nondiegetic," *Beyond the Soundtrack*, ed. Daniel Goldmark, Lawrence Kramer, and Richard Leppert (Berkeley: University of California Press, 2007), 184–202.

3. See David Neumeyer, "Diegetic/Nondiegetic: A Theoretical Model," *Music and the Moving Image* 2, 1 (2009): 26–39; Giorgio Biancorosso, "The Harpist in the Closet: Film Music as Epistemological Joke," *Music and the Moving Image* 2, 3 (2009): 11–33; and Jeff Smith, "Bridging the Gap: Reconsidering the Boundary between Diegetic and Non-diegetic Music," *Music and the Moving Image* 2, 1: (2009): 1–25.

4. Annahid Kassabian, "The End of Diegesis as We Know It?" *The Oxford Handbook of Audiovisual Aesthetics*, edited by John Richardson, Claudia Gorbman, and Carol Vernallis (New York: Oxford University Press, 2013), 89–106; Kassabian, *Hearing Film: Tracking Identifications in Contemporary Hollywood Film Music* (New York: Routledge, 2001).

5. Guido Heldt, *Music and Levels of Narration: Steps across the Border* (Chicago: Intellect, 2013).

6. Tobias Pontara, "Interpretation and Underscoring: Modest Constructivism and the Issue of Nondiegetic versus Intradiegetic Music in Film," *Music and the Moving Image* 9, 2 (2016): 39–57; and Valerio Sbravati, "Story Music/Discourse Music: Analyzing the Relationship between Placement and Function of Music in Film," *Music and the Moving Image* 9, 3 (2016): 19–37. In addition to all of the aforementioned essays, the diegetic/nondiegetic distinction also has a prominent place in a recently published discussion among film music scholars. See Annahid Kassabian (convenor) with Elena Boschi, James Buhler, Claudia Gorbman, Miguel Mera, Roger Moseley, Ronald Sadoff, Ben Winters (contributors), "Roundtable: Current Perspectives on Music, Sound, and Narrative in Screen Media," *The Routledge Companion to Screen Music and Sound*, ed. Miguel Mera, Ronald Sadoff, and Ben Winters (New York: Routledge, 2017), 108–24.

7. See Ben Winters, "The Nondiegetic Fallacy: Film, Music, and Narrative Space," *Music & Letters* 91, 2 (2010): 224–44; and *Music, Performance, and the Realities of Film: Shared Concert Experiences in Screen Fiction* (London: Routledge, 2014).

8. Winters, "Nondiegetic Fallacy," 3.

9. Daniel Frampton, *Filmosophy* (New York: Wallflower Press, 2006), 7.

10. Ibid., 77.

11. Winters, "Nondiegetic Fallacy," 20.

12. Marie Laure-Ryan, "Fiction, Non-Factuals, and the Principle of Minimal Departure," *Poetics* 9, no. 4 (1980): 406.

13. Michel Chion, *Audio-Vision: Sound on Screen*, trans. Claudia Gorbman (New York: Columbia University Press, 1994), 6.

14. David Neumeyer, *Meaning and Interpretation of Music in Cinema* (Bloomington: Indiana University Press, 2015), 3.

15. Frampton, *Filmosophy*, 169–82.

16. See Todd Berliner, *Hollywood Aesthetic: Pleasure in American Cinema* (New York: Oxford University Press, 2017).

17. David Neumeyer, "Source Music, Background Music, Fantasy and Reality in Early Sound Film," *College Music Symposium* 37 (1997): 15–17.

18. For more on the particularities of Edgar Wright as a sound stylist, see Amanda McQueen, "'Bring the Noise': Sonic Intensified Continuity in the Films of Edgar Wright," *Music, Sound, and the Moving Image* 7, 2 (2013): 141–65.

Chapter 15

The End(s) of Vococentrism

James Buhler

Vococentrism as Concept

After 1930, first in the United States and quickly thereafter elsewhere, the industry pursued a policy of codifying practices for producing sound film. The wide-ranging practices of the transition years winnowed to an increasingly ordered set of practices defined by the principles of what Michel Chion has termed *vococentrism*.[1] Chion famously claims that there is no soundtrack. Yet Chion does not deny that the voice organizes the soundtrack. Chion writes: "There are voices, and then everything else. In other words, in every audio mix, the presence of a human voice instantly sets up a hierarchy of perception."[2] This inherent hierarchy marked the humanism of the sound film, but also its anthropocentrism. For Dorothy Richardson, it also inscribed the sound film much more strongly within the patriarchal order than did the silent film.[3] In any event, the classical era sound film was in essence defined by this deference to a naturalized hierarchy of perception, which constituted the coordinates of a perceptual realism. Whether that hierarchy was actually natural and innate or just so heavily socialized as to form the second nature of ideology has been disputed, but few would deny that the classical style was organized to appeal to the dominant perceptual regime or that this regime has all the appearance of something immediate and natural; it strikes us, as Chion puts it, instantly, automatically.

The system of vococentrism determined a set of practices that established the centrality of the voice in the classical sound film, but more importantly vococentrism signified that everything in sound film passed through the voice, even when the voice was absent. Chion draws an analogy with anthropocentric vision—how perception organizes space around human bodies and faces—and argues that this is how we attend to sound as well. "The presence of the human voice structures the space that contains it."[4] Alfred Hitchcock, Chion notes, turned the face into his dominant compositional principle. "For Hitchcock, 'the position of the face determines the shot composition,'" and, Chion says, he "had only to transpose this lucid remark to the aural register: the first thing people hear is the voice."[5] Vococentrism for Chion thus asserts the centrality of the voice and the subjugation of the other components to it.

Without calling it vococentrism, David Bordwell develops a similar analogy for the practice of the classic Hollywood sound film:

> In sound cinema the voice became as central to the sound track as the human figure was to the image track. Like bodily build and facial expression, the voice individuates, it characterizes, it marks traits for narrative development, it gives access to psychological-casual factors. . . . In Hollywood, dialogue constitutes the chief vehicle of narrative action and must be personalized no less than body, face, and space.[6]

From very early in the sound era, sound film was centered on the vocal component of the soundtrack, at first through what I call *the rule of mimetic synchronization*—the demand that the source of the sound be accounted for in the image—and later through the more flexible system of vococentrism itself; and if it would not be correct to say that images generally illustrate the voice under the system of vococentrism, it is also true that the dialogue does not supplement the image. Instead, they are drawn into a complex relation that produces an effect of narration.

Vococentrism required that dialogue be the central element of the soundtrack, but David Neumeyer in his extensive development of Chion's idea notes that in the classic sound film vococentrism demanded neither the ubiquity of dialogue nor that it would always feature prominently.[7] In this respect, vococentrism was the theoretical side of the intermittent system that had evolved from the part-talkie, those films from the early transition period that featured an oscillation between the techniques of silent film and those of the talkie. Intermittence was also one important difference of the system of vococentrism from the rule of mimetic synchronization, which was essentially the theory of the 100 percent talkie. Early talking film—the 100 percent talkie—ensured the centrality of dialogue by insisting on the rule of mimetic synchronization stemming from the conception of sound film as the theater of reality, as "total cinema."[8] In this understanding, sound film was essentially a recording of profilmic action. But filmmakers quickly learned that vococentrism and mimetic synchronization need not constitute an identity, and so a theory of vococentrism cannot appeal straightforwardly to the image.

Although Chion draws an analogy with the face, he does not pursue the analogy to a proper conclusion.[9] What does it mean for the face to be central to cinematography and editing? It certainly does not mean that every shot is a close-up, or that every shot is of a face, or that the face dominates every shot that contains it. In the classical sound film, vococentrism in fact established and balanced a set of representational principles rather than adhering exclusively to recording and the rule of mimetic synchronization to regulate its usage. It permitted both synchronous and asynchronous use of sound; it allowed both source and accompanying music depending on representational needs; it regulated foreground and background layers in terms of narrative clarity and pertinence; and it presumed that the edited sequence took precedence over the individual shot and constructed the soundtrack to enhance the continuity and coherence of the sequence. It was also, as many noted and feared, anthropocentric and individualizing to an extreme. If a tendency toward psychological realism constituted its most troubling ideological commitment, the centricity of the voice regulated the composition of audiovisual figures and their interpretation without fixing the figures in advance. In classical style, the centricity of the face meant only that the image was always interpreted in terms of the face, that the placement and displacement of the face were of primary concern. And it is in this sense that we should understand the voice and the soundtrack under vococentrism: the soundtrack is always interpreted in terms of the voice.

Vococentrism as Classical Style

How did vococentrism come to be? Is vococentrism necessary? What are the goals of vococentrism? What are the challenges of vococentrism? What representational possibilities does vococentrism foreclose? We can look to the codification of the soundtrack during the transitional era to get preliminary bearings on these questions.

Although filmmakers such as Charlie Chaplin, René Clair, Fritz Lang, Vsevolod Pudovkin, and Sergei Eisenstein resisted the audiovisual figure of synchronized dialogue, commercial filmmaking after 1930, whether in Hollywood or internationally, increasingly meant talking film with synchronized dialogue. Vococentrism dominated not so much because it was realistic, but rather because it was able to appropriate and transform in a productive way the basic principles of the silent film practice of narrative filmmaking.

Although vococentrism insisted on the centrality of dialogue, dialogue was not ubiquitous on the soundtrack the way music was ubiquitous in the silent era or that synchronized dialogue featured prominently at every moment in the talking film. As David Neumeyer and I argue,

> Although the principle of vococentrism states that the position of the voice determines the composition of the sound track, this means only that the placement is always of central concern, never a contingent factor. It does not imply that the voice is always centered any more than the face is always centered and in medium close-up in the image track. Vococentrism in this sense claims only that we recognize in an immediate way when the voice has moved off-center and interpret the configuration accordingly as an expressive effect or as an excessive stylistic flourish.[10]

Some films, especially early in the transitional era, were edited so that each new line of dialogue motivated a cut. But the importance of the reaction shot as an audiovisual figure was understood almost immediately, as was the potential for sound effects, and to some extent music, to complement and contextualize the voice, to make a setting for it. René Clair famously appreciated the way offscreen sound in *The Broadway Melody* (1929) turned reaction into an affective power: "We hear the noise of a door being slammed and a car driving off while we are shown Bessie Love's anguished face watching from a window the departure we do not see."[11] As is often the case in these kinds of descriptions, Clair's memory of the sequence was not precise, and his memory drew somewhat faulty inferences from the sequence. We see and hear the car door slam as a synchronized figure (Figure 15.1a), and this is followed by a shot of Bessie Love's face showing anguish (Figure 15.1b). The syntax is actually characteristic of the silent film tradition, with the affect-laden reaction shot succeeding a shot of the event that gave rise to it, and without audio counterpoint. The next shot (Figure 15.1c) goes to Eddie (Charles King), and then returns to Love's face (Figure 15.1d), which is only now paired with the sound of the departing car. But Love's face here has changed: it shows less anguish than it seems to plead with Eddie. That is, the second shot is not so much the expression of the character's interiority as it is a communicative act seeking to move Eddie into action. The syntax is again primarily that of the silent film. But Clair's attention to this sequence suggests that the sound intervened into the silent film syntax and altered it: in Clair's memory the sound shifted from the second shot of Love (15.1d) to the first (15.1b), and the anguish became a response not directly to the shot showing Queenie (Anita Page) getting into the car but to the sound of the car departing. Clair thereby transformed the sequence into something of an allegory of the coming of sound. Sound acquired power when it marked a loss of vision, but this loss was paid for with added pathos. In this way, Clair's memory turned the sequence not just into an allegory for the coming of sound but also into a prototype for the reaction shot that would be crucial to developing a syntax for the sound film that was distinct from the silent film.

Figure 15.1: Sequence using reaction shot in *The Broadway Melody* (1929).

The importance of the reaction shot to classical style is that it recognizes that dialogue and sound are not merely caused but that they also carry an effect and that sometimes the effect is more pertinent to narrative understanding than is the place of its enunciation.[12] Pudovkin posed the following rhetorical question that emphasizes that dramatic function of reaction: "Would a director of any imagination handle a scene in a court of justice where a sentence of death is being passed by filming the judge pronouncing the sentence in preference to recording visually the immediate reactions of the condemned?"[13] Music, too, figured in realizing the aesthetic potential of the reaction shot inasmuch as a well-placed musical stinger could help anchor an expression passing across the listening face to a particular word in the dialogue, registering its force like a psychological sound effect. In this way, music helped facilitate the emergence of the reaction shot as a distinct and key feature of sound film.

Reaction shots occurred in silent film—the brief sequence I discussed from *The Broadway Melody* illustrates how they might be used—but, without being set in an audiovisual counterpoint determined by an expectation of synchronization, they lacked the same force. Such practice persisted long into the sound era, such as in *King Kong* (1933), where Anne (Fay Wray), bound for the sacrifice, awaits the arrival of the monster, who is introduced through a combination of sound and the panic on Anne's face. The screen test on the ship where Denham's (Robert

Figure 15.2: Comparison of reaction shots in *King Kong* (1933).

Armstrong) asynchronous dialogue guides Anne's reaction to an imagined menace grants to sound a power of suggestion that is enhanced by withholding the corresponding image and displacing it with the reaction (Figure 15.2a). The action that this scene foreshadows—the appearance of the monster (Figures 15.2b and c)—is actually much less arresting, since the visual strategies of the actual revelation of Kong are more in line with traditional silent film syntax of showing supplemented by sound. And it is perhaps worth noting that the sound for the sequence consists primarily of music, roars, and screams.

If reaction shots generally needed to be formulated somewhat differently in silent film, reactions are certainly used on stage as well. But unlike sound film, any reaction on stage must be played broadly enough that the gesture can be read from the audience, and the stage has no method like cutting to a close-up to ensure that the spectator's attention falls squarely on the listening rather than the speaking body. Finding drama in the subtle play of the face in reaction to the flow of dialogue (or other diegetic sound stream) is distinctive to sound film, and music helped highlight this possibility.

The prototype for the distinctive reaction shot of the sound film was discovered early. Its contours are already discernible in *The Jazz Singer* (1927), in Al Jolson's first performance in the film at Coffee Dan's (Figure 15.3a). During the song, the image presents a cutaway showing Mary's (May McAvoy) reaction to hearing Jack, Jolson's character, sing as she pauses on the stairs just after entering Coffee Dan's (Figure 15.3b). Similar cutaway shots focusing on the reaction of the listening face occur during each of the performance sequences in the film. Many of these—"Blue Skies," "Mother of Mine," and "My Mammy"—trace the mother's reaction as Jack's performance continues on the soundtrack. She even speaks, via intertitle, during "Mother of Mine," and the father's fatal word of dialogue is motivated by a reaction shot registering his distaste for Jack's jazzy version of "Blue Skies." Cutting into a musical performance scene to show either diegetic audience reaction or some sort of backstage hijinks is a common strategy for narrativizing the performance and eroding the autonomy of the number.[14] Something similar holds as well for the level of the shot in sound film, where the unity of image and voice can make a sequence that is cut to follow lines of dialogue devolve into a series of more or less autonomous shots. The reaction shot was one solution that allowed filmmakers to assert the precedence of the narrative sequence over the

Figure 15.3: Mary listens to Jack in *The Jazz Singer* (1927).

autonomy of the individual shot, and in this way the reaction shot effectively assimilated asynchronous sound into the incipient system of vococentrism.

Through audiovisual figures such as the reaction shot, vococentrism effectively recast the three dominant principles of silent film music—synchronization, continuity, and subjugation—as powers within a determining hierarchal order of foreground and background. As Hannah Lewis and I argue,

> Centricity rewrites the principle of synchronization as a marker of import, the site of meaning that assures the appearance of subjectivity and its hegemonic status. Continuity becomes the power of background, the guarantor that the image presents only a view, a fragment of a world that extends indefinitely beyond the frame. Continuity also establishes the more or less neutral ground of asynchronous sound against which the synchronization of the foreground figure stands out in contrast. Finally, vococentrism redeploys subjugation to unlock its full syntactical power, that of the hierarchy itself; but subjugation pertains not simply to music and effects vis-à-vis the voice or the soundtrack vis-à-vis the image, but ultimately to the subjugation of everything to narrative, the cinematic form of meaningful action.[15]

The basic claim here is that vococentrism was the system of sound film that appeared when narrative was given voice. The implication of this claim, in other words, is that narrative resisted being realized through only the rule of mimetic synchronization. The latter yielded only the reproduction of dramaturgy. Vococentrism, by contrast, organized the codification of classical style along narrative lines, extending both to the representation as well as to its production.

The seven rules that Claudia Gorbman famously identifies as characteristic of the classic style—invisibility, inaudibility, signifier of emotion, narrative cueing, continuity, unity, and the escape clause—would then all be manifestations of this basic principle of vococentrism.[16] Invisibility and inaudibility subjugate production to narrative. Signifier of emotion and narrative cuing relate to the setting of voice in relation to narrative, that is, they establish the emotional and narrative context of the vocal utterance and synchronized music to the narrative. Continuity determines the narrative conditions of the voice's centricity. Unity is a formal value, but it also relates indirectly to continuity: it helps establish that the representation is aesthetically convincing and internally coherent. The escape clause ensures that the voice is legible and that any displacements are read as significant, so that the centricity of the voice is itself subjugated to the narrative significance that it bears.[17]

Vococentrism in the Age of Intensified Continuity

Thus far I have been arguing that vococentrism is a basic premise of classical style. Indeed, perhaps it is simply another name for the classical continuity system of sound film conceptualized from the standpoint of the soundtrack rather than from the image. That intuition in turn leads me to leap far ahead from the transition to sound and the codification of the sound film as vococentric and to consider vococentrism and the so-called crisis of contemporary cinema that has emerged with digital filmmaking.[18]

If avant-garde and international cinemas have historically offered regular challenges to classical style and continuity, today's challenges to the classical continuity system take place routinely in mainstream commercial filmmaking, as the litany of offenses regularly brought against action films especially for violating accepted canons of film continuity and coherent storytelling readily attests. Some, like Eleftheria Thanouli, Justin Wyatt, Geoff King, and Carol Vernallis among others, have argued that a new "postclassical" style organized around impact, sensation, and a fraying of the narrative thread has emerged,[19] whereas others, especially David Bordwell and Kristin Thompson, see a basic persistence of the continuity system and classical storytelling that, though extended and intensified—Bordwell famously calls the techniques of contemporary filmmaking "intensified continuity"—nevertheless still delivers a narrative that is clear and unified.[20] Although there is a fair amount of agreement that the visual style of contemporary cinema is structured around the techniques that Bordwell identifies—fast cutting, close framings, mobile camera, and bipolar extremes of lens lengths—there is no consensus to the conclusion that Bordwell draws that these devices are in fact used to tell essentially updated classical stories. And Bordwell in particular is more likely to condemn a film like *The Bourne Ultimatum* (2007) for violating classical canons than he is to accept that a different aesthetic principle like sensation or impact might be deforming standards of continuity in order to reorganize the film along other lines.[21]

Here, I want to focus for a moment on the attribute of close framing. When widescreen cinema first came into being, the large and wide screen initially discouraged close-ups as presenting an overly magnified view on the one hand and as running counter to what was generally thought to be the widescreen's natural predisposition toward slower cutting rates. To fill the space, scenes were generally staged so that multiple figures would be present in the frame, and the space between the characters was then treated much more dynamically. And with the large screen size, the figures themselves were easily legible, even when they were scattered about the screen. This widescreen, however, caused issues when translated to television, where letterboxing preserved the aspect ratio (and the dynamism of the represented spaces) but at the expense of an illegibility of the characters, who are greatly—indeed on older televisions, ridiculously—reduced in stature compared to the big screen. Indeed, the wider the aspect ratio, and so the more impressively the film filled the theater, the smaller the characters would be when letterboxed on television. For this reason, the films were traditionally translated for television in what was known as pan-and-scan versions where the film would essentially be reframed for television in the editing suite. And increasingly over the '60s, '70s, and '80s, the films were shot with the television translation as the primary version (and this composition strategy was reinforced by the tendency of theaters to become smaller in size with a concomitant reduction in the size of the screen). Because of the limited screen resolution, pre-HD television greatly preferred close-ups, so filmmakers found ways to compose close-ups for widescreen in a way that they could also facilitate the translation to television. The result was a much faster cutting speed and an image that was increasingly structured to have a single focal point, two attributes that would become fundamental to intensified continuity in Bordwell's analysis. Though the widescreen image still tended to use space dynamically, this was now accomplished through off-center close-ups more than through the space structured by characters in, say, a 2-shot.

The result has been a shift from figures in medium and medium long shots that were characteristic even of dialogue scenes in both classical sound film and the first decade of widescreen film to a predominance of medium shots and close-ups even in action scenes. Bordwell laments the loss of kinetic movement in the modern action film, where the unified body in motion has been replaced by a series of close-ups that fragment the action and replace the grace of the singular movement with a frenetic energy that appears from the harsh juxtapositions of editing. Bordwell complains that the rapid editing and close-ups characteristic of intensified continuity atomize performance:

> Lengthier shots let the actor develop the character's reactions in detail, and force us to follow them. Classic studio cinema, with its more distant framings and longer takes, lets you follow the evolution of a feeling or idea through the actor's blocking and behavior. The villain in the average Charlie Chan movie displays more psychological continuity than the nasty agents in *Bourne Ultimatum*.[22]

Bordwell's meditation on shot length and distance suggests a fear of fragmentation, a longing for a lost wholeness that classical studio cinema promised. As Bordwell's clinically precise descriptions of the procedures make clear, the atomization and fragmentation of intensified continuity serve as attacks on the actor's body that evacuate the actor from the image, and action film generally pushes this process much further than do other contemporary genres.

In any event, I won't hope to resolve here this impasse over the extent to which intensified continuity has yielded a postclassical cinema, but I do think it might be useful to think about what has happened to vococentrism in the age of intensified continuity. With the parallel to the face that we have been tracing for vococentrism, we might expect that the new emphasis on the face in the visual style of intensified continuity would have a correlate to an emphasis on the voice on the soundtrack. Yet this does not appear to be the case. Carol Vernallis has argued for the importance of spectacle and sublime, figures of transgression, in understanding strategies of both visual and soundtrack construction in postclassical cinema—and indeed in contemporary media in general.[23] Mark Kerins, similarly, argues that Bordwell's conception of intensified continuity misses important ways in which the soundtrack has transformed contemporary cinema away from the classical continuity system and evolved a fundamentally new conception emphasizing impact.[24] Miguel Mera takes Kerins's approach a step further in arguing for a conception of 3D sound in films like *Gravity* (2013).[25] Arguing somewhat against Kerins, Jeff Smith agrees that the "impact aesthetic" is an important consideration for contemporary cinema but suggests that an impact aesthetic is not at odds with classical continuity and narrative strategies. And I imagine he would similarly understand contemporary spectacle as being managed much as Hollywood managed spectacle in the classical studio era—as primarily an expressive effect. If I understand Smith rightly, he thinks that impact is more a means of intensifying the classical elements than of subverting them or displacing them. In any case, Smith identifies six correlates to intensified continuity on the soundtrack. He usefully enumerates them as follows:

1. Increased volume
2. Low frequency effects
3. Expanded frequency range
4. The spatialization of sound
5. The "hyperdetail" of contemporary Foley work
6. The use of nondiegetic sound effects as stylistic punctuation[26]

Let me add seven of my own:

1. Expressive sound effects like R2D2, BB8, or Wall-E; but also ambiences that hum with affect
2. A disinclination to use music to score identity
   a. Athematic gestural music that underscores character's affective poses rather than sharply delineated themes that mark character's identity
   b. Wispy, affect-laden themes that evoke conventional tropes, moods, and musical topics but that disassociate identity or score dysphoric moods such as alienation
3. Blurring of the distinction between sound effects and music to the point that we often cannot know whether a particular sound was produced by the music or sound department
4. Use of intense choral music in underscoring to signify the mystical and the epic

5. Prominence of percussion ("cinematic drums") in underscoring
6. Organization of soundtracks around explosion points rather than screaming points
7. Systematic use of offscreen sound, especially voices, that we expect to be synchronized

Smith's correlates to intensified continuity mostly concern ways that technology enhances the immersive effect of cinema, increasing the options for filmmakers to render the fictional world with increased sonic detail and also using sound so that audiences feel the action. Smith's first five correlates are all presented as supplemental to the basic continuity system. Rather than the details and impact organizing the storytelling in new ways, they instead serve primarily to add new intensities to the narrative. The sixth correlate, nondiegetic sound as stylistic punctuation, concerns the overtness of the narration; that is, nondiegetic thumps and swooshes are sonic stylizations that draw attention to the narrative level of storytelling, usually coloring the narration with a conspiratorial tone.

In the Bourne films, for instance, the use of nondiegetic sound to accompany the appearance of bits of computer text suggests the presence of a narrational agency giving pieces of information, almost as if from surveillance, but at a higher level than anyone in the film has access to. Another notable feature is the use of subtle nondiegetic thumps and swooshes to emphasize cuts, zooms, and reframings. Sometimes the sound design appropriates diegetic sound or elements that float between diegetic and nondiegetic for emphasis. One interesting facet of this practice, however, is that these elements do not so much intensify the image in a centripetal fashion, in the sense of clarifying the image; rather the intensity is used to throw the details out as enigmas that signify that meaning will obtain, if at all, only at some larger level. This is one way the film renders its conspiratorial tone.

The resistance to these nondiegetic sounds to cohere into intensifying figures often applies to the other elements as well. And from the standpoint of vococentrism, it is noteworthy that none of the devices Smith identifies figures the voice; indeed in all cases, the intensities are obtained primarily by displacing the voice from its position of centrality. This, in fact, differs markedly from Bordwell's description of the visual strategies of intensified continuity, where intensity seems, at some level, a measure of the obsession with the face, with medium close-up passing to medium close-up in an ever-accelerating series.

The correlates I added to Smith's inventory do nothing to change this tendency.

Expressive Sound Effects

Expressive sound effects, for instance, may borrow from the order of vococentrism in a way that anthropomorphizes: R2D2 and BB8 from Star Wars, Wall-E from the eponymous film. But the unintelligibility of these "voices" nevertheless means they resist full assimilation to vococentrism, at least for the audience. Another way of putting the general situation is that where the image of intensified continuity is centripetal, the sound is centrifugal.

Athematic Gestural Music ("Corporate Classicism")

The turn from strong thematic profiles to a gestural scoring focused more on mood and affect has become a common observation on contemporary film scoring,[27] and much the way Bordwell attacks the visual strategies of the contemporary action scene for its atomization of the kinetic figure, so, too, many critics of contemporary film scoring lament the loss of thematic identity in film scoring. The most common target of this new style, which Nicholas Reyland has called *corporate classicism*, is Hans Zimmer. Reyland sees the opening sequence of *The Dark Knight* (2008) as prototypical:

> The opening minute of action begins with a discomforting metallic string pedal (Joker's leitmotif) accompanied by a ticking time-bomb beat layer for high pitched but untuned percussion; a low thrum of tension is thereby induced in the audio-viewer through culturally conditioned and mandatory embodied responses.
>
> A bass boom effect occurs on the cut to live action; tension mounts via the music's slowly intensifying dynamics and the camera's expressive zoom.[28]

And he summarizes more generally:

> [One] key trait of corporate classicism [is] its stark rationalisation of traits of the classical Hollywood scoring style which dominated the cinematic mainstream between the 1930s and 1980s. . . . Melody, most strikingly, is entirely absent: the heroes and villains of modern blockbusters get few big themes.[29]

Wispy, Affect-Laden Themes ("The Metaphysical Style")

Against this, although less concretely, Reyland also identifies a *metaphysical style*, which utilizes similar techniques and abstractions without, however, entirely abandoning melody, or what I would call articulated thematic structure. These articulated melodies, however, are often associated with loss, alienation, and suffering.[30] As Reyland notes, "A body in pain craves visions of transcendence." And the musical tunes mark not just the longing, but indeed the status of an identity that is not yet. That is, these tunes do not score a fixed identity any more than the athematic style of corporate classicism does. These contemporary characters are moved, not moved to action; the characters pose, tensed with affect, but they observe and feel, perhaps because they do not know who they are, who the film calls them to be. The music follows suit. With these tunes, as with the athematic style, the concerns remain the portrayal of affect and gesture, not identity.

Blurring of Effects and Music

Many of the examples of contemporary action cinema feature extensive blurring of sound effects and music, and the result is often a stylization of the soundscape—and music under this description is nothing but the absolute stylization of the sound design—that confuses our distinctions about the world. As Kevin Donnelly argues,

> The status of many of the sounds remains unclear: they might be diegetic, or they might be part of the scary musical furnishings of the film. Indeed, deep sub-bass rumbles and metallic sounds with a wide frequency range have exploited the dramatic and psychological possibilities of an extended range of bass and treble tones available to 5.1 Dolby sound and Chion's multispeaker superfield.[31]

In any event, a world rendered with music and digital effects is, as Chion long ago pointed out, not a world of reality but a representation that attempts to get us to feel the impact of the world. Music focalizes feeling and renders emotion-as-we-hear-it.[32] This is how most contemporary cinema has approached the confusion. But it is also possible to confuse the distinction in the other direction and create an equally stylized effect by lifting a sound out of the diegesis and into the music and thereby transform it into a motif. In the virtuosic opening sequence of *Atonement (2007)*, the typewriter sound is abstracted from the diegesis, nondiegetic typing sounds accompanying Briony's (Saoirse Ronan) brisk walk to show her just completed manuscript to her mother (Figure 15.4). The typing sound turns

Figure 15.4: Briony and the typewriter in *Atonement* (2007).

sinister and conspiratorial, like the ticking time-bomb percussion that Reyland identified in *The Dark Knight*, recurring in the film like a leitmotif but not to underscore identity and action; if anything, the recurrence emphasizes and collects together the traumatic confusions of identity that pass in the film between diegetic reality and diegetic fiction.

Epic Choir

The loss of "sacred contact" in the digital image seems to have been met by an epic inflation of music on the soundtrack.[33] If the system of Dolby stereo in the 1970s was affirmed by the sonic spectacle of the symphony orchestra, the system of digital cinema has been affirmed by the sonic spectacle of the epic choir. The communal body of human voices compensates for the turn to digitalization. Though the epic choir in film presents different faces, including the mystical and the angelic, its most common face is mythic fury, often evoking "O Fortuna" from Carl Orff's *Carmina Burana*. The nondiegetic choral sound is not novel to contemporary film—it has been used through almost the whole history of scoring films—but like contemporary ubiquity of the so-called "shaky cam," the choir remained an unusual choice, reserved for special occasions. Religious films, such as *The Robe* (1953), often made extensive use of it. *The Robe* displays both the mystical and the angelic face. *The Omen* (1976) even makes frequent use of the face of demonic fury. But the sound of the massed choir is now a reasonably common scoring choice, and if it retains a connotation of the epic and the implication that powerful mythic forces are at work, that, too, perhaps tells us something about the obsessions of contemporary filmmaking.

Cinematic Drums

The persistent recurrence of percussion has been a hallmark of scoring since at least 2000. Although initially incorporated as part of a retooling of film scoring to accommodate more contemporary popular music styles, the percussion layer, with its increasingly large array of exotic instruments, has quickly evolved into something quite different from a popular music drum track. Reyland's description of a ticking time bomb seems apt, and the relentless urgency of the percussion—both machinelike and yet with intricate cross-rhythms and syncopations dropping musical bombs—seems to hurtle sequences forward toward an apocalyptic conclusion punctuated by a final explosion.

Organization around "Explosion Points"

With the emphasis on affect and feeling the world, language and dialogue are no longer the central concern. If the scream—think about *King Kong*—was the limit of synchronized dialogue in the age of vococentrism, this was because the

Figure 15.5: "The unflinching walk" in *X-Men Origins: Wolverine* (2009).

soundtrack, and much of filmic representation, was structured around the voice.[34] As Reni Celeste notes, contemporary film, especially contemporary action film is structured around explosion points, not screaming points.[35] Explosions propel and punctuate the action, and yet the characters themselves can often seem strangely indifferent to the chaos and destruction they cause, as they coolly light the fuse and walk away while the explosion rocks the auditorium with low frequency effects (see Figure 15.5), a trope dubbed "the unflinching walk."

Systematic Use of Offscreen Sound

Films today make frequent use of offscreen sounds and voices, which has the effect of decentering the figures in the image, or at least positioning them in a space that extends far from the screen edges. Such sounds and voices can be acousmatic, coming from speakers, headphones, and telephones with vague sourcing in the image, such as Samantha (Scarlett Johansson) in the film *Her* (2017). They are sometimes used in conjunction with a mobile searching camera to distend the image frame so that "sync points" seem to occur just beyond the frame edge, such as when Bourne (Matt Damon) strangles Desh (Joey Ansah) just offscreen in *The Bourne Ultimatum* (2007). Sometimes the sound shifts about the surround field to convey the sense that the body in the image is itself in motion, creating the effect of a kind of decentered center, as, for instance, when astronaut Ryan Stone (Sandra Bullock) tumbles through space in *Gravity* (2013). More than ever the hierarchy of onscreen and offscreen seems to break down, as sound goes one way and the image another. Often the point seems to be one of withholding or at least attenuating synchronization cues in order to create an ambiguity that shifts the emphasis from meaning and deeds to gesture and affect. In this respect, contemporary soundtracks seek less to make action intelligible than to place us in its midst, to make us feel the action.

Conclusion

The list presented here is by no means exhaustive and is just a sketch of a typology of characteristic figures for the postclassical soundtrack. Drones and ostinati; synthesizers and digital effects; re-pitching and reversing samples; risers and hits; braams and whooshes—these and many other techniques of contemporary composition and sound design figure as basic compositional devices, but many, such as the syntactic pair rise and hit and the braam (popularized by its use in *Inception* [2010]), are also rudimentary gestural types that are arresting and affective, but do not seem fully explained as expressive effects nor are they primarily at the service of supporting a soundtrack hierarchy with the voice at its center. In commercial cinema, narrative still dominates the conception, to be sure, but that narrative is more complexly rendered and it no longer requires the voice to integrate the soundtrack.

Where does this leave vococentrism in the age of intensified continuity? Steven Shaviro notes that in contemporary film, "a jagged collage of fragments of explosions, crashes, physical lunges, and violently accelerated motions" no longer produces a "sense of spatio-temporal continuity; all that matters is delivering a continual series of shocks to the audience."[36] For Mark Kerins, the digital surround technology of contemporary cinema has reversed the cinematic hierarchy that lay at the heart of classical style. Today, he says, the soundtrack rather than the images "provides continuity and stability" so that the images can situate the audience in the middle of the action.[37] If so, the soundtrack has achieved its new place of centrality in contemporary cinema by allowing the old vococentrism to fade. Intensified continuity has ushered in the end of vococentrism, which in a sense recognizes the way marks of identity and subjectivity in contemporary cinema have given way to figures of gesture and affect.

Notes

1. Michel Chion, *The Voice in Cinema*, trans. Claudia Gorbman (New York: Columbia University Press, 1999), 5.

2. Ibid.

3. Dorothy Richardson, "Continuous Performance: The Film Gone Male," *Close Up* 9, 1 (1932): 36–38. For more on Richardson's interpretation on the sound film, see James Buhler, "Cinematic Listening and the Early Talkie," *The Oxford Handbook of Cinematic Listening*, ed. Carlo Cenciarelli (New York: Oxford University Press, forthcoming).

4. Chion, *The Voice in Cinema*, 5.

5. Ibid., 6.

6. David Bordwell, Janet Staiger, and Kristin Thompson, *The Classical Hollywood Cinema: Film Style and Mode of Production to 1960* (New York: Columbia University Press, 1985), 302.

7. David Neumeyer with contributions by James Buhler, *Meaning and Interpretation of Music in Cinema* (Bloomington: Indiana University Press, 2015).

8. André Bazin, *What Is Cinema?* vol. 1, trans. Hugh Gray (Berkeley: University of California Press, 2004), 17–22.

9. James Buhler and Hannah Lewis, "Evolving Practices for Film Music and Sound, 1925–1935," in *Cambridge Handbook to Film Music*, ed. Mervyn Cooke and Fiona Ford (Cambridge: Cambridge University Press, 2016), 24.

10. Neumeyer, *Meaning and Interpretation of Music in Cinema*, 101.

11. René Clair, *Cinema Yesterday and Today*, trans. Stanley Applebaum (New York: Dover, 1972), 94.

12. Buhler and Lewis, "Evolving Practices for Film Music and Sound," 24–25.

13. Vselovod Pudovkin, *Film Technique and Film Acting: The Cinema Writings of V. I. Pudovkin*, trans. Ivor Montagu (New York: Bonanza Books, 1949), 161.

14. Jane Feuer, *The Hollywood Musical*, 2nd ed. (Bloomington: Indiana University Press, 1993), 42.

15. Buhler and Lewis, "Evolving Practices for Film Music and Sound," 26.

16. Claudia Gorbman, *Unheard Melodies: Narrative Film Music* (Bloomington: Indiana University Press, 1987), 73–91.

17. James Buhler, *Theories of the Soundtrack* (New York: Oxford University Press, 2019), chapter 6.

18. For a recent summary, see André Gaudreault and Philippe Marion, *The End of Cinema? A Medium in Crisis in the Digital Age* (New York: Columbia University Press, 2015).

19. Eleftheria Thanouli, "Post-Classical Narration," *New Review of Film & Television Studies* 4, 3 (2006): 183–96; Justin Wyatt, *High Concept: Movies and Marketing in Hollywood* (Austin: University of Texas Press, 1994); Geoff King, *New Hollywood Cinema: An Introduction* (New York: Columbia University Press, 2002); Carol Vernallis, *Unruly Media: YouTube, Music Video, and the New Digital Cinema* (New York: Oxford University Press, 2013).

20. Kristin Thompson, *Storytelling in the New Hollywood: Understanding Classical Narrative Technique* (Cambridge: Harvard University Press, 1999); David Bordwell, *The Way Hollywood Tells It* (Berkeley: The University of California Press, 2006).

21. James Buhler and Alex Newton, "Outside the Law of Action: Music and Sound in the Bourne Trilogy," in *Oxford Handbook of Sound and Image in Digital Media*, ed. Carol Vernallis, John Richardson, and Amy Herzog (New York: Oxford University Press, 2013), 325–49.

22. David Bordwell, "Unsteadicam Chronicles," in David Bordwell and Kristin Thompson, *Minding Movies: Observations on the Art, Craft, and Business of Filmmaking* (Chicago: University of Chicago Press, 2011), 173–74.

23. Carol Vernallis, "Accelerated Aesthetics: A New Lexicon of Time, Space, and Rhythm," in *Oxford Handbook of Sound and Image in Digital Media*, 707–31.

24. Mark Kerins, *Beyond Dolby (Stereo): Cinema in the Digital Age* (Bloomington: Indiana University Press, 2011), chapter 4, esp. 118–23.

25. Miguel Mera, "Towards 3-D Sound: Spatial Presence and the Space Vacuum," in *The Palgrave Handbook of Sound Design and Music in Screen Media: Integrated Soundtracks*, ed. Liz Greene and Danijela Kulezic-Wilson (London: Palgrave Macmillan, 2016), 91–111.

26. Jeff Smith, "The Sound of Intensified Continuity," in *The Oxford Handbook of New Audiovisual Aesthetics*, ed. John Richardson, Claudia Gorbman, and Carol Vernallis (New York: Oxford University Press, 2013), 338.

27. Janet Halfyard, "Cue the Big Theme? The Sound of the Superhero," in *The Oxford Handbook of New Audiovisual Aesthetics*, 171–93; James Buhler and David Neumeyer, *Hearing the Movies: Music and Sound in Film History*, 2nd ed. (New York: Oxford University Press. 2016); Nicholas Reyland, "Corporate Classicism and the Metaphysical Style: Affects, Effects, and Contexts of Two Recent Trends of Film Scoring," *Music, Sound, and the Moving Image* 9, 2 (2015): 115–30; James Buhler, "Branding the Franchise: Music, Opening Credits, and the (Corporate) Myth of Origin," in *Music in Epic Film: Listening to Spectacle*, ed. Stephen Meyer (New York: Routledge, 2017), 3–26; Frank Lehman, "Manufacturing the Epic Score: Hans Zimmer and the Sounds of Significance," in *Music in Epic Film*, 27–55.

28. Reyland, "Corporate Classicism and the Metaphysical Style," 118.

29. Ibid., 117.

30. For an analysis of one of these characteristically wispy melancholic themes, see Buhler and Newton, "Outside the Law of Action."

31. Kevin Donnelly, "Extending Film Aesthetics: Audio Beyond Visuals," in *The Oxford Handbook of New Audiovisual Aesthetics*, 360.

32. Buhler, *Theories of the Soundtrack*, chapter 6.

33. Rick Altman, "Four and a Half Film Fallacies," in Altman, ed., *Sound Theory/Sound Practice* (New York: Routledge, 1992), 43.

34. Chion, *The Voice in Cinema*, 75–79.

35. Reni Celeste, "The Frozen Screen: Levinas and the Action Film," *Film-Philosophy* 11, 2 (2007): 15–36 (26–28).

36. Steven Shaviro, "Post-continuity: Full Text of My Talk," *The Pinocchio Theory* (blog) March 26. http://www.shaviro.com/Blog/?p=1034. Accessed June 25, 2019.

37. Kerins, *Beyond Dolby (Stereo)*.

Contributors

JULIE BROWN is professor of music at Royal Holloway, University of London. She is contributing editor with Annette Davison of *The Sounds of the Silents in Britain* (2013), has directed two silent film score and musical ephemera re-creations, and published on a range of other screen music topics. Her other books include *Schoenberg and Redemption* (2014), *Bartók and the Grotesque* (2007), and the edited collections *Western Music and Race* (2007), and (with Nicholas Cook and Stephen Cottrell) *Defining the Discographic Self: 'Desert Island Discs' in Context* (2017).

JAMES BUHLER teaches music and film sound at the University of Texas at Austin. He is author of *Theories of the Soundtrack* (2019), coauthor of *Hearing the Movies: Music and Sound in Film History* (2016), now in a second edition, and a coeditor of *Music and Cinema* (2000).

MARCIA J. CITRON is Lovett Distinguished Service Professor of Musicology Emerita from Rice University. Her research focuses on the intersection of opera and film, and she has published two books on the topic: *Opera on Screen* and *When Opera Meets Film*. Citron has also written on gender in music, including *Gender and the Musical Canon*. In 2012, she received the lifetime-achievement award of Honorary Membership from the AMS.

ERIC DIENSTFREY is a Postdoctoral Fellow in American Music at the University of Texas at Austin. His research has appeared in *Film History* and *Music and the Moving Image*. His article "The Myth of the Speakers" received the 2017 Katherine Singer Kovács Award from the Society for Cinema and Media Studies.

ERIK HEINE is professor of music at Oklahoma City University, where he has taught since 2005. He is the author of the book *James Newton Howard's Signs: A Film Score Guide*, published by Scarecrow Press in 2016, and his work has appeared in the anthologies *Contemplating Shostakovich: Life, Music, and Film* (eds. Andrew Kirkman and Alexander Ivashkin) and *Sounding Funny: Sound and Comedy Cinema* (eds. Mark Evans and Philip Hayward), as well as *Music Analysis* and the *Journal of Music Theory Pedagogy Online*.

JULIE HUBBERT is associate professor of music history at the University of South Carolina. She is the author of *Celluloid Symphonies: Text and Contexts in Music History* (University of California Press, 2011) and has written articles on a variety of film music and media topics, from silent and documentary film to Scorsese, that have appeared in a variety of journals and essay collections. She is currently working on a book on music in New Hollywood film.

HANNAH LEWIS is assistant professor of musicology at the University of Texas at Austin. Her research focuses on film music, music and visual media, early-twentieth-century French music, and musical theater. She is the author of *French Musical Culture and the Coming of Sound Cinema* (2019), and her work has also appeared in the *Journal of the American Musicological Society*, the *Journal of the Society for American Music*, *Musical Quarterly*, *The Cambridge Companion to Film Music*, and the *Journal of Musicological Research*. She is currently working on a new book titled *Rodgers and Hammerstein On Screen*.

BROOKE MCCORKLE is an assistant professor of music at Carleton College and the coauthor of *Japan's Green Monsters: Environmental Commentary in Kaijū Cinema*. Her publications address topics ranging from film and television music to Wagner reception in Japan. She is currently writing a book about the all-female Japanese punk trio, Shōnen Knife.

CARI MCDONNELL received her PhD in music theory from UT-Austin in 2015 with a dissertation that examines the ways in which vaudeville, radio, recording, and television influenced the style and production of the Hollywood film musical during the studio era. She resides in Austin as an independent scholar.

DAVID NEUMEYER is professor emeritus of music, Sarah and Ernest Butler School of Music, The University of Texas at Austin. He is the author of *Meaning and Interpretation of Music in Cinema* (2015), coauthor of *Hearing the Movies: Music and Sound in Film History* (2009; 2d edition, 2016), and editor of *The Oxford Handbook of Film Music* (2014).

NATHAN PLATTE is associate professor of musicology at the University of Iowa, where he also holds an affiliated appointment with the Department of Cinematic Arts. His research explores film music and sound of Hollywood's studio era from a variety of angles, including the process of film scoring, the intersection of technology and music, the role of studio orchestras, and soundtrack albums. Platte's most recent book, *Making Music in Selznick's Hollywood* (2018), illuminates the collaborative efforts behind the film scores for *King Kong, Gone with the Wind, Rebecca,* and *Spellbound,* among others.

KATHERINE QUANZ received her PhD from Wilfrid Laurier University and currently works at the Harry Ransom Center at the University of Texas at Austin. Her work on sound design history and aboriginal media has appeared in *Velvet Light Trap* and the anthology *Cinephemera*. She is currently working on a monograph titled *The Sounds of Satellites: The Postproduction Sound Network among Hollywood, Toronto, and London.*

JEFF SMITH is a professor in the department of communication arts at the University of Wisconsin–Madison. He is the author of *The Sounds of Commerce: Marketing Popular Film Music* and *Film Criticism, the Cold War, and the Blacklist: Reading the Hollywood Reds.* Smith is also a new coauthor with David Bordwell and Kristin Thompson of the eleventh edition of *Film Art: An Introduction.* He is currently at work on a book-length study of music in Hollywood films of the 1930s.

JANET STAIGER is William P. Hobby Centennial Professor Emeritus in Communication and Women's and Gender Studies at the University of Texas. She particularly attends to questions about situated and historical authorship, audiences and reception, and positionalities of gender and sexuality. Among her recent books are *Political Emotions* (2010, coeditor), *Media Reception Studies* (2005), *Authorship and Film* (2002, coeditor), *Blockbuster TV* (2000), and *Perverse Spectators* (2000).

ROBYNN J. STILWELL is a musicologist who teaches in the music, dance, writing, and film and media studies programs at Georgetown University. Her research interests center on the meaning of music as cultural work and music as an expression, or impression, of movement and space. Publications include essays on Beethoven and cinematic violence, musical form in Jane Austen, rockabilly and "white trash," figure skating, French film musicals, psychoanalytic film theory for female subjects, and the boundaries between sound and music in the cinematic soundscape. Current projects include a historical study of audiovisual modality in television and music and sound in podcasts.

Index

The University of Illinois Press
is a founding member of the
Association of University Presses.

Composed in 10.75/13 Arno Pro
with Trade Gothic LT Std display
by Lisa Connery
at the University of Illinois Press
Cover designed by Jennifer S. Fisher
Cover illustration: Image of man from *Pik Nik ha il do di petto* (1911). Courtesy of the Desmet Collection, EYE Filmmuseum, the Netherlands, with kind permission. Soundwave image (Shutterstock.com); music sheet (© iStock.com/blackred).

University of Illinois Press
1325 South Oak Street
Champaign, IL 61820-6903
www.press.uillinois.edu